THE ACCOUNTING HALL OF FAME

The Ohio State University

Thomas J. Burns Series in Accounting History

VOLUME 4

Philip L. Defliese: A Collection of His Writings

Philip Leroy Defliese
1915 – 1997

PHILIP L. DEFLIESE
A Collection of His Writings

Edited by

Edward N. Coffman
Virginia Commonwealth University

Daniel L. Jensen
The Ohio State University

The Accounting Hall of Fame
THE OHIO STATE UNIVERSITY
Max M. Fisher College of Business
1999

Manufactured in the United States of America
Printed on acid-free paper

ISBN 1-883356-04-0

TABLE OF CONTENTS

Standard Setting: The Accounting Principles Board and Beyond

Accounting for Leases

Fundamental Accounting Concepts and Objectives

Accounting for Changing Prices

Accounting for Income Taxes

The Role of the Accounting Profession

EDITORS' PREFACE

This volume brings together the writings of Mr. Philip L. Defliese in recognition of his contributions to the profession of accounting. Through the years, many individuals have made significant contributions to the growth and development of the accounting profession. Sixty-one such individuals, including Philip L. Defliese, have been elected to The Accounting Hall of Fame at The Ohio State University since the Hall was established in 1950. The scholarly contributions of many of these important accountants are dispersed in difficult to access periodicals, books, and manuscripts and are in danger of being forgotten. The record of contributions by accountants who, like Philip L. Defliese, made their careers outside academe are particularly vulnerable to being lost. For those who wrote and published little, one hopes that writers of history and biography will capture their contributions. But for those who wrote significantly, as did Philip L. Defliese, published collections of their works have an important role to play in preserving unpublished materials and in collecting published materials that are difficult to locate.

This volume is the fourth in a series presenting the collected works of Hall of Fame members whose works have not been collected and published elsewhere. The series was established in 1992 and named the Thomas J. Burns Series in Accounting History in recognition of his twenty-five years of administrative service to The Accounting Hall of Fame.

A chronological bibliography of Mr. Defliese's writings and speeches appears at the end of this volume. The bibliography includes the writings and speeches that we were able to locate through searches of bibliographic sources including *The Accountants' Index* as prepared by the American Institute of Certified Public Accountants. Copies of all items in our bibliography were located, except for the address presented at the annual meeting of the American Institute of Certified Public Accountants in September 1960 entitled, "Audit Report Problems of Regulated Companies." The search has demonstrated to us the many impediments to compiling a complete bibliography for a prolific writer with a long career.

In selecting the works to appear in this volume, we have attempted to present items that reveal Mr. Defliese's views on accounting and his professional philosophy. We have attempted to minimize redundancy by reproducing just one version of similar papers or speeches. An editors' footnote identifies the source of each item reproduced and cites duplicate or nearly duplicate items that are omitted from the collection.

We have endeavored to reproduce Mr. Defliese's writings as they originally appeared. Typewritten manuscripts are printed as they appear with only minor editorial changes and typographical corrections. Similarly, published materials are reproduced using Mr. Defliese's complete text; however, some editorial and stylistic elements of the book or journal are omitted in the interests of a uniform style. Occasionally, we have made comments and explanations in footnotes to the articles and speeches reproduced here. These are identified as "editors' notes" and printed in italics.

Mr. Defliese's works are arranged in nine groups of related articles: (1) the practice of public accounting at Coopers & Lybrand, (2) audit procedures and auditors' responsibilities, (3) public utility accounting, (4) standard setting: the Accounting Principles Board and beyond, (5) accounting for leases, (6) fundamental accounting concepts and objectives, (7) accounting for changing prices, (8) accounting for income taxes, and (9) the role of the accounting profession. Most of these groups include writings spanning a decade or more, evidencing Mr. Defliese's long-term interest in the topics he addressed.

We are grateful to Mr. Press C. Southworth III of PricewaterhouseCoopers, the Thomas J. Burns Trust, the Department of Accounting and Management Information Systems at The Ohio State University, and the Department of Accounting at Virginia Commonwealth University for supporting this project. We are also grateful for the invaluable assistance of Dr. Susan Morecroft at Fayetteville State University and Jeanne Scott, Interlibrary Loan Borrower, at Virginia Commonwealth University. Our appreciation is also extended to Bing (Andy) Sun and Nhu Uyen (Winnie) Tran, students at Virginia Commonwealth University, for their assistance in processing and proofing of these materials. Finally, in addition to acknowledgments elsewhere, we wish to acknowledge Dhia D. AlHashim, Roderick K. Macleod, James W. Robertson, *Accountancy*, American Accounting Association, American Institute of CPAs, *Business Week*, *The CPA Journal*, Conference of Accountants at The University of Tulsa, Financial Executives Institute, Institute of Chartered Accountants of India, Lafferty Publications, McGraw-Hill Companies, New York Times Co., PricewaterhouseCoopers LLP, RIA Group—*The Journal of Taxation,* and The University of Alabama (Culverhouse School of Accountancy) for permissions to reproduce Mr. Defliese's writings in this volume.

July 1999

Edward N. Coffman
Virginia Commonwealth University

Daniel L. Jensen
The Ohio State University

A BIOGRAPHY
of
PHILIP L. DEFLIESE

PHILIP LEROY DEFLIESE, the son of Philip and Frances Ankenbrand Defliese, was born February 11, 1915, in Queens County, New York City.[1] He attended Brooklyn's Bushwick High School, graduating in 1931. After graduation from high school, at the age of 16, Defliese took a full-time job as a mail-boy with New York Title & Mortgage Company and began attending evening classes at the City College of New York (CCNY). He earned a B.B.A. (cum laude) with a double major in accounting and education from CCNY in 1938. By that time, he had been promoted to the accounting department at New York Title & Mortgage Company.

Upon receiving his bachelor's degree, Defliese left New York Title & Mortgage to become a full-time "permanent substitute" accounting teacher at Grover Cleveland High School in New York City, where he taught for the next four years. He noted that his decision was partially motivated by finances: as an accountant, he made $32 per week, while as teacher he would make $8.50 a day. He continued to take evening courses at CCNY and earned a M.S. in business education in 1940. He later completed all the coursework for his Ph.D. in education at New York University, but never finished the dissertation. In 1975, Villanova University granted Defliese an honorary Doctor of Commercial Science degree.

In 1942, Defliese passed the CPA exam and was hired by Lybrand, Ross Bros. & Montgomery (later Coopers & Lybrand) as a "permanent temporary" junior in public accounting. About a year later, he left the firm to serve in World War II (1942-46). He entered the U.S. Navy as a midshipman under the V-7 program at the University of Notre Dame and was commissioned as an ensign, with a specialty in antisubmarine warfare. After three years of sea duty in the Pacific and Alaska, he was honorably discharged as a lieutenant and spent the next year (1947-48) teaching accounting as an assistant professor at Adelphi University in Garden City.

Defliese was certified as a CPA in 1947 and returned to Lybrand, Ross Bros. & Montgomery in 1948. He requested a three-part assignment: performing audit field work, teaching at the office training school, and assisting the firm's SEC

---

[1] This biographical profile builds upon information contained in Thomas J. Burns and Edward N. Coffman, eds., *The Accounting Hall of Fame: Profiles of Fifty Members* (Columbus, OH: College of Business, The Ohio State University, 1991).

specialist.[2] He directed the staff training programs of the New York office in the postwar period and later organized all of the firm's training programs on a national basis. He continued to pursue his interests in education during some of his earlier years at Lybrand, teaching as an adjunct professor at Pace University from 1950 to 1956. He became a partner in the firm in 1956 at the age of 41 and he served as the firm's national director of accounting, auditing, and SEC services over the period 1962-68, and chairman of the firm's practice committee.

After entering the partnership, Defliese became more active with the AICPA. He was a member and chairman of its Committee on Auditing Procedure (member, 1957-59; chairman, 1959-62). He later considered his work on the clarification of fraud detection responsibilities and qualified opinion criteria to be among his most significant contributions to the profession.[3] His other AICPA committee activities included serving as member of the Practice Review Committee (1962-65), chairman of the Committee on Specialized Audits (1960-62), and member of the Committee on Relations with Bankers and Other Credit Executives (1965-69). He was a member of the AICPA Council, the Institute's governing committee—first as an elected member from New York (1964-67) and later as a member at large (1969-74). He also served as a member of the New York State Board of CPA Examiners (1964-69).

In 1968, following a period of rapid growth for Lybrand, Ross Bros. & Montgomery, Defliese was elected to succeed Walter R. Staub as managing partner and chairman of the executive committee of the firm. At the time, the firm had 367 partners and 4,200 professional and administrative staff people in 61 offices in the United States. In areas outside the U.S., the firm had offices or was represented in 234 cities in 57 countries.[4] In that same year, the courts found against two Lybrand partners in the much publicized Continental Vending Machines case. Defliese, who was known as "a forceful leader with a solid reputation for integrity,"[5] guided his firm through this difficult period:

> He insisted upon introducing more rigorous rules in accounting and auditing practice to strengthen the quality of financial information provided by the Firm. He also hired Harris J. Amhowitz, a lawyer from Hughes, Hubbard & Reed in New York, to serve as in-house legal counsel and assist in the development of new policies to reduce legal exposure and to develop ways to minimize the burdensome costs of professional liability insurance. The

---

[2]Burns, Thomas J., "1987 Accounting Hall of Fame Induction, Philip Leroy Defliese," *The Accounting Historians Journal* 14 (Fall 1987): 93-94.

[3]"Response by Philip Leroy Defliese, 1987 Accounting Hall of Fame Induction," *The Accounting Historians Journal* 14 (Fall 1987): 94-97.

[4]"Lybrand's Executive Changeover: A View from the Top." *Lybrand Journal* 50 (1969): 3-6.

[5]Coopers & Lybrand LLP, *Building Values and Traditions: One Hundred Years of Coopers & Lybrand* (New York: Coopers & Lybrand LLP, 1998), p. 52.

Firm also established its own political action committee (PAC) in Washington to support a broad array of initiatives.... [6]

In 1973, an international merger changed the firm name to Coopers & Lybrand, an event that symbolized Defliese's philosophy. Upon his election to managing partner, he said, "It will be a period which we must start by not being satisfied with the status quo—no matter how good it is. Change is essential—we never reach perfection."[7] He carried this philosophy forward as he continued to push for accounting and auditing reforms following his retirement from the firm in 1976.

Defliese was the chairman of the Accounting Principles Board for its last three years of existence (1970-72.) He had been a member of the Board since 1964. Reflecting back on his career in 1987, he said his greatest satisfaction had come from his involvement in standard setting.[8] He had a hand in writing 26 often controversial APB opinions; significant among them for his involvement were, APB 11 "Accounting for Income Taxes," APB 15 "Earnings per Share," APB 16 "Business Combinations," and APB 17 "Intangible Assets." During his tenure, Defliese said the APB was moving "more toward a reflection of the economic facts of life...and away from the transaction-oriented accounting" traditionally taught in school, and warned that, by necessity, "accounting is going to get more complex rather than more simple."[9] By the time the Financial Accounting Standards Board replaced the APB in 1973, the APB had issued a total of 31 Opinions and numerous audit guides and position papers. Defliese ensured that the FASB received summary documents describing the pros and cons of proposed solutions to the very controversial topics that the APB worked on but was unable to resolve during its tenure, including: marketable securities, intangible drilling costs of the oil and gas industries, lease capitalization, and diversified companies.[10] After the FASB assumed its standard-setting responsibilities, Defliese served as a member of the Financial Accounting Standards Advisory Council of the FASB for a year and a half (1973-74). The AICPA awarded its 1972 Gold Medal Award for distinguished service to the profession of accounting to Defliese while he was still chairman of the Accounting Principles Board.

---

[6] *Ibid.*, p. 53.

[7] "Lybrand's Executive Changeover: A View from the Top." *Lybrand Journal* 50 (1969): 3-6.

[8] Response by Philip Leroy Defliese, 1987 Accounting Hall of Fame Induction," *The Accounting Historians Journal* 14 (Fall 1987): 94-97.

[9] "Defliese Tells Council What's Ahead for the Accounting Principles Board," *The CPA* (American Institute of CPAs) 51 (June 1971): 8.

[10] "Defliese Itemizes APB's Agenda," *The CPA* (American Institute of CPAs) 52 (June 1972): 15.

A positive, progressive approach also characterized Defliese's chairmanship of the AICPA's Board of Directors during a period in which public accountants were receiving significant untoward press. As he started his 1974-75 term, he warned against negativism, stating that "prophecies of doom are often self-fulfilling," and made it his goal "to turn around the image of the profession and make it more affirmative."[11] As chairman, he continued to press for critical re-examinations of fundamental accounting concepts. For instance, he called for the inclusion of the cost of equity capital formation in the determination of net profit.[12] He argued that the practice of omitting those costs had the economic consequence of impairing capital investment.[13] In criticizing the present accounting practice, Defliese recognized that he was challenging what he called "a deep-rooted professional bias"[14]—the completed-transaction orientation of accounting.[15]

Defliese stepped down from the leadership position at Coopers & Lybrand in 1976, after attaining their mandatory retirement age, and in 1977, he joined the accounting faculty at Columbia University, where he taught for 11 years and was awarded the status of professor emeritus.

Defliese served on the Conceptual Framework Committee of the AICPA, the FASB Task Force on the Conceptual Framework for Financial Accounting and Reporting (1973-84), and the FASB Task Force Subgroup on Measurement of the Elements of Financial Statements (1978-84). He was the first chairman of the New York City Audit Committee (1979-84). He served as a member of the Governmental Accounting Standards Board from its formation in 1984 until 1990. He served as a member of the Financial Accounting Standards Committee of the American Accounting Association (1981-82).

Defliese was also active in the New York State Society of CPAs. In addition to serving as vice-president for a year (1974-75) and a member of the Board of Directors for three years (1970-72), his service included membership on the Awards (1965-66), Auditing Procedure (1957-59), and Education and Personnel

---

[11]"Philip L. Defliese, the AICPA's New Chairman," *The Journal of Accountancy* 138 (December 1974): 44, 46.

[12]"Defliese Calls for "Cost of Capital" Disclosure," *The Journal of Accountancy* 139 (May 1975): 25.

[13]Philip L. Defliese, "What Makes Profits Look 'Obscene'," *Business Week* (August 4, 1975): 10-11.

[14]*Ibid.*

[15]However, Defliese was not alone in his thinking. In 1975, the Treasury Department released a study that ranked the United States among the lowest of the industrial countries in terms of real economic growth. The study identified a relatively low investment of output as a cause for the problem and suggested, among other remedies, the use of accounting methods that adjust earnings for the replacement cost of capital. (Schachner, Leopold. "An Accounting for Cost of Equity Capital." *The CPA Journal* 45 (December 1975): 13-17.)

(1954-57) Committees. He was also chairman of the Society's Accounting Practice Committee (1966-67) and a member and chairman of the Professional Development Committee (member 1966-67; chairman 1958-59). Defliese served as a director of several companies and as a consultant to the U.S. Defense Department.

Defliese was inducted into the Ohio State University Accounting Hall of Fame in 1987. He received the Public Oversight Board's 1995 John J. McCloy Award in recognition of his distinguished career and service to the accounting profession. He was a member of Beta Alpha Psi, Beta Gamma Sigma, and Delta Pi Epsilon. He was a founding trustee of the Baruch College Fund.

Defliese spoke before many professional groups. One of his last interactions with the academic and professional community was at the December 1996 research conference of the Academy of Accounting Historians where, as a panelist, he provided insightful reflections on the historical development and importance of the CPA examination. A prolific writer, he wrote extensively on accounting and auditing topics and he was the co-author of four editions (8th-11th) of *Montgomery's Auditing*—the classic text on auditing—including the first college edition (the 10th). Defliese also co-edited *Current Value Accounting: A Practical Guide for Business* (1977).

Defliese married Pauline Harnisch on April 28, 1946; they had one daughter and two sons. His hobbies included sailing, hiking, water skiing, and golf. He was active in the local Boy Scouts of America (1927-54) and earned their Silver Beaver Award (1947) for outstanding service to youth. Philip L. Defliese died on October 27, 1997, at the age of 82.

THE PRACTICE OF PUBLIC ACCOUNTING AT COOPERS & LYBRAND

STAFF TRAINING AT A NEW CLIMAX—AN INTRODUCTION†

by

Philip L. Defliese

IN a profession such as ours it is well recognized that the quality of its services is dependent largely upon the education and training of the men in it. Like medicine and law, public accounting cannot rely solely upon academic training —on-the-job training and in-service training must further the effort begun by professional schools and colleges.

While on-the-job training is recognized as the best, it has the disadvantage of being slow. Additional steps are needed in a fast-moving profession. This was realized as early as 1902, when the firm established its first training class, which was conducted in the evenings. In those days the objectives were somewhat different—the trainees had need for basic education in accounting and auditing, and assistance in preparation for the CPA examination. As the schools and colleges gradually assumed responsibility for these areas, the emphasis in staff training shifted to our present-day objectives—to bridge the gap between the theoretical and practical and to accelerate the progress of the men on the staff so that top-level responsibility may be assumed as early as possible.

For years many of our offices had offered staff training schools to all beginning men. These courses were generally of a similar nature, divided into elementary and advanced courses given in the first and second years, respectively. While these courses had served their purposes well in the past, it was apparent that more could be accomplished by centralizing these activities and having the beginning men of all offices reside at a university campus for the duration of the courses. Accordingly, the firm's first Central Training School was held this year in August at Drew University, Madison, New Jersey. The magnitude of our training responsibility can best be envisioned by considering the number who attended—150 men and 11 faculty members.

The current age of specialization has added much to our training responsibility. Experience has shown that the diversified background of the auditor is a distinct advantage to the specialist, making it desirable to recruit Tax and Management Services specialists from our audit staff. Here again, development is accelerated best by formal training programs designed for each level of achievement within the specialization and offered at the most suitable time. From humble beginnings these courses have also developed to a point

†Reprinted from *L. R. B. & M. Journal*, July-September 1957, pp. 8-9, with permission of PricewaterhouseCoopers LLP.

where they now have become national in character. They are, nevertheless, integrated programs. In medicine, the heart specialist must first be a qualified general practitioner, and the general practitioner must be somewhat of a heart specialist. The situation is the same public accounting—the auditor must also be somewhat of a Tax and Management Services specialist. Our Tax and Management Services courses, therefore, also aim to give the auditor a broad background in these fields. It is still one profession.

Once trained, we cannot stand still and rest on our laurels—there is the constant need to keep current, exchange ideas, develop, strengthen the ties. This need has been met by our annual national and regional conferences of supervisors and specialists where the men directing the engagements in their respective fields meet to help each other accomplish this objective—a never ending program. Most of what is learned at these conferences is brought back to the local offices and disseminated by means of local staff meetings.

The gradual evolution of these staff training programs has reached a new climax this year. In order that our clients and all members of our organization may have a better understanding of these programs, this issue of the *L. R. B. & M. Journal* has been devoted to staff training. The four articles which describe these programs are:

Central Training School—the new national training program for first and second year audit staff men.

Tax Training Program—the comprehensive tax program for audit and tax men at all levels.

Management Services Training Program—covering all areas from cost accounting to Electronic Data Processing.

Annual Staff Conferences—the way supervisors and specialists keep current and exchange ideas.

It should not be assumed that the millennium in staff training has been reached; it is only a plateau. Improvements, changes, new courses, all are already being planned. It can be expected that as new areas are developed within the profession, and as some or all of the new and old areas are embraced by the academic institutions, the emphases in our staff training programs will shift again. Our line-up a decade hence will be different, I am sure.

The State of the Firm—1970: NEW DECADES DEMAND NEW CONCEPTS†

by
Philip L. Defliese

NEW decades suggest new beginnings and demand new concepts. By this measure, the Lybrand organization has already renewed itself seven times in this century. Our Firm has grown up with this country, mirroring, from its start in 1898, the growth of the profession. Working from our essential auditing base, we started the century serving businesses in an overall financial capacity. To retain this approach, in varying degrees—through seven decades which brought revolutionary changes in financial reporting, taxation, operations, and technology—our relationship with our clients has had to become multidimensional. This relationship will intensify, and may well mean that the ideal Lybrand practitioner of the 1970s will, in addition to being an auditor, be a problem solver, an adviser, an innovator, a stimulator, and a catalyst.

If the 1960s were an especially restless and challenging time, then the 1970s must be a decade of response. Just as business, generally, incurred debts by producing finished goods—without always guarding against the environmental destructiveness of its products—so, too, did accountants incur obligations. We laid the financial foundations for a new series of commercial developments without always perfecting all the accounting techniques needed to measure earnings and balance results. In this sense, much of the current thinking and discussion on accounting principles is related to very recent developments—the rise of the conglomerates, the increased popularity of convertible securities, the general acceptance of the so-called "performance concept," and the resulting widespread attention paid to earnings per share. We, like society, have a backlog of unsolved problems.

AN AUDITING HERITAGE

Essentially, of course, we are auditors with an important heritage. At this writing, we are preparing the ninth edition of *Montgomery's Auditing*, which has been a basic text in educating generations of auditors. In this coming edition, attention is focused on the new tools of auditing, and on the important guidelines for coping with the complexities of the modern business environment. Last year we released our own computer-audit system, Auditpak, which we believe will not

†Reprinted from *Lybrand Journal*, 1970, pp. 3-8, with permission of PricewaterhouseCoopers LLP.

only enhance the verification aspects of auditing but also free the auditor for greater service as a source of business intelligence in the years ahead.

This decade, then, is likely to be a period of dramatic change in the scope of the auditor's activity and in the way he performs his work. Our audit philosophy, which emphasizes the importance of in-depth understanding of a client's operations within their industry framework, obligates our Firm to deal with changes as they evolve. The development of computer technology and the auditor's increased access to computers in the business world have already expanded our vistas. For the first time, the auditor will be able to process vast amounts of data on an economical and timely basis.

This capacity broadens the opportunity for discovery and points up the need for the development of even further auditing tools. Our Auditpak system can be an important step in this direction. We plan to expand the areas in which Auditpak may be applied, to develop other practical techniques the auditor can use in his attest function, and to diagnose conditions in a way that will further enhance the usefulness of our management letters.

As an accounting firm, we have been close to the center of a remarkable phenomenon—the emergence of a business economy without parallel in imagination, energy, and intelligence. The 1960s demonstrated not only the force of new developments but also the speed with which these developments could be absorbed into the economy. Midway through the 1950s, few could have envisioned the extent of the computer's participation in the economy of 1970. If achievement follows need, however, the 1960s saw the end of a postwar period of consolidation and a new reaching out by business, with resulting information and systems needs that only the computer could meet.

TECHNOLOGY FOR THE 70s

In our nonauditing practice, we responded early to the need to provide areas of EDP services and software on a timely basis. For continued timeliness, both our practitioners and our applied research group must keep us in the forefront of management sciences. Within our own organization, we have brought computer time-sharing to a point where we have terminals in 35 of our offices, with access for all divisions of the organization. We have adapted many programs, such as inventory analysis, to terminal time-sharing use for our clients. Underlying the advantages of time-sharing are the obvious needs for information delivered quickly and directly to the user on his own premises. Time-sharing is but one method of fulfilling these needs.

Our consulting practice will remain heavily committed to the managerial needs of our clients, a commitment that stimulated the growth of this practice to its present position of prominence. Surely, the increasing degree of sophistication in business foreshadows a massive demand for broader types of knowledge. The advance of technology and systems will continue to overshadow the more routine tasks, and will demand even higher degrees of intelligence and analysis. As part of our current research effort, we are applying such management science concepts as econometrics to the structure of businesses to facilitate preparation of budgetary guides. We also continue to train client personnel both in management techniques and, more recently, in the application of mathematical modeling and simulation techniques to a broad array of corporate problems.

Planning and control within Lybrand may offer a laboratory example of what might be expected in the next decade. We are currently exploring the use of mathematical decision-making models in our own Firm—which, incidentally, has quadrupled in size since 1960. Some of these techniques (which have been much discussed in business generally but, except for some bellwether operations, are barely implemented as yet) relate the business operation to prospective changes in the economy. This, roughly, involves analysis of various factors of the business correlated to economic indicators; it would enable us to study the effect of a great many possible changes in the economy on a particular operation, and obviously would result in greater precision in planning. Lybrand intends to continue pioneering in the use of these types of techniques, and to keep in close touch with the essential business technology of the 1970s and beyond.

Ultimately, the technology of the 1970s will affect many parts of a business. Our Firm is developing faster means of communication between its far-flung offices in ways that businesses generally are or soon will be interested in. Central to communications is the computer and the input and output it needs, and the quick dissemination of internal accounting information. Telecommunication is one key concept involving Teletype, leased telephone lines, and paper tapes that can be typed directly for computer use. Optical scanning is another important procedure that is drawing our attention because it offers, again in general, the possibility of machine reading and conversion of reports into magnetic tape. In essence, we are testing new methods for communicating with the computer, and all of these methods are available to us as products of our management science division.

The fact that these methods may now be treated as ordinary operational techniques is in itself a measure of how far business has come in a short time. Twenty or even 10 years ago, they were merely exotic, even fantastic, possibilities for some future generation. What we see now—in both looking back and looking ahead—is that we are, in fact, the generation that is effecting a new technological revolution in business.

THE BROAD COMMITMENT

Nor is technology our only area of action. Our profession's recent growth, which matches that of any industry in the 1960s, has been based on our ability to identify and satisfy important needs, to provide a kind of intelligence that must be at once multidimensional and eminently usable, and, finally, to be flexible enough to meet practical problems as they occur. As a source of professional intelligence, then, we are obligated to help meet the demands of a complex business environment, encompassing tax and financial reporting requirements and a continuing growth of multinational business. Also, since we in the accounting profession have an obligation to be both realistic and pragmatic, every client problem must be explored for both solution and opportunity.

Our international services division, working closely with our worldwide Coopers & Lybrand operation, not only is keeping a close watch on business problems and opportunities abroad but also is constantly striving to better communicate the sense of these to U.S. businessmen. Our efforts in this area have, in fact, been stepped up recently, as is reflected in a number of new Lybrand publications that feature information and intelligence on business conditions in specific areas. A highly developed training program brings staff from abroad into our schools and practice offices, and sends U.S. personnel abroad. Added to this is a yearly interchange of several hundred people throughout our international Firm. The goal here, of course, is to provide a high standard of worldwide proficiency.

Here in the United States, the decade closed with one of the most significant pieces of tax legislation ever enacted, the Tax Reform Act of 1969. It was known from the start, of course, that the Act would affect business broadly. As the legislation evolved over many months, however, it became increasingly complex. Containing many complications and new concepts, the Act and its development again pointed up our clients' need for new tax planning approaches. For us, therefore, it represented a particular test both of our organizational capability and of our will to respond quickly. By way of our Washington office and our tax research facility, we not only followed but also analyzed the legislation's changes as the bill moved through Congress. Within a few weeks of its passage, we were able to provide all of our clients with a comprehensive, analytical summary of the Act in our *Newsletter*, and to follow up with an extensive slide presentation still being given at many key points around the country.

This is one example of our response to change. In the broader sense, what is important to us is that we continue to help our clients in this vital area. Looking ahead, we can foresee many other possible changes in tax law, and a need, therefore, to help our clients plan effectively. Accordingly, our organizational emphasis is on training that enables us to send our clients tax practitioners who can bring them a knowledge of economics and accounting, and provide a creative overall approach.

THE MULTIDIMENSIONAL APPROACH

The approach must, in a sense, be a "total one." Here our organization is important; it must meet many overlapping needs—each of which may require a very specialized brand of expertise. Thus, our actuarial and employee benefit planning division, for instance, is being more closely integrated with audit, tax, and management services. Specialists in employee benefits have been placed in many Lybrand offices throughout the country. Obviously, the proportion of the payroll dollar going towards employee benefits has been growing, with strong, even vital, implications for tax and organizational planning. Even beyond this, however, we must continue to emphasize fresh ideas and procedures requiring broad participation by the many different disciplines within Lybrand. Our emphasis on this approach—in which we've actually created research and development facilities—has enabled us to come up with many new and important concepts for our clients. In building on this approach for the 1970s, we see an even more inclusive role for ourselves in the area of financial and operational planning.

Our approach, moreover, is supported by many important innovations in our own organization. We have, for example, an industry program, supported by a research facility, in which we continually seek to develop knowledge and expertise on those problems of our clients distinctive to their particular industries. In some instances, we have moved into the center of problem areas, such as hospitals, universities, and transportation, where we feel that accounting firms can and must make contributions. Paramount among the concerns of our society in the 1970s will be the health of our basic institutions; here, certainly, accountants, who have always been expert at bringing order, have much to offer.

We spoke earlier about the need to see a client's operation in its entirety. This requires that we provide not only new services but also better services. In plain terms, our staff must know more. This year, 3,000 members of our Firm, including 1,100 new recruits—the greatest number ever—will participate in our central auditing courses. We are devising methods of instruction attuned to the concept of greater involvement in a client's operation. We now use a seminar method of teaching, for example, that makes extensive use of case studies and encourages those attending the course to participate fully in solving problems.

Recognizing, too, that training must be a year-round function, we are expanding continuous on-the-job and local office training. Accounting is far more complex in 1970 than it was in 1960. And this is a challenge not only to us but also to the universities. On our part, it calls for greater liaison with colleges to help them train people who can meet the rigorous demands of our profession. Lybrand must commit itself increasingly to education, must invest more in its own staff training programs, and must start this investment in people, usually, at the college level.

A NEW OUTLOOK

In outlining just a few of our plans for the years ahead, we can see that the responsibilities of each practitioner are much greater now than they were a few years ago—that every position is becoming more intellectually demanding. We know, too, that we are requiring—even from our beginning people—a high degree of proficiency and a broad business outlook.

In today's changing world, most professional firms acknowledge that they have social as well as professional obligations. Our Firm is associated, either officially through specific sponsorship or unofficially through individual staff members, with a variety of social programs. While this participation attests to our willingness to contribute time and money towards solving some of today's major problems, we realize that much more is required of a firm with such widespread involvement in business and industry. We plan to intensify our social involvement, and for that reason we encourage staff members to cultivate their own social consciousness. We also plan to step up our hiring and training of increasing numbers of minority group members, since we feel that this kind of cooperation between the profession and the community will be essential in the 1970s.

Finally, we intend to benefit fully from our recent as well as from our past experience. The 1960s were an especially invigorating time of high growth and of new ideas, but obviously not everything in the decade was bright for the profession or for our Firm. The profession faces a backlog of important problems, and we ourselves also have a clear obligation to do better, to merit the position we have attained within that profession. It is a fact that as long as accountancy followed the principle of responding to the needs and demands of the broad marketplace, it progressed. Its progress faltered only when it failed to perceive the needs and demands or, perceiving them, acted too slowly in satisfying them. In this situation the public, through its spokesmen—the press, legislators, and even judges and jurists—expressed its displeasure. It is a tribute to the intrinsic strength of both our Firm and our profession that we were able to weather the storms, to come out of the decade strong and still forward-looking. Now, of course, we must increasingly ensure that we build on our essential historic strength. For us, that means to maintain a clear vision, to see even that which is problematic, and, above all else, to provide what is needed.

NEW ERA FOR AUDITORS: INTERIM REPORTS[†]

by
Philip L. Defliese

THE present era could well be characterized as the era of disclosure—the demands for more information, more facts, and more knowledge are accelerating in every area of American life, and most importantly for us, in financial reporting. Mere facts, however, are no longer enough in today's volatile economic climate. They must be current to be of any use during a period that is a paradoxical combination of double-digit inflation and burgeoning recession. In the face of constantly shifting figures, management decisions concerning such matters as sales forecasts, capital expenditures, and inventories cannot be made with any degree of authority without a timely frame of reference.

In response to this demand, Coopers & Lybrand is proposing to review—not audit—quarterly financial data and the supplementary historical accounting data included in annual reports. Although the profession has not yet set standards in those areas, we feel our action is justified by the urgency of the changing reporting environment. These expanded services will be offered, on an optional basis, for 1974 annual reports and for quarterly reports in 1975.

Independent accountants are uniquely qualified to assist the managements and directors of clients in fulfilling their responsibilities in meeting public demand for reliable information. By training and experience, auditors are well equipped to deal with this need. More importantly, they have developed a knowledge base about client operations, systems, and accounting polices that is not generally available.

One of the major advantages of the new service that I foresee is that we will be involved with our clients on a more or less continuing basis, without having to wait for year-end results. SEC Commissioner A. A. Sommer, Jr., speaking to the American Accounting Association last April, examined interim reporting at some length.[1] He said:

[†]A commentary on *The Changing Environment in Financial Reporting*, a 44-page manual on interim reporting issued by Coopers & Lybrand in 1975. Reprinted from the *Financial Executive*, December 1974, pp. 22-24, 26, 28, 32, copyright 1974, with permission of the Financial Executives Institute, 10 Madison Avenue, P.O.Box 1938, Morristown, NJ 07962-1938. (973) 898-4600.

[1]"The SEC and the Accounting Profession: 'Creative Tension'" by SEC Commissioner A.A. Sommer, Jr., at the 25th annual meeting of the Northeast Regional Group of the American Accounting Association, Philadelphia, April 19, 1974.

...There are strong pressures upon auditors to expand their involvement in the total financial reporting process. It has been suggested that they assume responsibility for the integrity of all financial information in annual reports and that, in addition, they have responsibility for press releases including financial information. Similarly, it is suggested that they be more intimately involved with interim statements.

This proposal has particular importance, it seems to me. Increasingly the market appears to be a short-term market; a single bad quarter can often have excessive impact upon the price of an issue of securities; hence, there is great temptation on the part of management to use various devices to smooth out earnings. Only if the independent auditor is involved in the interim reporting process can this temptation be thwarted.

While there are occasional misleading or inaccurate reports, most unaudited quarterly reports are highly reliable. But it is distinctly to management's advantage to issue accurate information so that the company's credibility is in no way jeopardized, and the business and financial communities are naturally concerned that the very few misleading or inaccurate reports not be considered typical.

Within this context, Coopers & Lybrand will institute a new service: we will review, upon request, quarterly results before they are published to reduce the possibility of errors or omissions. We plan to do this by reviewing the accounting principles and procedures, their consistency with those used for annual reporting, and appropriateness of any modifications of principles made for interim reporting. This review would be a periodical inquiry, using expertise and knowledge of the company together with our reading of financial statements and comparing them with previously issued quarterly and annual financial statement. We have been doing this for some time now on an informal basis for a number of clients who have requested it.

These proposals are being made on a preliminary basis—as a discussion draft. In this manner, we can evaluate comments and suggestions from clients and other concerned members of the business and financial community before releasing a final implementation draft in 1975.

Since auditing interim quarterly data is uneconomical, we are proposing to review rather than audit.

We are prepared to issue a report [see Exhibit 1] for the chief executive officer and the client's board of directors. The report will detail the nature of the limited review and indicate that no adjustments of the company's representations are proposed. Because we are not performing an audit, we cannot, of course, issue an opinion in the usual form.

The interim review is subject to certain conditions. Reasonably reliable financial statements must be available on a regular and timely basis, and interim estimates will require supporting documentation so that their reasonableness may be assessed. Since extensive background knowledge is required to perform this type of review, we will obviously be unable to perform this service for clients unless we have previously audited their annual reports.

The review report is basically intended for management and the board of directors. When, however, a client wishes to disclose to its shareholders that its interim reports have been reviewed, we will provide an appropriate report for publication [see Exhibit 2].

QUARTERLY AUDIT IMPRACTICAL

The value of quarterly financial statements is their timeliness and their usefulness as indicators of performance for the whole year. These two characteristics of interim financial statements make the conventional audit impractical because the time and costs of performing such audits—in terms both of professional fees and of increased internal accounting expenses—would offset the benefits.

It is of crucial importance that interim financial reports be issued as soon as possible after the close of a fiscal quarter in order to give users of these data time to reassess whatever judgments they may have made with respect to investments in the company. Studies have shown that the delay between the close of the period and the publication of financial information is roughly twice as great for the annual audited financial statements as it is for quarterly financial information.

THE QUARTERLY REVIEW

The potential benefits of the review of quarterly financial data are so important that some form of reporting this data within existing standards is warranted. Further, a review encompassing a formal program of inquiries, a reading of the financial statements, and a comparison of data between periods, which is less than an audit, will increase the user's confidence in quarterly data. The users of our reports must recognize that the interim financial statements are still unaudited. They must also recognize that, while we will report upon all significant matters affecting the financial data that come to our attention, we cannot guarantee that all significant matters would come to our attention as a result of our review.

In reviewing interim financial statements and summarized interim financial data to support his report, the auditor would be required to make "inquiries" into several diverse areas. The depth and extent of the inquiries are, of course, a judgmental matter.

Inquiries cannot take the form of a simple mechanical exercise involving asking a few questions and noting the responses. On the other hand, the auditor should not be expected to examine sufficient, competent evidential matter because he is not conducting an audit. It is here that the review procedure differs from an audit. In the review procedure, the auditor is satisfied if an answer is logical and consistent with his knowledge of the client. Only if the inverse is true will he ask further questions and pursue the issue. In an audit, the auditor wants all responses documented.

UNDERSTANDING REPORTING PRACTICES

Before any review procedure is begun, the client's interim reporting practices will be recorded. Because of the crucial nature of this knowledge base, both the manager and the partner will interview the chief financial officer. Further interviews may be conducted by other staff people under the manager's supervision. The resulting record of the client's interim reporting procedures will be part of a carryforward file that is updated at each review date. The final record will be reviewed with the chief financial officer to ensure accuracy of information. He should send us a letter summarizing the company's interim reporting principles and practices in a format similar to but more detailed than the disclosure of accounting policies required by Accounting Principles Board Opinion No. 22, *Disclosure of Accounting Policies*. Obviously, the interim reporting practices should be reviewed for consistency with those used in prior quarters and previous fiscal year-end.

Any problems should be resolved immediately with the chief financial officer, and a description of their disposition should be included in the first report that is issued on a limited circulation basis.

BUDGETS

The auditor would familiarize himself with the client's budget for the current fiscal year and with its budgeting procedures because the budgets should form the basis for management control of the business. Before reviewing any quarterly financial statements, the chief financial officer, the chief executive officer, and any other appropriate personnel connected with the client's budgeting procedures should be interviewed.

The current year's budget should also be reviewed and compared with the results of the previous fiscal year. Any questions stemming from the comparisons should be resolved with the chief financial officer.

INITIAL REVIEW

During the first engagement to review a client's quarterly reports, the auditor should generally also review the unaudited reports issued during the preceding fiscal year, using the same general types of procedures employed for the current year, while being aware of the audit results. Because the trend of revenues and income is an important analytical tool, this is obviously the most desirable procedure, and clients should be encouraged to use it.

The partner would also review the press release, the drafts of the quarterly stockholders' report, and the draft of SEC Form 10-Q, and indicate the disposition of items brought to his attention. The partner and the manager should have a closing conference with the client's chief financial officer and communicate any findings to the chief executive officer before the report is released.

FINANCIAL DATA OUTSIDE FINANCIAL STATEMENTS

A corporation's annual report to its stockholders generally contains a text, often a letter from the management, analyzing the company results and prospects and the basic financial statements. It often includes significant amounts of statistical and financial data. The kinds of information vary considerably, depending on the complexity of the reporting company, regulatory requirements, and management's desire to use the annual report to communicate with the shareholders. Although much of the historical financial data can be derived from the financial statements, other kinds of information are also presented. An incomplete but illustrative list would include: sales and earnings by divisions or product lines, backlog, mineral reserves or oil and gas reserves, number of employees, manufacturing floor space, retail store selling space, and research and development results.

In addition, much of the information is interpreted by comparing it to the company's or the industry's past performance, computing percentage increases and decreases, analyzing ratios, etc. The manner of presentation will also vary. The information may be included in the "president's letter;" in other narratives provided on divisional or product-line activity; in bar graphs, circle graphs, five-year and ten-year summaries; or in separate sections typically entitled "financial highlights" or "financial review."

INHERENT PROBLEMS

There are problems that an independent public accountant may face in assuming a responsibility for data outside the basic financial statements, however desirable his involvement. These problems arise not only from the auditor's reporting responsibility, but also from the way the data are displayed in the text of the annual report.

Simply stated, the primary problems in attesting to financial data outside the financial statements are as follows:

A. There are now no standards for setting forth the auditor's responsibility for reporting outside the basic financial statements. Most accountants agree on the general criteria holding that information in the annual report's main text should be consistent with the information included in the related financial statements. However, an auditor, having performed an audit, should know his client, and can and should comment on the annual report's nonfinancial aspects.

B. Some of the information included in the text has not been subjected to audit tests within the traditional scope of financial audits. Floor space and employee statistics are two examples. Although, in most cases, such data could be brought under audit control, the additional cost might not be worth the benefit in improving the usefulness of the information to the reader.

C. Dispersing the information throughout the text may draw the auditor into assuming a responsibility for all of the representations included. But he may not be prepared to judge such factors as forecasts, economic appraisals, market evaluations, etc. Any attempt by the auditor to protect himself by specifying the information for which he is assuming responsibility would involve—at least under present annual report format—submitting a lengthy and cumbersome report.

D. There are no standards governing the auditing procedures that should be applied to nonfinancial statement data. Some of the information represents management's interpretation of events or transactions that have occurred during the year. In common with all judgments, these represent considered opinion and not matters of fact. While auditors may be professionally competent, in most instances, to determine if these judgments are wrong they cannot judge if an opinion is the only one possible in the situation or, indeed, the most likely one. Management must retain the responsibility for the report.

A TEMPORARY SOLUTION

The accounting profession is working on the problems of reviewing and reporting on financial data outside the basic financial statements. Auditing standards requiring such reviews and setting forth procedures to be followed are being developed.

In the meantime, we intend to follow the program outlined below:

A. Coopers & Lybrand has always reviewed the historical accounting data to be included in the texts of our client's annual reports. The purpose is to make sure that the information is correct and does not conflict with the representations in the financial statements. Historically, this has not been viewed as an additional audit procedure distinct from those steps necessary to express an opinion on the financial statements. This requirement continues as firm policy. The procedure, however, does not and will not entail any explicit reporting in our opinion.

B. Under certain conditions, we are prepared to include in our opinion an explicit attestation of historical accounting information presented in the annual report other than in the normal basic financial statements. This attestation would be in the form of an additional paragraph in our standard audit report, which would read somewhat as follows:

> In addition, we have read the historical accounting information included in the nonfinancial statement sections of this annual report other than that labeled unaudited; have compared it to data taken from the audited financial statement; have subjected it to audit procedures; have verified its mathematical accuracy. In our opinion, such data are fairly stated in relation to the audited financial statements taken as a whole.

We are prepared to make the foregoing attestation only in connection with annual reports meeting the following conditions:

1. The historical accounting data covered by the above paragraph are derived only from the financial statement or data for which we have performed specific additional audit tests.
2. Data that provide details not derived from the financial statements, data that represent forecasting, or data that are not susceptible to audit tests will be so labeled and will not be covered by our report.

C. There may be other cases where these conditions are not met, but where the clients wants some attestation of financial data outside the basic financial statements. This problem can be resolved by placing all of the material for which attestation is desired in clearly segregated portions of the annual report and referencing our opinion paragraph to specific pages or sections of the annual report. The additional paragraph would read somewhat as follows:

> In addition, we have read the financial information derived from the financial statements examined by us, included in this annual report on pages xx to xx, have compared it to data incorporated in the audited financial statements, subjected it to audit procedures, and verified its mathematical accuracy. In our opinion, such data are fairly stated in relation to the financial statements taken as a whole.

CONCLUSION

Wider involvement could also lead to increased legal liability for accountants. Conversely, earlier involvement might prevent or at least minimize legal difficulties for both client and auditor.

We believe that the times demand positive action. As Sommer aptly states:

> The task that confronts all of us is to restore integrity in, and the confidence of the public in the integrity of, American corporate life....

Exhibit 1

DRAFT OF REPORT FOR ISSUANCE TO MANAGEMENT AND THE BOARD OF DIRECTORS

To the Chief Executive Officer and Board of Directors
XYZ Corporation

In accordance with our arrangement with you as set forth in our letter of , 19xx, we have performed the review procedures described therein with reference to the unaudited financial statements of XYZ Corporation as at March 31, 1975 and 1974 and the related unaudited summarized interim financial data included in the quarterly report to shareholders. Our review and inquiry were limited to the accounting principles and practices used by the Company in the preparation of such statements, their consistency with the prior year, and appropriateness for interim statement purposes. Based on this limited review and inquiry, we have no adjustments to propose with respect to such data. However, since such review procedures do not constitute an audit in accordance with generally accepted auditing standards, we cannot express an audit opinion on the data we have reviewed.

In addition, we noted the following items which we believe appropriate for your attention: [List items]

COOPERS & LYBRAND

City, State
Date

The sample report would be expanded in practice to include commentary that we considered appropriate. Such subjects as appropriate modifications of annual reporting principles, disclosure considerations, and the like should be included, as well as specific comments directed towards improving the interim reporting practices of the company. The CPA may also wish to include comments in this report, covering identified weaknesses in controls or operating problems that require management attention. This report is intended to have limited circulation because it will probably contain commentary on the interim reporting practices of clients and other matters of a type not normally presented to users outside the company. It presumes a level of knowledge of the company's systems and procedures not usually present outside the management and the directors of the company.

Exhibit 2

DRAFT OF REPORT FOR PUBLIC ISSUANCE
SHORT FORM

To the Board of Directors and Stockholders
XYZ Corporation

We have read the unaudited financial statements (not published herein) of XYZ Corporation as at March 31, 1975 and 1974 and the related unaudited summarized interim financial data included in this quarterly report to shareholders. We have also reviewed the accounting principles and the procedures used by the company in the preparation of such statements, their consistency with the prior year, and their appropriate appreciation for interim statement purposes in conformity with generally accepted accounting principles. Based on this limited review, we have no adjustments to propose with respect to such data. However, since such review procedures do not constitute an audit in accordance with generally accepted auditing standards, we cannot express an audit opinion on the data presented.

COOPERS & LYBRAND

City, State
Date

THE MANAGEMENT OF AN ACCOUNTING PRACTICE: A SEARCH FOR PRINCIPLES AND ALTERNATIVES[†]

by
Philip L. Defliese

INTRODUCTION

THE topic assigned to me—no choice was offered—seems like an odd one for an Accounting Research Convocation. I was told that the participants, heavily involved in research, teaching and related campus activities in the field of accounting and auditing, rarely have an opportunity to probe the inner-workings of a major public accounting firm, and would therefore appreciate learning how one operates and performs the decision-making role that is so essential to the credibility of our capitalistic system.

It was recognized that since my professional career was restricted to one firm—Coopers & Lybrand—my presentation would be limited to that experience. This would be overcome, presumably, by having my counterpart do likewise, and thus with exposure to the manner in which two of the eight major firms operated, a reasonable cross section of practice could be obtained. I believe that is probably so, but you will more likely find more similarities than differences.

ORGANIZATIONAL STRUCTURE

Although most jurisdictions within the U.S. permit professional organizations to incorporate, it is interesting to note that none of the Big Eight public accounting firms has opted to embrace the corporate form; they prefer to cling to the partnership format with which they have long been comfortable. I believe this is because all have examined the advantages and disadvantages carefully and have reached the conclusion that the complications of the corporate form—particularly from the legal standpoint—far outweigh the small tax advantages available. The legal complications I refer to should not be confused with legal liability—a matter that exists rather pervasively under either organizational form, and is generally assuaged by adequate insurance protection in either case. Ordinarily, partners of major firms have no equity interest in their

[†]Presented at the 1977 Accounting Research Convocation held at The University of Alabama. Reprinted from *1977 Accounting Research Convocation,* Jonathan J. Davies, ed. (University, AL: Graduate School of Business Administration, The University of Alabama, 1978), pp. 133-153, with permission of Culverhouse School of Accountancy, The University of Alabama.

firms other than the cash capital they contribute, plus their share of undistributed earnings, and with a large number of partners entering and retiring each year, the use of stock instead of partnership interests would unduly complicate the financial and legal aspects of organization. The recent changes in the tax laws permitting the substantial sheltering of self-employed pension fund contributions minimize any corporate tax advantages.

Because of the tremendous sizes of the major firms, it becomes necessary to operate, as a practical matter, along corporate lines and I have furnished you copies of the Coopers & Lybrand (U.S.) organization charts which demonstrate this rather vividly. Nevertheless, a partnership structured along corporate lines has both the best and worst of both worlds, perhaps with a tilt toward the better side.

As a partnership, we have the usual unlimited liability, rather well covered for the most part by insurance. Still, the youngest and most inexperienced partner can commit the firm and all his partners to an enormous liability (something not restricted to the young) and this has a sobering effect on all partners; in this respect they are all equal, even though profit shares are not equal.

Corporate lines of authority are usually very severe, and those of you that are close to the management scene, or teach it, know that an organization chart inhibits access to higher lines of authority; channels must be carefully observed. In a partnership, even though it may be structured along corporate lines, there is a commonality of interest, a congeniality, if you will, that permits departure from rigid channels. Partners are encouraged to talk freely and discuss their problems with one another, despite channels, in the interest of helping each other. Consequently, in reading these charts you should realize that there are, or could be, many dotted lines which are omitted for simplicity; they should be assumed. The interaction among partners of all levels is considerable and it is one of the greatest benefits we have. It makes for a feeling of one family, and we try to operate that way as best we know how. Surprisingly, this permeates the international scene as well.

THE INTERNATIONAL FIRM

The first chart presents merely an overview of the international firm of Coopers & Lybrand. It is a firm of firms, so to speak, and it would be too complicated to present a world-wide organization chart. The constituent firms are essentially autonomous locally and have joined in a world-wide association that binds all members and partners to the observance of uniform practice policies. Those policies are established by the International Executive Committee, upon the recommendation of international staff committees shown on the chart. This format is not unique; it parallels every other international firm because there is practically no other way for an international firm to operate. Each country has its own jurisdictional problems and the firms within it must operate autonomously even though bound by an international federation.

At present, the International Executive Committee is comprised of seven members—three representatives of the U.S. Firms, two from the U.K. Firms, and one each from Canada and Australia. As a rough guideline, firms with a complement of 1,000 or more are invited to join the Committee, with the result that the Committee has increased in the past and will probably do so in the future (at present, total personnel is approximately 20,000). International Policy statements covering all facets of practice are formulated by the relevant Committees with world-wide representation, and are then submitted for approval by the Executive Committee. In addition, the Executive Committee deals with all matters of administration and world-wide policies.

U.S. FIRM ORGANIZATION

As you would expect, an organization of our size—approximately of 7,600 in the U.S.—requires both a line and staff organization. And, as you would expect, the distinction between the two is sometimes fuzzy. Of course, the line organization has a pervasive management responsibility, and starts with the typical pyramid arrangement. In an enterprise of this magnitude, selection of top management becomes very crucial and we have developed a rather unique democratic process for this purpose. Recognizing that 660 partners could not possibly have an adequate knowledge or basis for voting, we restrict the franchise to the Firm Council, a body of approximately 70 partners* elected (by the Council itself) for terms of 6 years (like the U.S. Senate). There is no limit to the number of partners eligible for Council membership and an attempt is made to provide representation of all disciplines, as well as practitioners, administrators, and technicians. They are selected on the basis of their demonstrated ability, performance, judgment and business acumen. This group meets quarterly and discusses with the Executive Committee the business and policies of the Firm. This exposure equips them to perform their most important functions—the election of the Chairman and Executive Committee (and fixing their compensation), the admission of new partners, amending the basic partnership agreement, etc.—truly a parliamentary format.

The election of the management team takes place every three years. The names of all members of Council are on the ballots to elect the Chairman (this is done first) and the eight other members of the Executive Committee. On the first ballot (in each case) if an individual receives a two-thirds vote of the Council, he is elected. On the second ballot for Chairman, a majority vote is required. On the second ballot for the Executive Committee, those receiving the most votes are elected. On the second and succeeding ballots, the number of candidates listed is restricted to twice the number of remaining vacancies (but no less than four) selected from those receiving the highest number of votes on the preceding ballot. The voting is entirely secret, the ballots are mailed to a retired Council member who reports the count and destroys the ballots. We believe that this process brings to the fore those best qualified for the management role—based on the peer group's intimate knowledge of the available candidates. Once elected, the

---

*The term "partner" includes principals (non CPA specialists) who act as partners.

Chairman, with the advice and consent of the Executive Committee, selects the remainder of the management team as outlined on the organization chart. (It is interesting to note that, at present, two of the eight other members of the Executive Committee are not in any administrative position and actually report—from a line standpoint—to others on the chart.)

The Chairman is the Chief Executive of the Firm, and chief of operations, but the Executive Committee makes policy decisions and determines Firm position in all important areas. Chart II shows the organization of the Chairman's office—five Vice Chairmen and the General Counsel. Two of the Vice Chairmen (Domestic operations—East and West) are basically line, having direct responsibility for the operations of the 16 groups of offices and the Management Consulting and Actuarial Benefits Consulting Services organizations. The other three Vice Chairmen are basically staff, but operate as line managers within their areas. One is the Vice Chairman and Technical Counsel, who provides the top technical accounting and auditing advice to the Chairman, helping in the formulation of the Firm's positions in this area. The Vice Chairman-Domestic Operations—National is in charge of the National Office and all National Directors of the various disciplines (see following charts) report to him; these are essentially staff operations. The Vice Chairman—International (who is also a member of the International Executive Committee, together with the Chairman and one other U.S. Executive Committee member) provides liaison and administration to all overseas offices, operations, multi-national corporation audits, etc. The General Counsel is essentially the Firm's top lawyer (in house); with his staff he provides legal counsel on all litigation matters as well as a legal consulting service to practice partners as they need it in their auditing function. This legal-advice function has become one of the most valuable adjuncts to the practice of public accounting—a form of preventive medicine. Of course, outside legal counsel is also utilized when needed.

I have not expanded the organization chart as it relates to the line organization operated by the two Vice Chairmen-Domestic—East and West because it would follow the usual pattern of organization of operating branches. The offices of the Firm are organized into 16 groups of three to five geographically contiguous offices, each with a managing partner who organizes his office in pyramidical fashion, depending on size. One of the managing partners in each group (usually of the largest office in the group) acts as the group managing partner and has overall responsibility for operations of all offices within the group. We find this advantageous because movement of personnel is facilitated as needed by the ebb and flow of professional work requirements, inasmuch as the offices are relatively close. For example, the New York Group consists of the New York, Newark, White Plains and Long Island offices. This also provides diversified experience for the staff. In addition, duplication of administrative functions is minimized.

Chart III shows the various National Directors that report to the Vice Chairman in charge of the National Office; each Director has his own chart, which follows. As I indicated previously, these directors function essentially as staff, providing support to the line organization. They set policy for the operating disciplines and administrative functions—Accounting, Auditing and SEC Services, Tax Services, Practice Development, Finance and Administration (the Firm's internal accounting), Personnel Development, and EDP Development. Although basically staff, they interact with the line operations considerably; if shown, the dotted lines would clutter up the charts—the subsequent charts will provide some insight into this. The policies formulated are communicated by means of Policy Statements (and related supplementary memoranda), issued by each director under his authority, although occasionally a particular policy will require Executive Committee approval. As you can imagine, communication—clear, speedy, direct and unequivocal—is essential to the smooth operation of a huge professional organization. It is one of the most difficult and ever-present problems we face.

ACCOUNTING AND AUDITING SERVICES

The next five charts portray the responsibilities of the National Director of Accounting, Auditing and SEC Services. These services represent almost 70% of the Firm's practice and thus require considerable support. Four major activities are involved (Charts V-VIII). The first—Technical Services—is the Firm's research group—a nerve center which acts as a repository of all past and present research in the accounting and auditing field. When partners or professional staff in the field come across a new or difficult problem that requires considerable research, they contact the appropriate person in this directorate for the quickest and best answer the Firm has. Past positions, precedents, etc. are catalogued and accessed as needed. Most auditing problems revolve about accounting issues—something that isn't too well understood on the campus—and the type of research provided by Technical Services is the starting point toward their resolution.

Ultimate resolution of field problems frequently brings into play the Consulting Group (Chart VI). This group acts as the consulting arm of the practicing partners and staff. It is composed of seasoned audit partners who have demonstrated their ability to ferret out the relevant facts pertinent to an issue and to aid the practitioner in dealing with his client's problems. The interaction of the Technical Services Group and Consulting Group with the field personnel constitutes the fundamental manner in which public accounting is practiced.

Line and Staff Interaction. To understand how this interaction takes place, we must start with the field operation. A practice partner is in charge of every audit engagement; beneath him, depending on the size of the engagement, are one or more managers, supervisors, in-charge accountants (referred to in the past as "seniors") and staff accountants. In addition, a second partner is assigned to every engagement involving a public company or over 500 hours of audit time. The second partner acts as a form of quality control (described more fully later) and as a consultant on the engagement.

When an issue cannot be resolved by the first or second partner—after the assistance of the National Technical Services has been solicited—the matter is referred to the partner designated as the Consulting partner within the group (See

Chart VI). If the matter is still unresolved, and particularly if the client objects to the position taken, it is referred to the Associate Director next above, and so on until it reaches the top. Most problems are solved at the lower levels, but with the increasing complexity of business and transactions today, the Consulting Group is constantly busy at all levels. In many instances, representatives of the group will meet and negotiate with clients together with the practice partners. In this manner, the best talents of the Firm are brought to bear on the issues that require resolution—complete interaction.

Computer Auditing. The next chart (VII)—the Computer Auditing Assistance Group (CAAG)—portrays more of an operating group than a staff function. Engagements involving sophisticated computer installations need to be audited in a sophisticated manner. It is no longer desirable or feasible to audit around the computer—we must audit through the computer. Specially trained computer auditors (teams of the CAAG group located in each office group) serve as adjuncts to the regular audit teams for this purpose (see "Operating Staff"). With their expertise they focus on all the necessary control features of an installation, making many useful suggestions to clients. They are constantly developing new audit programs for the computers they service and thus expedite the auditing process while at the same time doing a more thorough job. They serve the audit partners in charge of the engagement and interaction is optimal.

QUALITY CONTROL

Finally, we get to the Quality Control Organization (Chart VIII). The importance of quality control in today's environment cannot be overemphasized. Our profession doesn't allow a margin for error. One blooper can wipe out 99,000 good audits; a firm's reputation is constantly on the line. Coopers & Lybrand has been developing its procedures in this area for over fifteen years, and has been applying the same techniques on an international scale for the last ten years. This is a form of "peer-review" process (similar to that recently proposed by the Institute) operating internally.

Pre-Release Review. I have previously referred to the second partner on each engagement as a form of quality control. He reviews the engagement when it is completed and before a report is rendered. His review is both procedural and substantive. Each engagement is controlled by an "engagement control sheet" upon which is listed—as a form of reminder list—all the Policy Statements that are relevant; adherence to these policies is attested to by the staff performing the work and the second partner assures himself that all procedures have been followed. (This is not to be confused with the audit program, which is just one segment of this process.) In addition, the second partner reviews the MAPS sheet (Matters for the Attention of Partners) on which the audit manager has listed all the items of accounting and auditing substance that he believes the first partner should review—including decisions already made; comments concerning the disposition of these items are required to be noted and second-guessing is not considered out-of-order in this exercise. These procedures are part of the pre-release quality control, and obviously are more important.

Post-Released Reviews. The Quality Control organization conducts post-release reviews and although these are after-the-fact, they provide an incentive for optimal staff performance because of a constant awareness that the work of each member of the organization will be randomly sampled for quality once every three years. Partner/Manager teams selected from practice are sent to different practice offices to review office procedures, reports, working papers, etc.; they cover every aspect of practice and issue reports of their findings. These peer reviewers are severer critics than outsiders would be. Most often the findings relate to weaknesses of documentation rather than errors of substance or judgment. Differences of opinion do sometimes emerge and they are arbitrated up through the chain of command; all in all, the process serves additionally as a training tool.

One additional responsibility assigned to Quality Control is the determination that partners and staff are financially independent of clients. This involves an elaborate communications network to make certain that no investments in clients are maintained.

PRACTICE DEVELOPMENT AND INDUSTRY PROGRAMS

The remaining charts (IX - XII) are self-explanatory for the most part, and perhaps of less interest to you as accounting researchers. The function of the Personnel Development directorate in the areas of recruiting, training, and development of staff and partners is rather obvious. Some explanation of the Practice Development Directorate is in order. While the ultimate objective of this group is the growth and enhancement of the Firm's practice, much of what they do is in the form of professional and practice enhancement. The publications group produces client letters, monographs, books, etc. for use by clients, staff and the profession. The industry research and related industry programs all serve a very useful purpose. Here again, their interaction with the Accounting and Auditing Technical Services and Consulting groups is quite evident. All major industries are assigned to practicing Industry Chairmen who coordinate all the Firm's activities (including research) in their respective industries. They serve as consultants to the field, aid in quality control reviews, and formulate the Firm's industry policy positions. Monitoring current developments in the industry is also a prime responsibility of an industry chairman.

In summary, a public accounting practice can survive and grow only if it is well organized to offer quality talent trained to provide a quality service to its clientele. Integrity, independence, and quality are the hallmarks of the accounting profession and all efforts must be directed to achieve this end.

Chart 1
Coopers & Lybrand (International)

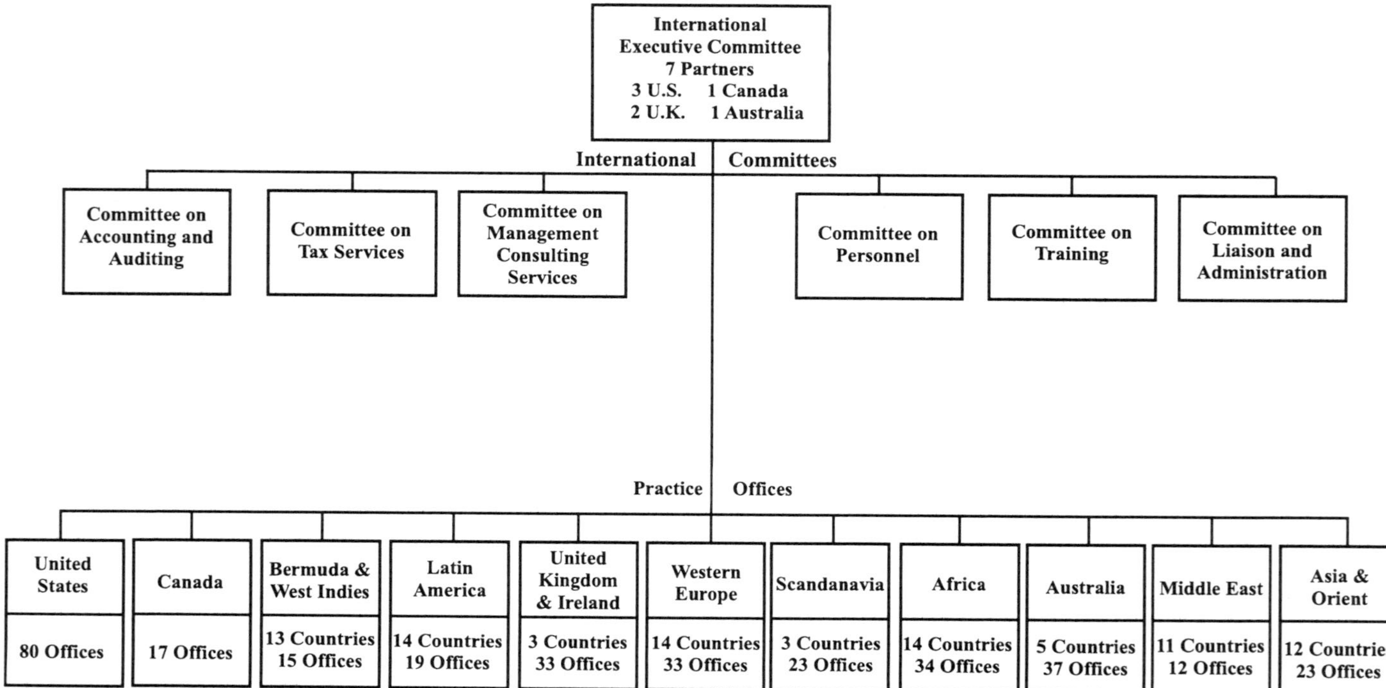

Chart II
Coopers & Lybrand
U.S. Firm Organization

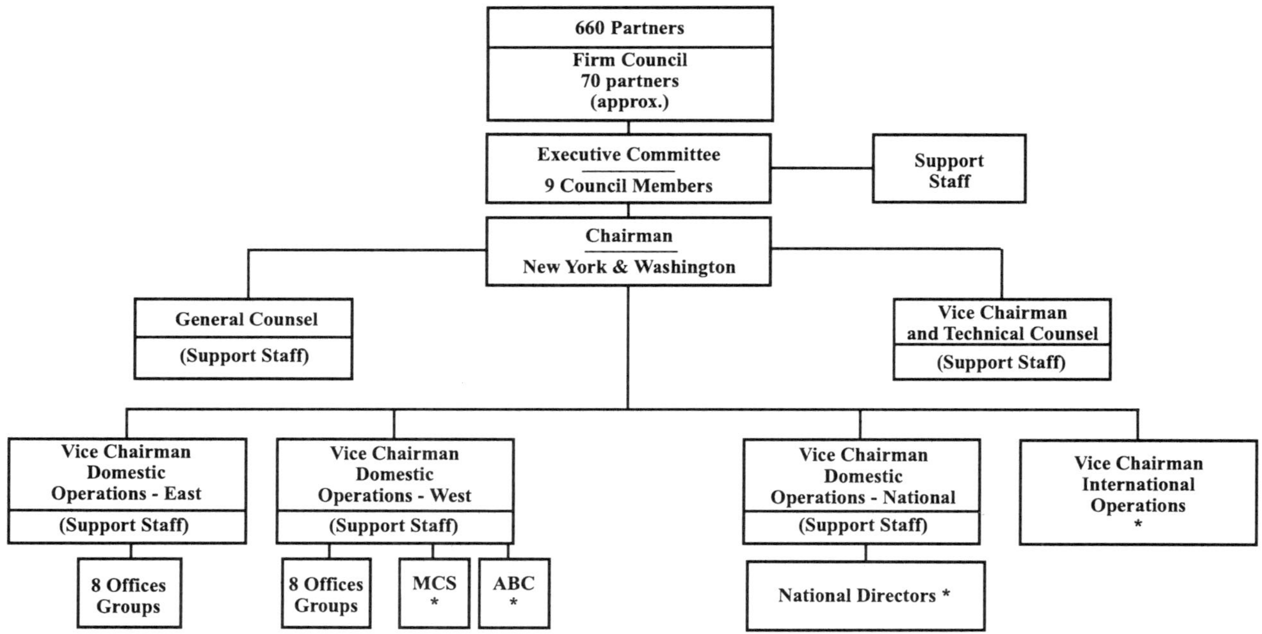

*See following charts

Chart III
National Headquarters' Staff

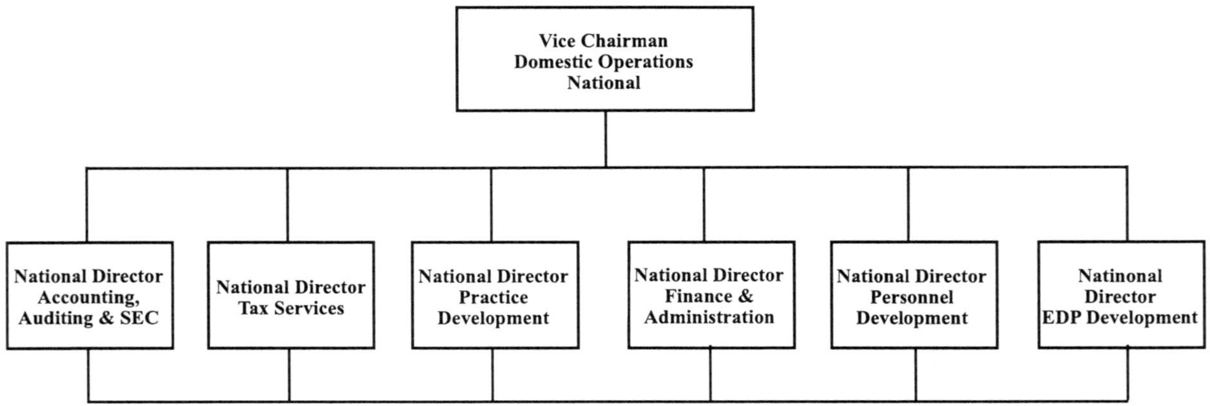

See following charts

Chart IV
National Accounting, Auditing
SEC Services Staff

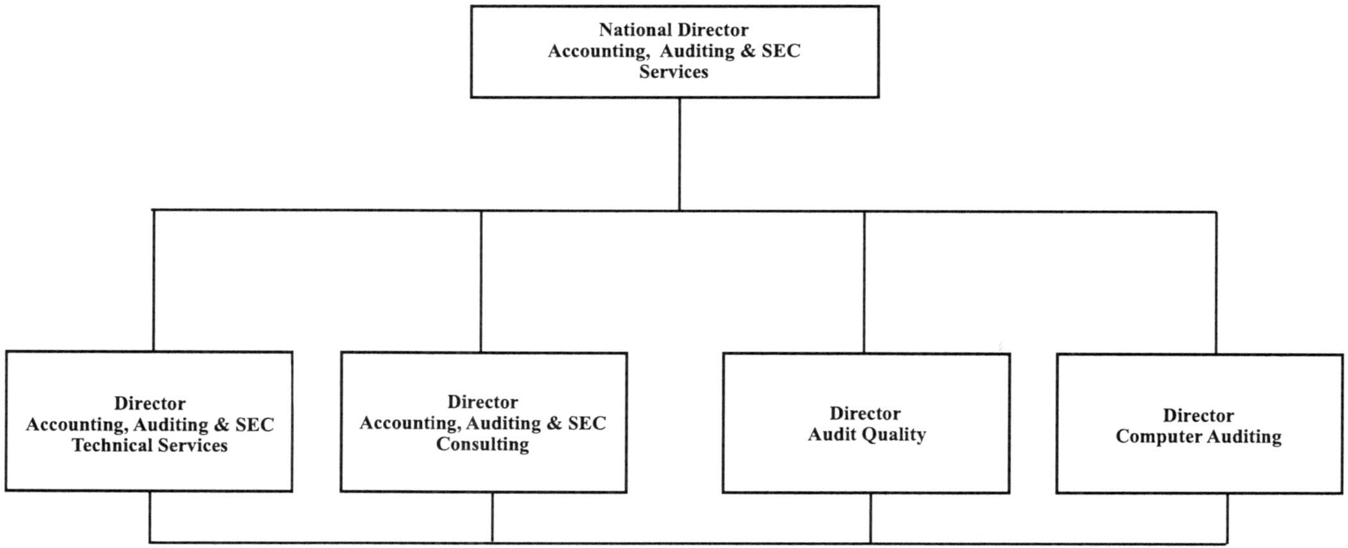

See following charts

Chart V
Accounting, Auditing & SEC - Technical Services

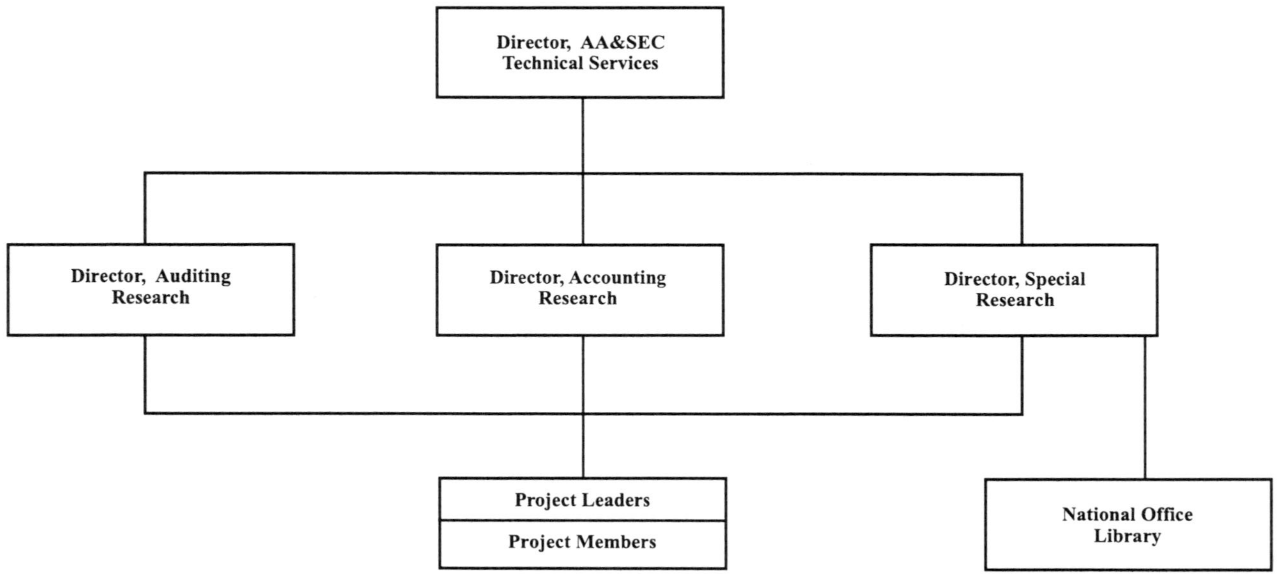

Chart VI
Accounting, Auditing & SEC - Consulting Services

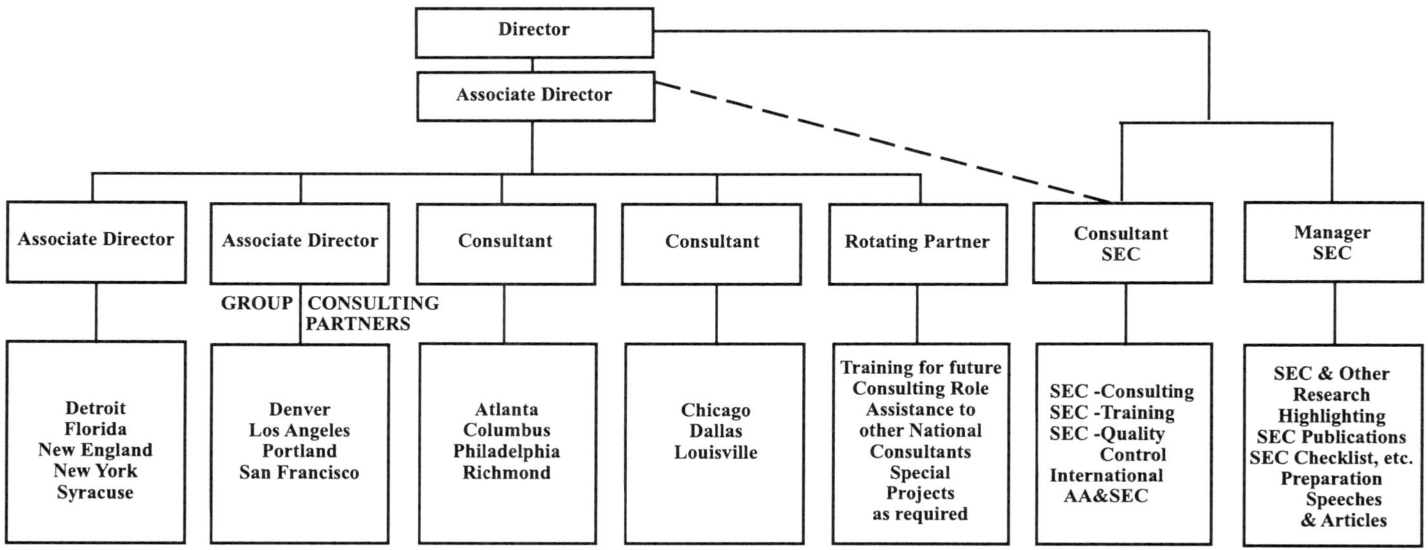

Chart VII
Computer Auditing Assistance Group

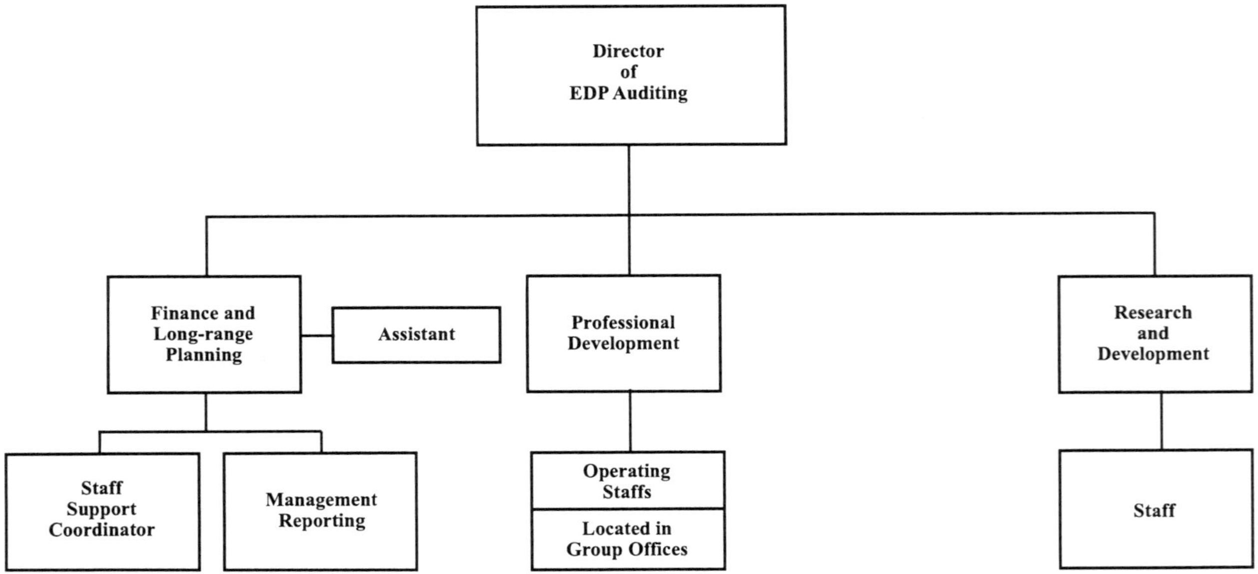

Chart VIII
Audit Quality Control

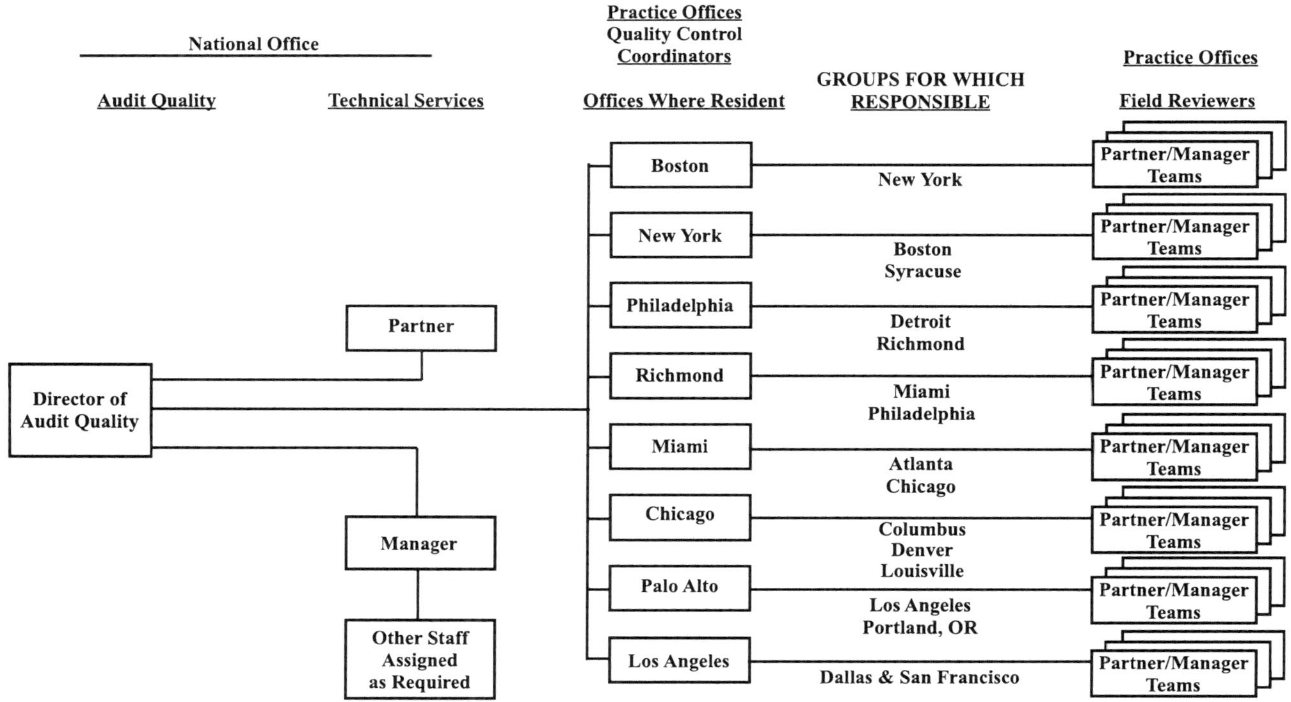

Chart IX

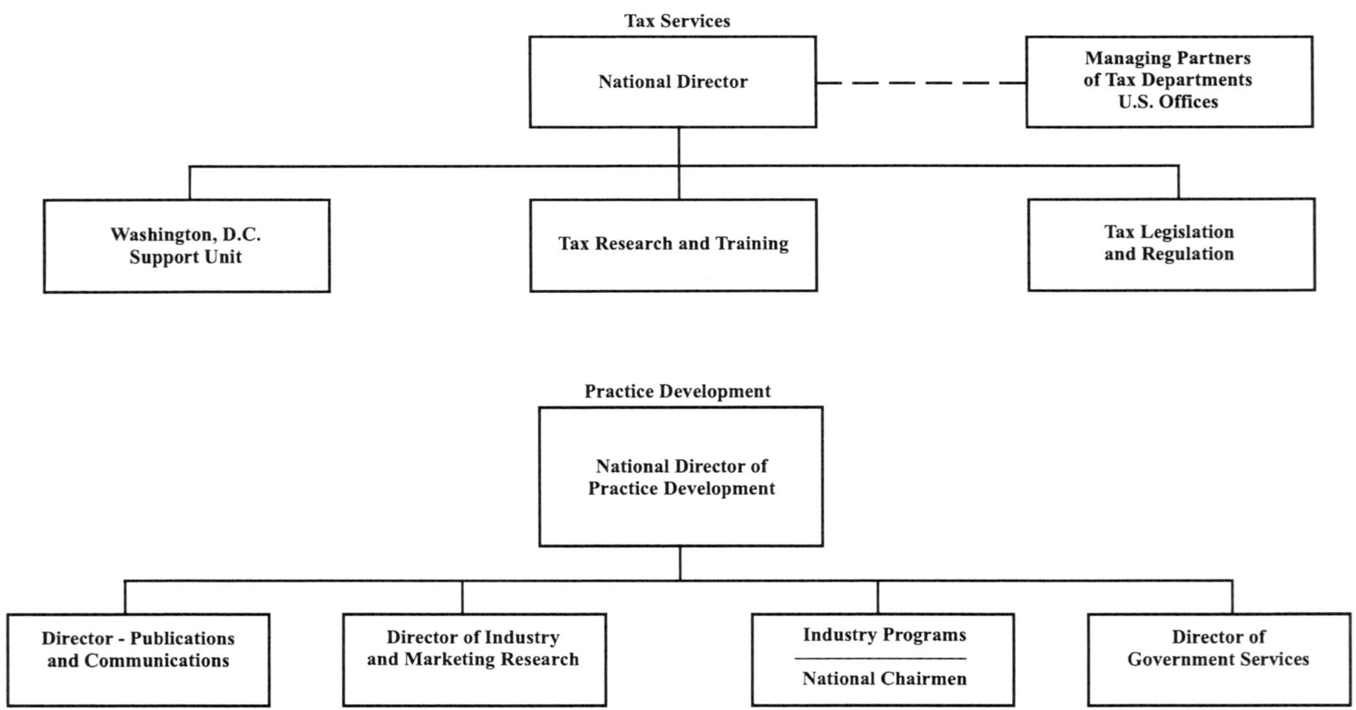
Tax Services
National Director
Managing Partners of Tax Departments U.S. Offices
Washington, D.C. Support Unit
Tax Research and Training
Tax Legislation and Regulation
Practice Development
National Director of Practice Development
Director - Publications and Communications
Director of Industry and Marketing Research
Industry Programs
National Chairmen
Director of Government Services

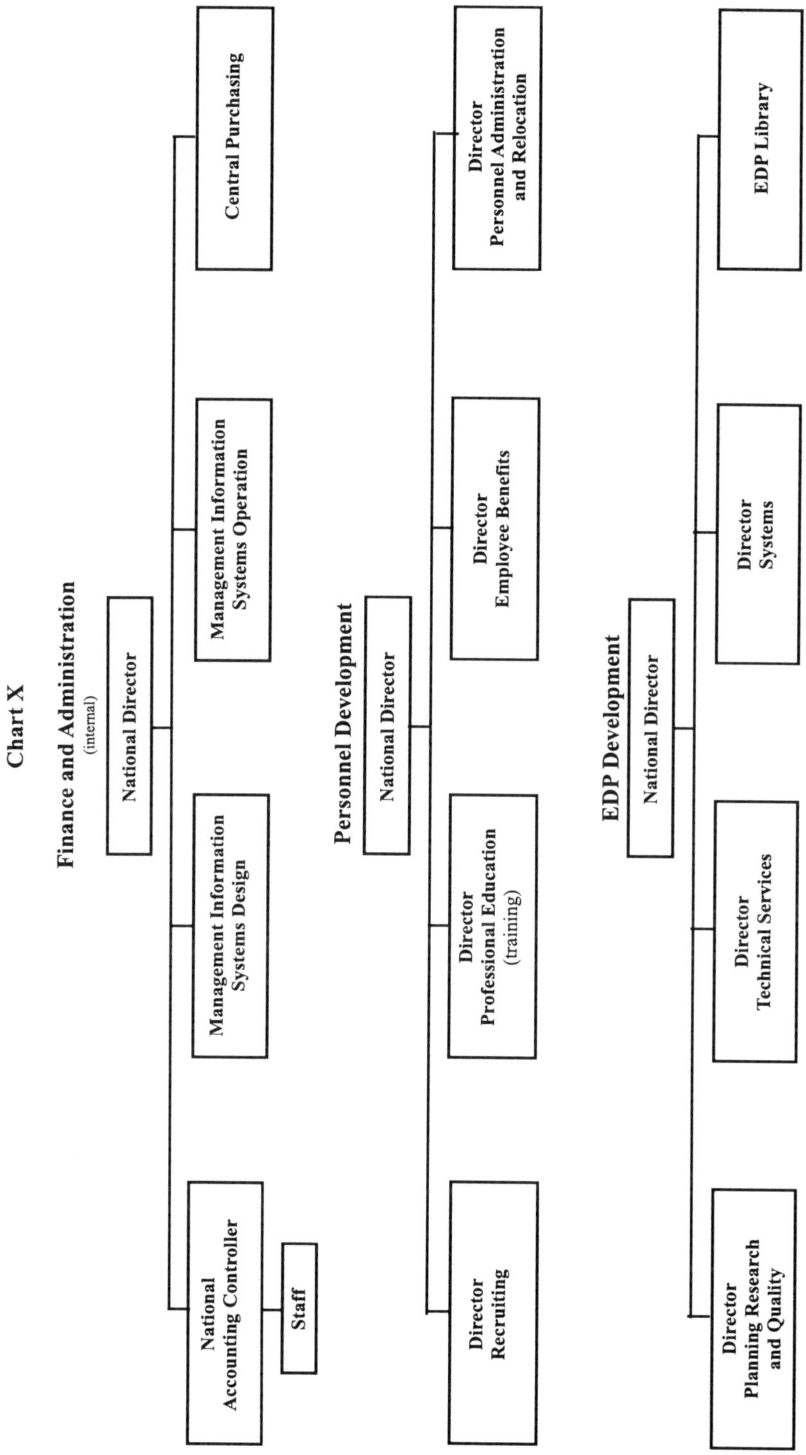
Chart X
Finance and Administration
(internal)
National Director
National Accounting Controller
Staff
Management Information Systems Design
Management Information Systems Operation
Central Purchasing
Personnel Development
National Director
Director Recruiting
Director Professional Education (training)
Director Employee Benefits
Director Personnel Administration and Relocation
EDP Development
National Director
Director Planning Research and Quality
Director Technical Services
Director Systems
EDP Library

Chart XI
International Operations

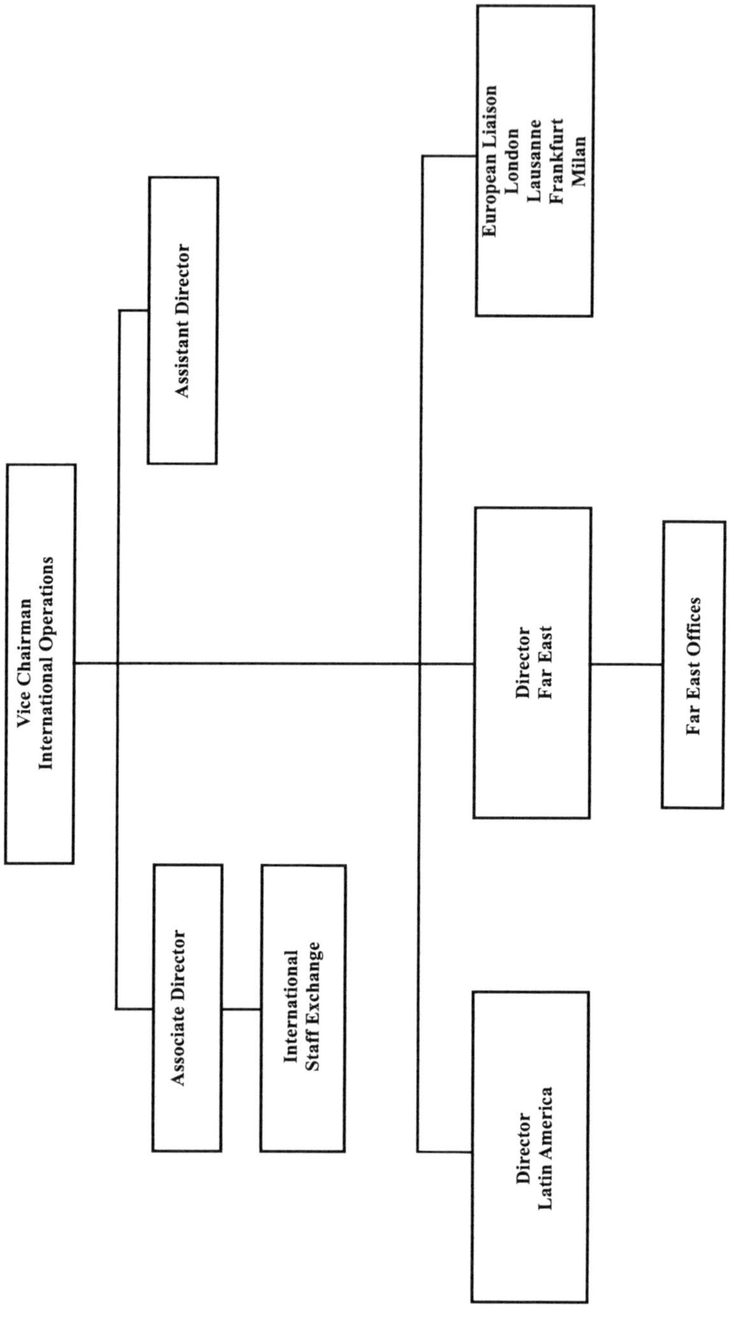

Chart XII
ABC (Actuarial Benefits Consulting)

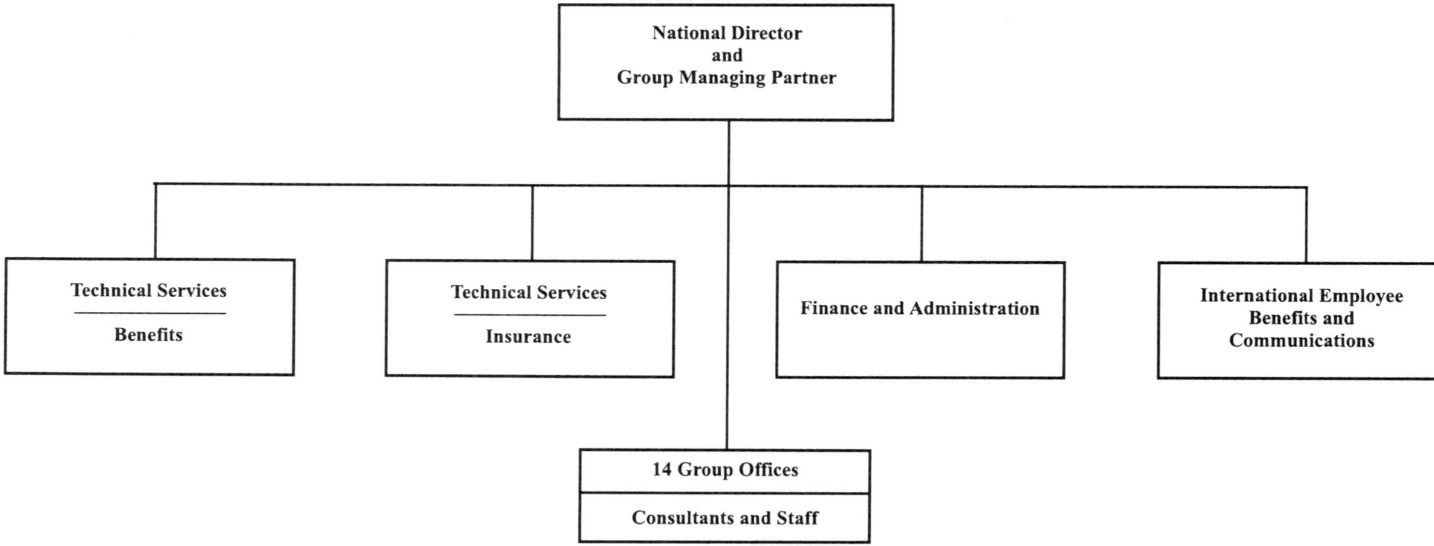

AUDIT PROCEDURES AND AUDITORS' RESPONSIBILITIES

AUDITING WHEN INTERNAL CONTROL IS INADEQUATE†

by
Philip L. Defliese

PUBLIC accountants have a continuing desire to perform their auditing work in an efficient and technically sound manner at the lowest practicable cost to clients. Since business today is experiencing a period of higher costs and lower revenue, this emphasis on efficiency is all the more imperative. Increased client insistence on minimum fees, in the face of such higher operating costs, has pointed toward the need for minimizing auditing procedures, without, of course, lowering standards of performance—the examinations should never fall short of generally accepted auditing standards. Nevertheless, a careful review of the purpose served by each procedure incorporated in an audit program will often lead to more efficient professional work.

NEED FOR MINIMIZING PROCEDURES

Most practitioners have some clients who are always desirous of obtaining an opinion on their financial statements at the least possible cost. These clients can be classified generally into two types. One type, usually a small or medium-sized company, is interested only in the certification required for credit or reporting purposes, and has little or no interest in any other benefits that may be derived from an audit. The internal controls of such a client are often something less than adequate. The other type of client represents the opposite extreme. This is usually a large organization with extensive internal controls, employing internal auditors, systems and tax specialists, and the best management obtainable. Although this client respects the ability of the independent auditor, as well as the need for his services, he feels self-sufficient in practically all related areas. He wants the auditor to pare his program to the minimum, without sacrificing quality, in an effort to reduce the cost of the audit, and still be available for consultation.

The auditor must employ all the ingenuity he can muster to accommodate the wishes of these clients and still maintain his standards. He should periodically analyze his programs with a view to minimizing procedures so that he may provide the most competent and efficient examinations for the lowest possible

---

†Presented at the Fifth Annual Tax and Accounting Seminar, State University of Iowa, September 1958. Reprinted with permission from *The Journal of Accountancy*, September 1959, pp. 37-43,

fees—an objective appreciated by all clients. Many of the suggestions given here are applicable to all examinations, regardless of the adequacy of internal control.

It is assumed, for the purposes of this discussion, that the client is desirous of obtaining the auditor's opinion on his financial statements at the *least* possible cost, and is determined not to pay for any "extras." It is also assumed that the client understands the limitations of such an examination and, nevertheless, does not wish to pay additional fees for any fraud-detecting procedures which the auditor might recommend as the result of his review of internal control. The client should understand fully, and furnish his written acceptance of, the profession's position concerning responsibility for the detection of fraud.

RESPONSIBILITY FOR FRAUD DETECTION

For years the public accounting profession, through its official pronouncements, has taken the position that the ordinary examination leading to the expression of an opinion on financial statements is not designed *and cannot be relied upon* to disclose defalcations and other similar irregularities. It has emphasized that the auditor is not an insurer or guarantor. Strict adherence to the highest standards of auditing and professional care cannot assure the detection of fraud. Even if the auditor extended his examination to a point where its cost would be prohibitive, there could be no such assurance, particularly in the event of collusion.

In recent years this position has been questioned in the course of certain litigation arising from undetected frauds. As a result, some confusion on the issue has arisen. Adding to the confusion is the statement in the Codification of Statements on Auditing Procedure that the auditor ". . . relies upon the integrity of the client's organization unless circumstances are such as to arouse his suspicion, in which case he must extend his procedures to determine whether or not such suspicions are justified." This ambiguous statement is unfortunate because, taken out of context, it might be considered contradictory to the basic position of the profession on fraud. Nevertheless, it does indicate that the auditor is not indifferent to the possibility that fraud may exist.

APPARENT IRREGULARITIES

Although the auditor's examination is designed solely for the purpose of providing him with the basis for an opinion on financial statements, it may disclose indications of the possibility of loss through defalcations and similar irregularities. When such indications are disclosed, the auditor should satisfy himself whether or not the potential loss is of such magnitude that it might affect his opinion on the financial statements. He should take into consideration the circumstances in which his suspicions were aroused.[1] For example, peculations from an impress fund would normally be expected to be of less consequence than those arising from "lapping" of accounts receivable collections. In any case, the client should be fully advised of the situation. If the auditor has established to his own satisfaction that the probable loss is not so material as to affect his opinion, the decision whether or not to pursue the matter further should be made by the client. On the other hand, if the auditor has reason to believe that a material discrepancy exists, he has no alternative but to request that the amount be reasonably determined. Whether initial determination of the amount involved is to be made by the client, or by the auditor as an additional assignment, would be decided by the client. If determination of the amount is made by the client, the auditor should satisfy himself of its reasonableness by appropriate tests.

Much of the confusion concerning the auditor's responsibility for detection of fraud stems from the historical origin of auditing and the impression the public (and many auditors) still has of the auditor's function. Fifty years ago the auditor was employed for the purpose of detecting fraud (on the part of management as well as employees) about as often as he was to express his opinion on financial statements. However, the expansion of business, with the concomitant improvement in internal controls, has minimized the need for the auditor as a fraud detector. Nevertheless, a large segment of the public still looks upon the auditor as primarily concerned with the detection of fraud, and lawsuits are still being entered against auditors for failure to uncover fraud mainly because many clients do not understand clearly the limitations of the ordinary examination. Continued education of the public and the use of letters of arrangements with clients will, we hope, ultimately resolve this problem.

PROFESSIONAL LIABILITY TO THE PUBLIC

In the final analysis, an auditor is not responsible for the detection of fraud, but rather for negligence in carrying out his examination leading to his opinion. This is a responsibility which goes beyond the area of fraud detection. His performance is governed by generally accepted auditing standards, which embrace the satisfactory completion of certain required procedures, the careful selection of other procedures, and the exercise of due professional care in all his work. Any examination made in accordance with generally accepted auditing standards ordinarily should not give rise to a cause of action for negligence when an undetected major error or major defalcation later comes to light. Of course, in a well-conducted audit it is extremely unlikely that major frauds or major errors would remain undetected; our procedures should more often than not disclose material errors in fairness of presentation of financial statements due to fraud. This is particularly true with respect to the balance sheet. When fraud has been

---

[1]Ordinarily, suspicion would be aroused only by evidence pointing toward a possible defalcation, in which case the auditor should take appropriate action. "Suspicion" should not be confused with the normal alertness with which the auditor would proceed when he knows internal controls are weak.

concealed through improper charges to the income account, substantial extension of audit tests might not bring it to light, particularly if collusion is present. Such undetected charges should not ordinarily negate the auditor's opinion on the income statement merely because they have not been so classified and segregated, since it is well recognized that the auditor's opinion relates to the financial statements taken as a whole, and not to any one item in the statements taken by itself.

In this connection, one can draw certain analogies with the medical profession. The ordinary medical examination made by a physician, whether for insurance, employment or personal reasons, follows a well-known pattern which is far from all-inclusive. There have been many cases of persons succumbing from heart attacks or cancer soon after such an examination. I doubt whether many lawsuits are filed against doctors in such cases for failure to detect a latent defect having fatal implications. By arrangement, some physical examinations are more extensive, involving electrocardiograms and series of X-rays. Even these may not reveal imminent illness. When a physician uncovers a clue to a possible difficulty he will usually recommend additional consultation and tests; the choice of extending the examination then rests with the patient. The physician knows that he cannot guarantee the nonexistence of defects because nothing, not even complete dissection, will give such assurance. When treating an ill patient, the physician does his best, but guarantees nothing; a surgeon usually points out to his patient that the surgery may not cure the complaint. The physician is liable to his patient only for negligence in his performance, for errors of omission or commission, *as measured by standards recognized within the medical profession.* The public accountant's position with respect to responsibilities to his clients is parallel to that of the doctor. With respect to third parties, there would rarely be a cause of action for an undiscovered fraud unless the balance sheet were materially misstated—a rarity today.

REVIEW OF INTERNAL CONTROL

Any consideration of the selection of auditing procedures to be followed, their timing, and the extent of their application must depend largely upon the auditor's evaluation of the effectiveness of his client's system of internal control.[2] Regardless of the terms agreed upon when the auditor was retained, if he is to express an opinion on financial statements he has an obligation to make a thorough review of those areas of internal control which affect the reliability of the accounting records. This review is needed not only for the purposes of his examination, but also to advise his clients of existing weaknesses and to recommend corrective measures.

---

[2] Not long ago the term "internal control" was adopted, for convenience, as a shortened version of the term "internal control and internal check" and its definition was broadened to cover all types of controls, including administrative controls. "Internal check," which refers to those controls designed to safeguard assets, was deemed to be included in the broad term "internal control."

In evaluating internal control the auditor must not lose sight of the objectives of the different areas included in the broad concept of internal control. Administrative controls, such as performance reports, training programs, and time and motion studies, have as their objective operational efficiency. Accounting controls have as their objective the reliability of the records, that is, the accurate and suitable recording and summarization of authorized financial transactions (internal accounting control), and the safeguarding of assets (internal check). These designations are distinctions in principle only, for in practice it is possible, and frequently necessary, for a particular procedure to serve all three purposes. Consider, for example, sales tickets turned in by route salesmen. If the tickets are prenumbered and the salesmen are required to account for the sequence of numbers, internal accounting control is achieved. If this accounting is made by an independent person, internal check is strengthened. If the independent person, in the course of examining the tickets, also tallies the number of stops, sales made, items sold, etc., by each salesman, internal administrative control is furthered. Note also that if the tally is made by personnel of the sales department, the objectives of all three areas may be realized entirely beyond the confines of the financial and accounting departments.

THE ADMINISTRATIVE AREA

The auditor is not concerned with administrative controls in the ordinary examination unless they have an important bearing on the reliability of the accounting records. Although he is naturally interested in them, and obtains a good knowledge of them, he is not obligated to report upon the efficiency of the organization nor upon the "hows" and "whys" of the results. He need not evaluate operational efficiency since the figures speak for themselves. This does not mean that he is oblivious to his surroundings; in the course of his examination he may well have occasion to recommend improvements in this area. However, when he finds internal accounting control or internal check weak or missing, he must ascertain whether alternative controls exist, particularly in the administrative control area. Referring back to the route salesman illustration, for example, if no accounting for sequence of sales tickets is made at all, but the sales and production departments "tie in" physical movement of all goods handled by the route salesmen, the apparent weakness in internal accounting control and internal check is overcome by an administrative control. It would be safe to say that the presence of certain administrative controls *may* provide the auditor with a basis for *limiting* his examination, but their absence would rarely require him to *extend* his examination.

Since internal accounting control and internal check bear importantly on the reliability of the financial and accounting records, the auditor must make a careful review and evaluation. If these controls are weak or lacking, his program must take this fact into account. However, it is in adjusting his program to these conditions that the auditor may have difficulty, since he is entering an area requiring the exercise of fine judgment, with very little authoritative literature to guide him.

Efficient internal accounting controls, in the absence of dishonesty, are sufficient to produce reliable records. If such controls are weak or lacking, the auditor has no alternative but to consider the need for extending his examination in order to supplement the absent controls with audit tests or over-all checks and comparisons, although it would be seldom, if ever, necessary to apply *all possible* audit procedures for the *entire* period under review. For example, if no proper review is made of the account classifications to which voucher charges are assigned, he might extend his examination of voucher charges; if numerous errors of significant dollar amount were disclosed, he might well carry his tests further. If no cost system existed, his examination of purchases and production records might require expansion in order that he may be satisfied that the costs of inventories are reasonably determined; he may also, in the absence of record-keeping procedures which provide a satisfactory alternative, require that the physical inventory be taken at the year end instead of at an earlier date.

PURPOSES OF INTERNAL CHECK

Internal check is designed to supplement internal accounting control by furnishing means of safeguarding assets against manipulations of dishonest employees concerned with accounting functions. Since the auditor does not assume responsibility for the discovery of defalcations, the question may be raised why he need devote any time and attention to investigating and evaluating internal check. As indicated previously, the auditor is not indifferent to the possibility that fraud may exist; on the contrary, his program is designed in such a manner that material fraud concealed in the balance sheet is often discovered through the application of recognized audit procedures. However, substantial extension of audit tests, or even complete coverage, might not uncover fraud concealed in the income account. Of course, the presence of collusion or clever forgery may prevent the discovery of fraud in any case.

Weaknesses in internal check thus do not ordinarily require extension of audit tests, per se. Instead, they may require the shifting of procedures from interim dates to the year end in order that there may be greater assurance of the fairness of the balance sheet. Cash counts and reconciliations, security counts, physical inventory taking, and confirmations of receivables are illustrative of procedures that may be performed at the year end when internal check is weak; in extreme cases coverage may be extended at that time, e.g., a larger percentage of receivables may be confirmed. When internal check is extremely weak, but internal accounting control is adequate, examination of year-end balances would obviously take precedence in emphasis over routine procedural testing.

INTERNAL CHECK AND THE AUDIT PROGRAM

Since the distinction between internal accounting control and internal check may be obscure in practice it seems desirable to illustrate it and describe its effect upon the audit program. For example, periodic (usually monthly) reconciliation of the bank balance with the book cash balance is a requisite of good internal accounting control because it offers an opportunity to check the accuracy of the book records through comparison with a record maintained by another party, in this instance an outside agency (the bank). Such reconciliations regularly made by an assistant cashier, who reports to the cashier, contribute to good internal accounting control but offer very little in the way of internal check because the assistant cashier lacks independence. To some auditors, this weakness might signal the need for additional procedural testing of cash activity, and several months may be reviewed when one month (or possibly less) might ordinarily suffice. Close analysis will show that, barring dishonesty, the additional testing would reveal little or nothing, since good accounting control already existed. And, if dishonesty were present, a review of all transactions during the year might not reveal it, especially if collusion were also present. The only solution to this problem is to take those steps necessary to assure himself of the fairness of the amount of cash shown on the balance sheet by *shifting* his testing, reconciliation procedures and confirmations to the balance sheet date. To extend his procedural testing of transactions during the year would be evidence that he is searching for something which he states he has no responsibility for finding; furthermore, he knows he can never be completely assured that it does not exist.

Management has the responsibility for the establishment and maintenance of a good system of internal control in order to assure the reliability of the accounting records and the safeguarding of the company's assets. The auditor has the obligation of informing his client of weaknesses in the system and of recommending appropriate changes—management has the choice of accepting or rejecting the auditor's recommendations. Many weaknesses in internal check can be corrected easily without additional cost. Perhaps a shifting of work assignments is all that is required. Most recommendations are adopted unless they involve personnel reassignment deemed impractical from an organizational standpoint, or the expenditure of funds is disproportionate to the benefits to be derived. It is incumbent upon management to calculate such risks as it does the many other risks of doing business.

However, the auditor must give consideration to existing conditions in designing his program. When controls are weak or lacking, he must, in appraising their effect upon his program, similarly calculate the risks in terms of the likelihood of such weaknesses having a material effect upon the reliability and integrity of the records. In this respect the internal control questionnaire, normally an extremely helpful tool in auditing, is subject to misuse if, as the result of a series of unfavorable answers, the auditor alters his program without first considering whether the weaknesses involved could lead to discrepancies which would materially affect his opinion.

WEAKNESSES IN INTERNAL CHECK

Perhaps the weaknesses found most often are in those controls relating to internal check. This is generally the case for two reasons. First, most organizations, regardless of size, find they cannot operate without an accounting system, so they usually have some semblance of good accounting control. Second, internal check depends largely upon the "independence" of the person checking on the other and this is more difficult to achieve in smaller organizations; in larger organizations it may be lacking because a careful study has never been made of the organizational relationships of the personnel involved.

Weaknesses in internal check, however, would rarely increase substantially the audit time devoted to an engagement when good internal accounting control exists. Since the auditor does not assume responsibility for the detection of fraud, his major concern is to see that his opinion is well-founded—that the financial statements are not materially misstated. As indicated previously, this would generally influence the timing of his procedures rather than the extent of his testing operations. As another example, when good internal accounting control exists over the recording of transactions in marketable securities, but the custodian of the securities is the only person required to be present to obtain access to the safe deposit vault containing the securities—an obvious weakness in internal check—it is unnecessary to extend the related testing procedures since the *records* can be considered reliable. Instead, it would be desirable to examine the securities on or about the balance sheet date in order to see that such securities agree with the records. The same principle can be applied to similar situations involving other assets. As mentioned before, if the assistant cashier does all the reconciling, and the usual testing of cash transactions indicates good accounting control, the only other concern the auditor need have is with respect to the year-end cash balance. If the cashier has extracted funds and somehow has kept this fact hidden from the assistant cashier or mollified him in this respect, the auditor should be able to detect it if he makes his counts, reconciliations and confirmations at the year end. Lack of independence on the part of persons handling credit, billing, shipping and collection functions would (assuming good accounting control) only require a shifting of the physical inventories and confirmations of receivables to the year end rather than an exhaustive study of the transactions. It should be apparent, however, that such steps are needed only when there are *major* weaknesses in internal check.

There will be many instances where weaknesses in internal check will have little or no effect upon the audit program. If the paymaster or person distributing pay, for example, is also in charge of all payroll preparation procedures, we know that an opportunity for padding the payroll may exist. Since the auditor has not been retained to discover payroll padding as such, but to express an opinion on the financial statements, he has no responsibility to extend his usual payroll testing in an effort to determine whether the paymaster has padded the payroll. He will make certain payroll tests in order to determine whether good accounting controls are present and to see that the pay charges are properly reflected in the accounts. In the course of such testing he will always be alert to the padding possibility, regardless of internal check, but he need not extend such testing in an effort to detect fraud.

WEAKNESSES IN INTERNAL ACCOUNTING CONTROL

As stated previously, most businesses today, regardless of size, cannot operate without a reasonably good accounting system. Even the one-man bookkeeper operation—although usually devoid of internal check—can have an excellent accounting system provided the bookkeeper has a knowledge of internal accounting control procedures and conscientiously follows them.

Consequently, it will be rather unusual to find a situation where internal accounting control is completely lacking. More often the auditor will be confronted with a series of minor weaknesses which he needs to evaluate in terms of possible effect on his program. As in the case of internal check, before adjusting his program, the auditor must appraise the possibility of a particular weakness or a combination of weaknesses producing a material discrepancy which may affect his ability to give an opinion. In addition—and this does not apply in cases of weaknesses in internal check—the auditor may take into consideration whether the ability, experience and attitude of the people doing the work (as evidenced by the results of his tests) is such as to overcome the weaknesses in the system. For example, the absence of a chart of accounts or an adequate accounting manual need not disturb the auditor if, by reason of his observation and normal testing, he is satisfied that the chief accountant is qualified for his job and is efficiently performing it. When receipts of cash are not deposited daily and intact, it is not necessary to extend unduly the volume of testing applied to cash receipts unless the preliminary tests revealed serious consequences from this lack of control.

TESTING INTERNAL CONTROL

This means that while an auditor has a valid basis for restricting his procedural testing operations in the presence of an exceptionally good system of internal accounting control (as proved by limited testing), it does not follow that he must expand his testing when the system of internal accounting control is something less than adequate, unless the testing shows that, because of the looseness in the system, errors of consequence are being made. Accordingly, broad extension of testing should be avoided unless there is clear evidence of its need in order to satisfy the auditor of the reliability of the accounting records.

A recognized method of testing internal accounting control procedures is the tracing of several diversified transactions from their origin to their conclusion. For example, a purchase of materials may be traced from its requisition by production personnel to the clearance of the check which paid for the purchase. The auditor scrutinizes all the paper work and procedures established for the processing and payment of such an order, making note of any deviations from standard company procedure and of any weaknesses in the procedures adopted. The transactions reviewed are usually selected in a manner designed to provide the auditor with a good cross section of the client's activities, thus constituting a good over-all review. When the established internal accounting control procedures appear to be less than adequate the auditor may increase the number of transactions selected for such a review in an attempt to form a basis for his opinion on the reliability of the accounts. If he can be satisfied by this review that the accounts are reliable, there is little need for him to extend the volume of his procedural testing.

DECIDING HOW MUCH TO TEST

When there are serious voids in the accounting system, steps must be taken which will contribute to the auditor's basis for his opinion. If a company has no cost accounting system, the auditor must devise some reasonable method of arriving at costs with which to test the pricing of the inventory. This will vary with the nature of the inventory and its materiality in relation to the financial statements. When serious weaknesses exist in the processing of orders—in the billing, shipping and collecting areas—the auditor must concern himself with the effect thereof upon the balance sheet amounts of cash, receivables and inventories. In this case, year-end examinations again may be employed in lieu of extensive testing. However, since such weaknesses might result in unrecorded receivables, *limited* tests may be made to determine whether unrecorded shipments are being made.

Gross profit margins which are in line with a particular industry or with a company's price structure or past performance may be acceptable alternatives to extensive testing in the face of serious weaknesses of internal accounting control. However, historical margins should be considered suspect when the same weaknesses have existed for a long period of time.

Certain types of procedures have over the years become traditional in our auditing practice and are being continued, I suspect, because clients expect them. They originated in the era when fraud detection was the primary objective and are continued despite the fact that this is no longer the purpose of the examination. Outstanding in this group is the "surprise count" of cash, notes, securities and other negotiables. Of course, when a count is made it is preferable to have it made on a surprise basis. But if internal check is good, there may be little need for a count or a surprise. If internal check is weak, then the count should be made at or about the year end, and this reduces the surprise element. It seems that surprise counts made in addition to regular counts at year end can have as their purpose only the detection of fraud. Some auditors may justify this additional procedure as a means of evaluating routine accounting procedures; it seems that our other tests could establish this. Surprise counts made by the client during the year are highly recommended as a good means of internal check. By separate arrangement, the independent auditor may perform this function for the client in conjunction with the regular audit.

Witnessing a payroll pay-off, sometimes done by auditors in opinion audits, is another traditional procedure which may be placed in the same class as the surprise count. It can have as its purpose only the determination whether the payroll is padded with fictitious employees—at that particular time! A shrewd dishonest paymaster could readily guess when the best time to pad would be. Consequently, the procedure produces an inconclusive result in most cases, is rarely needed at all when internal check is good, and certainly would hardly ever have an effect on the auditor's opinion of the financial statements.

MINIMUM PROCEDURES

The minimum procedures required to express an opinion on financial statements are readily ascertainable if the auditor will examine carefully, in the light of his evaluation of the adequacy and effectiveness of internal accounting control and internal check, the purpose served by each element in the procedures before he incorporates it in his program.

The "New Look" at the AUDITOR'S RESPONSIBILITY FOR FRAUD DETECTION†

by
Philip L. Defliese

IN September 1960, the committee on auditing procedure of the AICPA issued Statement No. 30 entitled "Responsibilities and Functions of the Independent Auditor in the Examination of Financial Statements." The Statement was designed primarily to clarify previous pronouncements regarding the auditor's responsibility for fraud detection, and represented the result of three years of intensive study by the committee. In order that the profession might have a better appreciation of the many aspects of the problem which were considered in the course of its deliberations, the committee requested the author to write this article to explain the considerations which influenced the thinking of the members and served to bring about unanimous agreement on the Statement. Although the views expressed here regarding these deliberations are the author's and, therefore, in no sense official, it is believed that they fairly represent those of most members of the committee that approved the Statement.

The delay in getting this article published has been caused principally by the author's subsequent activities with the committee (and his own practice). Since publication of Statement No. 30, the committee has been busy preparing two other Statements, one of which has been published. This delay has provided an interval of time in which reactions to Statement No. 30 could be observed. The committee has received very few comments on the subject, so it may be assumed that the profession is generally satisfied that the objective was achieved.

THE NEED FOR CLARIFICATION

The subject of responsibility of the independent auditor for the discovery of fraud is one which has interested the public accounting profession and its writers for more than half a century. From its origin, auditing has been considered by many laymen as primarily directed toward the detection of defalcations and similar irregularities. Consequently, despite the pronouncements of the profession, there will always remain the possibility that a certain segment of the

†This article is based on a speech presented at the 1961 annual meeting of the California Society of CPAs. Reprinted with permission from *The Journal of Accountancy*, October 1962, pp. 36-44, copyright © 1962 by American Institute of CPAs. Opinions of the authors are their own and do not necessarily reflect policies of the AICPA. This article was reprinted in *The Pakistan Accountant*, July, September 1966, pp. 19-26.

general public may continue to believe that the auditor's prime objective is the detection of defalcations. However, the financial world's better understanding of the independent auditor's function in our modern business society has aided in the clarification of the profession's position in this sensitive area; the auditor's efforts are recognized today, at least by the businessman, as being directed toward offering assurance that management's financial statements are fairly presented.

While this subject has been under discussion in this country for many years, the public accounting profession's fundamental position has not undergone any real change of substance since the objective of the ordinary examination of financial statements became more clearly understood in the early part of this century. However, in previous pronouncements the committee had neither accepted unequivocally, nor denied unequivocally, responsibility for fraud detection in such examinations and, as a consequence, a large gray area had been opened within which varying positions (mostly a matter of degree) were taken by various authors. In the final analysis, their opinions on this subject never really differed to any substantial extent. In reality, the difficulty has been mainly a matter of semantics, with each writer choosing his preferred expressions and each reader choosing to read into such words his preferred interpretation.

The limitations of an audit have been recognized by the profession for so long that one wonders why clarification became necessary at this late date. The necessity for recognizing both the value and the limitation of an audit was well stated in an address by the late George 0. May some thirty-five years ago (long before the *McKesson* case broke) before the New Jersey Society of CPAs on the subject of "A Proper Courage in the Assumption of Responsibility by the Accountant." Mr. May, whose wise counsel served the profession so well, said:

> ...An audit is a safeguard; the maintenance of this safeguard entails an expense; and this expense can be justified only if the value of the safeguard is found to be fully commensurate with its cost. The cost of an audit so extensive as to be a complete safeguard would be enormous and far beyond any value to be derived from it. A superficial audit is dangerous because of the sense of false security which it creates. Between the two extremes there lies a mean at which the audit abundantly justifies its cost.
>
> The problem is to determine this happy mean, to insure that the auditor does not fall short of a reasonable discharge of his duties, and the investor or lender does not attribute to the audit a greater significance than it can, as a practical matter, possess. And it must be recognized that skilled dishonesty, especially collusive dishonesty, may at times and for a time deceive even the auditor who conducts what is regarded as a reasonable audit and that this should be so is not to be regarded as a defect in the system, since, as I have said, audit procedure represents a balancing of the consideration of risks on the one side and cost on the other. As a matter of fact, investors and lenders need protection against deliberate dishonesty less than protection against unsound practices and undue optimism....

CHANGE IN PURPOSE

There has been a general belief that the profession in Britain considered the detection of defalcations an objective of every examination and that some degree of responsibility in this area was, therefore, assumed. However, a recent article in *The Accountant* by D. D. Rae Smith, a chartered accountant in England, indicates that this attitude, if it ever existed, has changed. Mr. Smith wrote:

> ...In recent years there has been a growing recognition of the fact that the overriding purpose of an audit is the expression by the auditor of an independent opinion as to the truth and fairness of accounts examined by him, and not the detection of defalcations and errors. This has required a change of emphasis in audit procedures. The verification of large numbers of detailed transactions and balances should give way to a review and assessment of the system of internal control undertaken with the object of determining the extent to which the auditor can rely on it in framing his audit procedures....
>
> ...In the distant past audits no doubt had their origin in the natural distrust felt by one man for another in matters where the handling of money or other valuables was at stake. The function of the auditor then was to obtain an account of a man's stewardship and to assure himself that no misappropriation of funds had taken place. With the passage of time, as businesses developed and grew into complex organizations, this original concept of the auditor's function became impracticable and out-dated. Nevertheless, it is only in relatively recent years that it has begun to be accepted that balance sheets and profit and loss accounts are representations made by management as to a state of affairs and results of transactions; and that the function of the auditor is to express an opinion on those representations....
>
> ...The detection of fraud should not therefore be regarded as the main purpose, or even as one of the main purposes, of an audit. This does not, of course, mean that an auditor is in no way concerned with, or interested in, the discovery of frauds and defalcations. If proper application of the audit procedures necessary to enable him to express an opinion on the accounts he is examining would also discover a fraud or defalcation, then any failure by the auditor to make the discovery will be at this peril. But this should not obscure the fact that such a discovery is a by-product, and not the main purpose, of the auditor's work. The responsibility for safeguarding the assets of a business rests squarely with the management. They do not discharge this responsibility by having an independent audit.[1, 3]

Mr. Smith's remarks seem to have presaged a more official position on fraud detection adopted by Council of the Institute of Chartered Accountants in England and Wales in August 1961 in its first "Statements on Auditing," entitled, "General Principles of Auditing." This statement covers the essential elements of an audit required under the Companies Act of 1948 and the auditor's responsibility thereunder. With respect to fraud it says:

Fraud

> (26) Irregularities which arise in the conduct of the affairs of a company may be classified broadly into:
>
> (a) acts or defaults by an employee or a director which are committed without the knowledge of the board of directors; it is the responsibility of the directors to take all reasonable care that the system will prevent such irregularities or bring about their early detection
> (b) acts or defaults by the directors which are designed to mislead or defraud the members

---

[1] "Auditing: the Purpose and its Attainment" by D. D. Rae Smith, M.C., B.A., F.C.A., *The Accountant*, October 22, 1960, pp. 525-529.

(c) acts or defaults designed to defraud the Inland Revenue or other third parties (on which the Council has already issued its statement entitled "Unlawful Acts or Defaults by Clients of Members"[2]

(27) Material irregularities of the above character will normally be brought to light by sound audit procedures but there is nothing in the Companies Act, 1948, which specifically places a duty upon auditors to search for them or to examine the books and accounts with the object of discovering whether there have been defalcations or other irregularities by directors or employees of the company. Lord Justice Lopes pointed out in the *Kingston Cotton Mill* case:

> Auditors must not be made liable for not tracking out ingenious and carefully laid schemes of fraud, when there is nothing to arouse their suspicion, and when those frauds are perpetrated by tried servants of the company and are undetected for years by the directors. So to hold would make the position of an auditor intolerable.

(28) Although there is no statutory obligation upon the auditors to search for irregularities, the possibility of their existence will be a factor governing the auditors' approach to their work as described in paragraph 9 and in discharging their statutory duties. In normal circumstances they are entitled to rely upon the honesty of the directors and employees of the company. But if, in the course of their examination, their suspicions are aroused they have a clear duty to probe the circumstances to the bottom and to report appropriately to the members.[3]

CLIENTS' UNDERSTANDING NECESSARY

Probably the greatest deterrent to the achievement of a better and more publicized understanding of the profession's position has been the reluctance on the part of many practitioners to discuss the matter freely and openly with clients. (Clients should certainly have a clear understanding of the nature and limitations of an engagement before it is undertaken.) The reluctance of the past may have been caused by the broadness of certain language of the committee's prior statements which some may have believed would not be understood by their clients. It may also have been caused by the general lack of appreciation that examinations may be designed for many purposes. One such purpose may be the expression of an opinion on financial statements, another purpose may be specific fraud detection. A client may require or desire an examination for one or the other of these purposes, or they may be combined in one examination. When the point is reached where all auditors describe these distinctions to all clients, the profession's problems in this area will be fewer. There is a real need to emphasize the difference between the ordinary examination of financial statements, which is not primarily or specifically designed to detect defalcations, and the special

---

[2]See *The Accountant*, October 12, 1957, pp. 431-440.

[3]The reference to Mr. Smith's article and to the statement of Council of the Institute of Chartered Accountants is not intended to imply that the author believes complete agreement now exists between the British and U.S. positions on the matter of fraud. The author believes that minor differences still exist, but it is not the purpose of this article to discuss them.

examination which is specifically designed to detect defalcations—a special service which some clients (usually smaller organizations) need and should be encouraged to authorize. With respect to the latter, the auditor should make it clear that the additional procedures or tests performed are not necessarily conclusive and cannot be guaranteed.

This article is confined to the auditor's responsibility in connection with the ordinary examination.

When the committee on auditing procedure of the AICPA issued Statement No. 30, it stated that it was a clarification of the position on responsibility for fraud detection previously taken in the Codification of Statements on Auditing Procedure issued in 1951.[4] Although a clarification may be presumed not to be a change in substance, here again moot matters of semantics enter. For the record, it should be stated that a large majority of the committee believed that the substance of prior statements was not being changed.

The committee recognized that the language in the Codification may have left something to be desired. The queries received by the committee and the articles written on the subject pointed up the need for clarification.

Some members of the profession felt that the statement on page 12 of the Codification, which read

> The ordinary examination incident to the issuance of an opinion respecting financial statements is not designed *and cannot be relied upon* to disclose defalcations and other similar irregularities, although their discovery frequently results. [Emphasis in original statement.]

used language that was entirely too broad and which if taken out of context might give a misleading impression because everyone recognized that an examination designed to express an opinion on financial statements would, in some respects, require the performance of some procedures which would have the corollary objective of discovering material fraud. Certainly, the auditor could not risk overlooking the possibility of the existence of major fraud if he intended to render a valid opinion on the financial statements.

Within the same paragraph the statement was made that:

> . . . the auditor relies upon the integrity of the client's organization unless circumstances are such as to arouse his suspicion, in which case he must extend his procedures to determine whether or not such suspicions are justified.

The vagueness of the phrase "unless circumstances are such as to *arouse his suspicion*" led many auditors to question whether extensive procedures had to be undertaken whenever *any* type of weakness in internal control was manifest.

---

[4]The Codification had revised the language on this subject originally contained in the committee's Statement No. 1. The committee had not considered that revision as a change in substance.

Many members of the profession felt that the expression "defalcations and other similar irregularities" was too vague. Did it or did it not include all forms of fraud and, particularly, did it include deliberate misrepresentation by management (not involving the extraction of assets)? It should be noted that the term "fraud" had never been used by the committee in prior statements. Hence, there existed an obvious need for a broader and more complete statement which would seek to answer such questions.

THE NEW LOOK AT FRAUD

In the new statement, the subject of fraud in its broadest sense was covered by the committee. It was recognized that fraud could be found in either or both of two basic forms—that which constituted a deliberate attempt at misrepresentation by management (obviously directed at stockholders, credit grantors and other interested outsiders), and that which constituted a diversion of the company's assets in some form or another. The committee then proceeded to distinguish between these two types of fraud insofar as they affected the objectives of the auditor and his responsibilities. This is best summarized in paragraph 5 of the Statement, as follows:

> 5. In making the ordinary examination, the independent auditor is aware of the possibility that fraud may exist; financial statements may be misstated as the result of defalcations and other similar irregularities, deliberate misrepresentation by management, or both. He recognizes that any fraud, if sufficiently material, may affect his opinion on the fairness of the presentation of the financial statements, and his examination, made in accordance with generally accepted auditing standards, gives consideration to this possibility. However, the ordinary examination incident to the expression of an opinion on financial statements is not primarily or specifically designed, and cannot be relied upon, to disclose defalcations and other similar irregularities, although their discovery may result. Similarly, although the discovery of deliberate misrepresentation by management is usually more closely associated with the objective of the ordinary examination, such examination cannot be relied upon to assure its discovery. The responsibility of the independent auditor for failure to detect fraud (which responsibility differs as to clients and others) arises only when such failure clearly results from noncompliance with generally accepted auditing standards.

Careful note should be made of certain statements in this all-important paragraph.

There is the recognition that the auditor is fully aware of the fact that fraud may exist when he makes his examination and that, if a material fraud were to go undetected, his opinion on the fairness of the financial statements may be in error. This makes it clear that he cannot assume an attitude of indifference to its possibilities or consequences. It should be noted that the sentence used the word "may" concerning the possible effect of fraud on his opinion. This was done to recognize the fact that material fraud may not always affect financial position, results of operations, or the auditor's opinion on the statements. As an extreme example, discovery of a material defalcation buried in the income statement, for which no indemnification or recovery possibility exists, has no effect on the balance sheet and, although it may raise serious questions concerning proper classification in the income statement, it does not affect net income. This problem will be discussed more fully later.

The sentence which stated the basic position concerning defalcations in the Codification (previously quoted) has now been changed to read:

> However, the ordinary examination incident to the expression of an opinion on financial statements is not primarily or specifically designed, and cannot be relied upon to disclose defalcations and other similar irregularities, although their discovery may result.

Although this follows closely the former language of the Codification, it has been changed in certain important respects. The sentence is introduced with the word "however" in order to supply the necessary antithesis to the preceding sentence which indicates that an examination made in accordance with generally accepted auditing standards gives consideration to the possibility of the existence of fraud. This helps point out the inherent limitations to that consideration. The words "primarily or specifically" were inserted to avoid any implication which may have existed in the Codification that *none* of the procedures followed by the auditor was ever to be directed toward the possibility of the existence of major defalcations. Thus, it was recognized that a fair number of the procedures followed by the auditor to express an opinion on financial statements have the corollary (but not primary or specific) objective of discovering material defalcations.

ROLE OF THE AUDITOR

The close association between the objective of the ordinary examination and the attempt of the auditor to detect deliberate misrepresentations on the part of management is clearly stated. Although rarely expressed, this objective had always been implied in the committee's previous pronouncements. Because all types of fraud were now being described, this objective was included in the clarification; this emphasizes that the ordinary examination, while made on behalf of the client, results in an opinion on the financial statements which may be useful to third parties. Of course, the usual limitations of an examination always apply, and so the reader is warned that the ordinary examination cannot be relied upon to give complete assurance of the discovery of management misrepresentation.

The last sentence of the paragraph contains the first positive statement of the committee concerning the auditor's responsibility to detect fraud. It reads:

> The responsibility of the independent auditor for failure to detect fraud (which responsibility differs as to clients and others) arises only when such failure clearly results from noncompliance with generally accepted auditing standards.

This sentence should be carefully noted for a number of reasons. It recognizes the difference between the auditor's responsibility to his client and to third parties.[5] Existing case law on the liability of auditors points toward the general conclusion that while an auditor may become liable to his client for ordinary negligence, his liability to third parties arises only through gross negligence from which fraud (on the part of the auditor) may be inferred.[6] The sentence also emphasizes that this responsibility can arise only when the failure to detect fraud *clearly resulted* from noncompliance with generally accepted auditing standards. Noncompliance with respect to a procedure not related to the area in which the fraud occurred would not ordinarily create a responsibility for the auditor; thus, negligence, per se, would not result in responsibility. In summary, a responsibility can arise only when an auditor, through noncompliance with the standards, fails to detect material fraud which would ordinarily have been discovered in the proper performance of a procedure considered essential to the expression of an opinion on the statements.

AUDITOR'S RESPONSIBILITY TO CLIENT

Of course, it should be clear that with respect to responsibility to clients, the *noncompliance* with generally accepted auditing standards referred to was intended to mean only such noncompliance as was wholly the fault of the auditor: that is, deliberate, negligent, or completely unjustified. When the client places limitations upon the scope of examination, or there exists contributory negligence on the part of the client—including persuasion, coercion, or misrepresentation—the resultant noncompliance should not subject the auditor to a responsibility to his client. However, in the absence of a specific disclosure in his report of a limitation upon his examination, the auditor's responsibility to third parties for failure to detect material fraud, when such failure clearly resulted from noncompliance with the standards, may be unaffected by acts or omissions of the client.

Paragraph 5 makes reference to compliance with generally accepted auditing *standards* rather than with specific *procedures*. The reason for this should be apparent. Reference to compliance with *procedures* would result in confusion since there exists no official compendium of procedures required for the ordinary examination; furthermore, no such list could ever be prepared since specific procedures are always dependent upon circumstances. Since official literature does include a complete description of generally accepted auditing standards, together with substantial commentary, reference to these standards, as they apply to the objective of the ordinary examination, should be sufficient to define the limitations of the auditor's responsibility for fraud detection.

---

[5]Even though stockholders may elect or ratify the selection of auditors, they should be considered parties in this context (unless they are also part of management).

[6]See *Ultramares Corp.* v. *Touche*, 255 N.Y. 170, 174 N.E. 441.

THE NEED TO EXTEND PROCEDURES

In Paragraph 7 the committee came to grips with the question of the auditor's responsibility to "extend his procedures" when his "suspicions are aroused." This paragraph says:

> 7. When an independent auditor's examination leading to an opinion on financial statements discloses specific circumstances which arouse his suspicion as to the existence of fraud, he should decide whether the fraud, if in fact it should exist, might be of such magnitude as to affect his opinion on the financial statements. If the independent auditor believes that fraud may have occurred which could be so material as to affect his opinion, he should reach an understanding with the proper representatives of the client as to whether the independent auditor or the client, subject to the independent auditor's review, is to make the investigation necessary to determine whether fraud has in fact occurred and, if so, the amount thereof. If, on the other hand, the independent auditor concludes that any such fraud could not be so material as to affect his opinion, he should refer the matter to the proper representatives of the client with the recommendation that it be pursued to a conclusion. For example, frauds involving "lapping" accounts receivable collections, or frauds involving overstatements of inventory, could be material, while those involving peculations from a small imprest fund would normally be of little significance because the operation of the fund tends to establish a limitation.

This differs from the previous statement in certain important aspects.

It clarifies the previous statement on this point by indicating that action on the part of the auditor is necessary only when, in his opinion, the type of fraud suggested by the specific circumstances involved could be of such magnitude as to affect his opinion. This eliminates the need for automatic extension of procedures in all cases, and places emphasis on the over-all fairness of the statements rather than upon fraud detection.

In addition, reference is made to "specific circumstances which arouse his suspicion as to the existence of fraud." The insertion of the word "specific" was made to clarify the point that any vague circumstance or hunch which could arouse the auditor's suspicion was not intended. Certainly, some auditors are more suspicious than others. But the auditor recognizes that the large majority of people are honest; he is not assuming that everyone is guilty of fraud unless proven innocent. The intent here was to require a situation with enough factual evidence to give the auditor a good reason to believe that fraud may be present *before* he needs to evaluate the possible effect of the fraud.

A situation involving a complete lack of internal check *unaccompanied* by other factors pointing toward a fraud should not ordinarily arouse the auditor's suspicion. If this were not the case, an auditor would most likely be precluded from expressing an opinion on statements of a one-man bookkeeper organization. It is entirely possible for a one-man bookkeeper system to have excellent internal accounting control in the form of prenumbered vouchers, checks, invoices, receiving and shipping tickets, etc. The bookkeeper's systems and procedures can include controlling accounts, perpetual inventory records, periodic trial balances and bank reconciliations and *still* be devoid of internal check because there exists no one to check his work. Under these circumstances, when the auditor's tests reveal no discrepancies, and operating results appear to be as expected, the auditor would ordinarily have no basis for suspicion.

With respect to the relationship of internal check procedures to the question of fraud detection, it should be noted that the committee's Statement No. 29 on the auditor's evaluation of internal control, issued in 1958, stated:

> The committee has considered whether the part of the definition of internal control concerning the safeguarding of assets and the auditing standard concerning study and evaluation of internal control, taken together, are inconsistent with the statement in the Codification to the effect that, in the ordinary examination, the auditor does not assume responsibility for the detection of defalcations and other similar irregularities. The committee sees no conflict in this regard since the objective of the audit program (which is designed, in part, as a result of the evaluation of internal control) is to provide a basis for the expression of an opinion on the financial statements, taken as a whole, and not to detect defalcations or similar irregularities. In developing such a program, the auditor has a responsibility for evaluating internal controls designed to safeguard assets, and when such controls are weak or lacking his program should take this condition into consideration. This consideration might lead either to the extension of audit tests, or to the shifting of emphases or timing of the audit procedures; for example, counts, reconciliations, confirmations, or observations of certain assets (such as cash, receivables or inventories) might be made at the balance-sheet date rather than at an interim date.

The committee also described, by way of illustration in paragraph 7, types of frauds which would be expected to have a material and immaterial effect on the financial statements; it did not, however, illustrate the types of specific circumstances which could be expected to arouse the auditor's suspicion. These are very difficult to illustrate because it usually takes a number of factors to incite suspicion; hence illustrations would require lengthy recitations of all attendant circumstances. However, in order that there may be some guide in this area, listed here are some specific circumstances (not a complete list) which, in the author's opinion, may arouse the auditor's suspicion as referred to in paragraph 7, particularly when they appear in combination and are accompanied by poor internal accounting control, poor internal check, or both:

1. Trial balance difference which cannot be located.
2. Subsidiary ledgers which cannot be reconciled with control accounts.
3. Unexplainable differences disclosed by confirmation procedures, or unexplainable substantial lack of response to confirmation requests.
4. Unexplainable changes in operating ratios.
5. Material transactions incapable of documentation; many missing documents such as invoices, vouchers, checks.

Paragraph 7 makes reference to the need to reach an understanding with the proper representatives of the client concerning the proper course of action to be taken whenever the auditor believes that fraud may have occurred which could be so material as to affect his opinion. The question may arise, "Who is the proper representative of the client in such circumstances?" Is it the president, board of directors, or the stockholders? Here the judgment of the auditor should provide the appropriate answer. In assessing the evidence before him, he must consider the nature of the possible fraud and its various implications, and inform the management echelon which appears to be at least one level above that which may be involved. It would appear that only in unusual cases would the auditor be obligated to report such findings to stockholders. (This has no bearing on management's obligation to report to stockholders on all aspects of a company's operations.)

MINOR BUT SIGNIFICANT POINTS

There are also a few minor points made in the statement which are worthy of mention. Paragraph 6 reiterates the auditor's right to rely upon his evaluation of internal control in determining the timing and extent of his other auditing procedures for the purpose of expressing an opinion. It emphasizes that management has the primary responsibility for establishing good controls, and that even if the auditor were requested to extend his procedures to discover all fraud, his examination would be expensive and not necessarily conclusive. The paragraph points out that extended procedures would not necessarily uncover unrecorded transactions, forgeries and collusive fraud—a point that is well worth remembering since the same limitations apply to the ordinary examination.

Paragraph 8 re-emphasizes the fact that in no case is the auditor ever an insurer or guarantor and that if his examination was made in accordance with generally accepted auditing standards he has fulfilled all his obligations.

It should be noted that Statement No. 30 used the term "financial statements" throughout. No specific reference was made to the balance sheet or the income statement, and the reader might wonder whether the committee intended to imply that this clarification of the auditor's responsibility for the detection of fraud was equally applicable to both statements. There can be only one answer to this question—yes! The auditor gives his opinion on the fair presentation of financial position *and* results of operations; he does not discriminate, nor does he report that one is more or less fairly presented than the other, unless extenuating circumstances require him to do so.

The auditor must, however, be mindful of the fact that the objective of the examination is the expression of an opinion on the statements and not fraud detection, per se. While he is always alert to the possible existence of minor defalcations, which, if found, should be called to the attention of the client, their detection is not his principal objective. With respect to such minor defalcations as petty cash thievery, payroll padding, pocketing of minor currency sales or receipts, thefts of merchandise, and the like, the auditor's objective is aimed more toward training the client to prevent and detect them than toward specific detection on his own part. If the client realizes that it is not the auditor's function to search out all such possibilities—unless he is additionally engaged for this purpose—the client will usually take the necessary self-protective steps. Of course, auditors recognize that minor defalcations carried out over long periods can accumulate to major sums and that every effort should be made by the client to prevent this; constant vigilance spurred by the auditor is the only answer to this problem. Management has the responsibility for the preservation of the company's assets. If it fails in this respect, or in any other respect, the independent audit cannot be relied upon to cure the ills induced by poor management and stockholders should not expect that it will.

POSSIBLE METHODS OF FRAUD

Hence, the auditor's "awareness of the possibility that fraud may exist" (see paragraph 5) is exhibited by his concern whether, after he has made an examination with due care, an existing undetected major fraud can have an effect on his opinion on the statements. Expressed differently, the question is whether the readers of the statements, including third parties who may rely on their reasonableness, will be misled if a major fraud remains undetected. Before this question can be answered, the three methods by which major fraud may be perpetrated should be considered. They are:

1. Gross overstatement or understatement of net assets and results of operations—not involving the extraction of assets—perpetrated by management for the purpose of misleading taxing authorities or existing or prospective creditors or stockholders. Typical of this method are the overstated or understated inventory, the unrealistic valuation of receivables, unwarranted capitalization of expenses or expensing of capital items, the omission of liabilities, commitments, and contingencies.
2. Gross overstatement of net assets to cover up the extraction of assets. Typical of this method are the lapping of collections, the kiting of cash balances, the unrecorded loan, and the borrowed or falsified inventory.
3. Major extractions of assets charged off in the income account. Typical of this method are improper disbursements, diversion of sales or other income, write-off of accounts whose collection was diverted, and massive payroll padding.

It should be noted that the first two of these methods may have a substantial effect upon the balance sheet. Thus, if the examination of the balance sheet is emphasized, the likelihood of undetected fraud of these types is minimized. The third type affects the balance sheet by *understating* net assets, but only to the extent that a recovery of the theft may be possible. Unfortunately, such recoveries are usually limited or negligible, because thieves frequently squander or hide their loot and recoveries under fidelity bonds are necessarily limited. From the standpoint of some third parties, such as prospective stockholders and creditors, understatements of this type, even if material, would be less misleading because decisions to invest or extend credit would have been predicated upon "conservative" statements. (Existing stockholders may, however, be induced to sell.) Certainly, if no recovery is possible, the income statement is still a fair presentation of *net* results of operations. However, because the classification and proper disclosure of items within the income statement may be affected, a serious, and rather moot question concerning fair presentation of over-all results of operations would still exist, and the auditor should always be "aware" of this possibility.

IMPORTANCE OF BALANCE SHEET

Consequently, in the author's view, it should be obvious that, despite the ascendancy of the importance of the income statement from the security analyst's and creditor's point of view, the auditing emphasis (from a fair presentation standpoint and from a fraud standpoint) should still be on the balance sheet. An auditor's assurance of a valid opinion on the income statement is greater if he concentrates on the balance sheets at both ends of the period than if he devotes the equivalent time to the income statement. However, he knows that he cannot ignore auditing the income statement because his opinion on its fairness is predicated on more than just obtaining assurance regarding both balance sheets. His review and testing of a company's procedures and transactions must be such as to provide him with reasonable assurance that revenues and expenses have been fairly presented and that material omissions or distortions are not likely to have occurred. He should be alert to the fact that if major frauds are buried in the income statement, historical operating ratios and normal profits would probably be affected (unless the fraud is continued over long periods). Here the background of the auditor and his knowledge of the client's methods and operations should be more helpful than voluminous testing.

Statement No. 30 has attempted to place in focus the objective of the ordinary examination and the responsibility the auditor assumes in its undertaking. Generally accepted auditing standards are aimed at achieving this objective, and if examinations are made properly in accordance with such standards by competent auditors who are alert to the possibilities and probabilities in the fraud area, the likelihood of undetected major fraud will be minimized. However, the public should never lose sight of the fact that the auditor is never an insurer or guarantor, and that because of the possibility of colossal collusion, forgeries and unrecorded transactions, a master deception of the McKesson variety is still possible (although very unlikely) without the auditor being at fault.

A better appreciation of this problem can be achieved only by a program aimed at informing clients and the public of the objective and limitations of the ordinary examination. Now that there exists a better statement of the auditor's responsibility in this area, there should be no reluctance to discuss the matter frankly with clients. Small organizations frequently want an examination that has the detection of defalcations as a principal purpose. There is no reason why such an examination cannot be combined with the ordinary examination of financial statements. The additional expense involved in such a dual-purpose examination may be small in some cases; this should be carefully analyzed and then discussed fully with the client. Whatever the decision, the understanding of the nature of the engagement *and its limitations* should preferably be in writing.

The auditor should also emphasize the need for better internal control and fidelity insurance coverage. In most instances, these provide better protection (and indemnification) against defalcations, usually at less cost, than extended examinations by independent auditors.

PROFIT FORECASTS†

by

Philip L. Defliese

AS professional accountants, our interest in the subject at hand is substantial. We have studied it in some depth—both independently and through our participation in the relevant committee of the American Institute of CPAs.

Public use of profit forecasts is an idea whose time has *not* quite come. We at Lybrand, Ross Bros. & Montgomery have been investigating for some time the question of whether, how, and when to include forecast data in published financial information.

We have concluded that reporting such data in financial statements might ultimately be useful and beneficial to the investing public, but only when the relative degree of certainty and uncertainty entailed in financial forecasts can be clearly defined, expressed, and understood by the investing public. As a prerequisite to this, we see a crucial need for basic research and testing before the concept itself can be introduced on a universal, mandatory basis.

We believe that an overemphasis on forecasting at this time would be unwise, particularly in view of the large number of unsophisticated persons who, having no knowledge of the imperfect state of the art, would accept forecasts on face.

Our position is *positive* rather than reactionary. We want the concept to succeed, and, toward this end, I will offer the Commission our views on basic criteria for expanding financial reporting requirements, reinforced with details derived from our own extended study and thought. We believe that financial reporting has an obligation to maintain investor confidence. If a proposed new disclosure requirement will preserve that high level of confidence, it merits consideration; if it impairs it, there will inevitably be the risk of misleading investors, thereby destroying public confidence in those aspects of financial reporting that have proven reliable. If this should happen, the new reporting requirements will surely be abused. If the abuses get out of hand, chaos could threaten the whole system.

THE AUDITOR'S ROLE

Our own studies naturally started with the role of the auditor in a forecasting environment. Should the CPA be publicly associated with a forecast? We think

†The position of Lybrand, Ross Bros. & Montgomery submitted to the Securities and Exchange Commission on December 12, 1972 by Philip L. Defliese, Managing Partner. Reprinted with permission from *The CPA Journal*, March 1973, pp. 171-175, copyright 1973.

not. We see an important role for auditors reporting to knowledgeable parties—such as the board of directors—and we have recommendations on how this role might be structured. We are against the auditor's *public* association with forecasts, however, because of the cited issue of certainty and for a variety of other significant reasons.

First, there is the question of attesting to managerial assumptions, which must be at the root of all forecasts. Does the auditor have a rational basis for challenging managerial assumptions about the future? What particular qualifications do CPAs have for launching such a challenge in view of the fact that their discipline does not cover economic projections, marketing outlooks, or intuition?

Professional accountants do have a unique knowledge of business and business conditions, and they have both the discipline and the independence to constitute an ideal outside party to check on forecasts. Their role, however, must first be carefully structured so that they can effectively bring their training and their knowledge to bear, and, second, the auditors themselves need a period of experience with forecasts if good rules are to be formulated.

In short, CPAs have no standards by which to pass on managerial assumptions, nor do they presently have broad practical experience in dealing with such matters. At present, the CPA's expertise could best be deployed in the area directly allied to compilation and computation. And the accountant could furnish important professional services in these areas, even perhaps including the development of practical standards and generally accepted principles upon which forecasts could be compiled.

THE MANAGERIAL RESPONSIBILITY

Only management can determine the underlying assumptions of a forecast. Responsibilities cannot be transferred, in whole or in part, to auditors, or to any other party. In the United Kingdom, the "sole responsibility" for forecasts is borne by the company's board of directors. Therefore, in order for forecasting to be used in the United States, it must be made crystal clear to the investment community that all projections are dependent on future economic, legislative, and other circumstances, only some of which are under management's control. And, in point of fact, management assumptions are not auditable.

Now, even though the auditor can provide important aid, the nature of this aid would be difficult to describe directly to the investing public. In general, there must be a critical evaluation of all the various aspects of the public reaction to forecasts to ensure that these projections do not come to be regarded as the magic key to improved investment decision-making. This point is especially important if we are to avoid the type of overreliance on one aspect of analysis, as that exhibited by the overdependence on the single earnings-per-share figure by investors in the late 1960s.

It should be observed that forecasting in the form envisioned is essentially an extension of an internal operation—corporate budgeting—into the public arena. Corporate budgeting is a valuable and necessary operational tool, offering a framework for implementing management expectations and policies. Budgeting facilitates capital expenditures and shapes operations, but, even internally, it is used as no more than a basic guide, subject to periodic review and revision. While management uses such information, with suitable reservations as to its certainty, there can be no assurance that the investing public would exercise comparable restraint.

As a result, legitimate concern about reporting responsibility and the related legal liabilities could force management into an overly conservative stance, seriously limiting the utility of forecasts for external purposes. Furthermore, variations in approach could lead to substantial comparability problems between companies sensitive to liability problems and companies aggressively seeking to foster optimistic expectations. With so high a subjectivity factor, forecasts, in the aggregate, could become almost meaningless.

Likewise, management might often be constrained in preparing forecasts because they depend upon new marketing or product plans. These, of course, could not be disclosed without jeopardizing the company's competitive advantage.

RESEARCH: THE CRITICAL FACTOR

Thus, there are internal as well as external conditions militating against the premature inauguration of a forecasting requirement. We believe that these considerations create a compelling need for research in depth and for further experience before any mandatory rules are formulated. We don't suggest that these and similar problems are an absolute barriers against publication of forecasts; we only ask that they be given serious thought in any plan that would eventually be carried out.

We also recommend that strong attention be given to the need for educating the investing public, in advance, of any mandatory forecasting requirement, stressing that published forecasts represent opinion *not* fact, that no degree of precision has been attempted, but rather that forecasts cover a range of anticipated or desired results.

In point of fact, our country has had little experience with forecasting. That which we have had has been recent and inexact. It is certainly desirable to supply greater information to the investment community and to the public—and, toward this end, we are sympathetic to the aims of forecasting proponents. We urge that forecasts, however, be approached as one of several elements—such as more detailed and meaningful quarterly reporting—to be explored in an overall effect to better communicate financial information.

Those favoring the immediate implementation of mandatory requirements to publish forecast data point frequently to the United Kingdom as proof of the quick workability of the concept. But business is practiced quite differently in the United Kingdom. The capital market there only remotely resembles that of the United States, with its 32-odd million investors. The legal environment also differs substantially, a difference that must be emphasized in the face of arguments that legal liability on forecasts has presented no grave difficulties in

Great Britain. In fact, lawyers in the British Isles cannot take cases on a contingent basis; i.e., a litigant or plaintiff must always pay for the attorney's professional services independent of the outcome of his action. This fact is such a significant deterrent to their initiation of liability suits—and thus their low incidence—that it cannot be considered as a reliable precedent for the United States.

The composition of the capital market, the legal environment, the practice of business itself, even the social customs—all these constitute profound differences between the two countries and make it unrealistic to attempt to transfer directly the U.K. experience to the United States. We can learn much by examining U.K. forecasting practices—which have been restricted to merger situations and prospectuses, and which allow errors of up to 10% (with rumors of out-of-court settlements). But we need our own studies and experience, if we're to establish an atmosphere conducive to intelligent and reliable forecasting.

THE NEED FOR STANDARDS

In this context, it is wise to recall the general background of reporting by lines of business, an important reporting concept, which, however, was carried out without accurate definitions. To date, some feel that this reporting has been plagued with inadequacies—traceable in large part to a lack of guidelines for preparing such data and even, in part, to the absence of a clear-cut definition of what precisely is meant by "lines of business." In many instances, the results have been so substantially uncertain that product-line reporting has been of little or no value to financial-statement users.

Assuredly, the adoption of a forecasting requirement should be based on explicit standards. Yet we presently have no generally accepted guidelines for the preparation of forecasts, nor any plain, widely accepted definition of what a forecast means. In our own Firm, we have defined a profit forecast as follows:

> A profit forecast is a prediction of what profit will be for some period in the future based on certain assumed happenings, both within and outside the control of company management. A profit forecast is one expressed numerically or in a narrative containing words enabling the reader to approximate future profits by an arithmetical process.

EVOLUTION VERSUS IMPOSITION

Generally, what we have outlined is merely a broad perspective of the problem related to published forecasts. These are noted as both areas of study and as examples of the types of difficulties that must be dealt with via research and testing. The latter might be accomplished by allowing forecasting, first on a voluntary basis, and then studying the results to find what they yield in the way of pitfalls. In this way, we may also evolve a logical approach, rather than impose an arbitrary rule with which both the business and investment communities would have to conform.

We believe that, at the appropriate time, the voluntary inclusion of forecast data in annual financial reports should be encouraged. This makes for evolution of custom, and would ultimately simplify the SEC's work. It also allows for a period of education in which investors would gradually come to understand the true limitations and relevance of these forecasts, recognizing clearly that the CPA is not attesting to the accuracy of the forecast.

We recommend immediate attention to defining forecasts and establishing machinery for studying experience. The goal in this effort should be the establishment of explicit guides and standards. While flexibility will obviously be needed, published forecasts will be useful to financial-statements readers only if they are based upon a consistently applied and rational set of principles. Such principles should apply to both the development of the forecast assumptions and the computation of the projection.

Limiting the accountant's opinion to the forecast compilation only, as some have suggested, would not, in our opinion, weaken the implication that forecast data is comparable to other financial data. Even if this were not the case, the certification of forecast compilations would raise many substantial technical problems. Even accountants themselves differ on what compilation means and what the independent accountant should do before rendering a report, even on compilation. Furthermore, opinions vary as to whether we deal with mathematics only, or the reasonableness of the numerical assumptions and, if they are reasonable, how they have been checked.

REPORTING TO A THIRD PARTY

This does mean, however, that we do not see an important role for independent accountants in auditing forecast information. On the contrary, we believe, as we noted earlier, that accountants should systematically review and report on forecasts, but privately, to an informed third party, rather than publicly, in annual reports. The third party might be an underwriter or a board of directors. In fact, we would suggest that directors—or committees much like audit committees—be encouraged to serve in this area. The auditor should be able to aid such a group by freely disseminating information and intelligence to it without undue fear of wrongly influencing investors. The report to these directors could be in the form of a letter that would allow the accountant scope to describe the procedures he had followed, and to express his views as to the compilation of the data and whether it adheres to Generally Accepted Accounting Principles.

The inclusion of forecasts in annual financial statements would also raise important questions as to the form and the relative validation of forecast data. We strongly suggest:

1. that such data should be presented separately from historical data, and
2. that independent accountants should not, in any way, be directly associated with published forecast data.

We base our suggestions on the issue of the relative certainty that financial-statement users are likely to assume. We believe that every effort should be made to maximize forecast certainty and to minimize the risk of the investing public's assumption of an unwarranted *degree* of certainty.

Thus, because historical data and forecast data are inherently different, we, as accountants, are keenly sensitive to the possibility that their direct association could suggest a greater degree of certainty for forecasts than is justified.

Similarly, an accountant's report associated with the forecast could add undue weight and overemphasize the usefulness of the data. For the foreseeable future, forecast information would be derived by methods differing so markedly from those used for developing other financial information that inclusion of the forecast in the accountant's opinion letter would be inappropriate and misleading.

In conclusion, we strongly believe that a forecast requirement, although theoretically desirable, would be highly premature at this time. Instead, we recommend that the SEC take the initiative in establishing an ad hoc body composed of interested parties, plus the necessary technical advisers, to conduct an intensive investigation of problems, approaches, and alternatives in developing reasonably reliable and consistent forecast systems. We suggest that a two-year period of research followed by three years of voluntary compliance in which actual experience may be studied. Such an investigation or feasibility study could well lay the groundwork for effective forecast reporting without some of the associated difficulties we have cited today. Thank you.

LUNCHEON ADDRESS: PERSPECTIVES ON AUDITOR'S RESPONSIBILITIES†

by
Philip L. Defliese

MR. Chairperson, honored officers and directors, and fellow job hoppers: I used to attend your meetings quite regularly back in the 1950s, and all I can say is things haven't changed very much. I see the resumes flying like mad. But certainly it's great to rejoin the group and to meet with a number of old friends. I did get seduced by Dr. Savage of Adelphi [University] many years ago and took an assistant professorship there. However, I soon saw the error of my ways and went back to Lybrand.

If I may be entitled to a slight commercial, in view of the fact that we participants are providing voluntary services, I think you'll find that the new [ninth] edition of *Montgomery's Auditing* is a complete rewrite, and it will, of course, contain the Coopers and Lybrand approach to auditing which de-emphasizes statistical sampling. I would like to say one other thing concerning the book. In preparing the preface, we were really intrigued as to how we might communicate our general philosophy. Obviously we had to restrain ourselves from discussing current hot issues in accounting and auditing, because the book is basically a reference work and not a prospectus in any sense. We reviewed the prefaces of Montgomery's first eight editions, starting back in 1912, and pieced together a number of quotes which I think you will find very interesting. They will read as if they were written yesterday, and you'll get the impression that perhaps this profession of ours hasn't changed very much over the years. But there is one thought I would like to furnish you which I think really puts it all together. In 1921, Montgomery said that good accounting practice is the practice of good accountants. I think there is some meaning to that. In 1934, right after the bubble of the 1920s and some of the scandals that came out as a result of the investigations which led up to the FCC, he made the comment that good accounting practice and good business practice cannot long remain apart and I think that, too, has a great deal of relevance in our environment today. There is no doubt that the auditor today is being expected to assume a greater role than he ever has and the question is whether or not the profession is going to live up to that demand. I think it is, and I'll explain why. I'd like to add, however, the disclaimer that the comments I make on my own are not necessarily the views of

†This article is based on the dictated script for a speech given at the 1975 Annual Meeting of the American Accounting Association, which was published under the title, "Luncheon Address," in the *Collected Papers of the American Accounting Association's Annual Meeting* (Tucson, Arizona), pp. 405-411. Reprinted with permission of the American Accounting Association.

the AICPA. I think, however, most of what I say will have a great deal of relevance to what the Institute is doing and thinking.

AUDITOR RESPONSIBILITY

This increased responsibility that is being thrust upon us as time goes on is something which the profession has to react to. The question is whether we will react to it voluntarily or whether we will react to it involuntarily. Until recent times the profession more or less has had to be pushed. Some of us did more pushing than others but with out the push we would have not responded. I do see some signs today of a profession that is responding to the demands of our society. You might say the public accounting profession is going through its own post-Watergate fallout—the results of some of the practices of the go-go period of the 1960s. We've seen now the result of the cases of Equity Funding, Four Seasons, and National Student Marketing. The question is whether or not these are the failures of the accounting profession, the failures of regulatory commission, or the failures of business itself; or whether or not we have really learned, so to speak, the lesson of Continental Vending. Certainly Continental Vending was a sign for people to follow, especially since it was a case that was not prosecuted by the SEC and a case that never lost a dime for any investor. Nevertheless, it had a moral that we as a profession should have been concerned about. I think these cases have indicate that perhaps we've been over-emphasizing accounting principles and overlooking the need to strengthen our auditing procedures. If you analyze the cases today, by and large they constitute auditing lapses rather than accounting lapses. For that reason we need to really give consideration to the approach to auditing.

These cases also, of course, emphasize the need for a re-examination of responsibilities for management fraud. Today practically everyone accepts the fact that the ordinary examination isn't designed and can't be relied upon to detect defalcations and the like. But on the question of management fraud, we have another issue: I think that, no matter what we do, the public will never accept the notion that we are not responsible for management fraud. This may need a call for re-examination of our procedures, our approach to auditing, and all the rest. Unfortunately, we do not have the subpoena powers or the investigatory powers of the SEC or the Justice Department.

For this reason, we have asked a special commission [the Cohen Commission] to determine what the auditor's responsibilities are in this area and hopefully, by 1976, we will have a report which may indicate the need for some changes. Actually, in the final analysis, I think the old fraud statement that we have will probably still prevail. After all, it does point up the fact that the auditors should be aware of the possibilities of management misrepresentation. It is what the auditor does about that awareness that needs some redefinition, rather than the question of whether or not there needs to be a broader responsibility.

Recently, the Auditing Standards Executive Committee issued two new statements which I believe probably have not yet reached you. They are Statements on Auditing Standards No. 5 and No. 6. SAS No. 5 deals with the question of presenting fairly. What does that mean? Does it mean something beyond its traditional interpretation? Does it mean presents fairly in the abstract rather than in conformity with generally accepted accounting principles? I think you will find that the "presents fairly" statement does not really state much more than what prevailing practice was, and that is that. Implicit in the determination of whether or not financial statements present fairly was the concept that accounting principles were applied that were appropriate to the circumstances. Now I think it is quite possible that, in the last decade or so, that concept was not always uniformly applied—that as long as it was a generally accepted, whether or not it was appropriate in the circumstances, it was acceptable. This is now finally articulated making it incumbent upon the auditor to reach a conclusion that the principles used are appropriate in those circumstances. I think this comes close to the true and fair concept that the British use. I think that basically that there has been very little difference in the past between the British concept and the presents fairly concept that we use. Obviously, auditors should not close their eyes, but should be willing to share judgment with management concerning the proper selection of principles.

The same applies to SAS No. 6 on related party transactions. Here again I believe that finally we have a rather definitive articulation of what a related party transaction is and what alertness the auditors should have concerning its discovery. I believe this will be helpful in detecting management fraud. What it boils down to is that there is again a further thrust of responsibility onto the auditor to share the judgment with management in the presentation of financial statements. I know this is an anathema to many auditors because they feel the financial statements are management's representation. Well, I see nothing inconsistent with that and the sharing of the judgment in the opining on those financial statements. To me, obviously one must come before the other, but certainly we can share that judgment and provide our readers with greater assurances to the acceptability of the presentation. Consequently, I think we can see that the public is expecting more from the auditors than ever before, and auditors will accept it readily if we restore the credibility that I think will certainly be restored after this purging storm through which we're passing.

DISCLOSURE OF ILLEGAL ACTS

The SEC through its injunctive proceedings and class actions has pointed up to the public that we have this responsibility and this responsibility has been exposed to such an extent that we obviously need to react to it. At the same time, however, business is having its own post-Watergate fallout. We have found a tremendous number of disclosures concerning political contributions, both domestically and abroad, and bribery in foreign countries in order to obtain advantageous contracts or positions. The real question is what is the auditor's role in that environment. It creates a dilemma really because, in the past, auditors have taken the position, and I think rightly so, that their job is to express an opinion on the fair presentation of financial position and results of operations. To the extent that any activity did not create a cloud over either financial position or results of operation that activity was not required to be disclosed. But we now find that the SEC takes a different view and insists on disclosure. Of course, it attempts at the same time to impose different standards of materiality than we have experienced in the past, and I think that will create further problems for us. In a sense the auditor is being placed in the role of monitoring the morals of our business society. Maybe this is all right and maybe that is what the role of the auditor should be. But, if it is the case, it's something that needs to be well defined with guidelines expressed as such so that we will know what the game is all about. We cannot suffer through any attempt to apply these standards retroactively. The American society has been largely opposed to the imposition of an ex-post-facto approach, whether in law or elsewhere. Here again we find ourselves perhaps being judged on standards that didn't exist at the time of the actions in question. This is always a problem and it is frequently a problem in the courts.

This is not to say that I or the Institute or anyone condones illegal or immoral activities, and I think it would be delightful if we could impose abroad some of the standards of behavior that we accept rather readily in this country. But the question is whether or not disclosure after the fact can result in self-fulfilling prophecy. The Institute had a number of discussions of this subject with the commissioners and staff of the SEC. I dare say that we got some rather mixed views on what the issues should be and what the guidelines should be. For example, some expressed the view that the auditor has a responsibility to disclosure illegal or immoral activities, assuming that he finds them. An auditor cannot disclose something he cannot find. Whether or not his auditing procedures should be aimed at finding them again is another issue that needs to be sorted out. But when he does find an act that might be considered either illegal or immoral they feel a disclosure should be made and that the basis of disclosure should be the impact upon the company's financial position and results of operation. Well, obviously, that creates a more or less self-fulfilling prophecy because if something must be disclosed that would ultimately be advantageous or disadvantageous by virtue of its disclosure, the auditor faces a dilemma.

My firm recently had a case in point. As a result of our normal auditing procedures, we found that there had been a bribe of a government official in another country and the bribe made it possible to obtain a rather substantial contract. This contract made the difference between a profit or loss to the company that year and therefore was significant in that respect. In discussion with the SEC, they insisted upon its disclosure, including a disclosure of the country in which these things took place. Now, these are new standards which are being imposed retroactively. Obviously, had the company known this would be the ultimate outcome, its actions might have been different. The impact upon the company of such a disclosure remains to be seen. In the long run investors are going to be hurt rather than helped by this kind of disclosure. Well, so much for the new look in the responsibility for the auditor in disclosing unusual transactions, unusual actions, on the part of a company.

INTERIM FINANCIAL STATEMENTS

Let me move now to another area of dispute within the profession, which is still to be resolved to a large extent; that is interim financial statements. I believe that the public wants some assurance of the reliability of interim financial statements. The question of reliance upon interims is well established. Market quotes react rather severely to interim financial statements; consequently, there is a great deal of reliance being placed upon those numbers. Therefore, I think its axiomatic that the public would want them to be as reliable as possible. We also know that interim financial statements can never be as reliable as those that might be ultimately audited. Nor do we feel that auditing of interim statements should be a requirement. The question is what can be done in order to provide this reliance.

In 1974, we had two very dramatic examples of what can happen in interim financial statements. Chase Manhattan Bank had to withdraw its second quarter results because of a later discovery that it failed to use the correct principles in valuing its bond portfolio. In the ICN Pharmaceutical Company case, when the auditors came in to audit in the fourth quarter, they found the first quarter's results were totally misstated and had to be revised. Of course, in the Chase situation, the impact upon the stock wasn't very great because they were able to assure shareholders that the results of the year would not be too badly depressed and so everything was fine. In the ICN situation, of course, the market went crazy and at the same time you had lawsuits coming out of your ears, against management and the auditors as well. So dire results can follow if interims are not reliable.

The question is can interim financial statements be made reliable through a process something short of auditing. I think you've read some of the material that has been issued on this topic. The Institute's Committee on Auditing Standards has an exposure draft out in which it outlines what can be done and what kind of assurance can be given to management. As you know Coopers & Lybrand initially opposed this. We believed that those comfort letters should be made available to the public, but in the interest of harmony we have withdrawn from that position and agreed to accept the Institute's position on keeping the comfort letter, so to speak, private to management. Again, I think we find a great reluctance on the part of the profession to move ahead and accept responsibility where obviously there is a need. Now there may be some dispute over that need, but I believe that the public is expecting more of us than we have recognized. Our experience with comfort letters in registration statements has been absolutely excellent. There have been no lawsuits predicated upon failures in those comfort letters. Even though they have been kept totally private, so to speak, everybody knows they exist and they could easily be subpoenaed in the case of a law suit. Thus they have been exposed considerably and for any attack. But those attacks have not come. So with that experience I think we can, I am sure we can, devise some technology that will provide greater assurance.

Ultimately the public will be benefitted through this process but I think there is a need to go about it slowly. There is no question in my mind that many companies are not yet ready for this process and, therefore, it must be voluntary.

There are many companies today, including many of the smaller companies, which went public and were probably traded over the counter, that are not yet fully geared out to the production of reliable interim results. Their financials were more or less put together with bailing wire back in the 1960s when they went public and—as a result of a rather disinterested SEC and accounting profession—no attempt was made to determine whether or not their internal systems were such as to produce reliable results on an interim basis. Usually they waited for the auditor to come in and make 85 closing adjustments before the annual report went out. That era has passed and we as a profession have to move ahead and accept a greater role. In fact, I would predict that within the next decade or so our auditing reports will include some opinions concerning internal control and management systems, so as to provide investors with some indication of how good the internal processes are. So much for interim reports.

FORECASTING

Let me get down to the last area in which I believe the auditors will find an expanded role—forecasting. Now many accounting firms today are making projections, particularly as they relate to feasibility studies for everything from health care operations to real estate operations. Many of these projections include opinions of the auditors to the effect that the numbers are put together properly and that good accounting has been applied. In some instances you will find that they will state that the assumptions are reasonable. So this is not a new exercise as far as the public accounting profession is concerned.

We all know that any company worth its salt has a budget or a forecast for the coming year. The real question is to whether or not the investor, and particularly the prospective investor, is entitled to know what their view is concerning what the future year holds. Here again I think we need to walk before we can run. Forecasting has to be on a voluntary basis. We have to experiment with it; we have to produce the guidelines and the Institute committees are working on those guidelines now so that the question of liabilities concerning improper forecast will be minimized. I think that ultimately the CPA will be expected not only to opine concerning the propriety of the forecast from both the mathematical and accounting principles standpoint but also on the reasonableness of its assumptions. Here again many people will say this is something outside the province of the auditor. Altogether too frequently we hold ourselves outside when in many respects we as auditors are probably closest to the situation. In many cases we are even closer than management. We can tell readily whether or not a projection or an assumption is reasonable in the circumstances in which we find them.

Some people say that opining on forecasts of this sort will affect our independence, that we will thereby be somewhat influenced at year end in order to make a forecast come true. I think this is a slur on the integrity of the profession. Hopefully that concept will diminish and people will recognize that we can produce an opinion that is worth the paper its written on and that will hold up regardless of what the final outcome may be. I would certainly be disappointed if any direction were taken toward limiting the independent auditor's role in this respect. I do believe that our independence has to be demonstrated, and I think that the actions of the firms of the last few years have demonstrated that rather well.

We are also going to be asked to perform new functions in a number of other areas. The passage of the pension reform act has again thrust us into the area of pension reporting. Many firms, of course, do have actuarial services and we will be assuming a role of passing upon the reasonableness of pension determinations. I think this is all for the good, because we should be willing and able to accept that responsibility. A number of other new issues have been discussed during the course of your meeting. We are obviously getting more involved in price levels, fair value, capitalization of interest, cost of equity capital, and we are also going to be involved in the quality control peer reviews and accreditation problems. These additional responsibilities are here. I think we have the capability of assuming them, and I think the future of the profession will be enhanced by our willingness to assume this responsibility. Thank you very much.

DEFINITION OF MATERIALITY: The Multi-Facet Perspectives— THE ACCOUNTANT'S VIEW†

by

Philip L. Defliese and Roderick K. Macleod

THE PRE-WATERGATE, PRE-FASB VIEW

BELOW is reproduced, with the publisher's permission, the section on materiality contained in the recently published ninth edition of *Montgomery's Auditing*.[1] It deals with the concept as it relates to accounting determination and disclosure solely from the point of view of an auditor engaged in an examination of published financial statements, and it was written shortly before the beginning of the current intense scrutiny of the subject. Note that it *does not* deal with the effect of materiality on the auditing process; this is dealt with in another section of the book and is not relevant to this discussion.

The reproduced paragraphs illustrate that the subject of materiality is and has been a difficult question and one which the accounting profession hasn't dealt with adequately. The section follows:

MATERIALITY

Need for a Materiality Standard

A materiality standard is a practical necessary in both auditing and accounting. Allowing trivia to complicate and clutter up either the auditing process or financial statements is wasteful and disorderly. Worse, it can cause inconsequential matters to obscure significant ones. Therefore, ignoring "items not material" is well-accepted practice: they are not disclosed in financial statements, they require no comment in an auditor's report, and they need not be corrected or adjusted in the accounts.

The concept is simple, but applying it in practice is not. These are some of the major questions: How is materiality of an item measured?

†Reprinted from *Materiality: An Evolving Concept Under the Securities Laws*, Course Handbook Series Number 197, Douglas R. Carmichael and Alan B. Levenson, cochairmen. New York: Practising Law Institute, 1975, pp. 27-40. Reprinted with permission of Roderick K. Macleod.

[1] *Montgomery's Auditing*, 9th Ed., Defliese, Johnson, Macleod, Ronald Press 1975.

Is materiality related to an effect on net income? An effect on the trend of net income? An effect on the balance of an item? Is materiality to be judged on the basis of individual items, categories of items, or the total of all possible items affecting the statements under review? If the total, is it the gross total or the net total?

Materiality is even more perplexing in the details of practice. Are some accounts subject to a lower or looser standard than others? Common sense calls for variations in "guesstimates" to be treated differently from factually based judgments and both to be treated differently from clear-cut errors, but how?

We have long believed, with others in the profession, that a standard—either a Statement of Financial Accounting Standards by the FASB or a Statement on Auditing Standards—is needed to guide practitioners on the subject of materiality. The concept of materiality is highly complex, is understood differently by different auditors, and is constantly alleged to be abused. The FASB is presently wrestling with the subject.

Pervasiveness of Materiality Questions

All kinds of questions about accounting for and disclosure of various items and events arise during the course of every audit, even one that is impeccably "clean" because of diligent auditing. Each question must be dealt with as two questions: First, how should the item or event be treated on its own merits? And second, is it material enough that the way it is treated affects the fair presentation of financial position or results of operations in the financial statements? The answer to the first question is of consequence only if the answer to the second —the materiality question—is affirmative. How materiality and relative risk affect the auditing process is also discussed in Chapter 5 ["Auditing Procedures—Their Nature and Extent"].

Obviously, an item that is clearly material is dealt with on its own merits and is not part of the subject under discussion. Also, material items are much less likely to be overlooked or accounted for incorrectly. Most of the questions of possible adjustments or disclosures raised by an audit involve both the question of correct treatment and the question of whether the item or event is material. Even if an item or event is clearly too small to be important, the question has to be dealt with because of the possibility that it may combine with others to accumulate to a material total.

The following are examples of items and events giving rise to possible adjustments or disclosures that may or may not be material:

Simple errors in the accounts—a mistake in a computation, an invoice payable that was overlooked.

Events requiring disclosure as unusual or nonrecurring, or segregation as extraordinary—occasional sales of productive assets used in the business, a casualty loss in a subsidiary warehouse.

Items possibly requiring prior-period adjustments—settlement of income taxes, a lawsuit, or wage contract negotiations.

Changes in the business entity—acquisition of a subsidiary company, consolidation of a subsidiary not previously consolidated.

Voluntary changes in accounting principles—adoption of a standard cost system that results in incluing certain production variances in the expenses of the year of occurrence rather than in inventory cost.

Changed conditions requiring new accounting—a new sales policy involving more liberal merchandise return privileges or product warranties, a change in a labor contract of a subsidiary that necessitates accrual of vacation pay.

Judgments or estimates—an allowance for estimated bad debts or for estimated obsolescence of inventory that could be larger or smaller.

In each of the above examples, the generally accepted accounting treatment is clear, but it is not clear whether failure to follow it would materially affect the financial statements.

A client's accounting staff decides how to account for and disclose most items and events before an audit begins. That is true even if the auditor is routinely consulted in advance about significant transaction; it is not practicable to consult the auditor on every unusual transaction, and those not clearly material may be either overlooked or routinely passed without review. The auditor must independently evaluate those judgments and reach his own conclusions about accounting, disclosure, and materiality.

The most sensitive category listed in the above examples is probably the last—judgments or estimates—because of the uncertainties involved, but differences of opinion between management and an auditor are also possible, and perhaps likely, in each of the other categories. Of course, the auditor should first discuss differences thoroughly with the client with the objective of reconciling them. However, even with the best of relations between client and auditor, several differences of opinion will usually remain as suggested "audit adjustments."

In companies that issue financial statement data periodically, financial management is understandably reluctant to change its initial judgments about accounting and materiality. By the time the audit is in progress, earnings for the year or three quarters of the year have been tentatively determined and reported to the president, the board of directors, and in many cases even the public. Even when management requests review of the accounts prior to any interim or year end release, an auditor is unlikely to uncover all possible differences of opinion. Considerable embarrassment results if the preliminary figures are not borne out by the audited financial statements, even if the differences are small. Management, however responsible, is therefore interested in seeing that an auditor's suggested adjustments to the financial statements are "waived" as not material.

Score Sheets

Some auditors have adopted a general practice of keeping a record of potential audit adjustments, commonly called a "score sheet." As an audit progresses, each item, large or small, that an auditor thinks should or could be adjusted is first taken up with the client. Of course, if it is something the client has obviously overlooked or misjudged and there is agreement about its disposition, the accounts are adjusted and the item is of no further concern. If the client disagrees, or agrees but prefers not to adjust, the item is carried on the score sheet. The company under examination need not be especially complex to product a score sheet covering several pages of working paper.

The auditor evaluates the score sheet as one of the concluding steps of the audit. More often than not, no single account is materially affected by the score sheet entries and the cumulative pluses and minuses net to an insignificant effect on individual classifications in the financial statements. The auditor then completes the audit and issues his opinion on the financial settlements, and the score sheet becomes part of the evidential matter documenting his examination. It may also be useful in discussing with the client suggested improvements in his accounting procedures.

Sometimes, however, an auditor believes that the possible adjustments listed on the score sheet, although individually insignificant, accumulate to a total that is material to one or more of the items appearing in the financial statements—usually net income. The auditor then confers with the client to decide what to do.

The client may be able to produce further evidence to justify the initial treatment of some items or may agree to record some of them in the accounts or to disclose others. The discussions continue until enough score sheet items are resolved so that the auditor can conclude that the remaining items do not adversely affect the fairness of presentation of the financial statements.

Depending on the size and complexity of an organization, each score sheet item may have to be taken up with several levels of management. The first consultation, of course, is with the individual directly responsible, who must supply all the facts. Additional conferences may include his supervisor, and sometimes a plant controller and division controller, all of whom must concur in a decision. Often the deciding score sheet conference includes top management of the client company: the financial vice president and the chief executive. If discussions reach that level, two subjects should probed: how to resolve the current score sheet problems and how to prevent similar problems from growing to such a magnitude in the future.

Rules of Thumb

The essence of materiality is that insignificant differences do not matter. The question of how large a difference may be before it matters has never been definitively answered in the literature of accounting and auditing. It was addressed in the famous *BarChris* case,[2] and the decision in that case included a number of issues of materiality. However, the reasoning in the *BarChris* decision was so intertwined with the specific facts of the case that it does not provide general guidance. The determination is still left to individual professional judgment, which can only be guided by some rules of thumb that are by no means uniformly accepted.

The figure most often given for the point at which a difference becomes material is 5%. That is, if the item under scrutiny is within 5% of what it might otherwise be, the difference is immaterial. Obviously, any rule of thumb, such as 5%, must be used with great caution and careful judgment. Some times 5% is clearly too broad a range. For example, small variations in trends are considered significant in companies with operational stability, such as public utilities, and the limit of materiality must be reduce to 3%, 2%, or less; otherwise, "immaterial" items would affect the trend. In recent year, the trend of annual earnings (up or down) has become of paramount interest to investors; consequently, whether an item is of sufficient materiality to influence the trend must receive careful consideration. (See a reference to this concept in APB Opinion No. 20, paragraph 38.)

Sometimes materiality of an item or event is clearly a function of the nature of the account. Little or no error is tolerable if precision is desirable and achievable, as in capital stock accounts where accounting does not require estimates or judgments. In contrast, inventory valuations can never be made with precision, and the threshold of materiality may be relatively high.

Some auditors believe that the standard of materiality should vary with the nature of the difference. If the difference arises from a clear-cut error, the tolerance is smaller than for a judgment about classification

---

[2]*Escott et al. v. BarChris Construction Corp. et al.*, 283 F. Supp. 643 (S. D. N. Y. 1968).

or disclosure, and that in turn is smaller than for a difference in estimating collectibility, realizability, or some other uncertain future event.

Netting

The way items are added together or set off against each other can significantly affect evaluations of materiality. Some items or events are more significant than others, implying that some kinds should be evaluated individually while others may be evaluated in groups.

Netting separate items to determine the amount that is to be judged for materiality raises intricate questions that need careful attention. Is it acceptable, for example, to net the effect of an error against the effect of a change in accounting principle? Or to net an error in the beginning balance against an error in the ending balance? Clearly, both answers must be negative. Each change in accounting principle must be considered separately under the consistency standard, and APB Opinion No. 20 (*AICPA Prof. Stds.*, vol.3, Sections 1051 to 1051B) calls for estimates and evaluations of materiality to be made afresh every year. Also, netting material items to obtain an immaterial total obviously violates the third standard of reporting. Otherwise, we see no harm in netting of, for example, insignificant differences in estimates against insignificant errors.

Summary

It should be clear from the foregoing discussion that a materiality standard is needed and also that it will not be easy to find one that can adequately encompass all the possible combinations of pertinent circumstances. In the meantime, each auditor has to try his best to judge what information might affect a reader's interpretation of the financial statements. If a decision might reasonably rest on a disclosure, it is material; if not, it is immaterial. For example, if one is buying an asset or a company at price precisely measured by accounting results, small amounts become material; on the other hand, if one is buying or selling stock, prices may be affected by but are not derived directly from the financial statements, and a larger amount may have no effect on willingness to buy or sell. As rational as that criterion is, however, it is too subjective for easy or confident application.

Obviously, the above paragraphs focus solely on business transactions and their possible impact on financial statements, because that is the way accountants and auditors have always thought about materiality. Questions of legality and morality have always been translated into resulting actual or potential financial impact and then evaluated and accounted for accordingly. For example, an omission of payment of a local tax was a problem if the proper liability (including interest and penalties) was not accrued in the accounts, but not a problem otherwise; the possibility that defalcations might be concealed in the income statement could be ignored because that is where they would be accounted for if discovered.

TREND TOWARD CONSERVATISM?

Certain published financial statements indicate that some accountants are taking much sterner positions on what constitutes a material item, even in the conventional sense. For example, the following footnote appeared in the 1975 annual report of PVO International, Inc., accompanied by an *unqualified* auditor's opinion dated August 25, 1975:

> Certain of the foreign countries in which the subsidiaries and affiliates of the Company operate impose currency restrictions. During the last two fiscal years, the Company received a total of $1,170,000 in the United States from its investments in one country including, in part, a distribution of profits in excess of that reported for tax purposes, in possible violation of that country's withholding tax and foreign currency exchange laws. In addition, income for tax determination purposes has been reported in that country in the last two, and prior, fiscal years, on a basis which excludes certain transactions. Full provision has been made in the Company's consolidated accounts for the effect upon its financial statements of all taxes which may become payable in that country. In light of the uncertainty as to the likelihood any penalties will be assessed or their amount, if assessed, no provision has been made in the accounts for any possible penalties or fines relating to these transactions. The Company's net investment in that country was $937,000 at June 30, 1975, and the accompanying statement of income includes for this investment $658,000, after taxes, for the fiscal year ended June 30, 1975, and $203,000, after taxes, for the fiscal year ended June 30, 1974. The Company has voluntarily placed this matter before the Securities and Exchange Commission and it is currently under review by the Commission.

Since the footnote states that (1) full provision has been made for taxes which may become payable, (2) there is an uncertain likelihood of penalties, and since the note *omits* an indication of amounts of unpaid taxes upon which penalties could be assessed, most accountants in the past would have thought (considering that the opinion is unqualified) that the matter was not material enough to require disclosure. Since PVO's revenues for the year were $240 million, its net income $2 million, and its total assets $55 million, the question of materiality arises in the traditional sense. The subsidiary's net income, $658,000, is clearly material in relation to the $2 million of consolidated net income, but some accountants would say that comparison of those two numbers could be misleading, since it has nothing to do with the matter being disclosed. However, it becomes clear that the purpose of the footnote is not to raise questions about the dollar amounts recorded in the consolidated financial statements but rather to disclose unknown contingencies not recorded in the statements which arise as a consequence from possible violation of tax and currency exchange laws. While severe penalties or expropriation could wipe out the investment (not material), the discontinuance of a material segment of the income stream could affect the company's future operations. It is the amount of that contingency which could be of significance and to which a standard of materiality is being applied.

The above-quoted footnote illustrates the problems of doing anything at all in a rapidly changing environment. If the above disclosure had not been made, both the company and its accountants would have been subject, for a considerable period of time, to the possibility of accusations of having failed to live up to a standard which has yet to be developed. Instead, they have made statements, which seem to suggest that the company may be in some kind of terrible trouble, and which only careful analysis by accountants experienced in international operations can reveal to be a probably minor exposure. And having made that damaging disclosure is no guarantee that they won't still be subject to attack when the materiality standard is finally written, either for being too tough or not tough enough.

THE ACCOUNTING QUESTION

As noted above, accountants have always looked at materiality in terms of its potential financial impact on the reporting entity. Clearly, other concepts are being tested and examined. They can be stated in various ways, although each way must be considered tentative for the present. One way to state what appears to be happening in terms which are consistent with the accountant's traditional function might be approximately as follows: "The purpose of publishing financial statements is to report in a consistent schematic form on the quality of management as reflected in the adequacy of financial position and results of operations; therefore, everything bearing on the quality of management should be included in financial statements."

Stated that way, the debate on changing concepts of materiality should focus on whether financial statements should stick to reflecting financial position and results of operations, or should undertake the broader function of reporting on the quality of management, that is, give greater emphasis to performance stewardship than results of stewardship. If we could agree to stick to the former, then no basic change in our traditional approach to the concept of materiality would be required. If it is the latter, then we need to erect a whole, new structure of theory and practice—both accounting and auditing—to deal with the new concepts.

If we stay with our traditional concept, a high degree of professionalism will be required to keep from trying to hide ourselves in a thicket of trivial disclosures. Much as we abhor detailed rules and measures—because every rule only invites imaginative exceptions—it may be that, in the short run at least, a detailed definition of materiality having the force of law will be the only way to avoid intolerable hazards of irresponsible litigation.

THE AUDITING QUESTION

Whether or not financial statements disclose all of the known problems, large or small, auditors are faced with the additional question of what to do about the problems which may not be known to them. The client may know about the problem and choose not to mention it (or to conceal it carefully); the client may know about the item or incident and not realize it's a problem, or the client may be innocently ignorant. It doesn't matter—when the fat's in the fire, everyone is looking at the auditor in one way or another, seldom friendly.

No audit, however extensive and expensive, can uncover every questionable transaction or activity in a company of any size and complexity. Experience is constantly reminding us of the propensity of mankind to think up questionable practices. Therefore, the auditor's exposure is constant and virtually universal.

The profession is studying a formal response to this dilemma. When an authoritative position is reached, we will undoubtedly support and follow it. In the meantime, we believe our current audit procedures are adequate. What is needed in some cases is a clearer understanding between auditor and audit committee of just what is and what isn't examined and evaluated in the course of an ordinary opinion audit.

THE FASB DISCUSSION MEMORANDUM

In March 1975, the Financial Accounting Standards Board issued a Discussion Memorandum entitled "an analysis of issues related to Criteria for Determining Materiality." The memorandum is 152 pages long, 246 pages including appendices. It discusses at length the issues and questions touched upon in the above quote, as well as examining authoritative literature in this and other countries and presenting the results of a survey of users of financial statements. Considerable emphasis is given to environmental or qualitative aspects of materiality as contrasted with quantitative aspects.

The memorandum reaches no conclusions or recommendations, but rather, as intended, it sets off an intensive examination of the subject within the profession. That examination will come to a head when public hearings are held in May 1976. There are at this time many different opinions on what ought to be done, if anything. It remains to be seen whether the accounting profession will be able to take definitive action on its own until the current "evolution" of the materiality concept has run its course under the securities laws.

PUBLIC UTILITY ACCOUNTING

PUBLIC UTILITY ACCOUNTING—COMPARABLE OR CHAOTIC?†

by
Philip L. Defliese

ACCORDING to a Greek legend, the robber gang leader Procrustes required his victims and guests to sleep in a special bed of a certain size. If they were too short he stretched them to fit; if they were too tall, he lopped off the protruding ends. Thus, the demand for uniformity had its beginnings long ago.

Public utility accounting finds itself today in a similarly unenviable position. It is faced by the Federal Power Commission which is trying to establish uniformity although it fully recognizes the diversity of policies inherent in our multi-jurisdictional regulatory process. And, it is being badgered by financial analysts and others who, with an apparent lack of understanding of the relationship of accounting to the regulatory process, are demanding uniformity regardless of differing conditions. The subjects of these attacks are the public utility accountants and their independent auditors who, nevertheless, are seriously endeavoring to produce meaningful financial statements, and who recognize that comparability cannot be achieved by blindly applying a uniform rule to circumstances that differ but only by applying that principle which is most appropriate in each situation.

Perhaps the severest criticism which has been levied lately is that contained in the report of the Public Utilities Securities Committee of the Investment Bankers Association of America at its 1965 annual convention last December. Charges of inconsistency, confusion, and encouragement of alternative accounting practices from such a presumably sophisticated group cannot be ignored. This report received such widespread publicity in the press that I will quote several of the serious charges which it contained:

> Accounting variations have arisen because of the special tax concessions made by Congress.... There is real concern for the accounting confusion that has followed and the impact this has on the average investor. Differences in accounting practices have placed the average investor at a great disadvantage. It is a handicap with which he is unable to cope.Indeed, even the institutional investor finds it difficult to follow and determine comparable utility earnings .... the ways in which a utility may report earnings to its stockholders is almost infinite. At the very least it raises a question as to whether the accounting profession realizes how serious a situation has been created by the certification of so many variable principles and practices.... Much could be accomplished by a more

---

†Excerpts from speech before the National Conference of Electric and Gas Utility Accountants, New Orleans, May 2, 1966. Reprinted with permission from *The Journal of Accountancy*, August 1966, pp. 65-71, copyright © 1966 by American Institute of CPAs. Opinions of the authors are their own and do not necessarily reflect policies of the AICPA.

> pragmatic approach to the problem by the accounting profession.... If accountants would establish more precise standards, they would become the necessary catalyst in realizing the goal of comparability of financial statements.... If past patterns among state and federal regulatory bodies continue without more general agreement on accounting procedures, and members of the American Institute of CPAs continue to encourage alternative accounting practices, further confusion for the investor is inevitable. Reported earnings will fluctuate widely subject to regulatory whim with a consequence that can hardly lead to broader acceptance for utility stocks. At the least, it could result in a lessening of investor confidence in the quality of reported earnings. The American Institute of CPAs' Accounting Principles Board has recently voted to issue a new bulletin as its Opinion No. 6 which has the effect of suppressing present disclosure of the dollar amounts of flow-through resulting from the use of liberalized depreciation for tax purposes while straight-line is used for books. Thus, the investor will be placed even further in the shadows because even if he could understand the complex of alternative accounting principles now available, the financial statements would not show the dollar amounts. This action was adopted by the Accounting Principles Board with a number of dissents and with full knowledge that utility analysts consider this information to be a material fact in their analysis of financial statements.

I can assure you that this report caused a veritable furor in the public accounting profession. Nowhere in it was any mention made of the rate-making process, an appreciation of which is basic for a proper understanding of public utility accounting. In this respect, it is interesting to note that when Donald C. Cook, president of American Electric Power Company, took the IBA to task for this oversight, William N. Bannard, author of the report, and Albert Pratt, president of IBA, conceded "that accounting by a utility should conform to the regulatory requirements of the public body having jurisdiction over its rates" and that the "cause of the problem is the inconsistency of the rate-making philosophies of the various regulatory agencies."

The IBA report followed closely the substance of an article written by Alfred L. Burke, president of Duff and Phelps, Inc. in the September-October issue of the *Financial Analysts Journal* in which, again, practically no consideration was given to the effect of the rate-making process. He said:

> . . . there is no consistency in accounting practices with respect to deferred taxes due to accelerated depreciation and with the treatment of the investment credit, so that investors . . . must make their own adjustments if they wish to arrive at comparable figures.

Commenting on the IBA committee report in the *Public Utilities Fortnightly*, Owen Ely emphasized that certain large investment houses felt great concern over the fact that they now would no longer get the information they needed to make the adjustments to put all companies on a "comparable" basis. The report said:

> Per share figures presented for 102 electric utilities in the annual review of electric utility companies . . . showed 1964 earnings for 52 flow-through companies normalized as contrasted with the reported figures, and also gave a breakdown of the total adjustment as between accelerated depreciation and guidelines (combined) and the investment tax credit. For companies using flow-through the increase in earnings per share over the normalized figures averaged 19 per cent.

Mr. Ely also reported that:

> . . . Some of the partners of . . . a well-known accounting firm have consistently favored normalization . . . [and] place the responsibility for the present conditions on the American Institute of CPAs.

Thus it can be seen that complete agreement also does not exist within the accounting profession. Complete agreement, of course, is always too much to expect, and this is fortunate because only by independent expression of opinion can a learned profession progress. However, in a democratic society such as ours, progress can only be made by an understanding that the minority will adhere to the views of the majority, and I fully expect that this will be the case on this issue.

The recent action taken by the Accounting Principles Board in Opinion No. 6, modifying the disclosure requirements of Paragraph 9 of Accounting Research Bulletin No. 44 (Revised), was not a frivolous action. The subject had been under consideration for a considerable length of time by a subcommittee which had solicited the views of investment bankers and the appropriate committees of the Edison Electric Institute and American Gas Association. When the exposure draft was issued, comments on it were voluminous and penetrating, and in the end, what I consider to be a wise decision was made to discontinue disclosure of flow-through amounts, pending further study. My purpose today is to place that decision in its proper perspective and to provide the rationale underlying that conclusion.

HISTORICAL DEVELOPMENT OF REGULATED ACCOUNTING

Regulatory commissions have been with us a long time, so long, perhaps, that we fail to appreciate the role they play in our capitalistic society. Without them, it is quite possible that we would not have investor-owned utilities today, and perhaps we would be further along the road toward government ownership in general. Thus they have served a purpose beyond that of being mediators between shareholders and managements on one side and the customers on the other. As accountants, we owe even more than this to the commissions because of their contribution to the development of our art; in many areas they led the way.

Unfortunately, we cannot agree with all the accounting determinations which have resulted from this process. However, these are matters which cannot now be changed, and accountants must do what they will always have to do—find a means of expressing in accounting terms the economics of the situation as it exists.

Essentially, the major problem in public utility accounting centers around the application of the basic principle of matching costs and revenues—a principle which has been well-established in all areas of accounting for many years. Commissions and accountants have long recognized its interrelationship with the rate-making process. Belatedly, the AICPA gave official recognition in 1962 to this interrelationship in the addendum to APB Opinion No. 2, which stated:

> . . . if a cost incurred by a regulated business during a given period is treated for rate-making purposes by the regulatory authority having jurisdiction as applicable to future revenues, it may be deferred in the balance sheet at the end of the current period and written off in the future period or periods in which the related revenue accrues, even though the cost is of a kind which in a nonregulated business would be written off currently. However, this is appropriate only when it is clear that the cost will be recoverable out of future revenues, and it is not appropriate when there is doubt, because of economic conditions or for other reasons, that the cost will be so recoverable.

In reality, this was an affirmation of the principle adopted by the Board's predecessor, the accounting procedure committee, when it issued ARB No. 44 (Revised) in 1958. That Bulletin generally made mandatory deferred tax accounting for the difference between book depreciation and accelerated tax depreciation, but it added the now famous Paragraph 8, which read:

> Many regulatory authorities permit recognition of deferred income taxes for accounting and/or rate-making purposes, whereas some do not. The committee believes that they should permit the recognition of deferred income taxes for both purposes. However, where charges for deferred income taxes are not allowed for ratemaking purposes, accounting recognition need not be given to the deferment of taxes *if it may reasonably be expected that increased future income taxes*, resulting from the earlier deduction of declining-balance depreciation for income tax purposes only, *will be allowed in future rate determinations*. (Emphasis supplied.)

Obviously, the basic principle which was later affirmed in the addendum to Opinion No. 2 served as the basis for this exception. At that time, "flow-through" jurisdictions were not as numerous as they are today. Some accountants now believe that if the profession had held the line at that time, the trend would have been the other way. To have done this, however, the auditors would have had to require the flow-through companies to normalize or they would have had to qualify their opinions; neither course was acceptable to the public utility accountants and their auditors who were trying to reflect the economics of the situation.

Of course, ARB No. 44 (Revised) also added the now much debated Paragraph 9, which read:

> In those rare situations in which accounting for deferred income taxes is not appropriate, full disclosure should be made of the amount of deferred income taxes arising out of the difference between the financial statements and the tax returns when the declining-balance method is adopted for income tax purposes but other appropriate methods are used for financial accounting purposes.

At the time this paragraph was written, requiring the disclosure of such information seemed the best course of action by those who favored Paragraph 8 as well as those who opposed it. In view of the fact that the ultimate trend to flow-through could not be predicted, and the fact that there was always a lag on the part of commissions in adjusting rates, the information it required probably was then useful to investors. Now, of course, commissions have set their policies—with a greater trend to flow-through than we expected—and have adjusted their rates accordingly. Thus, accounting and rate policies are substantially in phase.

But I am getting ahead of my story. Let me go back to the history of the development of the rate-making process and its relation to accounting. From the beginning, the commissions have been faced with the problem of deciding which costs should be allowable, and how they should be determined and allocated. While variations in approach still exist in this area, most accountants will agree that the commissions, by and large, have done an able piece of work. In the process, however, they developed certain differences between public utility accounting and accounting in nonregulated industries, and these differences became generally accepted because they implemented the matching principle as it related to the rate-making process. Notable among these is the deferment of storm damage losses and costs of conversions of equipment. The purpose of deferment—to spread the impact over several years, and thus not influence rates radically—is well served in this field, but if it were not for the assurance of recovery through the use of compensatory rates in the future, this deferment would not be acceptable. In locations especially subject to recurring storms, reserves for storm costs not yet incurred serve the same purpose.

In the field of income tax accounting, the effect of differences between book and tax income was ignored for many years by all accountants, mainly because of its insignificance. Thus the deferment of the storm losses I just mentioned did not carry with it the need for the deferment of the tax benefit derived when, for taxes, such losses were written off immediately. Interest on construction was capitalized, but expensed for taxes; depreciation rates were in many cases lower for accounting purposes than those used for tax purposes (frequently referred to as the "normal spread"). As these matters evolved, no thought was given to deferment of the tax benefit and, as a result, many commissions firmly adopted the policy of allowing income taxes as a cost only on a cash-payable basis. Not until the arrival of certified emergency facilities, with the five-year writeoff for tax purposes, did a significant problem arise in this area. The huge disparity between book and tax income created by such rapid tax amortization could not be ignored, and the deferment of the tax benefit soon became accepted in many jurisdictions.

When accelerated depreciation for tax purposes came along in 1954, the Institute committee did not first deal with it in the same fashion as it had with amortization of emergency facilities. The first ARB No. 44 permitted alternatives; this proved unfortunate and subsequently ARB No. 44 (Revised) was issued. Some of the present confusion probably stems from this mistake and I am sure the accounting profession recognizes this.

This brings us up to date. At present, practices among the various rate-making jurisdictions vary all over the lot, requiring or permitting tax deferment ("normalization") or flow-through, sometimes within the same jurisdiction, on each of such items as accelerated depreciation, guideline lives and the investment credit. Flow-through is the more prevalent treatment given those items constituting normal spread, mainly, I believe, because those tax differentials have been consistently ignored in the past. In fact, I doubt whether a jurisdiction exists which "normalizes" all differences between book and tax income.

There is constant need to adapt accounting to these variations in order that financial statements may be meaningful in a real sense—not merely superficially uniform. We cannot alter the fact that the methods now being used by the commissions to determine income tax cost for rate-making are not uniform. As accountants, we have adjusted to the situation by permitting the accounting to follow rate-making. Thus, it is the accounting that is uniform—it is the rate-making that is not.

What is really confusing this issue is the fact that rate-making philosophies of the commissions are generally implemented in the form of accounting orders. A commission decides on what basis it will allow income taxes as a cost for rate purposes, and then issues the appropriate accounting order. Subsequent rate determinations give cognizance to the prescribed accounting, and a reasonable matching of costs and revenues is achieved which accountants must recognize. Understandably, lay observers get the impression that, by permitting such a variety of treatments, the accountants are sponsoring diversity in reporting. It is useless to debate whether the chicken or the egg came first in this area; the accountants cannot impair the matching principle for the sake of uniformity.

Thus, uniformity in the real sense can only be accomplished by achieving uniformity in rate-making policy. Whether this can ever be achieved while jurisdiction is shared by many state and federal agencies is a serious question. The accounting profession cannot insist upon the use of any particular philosophy of rate-making, nor can it favor one form of jurisdiction over another. In line with its present program to narrow the differences among accounting alternatives—a program which is being pressed forward more than is realized—the profession would prefer that the basic principles of accounting used by regulated companies should not differ drastically from those used by nonregulated companies. Thus, complete normalization throughout would be its preference. However, it is becoming clear that the tendency is in the opposite direction. The Federal Power Commission has indicated its preference for flow-through; this is evidenced by its intent to prescribe it for accounting purposes in proposed rule-making Docket R-264, and by its published statistics showing rates of return of normalized companies on a flow-through basis. Armed with the power granted to it in the *Appalachian* case to prescribe the accounting used in reports to shareholders, the FPC may someday be able to eliminate normalization for the sake of uniformity. The trend among state commissions seems to be in the same direction. Thus it appears that, even though the accounting profession would dislike it, uniformity, if it is to be achieved at all, may be achieved on a flow-through basis.

THE RECENT CHANGE

Let me return now to APB Opinion No. 6 which concluded that, pending further study, amounts of flow-through taxes need no longer be disclosed although disclosure of the fact that the flow-through treatment is used shall continue to be required. Paragraph 20 of that Opinion states:

When a company subject to rate-making processes adopts the declining-balance method of depreciation for income tax purposes but adopts other appropriate methods for financial accounting purposes in the circumstances described in Paragraph 8 [of ARB No. 44, Revised], and does not give accounting recognition to deferred income taxes, disclosure should be made of this fact.

Considerable controversy attended the Board's conclusion as indicated by the fact that seven members of the 21-member Board registered their dissents. Those who dissented did "not agree with Paragraph 20 . . . because it deletes a requirement in Paragraph 9 of ARB No. 44 (Revised) for the disclosure of information they consider to be essential in financial statements . . . . The intent of Paragraph 20 . . . is to continue the requirement for disclosure of the accounting practice followed but to omit the previous requirement for disclosure of the effect of the practice. Thus, in their opinion, the . . . Board is inappropriately sponsoring the viewpoint that investors and other users of financial statements should be told of the practice but need not be furnished the information to judge its significance."

DISCLOSURE VS. NONDISCLOSURE

In view of the past and continuing controversy associated with Paragraph 20, and the reference to its being effective "pending further study," I would like to review with you the principal arguments for and against disclosure advanced by representatives of the public utility industry, by security analysts and by CPAs. As a member of the subcommittee of the APB charged with the responsibility of considering the question of whether Paragraph 9 should be withdrawn, revised or left intact, I had the opportunity to hear at close range all of the pros and cons. The subcommittee held informal meetings with your representatives as well as representatives of the financial analysts.

The arguments for and against disclosure of amounts were quite numerous and, because they came from different sources, they were not always compatible with their own sides. Time does not permit a complete review, so I shall recite here briefly the more meaningful arguments advanced (a more extensive review of the major arguments is presented as an addendum to this paper):

ARGUMENTS IN FAVOR OF DISCLOSURE

(a) The amounts are needed to adjust earnings of flow-through companies to place them on a comparable basis with normalized companies.

(b) There can never be assurance that future commissions will increase rates to allow for the higher taxes; thus the disclosure is needed to evaluate this contingency.

(c) Flow-through may overstate income because rate reductions may not yet have taken place. Regulatory lag is understood by the analysts.

(d) Analysts should be given the information to use as they see fit; it can be disclosed in such a way as not to mislead.

ARGUMENTS AGAINST DISCLOSURE

(a) Since rates are adjusted to the costs that are allowed, a proper matching of costs and revenues is achieved in all jurisdictions regardless of the variations of treatment; thus any disclosure of amounts detracts from the appropriateness of the accounting.

(b) The cash basis of accounting for income taxes is too well established in flow-through jurisdictions to permit future commissions to deny recovery; courts would not allow such confiscation.

(c) *Required* disclosures should be such that the statements would be misleading without them; they should be capable of being used in a positive way. Flow-through tax benefit amounts, without disclosure of their related effect upon revenues, are misleading in themselves.

(d) The future increased taxes may never be paid because utilities will continue to increase, or at least maintain, their present plant accounts.

CONCLUSIONS

Rather than debate each of these issues separately, I shall attempt to explain how the majority of the Board reached its conclusion.

The validity of a reporting disclosure requirement, as in the case of an accounting principle, rests upon its usefulness and the soundness of the logic upon which it is based. I believe the disclosure called for by old Paragraph 9 became invalid largely because the regulatory bodies, many of which were uncommitted at the time it was adopted, have trended toward use of the flow-through method as a means of lowering rates or avoiding increased rates. It was originally thought that few commissions would adopt flow-through. Now the trend is evidenced by an increasing number of rate determinations based upon the flow-through principle and it appears likely that this trend may accelerate as a result of the FPC proposal to change from its former policy of permitting normalization to a requirement that the flow-through method be followed.

The reduction in tax expense arising from flow-through has a counteracting effect upon revenues without necessarily affecting the rate of return; when commissions prescribe flow-through, their purpose is obvious. In cases where revenues are reduced in an amount substantially equivalent to the reduction in tax expense, net income is not affected. In other instances, utility rates may not be permitted to increase. For example, a utility whose rate of return has been trending downward would presumably propose a rate increase. However, upon adoption of flow-through, the rate of return may be restored to a reasonable level and a rate increase may no longer be justified; a regulatory agency might urge such a course of action to avoid the alternative of increasing rates. The implication that net income has increased as a result of flow-through in all such cases would be misleading.

Even where a rate increase has been granted in a flow-through state, it is hardly logical to assume that the commission has ignored the effect of flow-through. During 1962, for example, the Ohio Supreme Court upheld the

Ohio Commission's ruling that only the taxes actually paid were properly allowable as operating expenses for rate purposes. As a result of the Court's decision, the Commission's ruling reducing the utility's (Cincinnati Gas & Electric Co.) requested increase of $2,238,000 to $879,000 (or about 39 per cent) was affirmed. In this case the flow-through method obviously prompted a substantial reduction in the amount of the requested rate increase; nevertheless, a rate increase was granted.

Of course, many things affect the income of a utility, with changes in the art and increased usage being of prime importance. Other factors which would ordinarily require a reduction in rates in the future may come into play and provide an offset to the increased rates which would otherwise be needed to cover the additional taxes which may become payable. Therefore, it is conceivable that essentially the same rate of return may be maintained by a utility although factors giving rise to that rate of return may change considerably. If and when our economy falters we can expect many other factors to come into play which will affect a utility's earnings—nonrecognition of taxes actually paid will not alone be the basis for such a determination.

It is also fairly obvious that by using the fair rate of return on unrecovered investment as the major determinant, commissions have established a uniformity within the public utility field that cannot be matched anywhere. When the prescribed accounting conforms with the rate-making philosophy of the commission (and management feels confident that such conformity in the future is reasonably assured), it cannot help but fairly reflect results of operations and portray the return intended. Thus, while commissions may vary in their policies regarding the timing of costs, they are matching these costs with the necessary revenues to achieve a reasonable late of return. When accounting accommodates itself to such variants, it is achieving a uniformity far beyond the dream of most accountants. Thus, disclosure of an amount which could be used to adjust the reported results of one company in order to make them comparable with those of another in a jurisdiction with a different rate-making philosophy is manifestly misleading.

Nevertheless, it may be appropriate, due to "regulatory lag," to disclose the amount of flow-through taxes during the first year or two after adoption of liberalized depreciation for tax purposes. This disclosure would alert the reader to the possibility that the sudden increase in earnings may not be permanent. If rates are high, the commission having jurisdiction will presumably take action to adjust them downward. Within a short period of time the rate of return will presumably return to a reasonable level. However, as I indicated previously, rates may be low and the adoption of flow-through may eliminate the need of a rate increase; disclosure in the early years in such a situation could be misleading as it would belie the greater return that has effectively been allowed.

LOOKING AHEAD

The earnest desire of investment analysts for uniformity in financial reporting by public utilities is fully appreciated by us all. The public accounting profession welcomes the challenge to strive for the desired uniformity; and we recognize our responsibility to lead in the efforts to promote such uniformity. But the analysts must recognize that we *have* achieved accounting comparability and that the present nonconformity exists in rate-making policies which are beyond our control.

The IBA report referred to previously expressed concern over the possibility that further accounting confusion may ensue. This is a concern which I share.

Such a situation would likely develop if the FPC (1) prescribes flow-through accounting for liberalized depreciation tax reductions and disposition of accumulated deferred tax balances, regardless of state rate-making authority, and (2) continues to assert that the financial statements in annual reports to stockholders conform to its requirements.

The Accounting Principles Board responded to this proposal of the FPC to require the flow-through method as follows:

> The committee recognized in ARB No. 44 that the position taken regarding the allowance of deferred income taxes by the various regulatory authorities for rate-making purposes should be controlling on the accounting followed by utilities. This is essential to a matching of revenues and expenses and, therefore, to a fair presentation of periodic income.
>
> The accounting authority of the Federal Power Commission extends to many utilities where the rate-making jurisdiction for a major portion of their services is vested in the state public utility commissions. For this reason it would seem essential that the provisions of the uniform systems of accounting be broad enough to permit either flow-through or the normalized accounting procedures, depending upon the rate-making policy of the regulatory body having jurisdiction.
>
> In the opinion of the APB the proposed rule-making set forth in the FPC notice of July 7, 1964, would result in misleading financial statements for public utilities where normalization of income taxes has been allowed for rate-making purposes. The Board recommends, therefore, that the proposed rule-making in Docket No. R-264 be reconsidered by the Federal Power Commission.

I think we can all appreciate the impossible situation public utility accountants and CPAs would face should both the FPC and the applicable state regulatory body insist that their respective (and differing) systems of accounts be reflected in the annual report to stockholders. In the *Appalachian Power Company* case, the FPC was upheld when it stated that its own accounting requirements and "not those of a state or of the company's own choosing, establish and govern the primary content of statements of financial condition which companies subject to its jurisdiction make to their stockholders." This dilemma was dramatically illustrated in the Montana Power Company 1964 annual report by the inclusion of two sets of financial statements, each presenting different financial positions. One set of financial statements conformed to the accounting requirements of the PSC of Montana (which determined most of the company's rates) and the other set conformed to the requirements of the FPC. Obviously, the resulting presentation arose not from confused public utility accountants and CPAs but stemmed directly from the conflicting requirements of the federal and state regulatory bodies having jurisdiction. Accounting was simply trying to serve two masters.

Most utilities have resolved such conflicts in the past by reporting to stockholders following the system of accounts prescribed by the regulatory body having jurisdiction over setting of rates for the major portion of revenues. This reporting practice makes a great deal of sense to me. It is to be hoped that the FPC will permit its continuance as long as serious conflicts exist between the respective systems of accounts of the FPC and state regulatory bodies.

I can assure you that the public accounting profession will continue to strive to solve the vexing problems pertaining to financial reporting by public utilities and, with your continued co-operation and counsel, substantial improvement will be forthcoming. I trust that my comments today have served to explain the reasoning behind the action taken by the APB in discontinuing the requirement to make the disclosures previously required. In doing this, it affirmed its view that public utility accounting was not chaotic, but comparable in the real sense because revenues and related costs are matched by regulation. This is one area in accounting in which comparability has indeed been achieved to a greater extent than in most others.

ADDENDUM

The major arguments in favor of and against disclosure of annual amounts of flow-through taxes considered by the subcommittee of the APB were:

ARGUMENTS IN FAVOR OF DISCLOSURE

(a) Investment decisions must be based as nearly as practicable on actual operating results, shorn of artificial factors such as flow-through of deferred taxes. Those taking this extreme view believe that results of flow-through companies must be normalized in order to establish fairness of presentation.

(b) Whether or not the current rate structure reflects the reduced current income taxes, there is no assurance that a regulatory agency at some future date will recognize the increased income tax as a proper charge against customers at that time, and will accordingly increase rates. A commission may reverse the decisions of prior commissions, or merely establish different guidelines for its own determination. Economic factors, including competition, may have greater impact than theoretical rate-setting processes. Because of the substantial amounts involved, disclosure of this possibility is essential for a fair presentation of financial position and operating results. Disclosure that a balance sheet asset has lost more of its "tax deductibility" than is reflected by the balance sheet is considered prudent. Those advancing this argument do not suggest that disclosure implies that the results of operations should be recomputed on a different basis but do believe that flow-through involves future contingencies which should be disclosed.

(c) Current net income is, or may be, overstated in those cases in which a rate determination has not been concluded since the tax reduction commenced. Disclosure of the amount of this possible overstatement is essential for a fair presentation of operating results for the current period. Further, even though a rate determination may have been concluded, it is not always possible to determine whether the regulatory agency specifically reflected the effect of the reduced income tax in the new rate for services; therefore, net income may be overstated. Analysts are aware of "regulatory lag" and the problems of determining whether a rate determination has given consideration to a specific cost reduction.

(d) Security analysts and investors should be furnished this tax reduction information to enable them to evaluate the earnings of the utilities operating in flow-through jurisdictions and to compare the results of operations and the future prospects of such utilities with utilities in "normalized" jurisdictions. Clear disclosure, including information as to the status of rate determinations, is essential for an informed judgment. A position against disclosure of information which many responsible people consider important is untenable in the long run. The requested information should be disclosed in language which is completely clear, accurate and understandable. Utility financial executives and public accountants can prepare note disclosures which will not be misleading and which will avoid the misuse of the information in which some financial analysts have indulged. The likelihood that analysts, or even average investors, will be misled by such disclosures of these amounts is minimal.

ARGUMENTS OPPOSED TO DISCLOSURE

(a) The rate-making process adjusts the utility's charge for services to reflect those costs which the regulatory agency determines to be proper; therefore a correct matching of costs and revenues takes place and no disclosure of the timing of the expensing or recovery of specific costs is necessary. Since average investors (and possibly some analysts) do not understand the theoretical concepts of rate regulation, it would be misleading to disclose the amounts of tax reductions because the tax reductions do not flow through to net income but instead flow through to the consumer in the form of lower rates. The substantial use of flow-through by regulatory commissions, and the APB's subsequent affirmation of the principle (Addendum to Opinion No. 2), has established the soundness of Paragraph 8. This was not too evident at the time Paragraph 9 was written; no doubt, "regulatory lag" was envisioned and a disclosure requirement was the temporary cure. If Paragraph 8 is considered good accounting, then any disclosure of the type previously required by Paragraph 9 is contradictory. As evidence of this, disclosure practice prior to issuance of Opinion No. 6 varied considerably—some regulated utilities disclosed the current and accumulated amount of income tax reductions; others did neither. In recent years this state of confusion testified to the fact that many companies recognized that the information could be misleading; they also knew that it was being misused.

(b) Future commissions will feel morally, if not legally, bound to follow a consistent pattern of regulation and allow the future increased income taxes as costs in future rate determinations. Rate matters involving the allowance of income tax cost only on a cash basis have been litigated and the concept of flow-through has received support from many different regulatory agencies.

Reversal of commission policy would be tantamount to confiscation as it would deprive the utility of its right to recover actual costs and to earn a fair return. The courts would not allow such confiscation.

(c) Disclosure of information necessary to make financial statements not misleading is a matter of judgment for the company and its auditors. When the APB specifies a required disclosure, it should be convinced that the omission of the information would make the statements misleading and that the reader should be able to use the information in some positive way; certainly, disclosures should not be required if they could be in any way misleading. Disclosure of the amount of the current year tax reduction might raise a question as to whether results of operations have been properly presented. The footnote disclosure would carry the inference that net income as shown on the income statement is overstated. Illustrative of this is the comment in the March *Fortune* article on Con Edison of N. Y., in which it was stated that "the flow-through method accounted for more than 30 per cent of Con Edison's per share earnings." Many analysts actually deduct from earnings the amount of flow-through disclosed in order to make comparisons with "normal" companies, and thus disregard the effect of rate determinations. Disclosure of the amount of the accumulated tax reductions at the balance sheet date would be meaningless and could be misleading. For many utilities, such a figure would represent a 12-year cumulative effect at December 31, 1965, and would total a substantial amount. Additional tax expense in future years necessarily would constitute an additional cost of rendering service and would be correspondingly reflected in rates. Many might consider the earned surplus balance as improperly stated despite an unqualified audit opinion.

(d) The entire concept of income tax allocation under these circumstances is academic, since utilities will continue to increase (or at least maintain) their plant accounts, and thus the book depreciation will never exceed the tax depreciation (barring a change in the tax law). Therefore, disclosure is not only misleading, but illogical. (This is an argument that goes far beyond the question of whether tax deferment relating to depreciation differences is ever appropriate for operations that are expected to expand, or remain stable, indefinitely.)

A NEW LOOK AT UTILITY RATE-MAKING[†]

by
Philip L. Defliese

IN the electric and gas utility industry, as in all other industries, accounting must keep pace with technological progress because it furnishes the financial communications on which the commercialization of all scientific advance depends. Accountants cannot cling to static concepts and expect the business world to rely upon financial statements based on principles and practices formulated many years ago. While the accounting profession realizes this (and, through the Accounting Principles Board, is accelerating its efforts to formulate principles attuned to present conditions), accountants cannot do it alone.

A key impediment to orderly and progressive accounting in the utility industry is, in fact, the diversity of policies pursued by the various regulatory agencies. What is needed to bring order is a broad approach to the currently unsettled and unsatisfactory conditions under which utility accounting now functions. This approach must include a program for cooperative effort and agreement among business management, utility commissions and accountants, and must also encompass serious consideration of accelerated methods of depreciation to encourage the implementation of an advancing technology.

NATIONAL CONFERENCE

The necessary first step is, of course, the voluntary agreement on what accounting methods should be used. To reach this agreement, a national conference of utility accountants, commissioners and CPAs should be formed. Establishing uniformity on a voluntary basis is the only orderly way to provide fair rates to consumers of this and succeeding generations and, at the same time, adequate returns for investors.

CPAs have worked, and continue to work, with the legal and banking professions on similar problems through joint cooperation, and I believe it can be done here. Adequate representation would, of course, be a problem in this undertaking, but I believe it can be done if all concerned are willing to have it done.

[†]Parts of this article are based on a speech made before the Electric Council of New England in fall 1967. Reprinted from *Lybrand Journal*, 1968, pp. 5-14, with permission of PricewaterhouseCoopers LLP.

There is no justification for the current confusion caused by the differing standards of the various regulatory commissions in a country as sophisticated in other areas as ours is. Nor is there any sound reason why generally accepted accounting principles applicable to nonregulated industries should not be guides for the presentation of financial data in thc public utility industry. Good accounting, applied with reasonable uniformity to the same set of facts, should be at the heart of all our financial representations.

ACHIEVING UNIFORMITY

The first step is for regulatory commissions to give increased consideration to their responsibility to the growing number of investors as well as to *all* generations of consumers. The second is to decide what constitutes good accounting for all rate-regulated companies. There is no justification for the continued proliferation of divergent practices in this area. For instance, if income tax normalization is continued as the general accounting rule, it should apply to all industries, even though commissions seem to be tending toward a preference for income tax flow-through.

Third, commissions and managements should be forward looking in their approach to this problem, particularly in the areas of depreciation, obsolescence and income tax allocation. Rapid technological developments certainly call for consideration of the use of shorter lives and accelerated depreciation to cushion an inevitably high rate of obsolescence and to provide tax funds for financing. Subway users of the deficit-ridden New York subways can testify how later generations pay for inadequate depreciation allowances made earlier.

New technological developments are coming at the fastest rate in history, and utility accounting must keep pace. In the electric utility field, for example, generating capacity grew sixfold, from approximately 40 million kilowatts 25 years ago to approximately 250 million kilowatts at the close of 1966. The Atomic Energy Commission recently forecast that nuclear power plants will produce between 120 and 170 million kilowatts annually by the end of 1980. Another major innovation is the huge coal-fired generating plant located at or near the mine-mouth, thereby eliminating coal freight costs, a development made economically feasible by the related development of extra-high-voltage transmission lines. In addition, pumped storage projects using the comparatively new reversible pump-turbine to pump water into reservoirs during off-peak hours, for use during peak hours, have received much attention. Such technological progress has enabled the electric utilities to meet the growth in the nation's electrical energy requirements and to improve their competitive position in relation to other energy sources. We are all familiar with the total and relatively swift replacement of steam locomotives by diesels, and are now witnessing the steel industry's dramatic shift from the open hearth to the oxygen furnace.

If such rapid technological obsolescence can occur in these basic industries, it would seem only prudent to give full consideration to the possible impact of technological developments in the entire utility industry. We cannot overlook the fact that within the next 25 years we may find our homes powered and heated by an economical power-pack which rests on a basement shelf and needs a recharge only once every few years.

Accounting Research Bulletin No. 44 (Revised) recognized accelerated methods of depreciation as meeting "the requirements of being systematic and rational." It said that "where the expected productivity or revenue-earning power of the asset is relatively greater during the earlier years of its life, or where maintenance charges tend to increase during the later years, the declining-balance method *may well provide the most satisfactory* allocation of cost." (Emphasis supplied.)

An accelerated method of depreciation, at least for certain classes of equipment, should be beneficial for the investor as well as the consumer, as it offers some protection against the risks of obsolescence and other contingencies—including, in an indirect way, the risk of inflation. Technological developments may well lead to a shortening of the *economic* lives of some of the present-day utility plants on which our depreciation provisions on a straight-line basis are now determined. Hence, the adoption of an accelerated method of depreciation and, possibly, guideline lives for rate-making and accounting purposes would be a conservative and prudent course. Consumers would benefit because of the greater incentive to apply low-cost technology more quickly. An interesting and welcome result would be that depreciation provisions for rate-making, accounting and tax return purposes would be in phase, and the current controversy over normalization vs. flow-through would therefore become largely academic.

PRICE-LEVEL ACCOUNTING

Price-level accounting is now on the threshold. In my view, this form of accounting is best applied in the utility field, and commissions should give it more serious consideration. The use of historical cost depreciation for accounting and rate purposes during periods of constantly rising price levels results in the investor's recovering his investment in cheaper dollars. In this respect the commissions break faith with their responsibility to investors. Some commissions have already recognized this and consider current fair value in setting rates.

Most of these proposals may suggest higher rates for consumers—a very unpopular notion, and one which will not be greeted cheerfully by many commissioners. I believe, however, that much of what I am recommending can be implemented without raising rates; instead, I believe, it can be done by stabilizing rates.

Most utilities are constantly reminding their customers that rates are currently bucking the rising price trend. When you consider that the consumers' cost of a KWH is generally at an all-time low, while the price of everything else seems to hit new highs regularly, it becomes desirable to analyze the circumstances carefully and decide whether the rate reductions are entirely merited. Some part is obviously attributable to the flow-through treatment. Eliminating this on a gradual basis could result in stable rates. The increased volume resulting from the present growth posture of the industry, and continued technical improvements, could lower operating costs enough to offset the cost of additional depreciation and normalized taxes. In this period of high income and high economic and inflationary activity, rate reductions seem out of place unless they are predicated upon a sound consideration of all factors involved.

ORDER OUT OF CHAOS

A key question, actually, is how to bring some order out of the chaos created by a multiplicity of jurisdictions and philosophies. State organizations cling to their right of freedom from federal jurisdiction regarding intrastate activities. Federal agencies take the same view on interstate matters—in fact, the federal agencies also reserve the right to disagree with one another. Each group seems to feel that rate-making within its own bailiwick should not be subject to rules made by the accounting profession (through the APB), although many of them do give some consideration to our views.

This situation will not change by itself. However, it is in the long-range interest of the commissions and of the financial community, as well as of the consumers, to see that this gap is bridged, and I believe that the time has come. Signs are already visible. For example, various committees have been formed to provide liaison between federal government agencies, CPAs and representatives of the utility industry. None of these, however, goes far enough. No one committee represents all the parties involved, and none of them has a purpose beyond the exchange of views.

Establishing uniformity on a voluntary basis seems to be the only way to bring order to this field. The obstacles are not insurmountable. One eminent accountant has suggested a federal accounting court to deal with these problems. In my opinion, the case law resulting from this process over many agonizing years would not bring unified or consistent results on a timely basis, if ever—another reason for establishing a conference which represents all parties concerned.

PRESENT REGULATORY SYSTEM

The federal or state regulatory commission itself is not a development of the past quarter century; it has been with us about 75 years. A commission's primary responsibility to the consumer is to see that he receives adequate service at a fair rate in a situation where no competitive service is available. Its obligation to the shareholder is to see him compensated for the cost of operations, including recovery of capital invested, and a fair rate of return on unrecovered capital. All of this is subject to judicial review.

There is still, however, one flaw in this process: the commissions not only determine what they consider a fair rate of return, but also set the rules by which costs of operations and unrecovered capital are determined. Since consumers are vocal and commissioners human, it seems not unlikely that, given a choice between an accounting approach which, in the long run is best for all consumers, and one which will result in the lowest possible rate for present consumers, many commissioners may lean toward the latter.

Accountants believe they also know something about rate of return, although they generally leave this determination to economists and financiers. But the determination of unrecovered capital and cost of operations should certainly be considered within the province of accounting. However, the need to develop accounting information as a basis for rate determination preceded the development of modern accounting theory. By establishing uniform systems of accounts for the companies subject to their jurisdiction, the commissions filled this void and, in fact, spurred the development of accounting.

Until recent years this worked quite well, and the development of these prescribed systems and general accounting theory went hand in hand. But we have now reached a point where general accounting is moving more rapidly and on sounder bases than before because the concerted efforts of a more sophisticated profession have developed better and more uniform accounting. On the other hand—and this is most important—we find commissions applying different accounting rules to the same set of facts, to the confusion of investors and the public.

RATE-MAKING PHILOSOPHY

Perhaps the best illustration of the confusion between rate-making philosophy and accounting is the recent development requiring rates to be set on the basis of flow-through of accelerated depreciation, even when the company is not electing an accelerated method for tax purposes. The Federal Power Commission has ruled that rates for two natural gas pipeline companies, Midwestern Gas Transmission Company and East Tennessee Natural Gas Company, must be based on the use of accelerated depreciation and flow-through even though the companies were using straight-line depreciation for tax purposes. The companies had been claiming accelerated depreciation but then switched to straight-line. The FPC concluded, in a 3-2 decision, that the use of liberalized depreciation for tax purposes resulted in a permanent tax saving and cited the increased tax payments resulting from management's decision to discontinue the use of liberalized depreciation as not a reasonable and prudent business expense which customers may properly be required to bear. In a dissenting opinion, it was stated that the election to adopt either liberalized or straight-line depreciation in computing federal income taxes involves risks and uncertainties which are best known to those who have an intimate knowledge of a particular company and is an individual management decision.

This intrusion upon management's judgmental prerogative is not completely unique. For example, the New York Commission has indicated that one of the factors to be considered in a rate proceeding is whether or not a company uses liberalized tax depreciation, and that the Commission in setting rates will give consideration to this factor. The Maine Commission has ordered compulsory flow-through for a utility which had changed to straight-line depreciation. The West Virginia Commission has used depreciation rates based upon the shorter guideline lives in computing the income tax of a gas utility for inclusion in its cost of service, even though guideline lives were not in fact used by the company.

From all of this one point emerges clearly: the accounting rules and rate-making philosophies or policies used or followed by commissions seem to be inextricably intertwined. It is difficult to see where one begins and the other ends. Commissions appear to be more concerned with the current rate charged the consumer than with their responsibility for providing a fair rate of return to shareholders which would stimulate utility growth, technological advancement, and improved service and ultimate economies to the consumer. It appears possible to decide upon almost any rate structure and then find the accounting to support it. This is probably not being done consciously, even though it has that appearance; but the area has become so confused that all parties concerned must find it difficult to find any rational basis for the result.

THE MAJOR PROBLEM

Obviously, the major problem creating this confusion is the proper treatment of the cost of income taxes for accounting and rate-making purposes. (There are other problems involving such items as pension costs, conversion costs, storm losses, etc., but these are not as universal.) Income taxes are a major operating cost, representing approximately 100 percent of the final net income available to shareholders, and thus have a considerable influence on rates. Accounting for income taxes does not present a problem as long as revenues and costs are included in tax returns on the same basis as they are presented in financial statements.

The impact of differing tax and accounting methods has been especially significant since 1954, when additional accelerated methods of depreciation were provided in the Code. Since then the disparity between the actual tax paid and the amount of tax expense considered proper for accounting purposes has widened. When guideline lives and the investment credit were added later, this disparity increased. Commissions were willing to allow companies under their jurisdiction to elect to receive these tax benefits, but they generally did not permit adoption of any depreciation methods for accounting and rate purposes beyond the traditional straight-line composite percentage methods based on normal life, with very little consideration for obsolescence. Unfortunately, tax-effect accounting, or "normalization," as it is called, was not firmly established at that time, and when the accounting profession took a firm stand in favor of normalization in 1958, some commissions had already set their policies requiring flow-through. Because exemptions were allowed for these, others followed suit.

A recent development that adds to the confusion is the amortization to income, over a relatively short arbitrary period, of the accumulated deferred income taxes which arose in years prior to a switch from normalization to flow-through.

LEGISLATIVE INTENT

When these amendments to the Internal Revenue Code were made, it was clear that the administrations sponsoring them wanted to spur the economy—not by reducing taxes per se, because a general rate decrease would have done that, but by stimulating the incentive for replacement of plant and equipment by providing a quick recovery of cost through accelerated tax depreciation, shorter lives, and actual cost reduction, i.e., the investment tax credit. The 1964 amendment to the investment credit section of the Code emphasized this intent by forbidding federal regulatory agencies to require flow-through in setting rates. A proposed bill (S 887), sponsored by Senator Russell D. Long and now before Congress, also emphasizes this, as its stated purpose is to prevent federal regulatory agencies from denying regulated industries the right to exercise business judgment in selecting their method of depreciation or in accounting for depreciation on a deferred tax-accounting basis.

Failure of the regulatory commissions to permit normalization in rate-making is thus contrary to our national tax policy. The action of the present administration in requesting first a suspension and then reactivation of the use of liberalized depreciation (and the investment tax credit) because of the state of the economy, while at the same time requesting an overall increase in rates, clearly indicates that these devices were intended to influence investment decisions and were not considered as tax reductions which could then be used to reduce rates to customers.

NORMALIZATION

Businessmen and accountants usually consider the depreciation charge as a recovery of the cost of investment in operating property through the price of the product sold and the tax allowance obtained. Underlying normalization accounting is the concept that an advance tax benefit is obtained when depreciation or other costs can be deducted for tax purposes earlier than they are deemed to accrue for accounting purposes and offset in later years when the situation reverses. Since 1958, it has been an established accounting principle that this advance tax benefit should be deferred until such time as the situation reverses so that the tax charge is always proportionate to the accounting charge—that is, they are matched, and thus net income is fairly presented. Some commissions have seen the merit to this argument and have prescribed normalization.

The Michigan Commission, in support of its policy of normalizing, has presented a number of significant points, including the following:

> Under all methods of computing income tax, the amount of depreciation allowance for tax purposes is identical on the same property. To borrow now future tax depreciation allowances in computing current year's tax is to incur increased tax liability over the remaining life of the property.... The inclusion of a charge for tax expense in the period in which a portion of future depreciation allowances is used by accelerated depreciation

avoids inequity between utility customers by assigning the cost to the accounting period in which the related income is produced and service is received by the respective customer....

FLOW-THROUGH

Because most utilities are in a rapid growth status, the advance tax benefits derived from using accelerated depreciation on additions usually are greater than the reversing effect on older equipment, and thus the net cumulative deferred tax benefit grows under normalization. Many commissions have concluded that the net reversing effect is so far in the future that it should be ignored. They contend that the tax expense allowed for accounting and rate purposes should thus be the amount actually paid, and say that if tax expense becomes greater than normal in the future, because no deferred tax benefit is available to relieve it, the higher taxes paid will then be allowed for rates at that time. Thus the present tax benefit is ordered to "flow-through" to income on a cash basis. However, because this has resulted in the lowering of rates, these benefits have flowed through to the consumer.

The assumption underlying "flow-through" in the case of utilities is that the cash basis of accounting is made proper by an explicit or implied regulatory promise to allow in the future any increased tax costs which may then arise because of this "cash basis" method of accounting. Managements of companies take the position that they have little choice but to accept this promise as creating an economic fact of life.

Those who support normalization point out fallacies inherent in the flow-through arguments. These include:

• Avoidance of the impact of the reversal of the advance tax benefit is predicated upon the perpetual existence of the company and a continued growth, or at least the maintenance of the present level, of plant facilities (and presumably on the continuance of present tax law). Obviously, this assumption is subject to challenge. Changes in taxing philosophy and the rapid scientific progress that is taking place can quickly change this picture. We have seen within our lifetime marked changes in the transportation field, particularly the railroads, and we are beginning to see it in other utility fields.

• Should the assumption of continued growth not be fulfilled, and the reversing process take place, commissions may not be able, or may be unwilling, to set rates to accommodate the proportionately higher taxes at that time. Failure of continued growth of an industry usually means that decline has set in because of competition from other sources or because of basic obsolescence. Forcing higher rates upon a dwindling supply of customers is difficult under these circumstances, as it would be during an economic depression; again, witness the plight of the railroads, particularly in passenger traffic. Even assuming establishment of higher rates were possible, there is still the nagging reality that a later generation of consumers will pay for the tax benefits which flowed through to earlier generations.

The present official AICPA position is that normalization should be the general rule; this is predicated on the matching concept. However, the accounting profession has permitted flow-through as an acceptable alternative to normalization for public utilities when there is reasonable assurance that future rate determinations will allow the increased income taxes resulting from the flow-through of the earlier deductions. Thus, accounting has had to adapt itself to these variations in order to reflect the rate of return allowed by commissions; the result is a matching of costs and revenues not based upon good accounting, but upon what a particular commission considers cost at a particular time, with implicit assurance that all costs will eventually be recognized and recovered.

INCREASING DILEMMA

The result of all of this is that all parties involved are confronted with a dilemma that could worsen as time goes on. Management has a responsibility both to investors and consumers; it is not anxious to overcharge its consumers. On the other hand, low rates predicated upon the flow-through of tax windfalls that prematurely utilize the tax deductibility of future depreciation charges can affect the investor's equity and his future return if the promise of later recovery cannot be met. A company may provide for this contingency, but then faces the possibility that its current earnings, relative to those of other companies, will appear to be depressed.

Commissions are faced with a similar dilemma: should they withhold these windfalls, and thereby keep rates at present levels, or should they pass them along by lowering rates and attempt to commit future commissions to an unknown rate structure? Many feel, or perhaps hope, that improvements in the art and increased volume will serve to allow rates to absorb what comes along later without increases. The question is whether this is possible when the absorption point is reached, or when obsolescence rears its ugly head and decadence sets in.

Independent auditors have to share essentially the same dilemma because they must evaluate management's judgment in deciding what the prospects are for recovering costs and obtaining an adequate return in the future so that current financial statements are fairly presented. While they can lean on the present exemption provided by the AICPA position (that permits flow-through), they know that ultimate realization through allowability by a future commission is a necessary prerequisite.

Aside from this theoretical discussion, there are certain significant factors that should be kept in mind concerning recovery of costs invested in plant. The cost of plant assets is recovered in two ways. The first element—depreciation—is charged to the ratepayer as part of the cost of rendering service. The second element—tax deduction for depreciation—is passed to the ratepayer as a reduction in the cost of rendering service. In essence, the utility recovers part of its invested cost from ratepayers and the balance from the government.

What happens, however, under flow-through when accelerated depreciation is used for tax purposes and straight-line on the books? The major part of the tax cost-recovery element is obtained in the early years and is handed over to the consumer in the form of reduced rates, and the reverse takes place in the later years; there is a retardation of cost recovery having somewhat the same effect as the old compound interest method of depreciation, now generally discarded. As the plant becomes older and its relative efficiency decreases, the cost of its service contribution increases. This doesn't make sense in an age of rapid technological advancement.

DIVERSITY OF JURISDICTION

The situation is further confused by the diversity of regulatory jurisdiction and approach, a diversity best illustrated in the accounting and rate-making treatment of income tax reduction arising from accelerated depreciation, the investment credit and guideline depreciation. A number of states prescribe various combinations of normalization and flow-through treatment, and the picture is further clouded by opinions or rulings of federal regulatory bodies whose jurisdiction overlaps those of state agencies. The FPC, for example, presently permits normalization when required or permitted by state regulatory agencies, although it favors flow-through. With the investment tax credit, the FPC presently accepts either normalization or flow-through. This confusion is intensified by examples of inconsistencies in accounting and rate-making within the boundaries of a particular state.

An interesting compilation of accounting variations on a company basis is included in the 1965 report of the Public Utilities Securities Committee of the Investment Bankers Association of America. Of the 85 utilities included in the study, 73 companies had adopted accelerated depreciation, but in accounting for the applicable income tax reduction, 40 companies normalized, 30 followed flow-through, and the remaining three partly normalized and partly followed flow-through. In accounting for the investment credit, 57 companies normalized, 27 followed flow-through and one partly normalized and partly followed flow-through. Of the 54 companies using guideline lives, 22 companies normalized and 32 followed flow-through.

CONCLUSION

These points taken in conjunction—technological developments which make yesterday's accounting principles inapplicable to today's industry, the numerous different accounting methods advocated by the various regulatory commissions, and the disagreement among the commissions themselves as to the extent of their respective jurisdictions—all make it clear that action is needed to put utility accounting on a more uniform basis. Utility accounting cannot be simplified; the utility industry itself is too complex for that. But the formation of a conference representing all the interested parties would do much to establish uniform principles and promote consistent procedures. With this, utility accounting may best perform one of the major functions of accounting in any area: keeping the lines of financial communication clear.

CHANGING ACCOUNTING OBJECTIVES FOR UTILITIES†

by
Philip L. Defliese

THE one thing on which all accountants will agree is that today the profession is in a state of turmoil. Criticism–internal and external–coupled with highly publicized lawsuits against major firms have reduced public esteem for the profession to an all-time low. The profession has attempted to counter this situation, by speeding up the activities of the Accounting Principles Board, by creating a study group to examine the mechanism for the establishment of accounting principles—headed by former SEC Commissioner Francis Wheat—and by creating a study group to examine the objectives of financial accounting—headed by Robert Trueblood.

There is general agreement today that financial statements do not present an accurate picture of the economic facts of life. The controversy arises over the question of whether they should strive for this objective and, if not, for what should they strive? The Trueblood group needs to resolve some very basic issues: (1) what type of financial statements do users want and how are the statements to be used? (2) should different users—investors, creditors, regulatory agencies, taxing agencies—receive different types of statements? (3) should current fair values, price level, or historical cost be used? (4) since users are concerned with the future, should forecasts of future years' operations be provided? (5) should accounting give recognition to social concerns and personnel resources?

It is time for [public utility] commissions to give greater recognition to their obligations to investors as well as consumers and to weigh the advantages of adequate return for investors (not to be confused with rate of return on rate base) as well as potential for capital appreciation with other indicia of utility performance. Otherwise, the utilities' attractiveness to investor capital may be diminished, to the ultimate detriment of the consumer.

The basic significance of depreciation itself should be re-examined. Depreciation is an important element of service cost in all rate proceedings, and in this age of spectacular technological, sociological, and environmental change, depreciation concepts must keep pace. Technological factors alone will spell shorter service lives for both old as well as new plants. Many facilities will be retired early to make way for nuclear plants. Huge pumped storage projects and

---

†An address before the annual EEI-AGA Accounting Conference, Chicago, Illinois, May 8-10, 1972, as reported in the *Edison Electric Institute Bulletin,* May/June 1972, pp. 107, 142. Reprinted with permission of the Edison Electric Institute. A somewhat longer version of this topic was published under the title, "Changing Accounting Objectives—What About Utilities?," in *Public Utilities Fortnightly*, July 20, 1972, pp. 17-21.

mine-mouth plants will operate at very high load factors until retired with little likelihood of reserve employment.

It would be wrong to assume that total service life will be comparable to life-spans of the past: high operating loads bring about changes in stress of metals. Certainly, environmental factors will have more impact on the service lives of utility plants. Here I need only mention the drive against overhead transmission wires of all kinds. If this march to the junk yard with its concomitant depressing effect on rates is ignored by accountants, the future capitalization of utilities will be imperiled.

The re-examination of financial accounting objectives by the Trueblood study group gives everyone an opportunity to take a hard look at the role of accounting in the financial and operational activities of business, and the capital market as a whole. Public utilities and their regulatory commissions cannot afford to neglect this subject because they cannot isolate themselves from the forces within our capitalistic society upon which their survival depends. Utilities should:

1. Re-examine the nature of the income statement and restructure it in a fashion that will be comparable and competitive with industrial companies.
2. Re-examine the basis upon which the rate structure rests, giving cognizance to the allowance of interest as an element of cost of service, and in particular to recognize current rates instead of embedded rates. Commissions have not control over the rate of interest that the market demands for utility debt capital. Therefore, they should be more concerned about allowing utilities to be competitive in the equity market than with clinging to sacred cows, their traditional preoccupation with the rate base and above-and-below the line allocations.
3. Modernize the depreciation concepts in keeping with the fast-moving technological period in which we find ourselves. In particular, obsolescence should be recognized *before* the fact rather than after it so that consumers will reap the benefits of progress that much sooner.
4. As a minimum, standardize the entire income tax area, and recognize tax benefits of accelerated depreciation and investment credits for what they are—return of capital. Otherwise the viability of utilities in the capital market will be imperiled. The notion of perpetuity—letting the next generation pay—may work for governments, but it will not be accepted by our sophisticated money marketers.

I sense a greater recognition of these problems, and I believe that the opportunities before us will not go unutilized. If the environment of the future is to be orderly and conducive to the living standards we envision for our posterity, business and government must be prepared to toss aside outmoded ideas and unproductive policies and make a new start. An important step in this direction is the strengthening of the real "power-structure" of our nation, the investor-owned utilities.

STANDARD SETTING: THE ACCOUNTING PRINCIPLES BOARD AND BEYOND

ACCOUNTING PRINCIPLES[†]

An Interview of Philip L. Defliese

Question: Has there been a preoccupation in the Accounting Principles Board with trying to deal with accounting abuses and attempts to manipulate earnings?

Answer: It's been uppermost in our minds.

We feel a very strong public responsibility to make certain that the reports to shareholders are as meaningful as we can make them. We're never going to achieve perfection in this area because accounting isn't that simple.

There are too many elements going into the determination of financial position as the result of operations when we're dealing with short periods of time—particularly periods as short as a quarter of a year. So our only hope is to achieve some measure of success in the direction of full disclosure of all of the elements that go into a determination and set guidelines that can be uniformly applied.

Q: Has the business community been shy about taking advantage of loopholes in accounting principles to gain advantage?

A: When you say, "business community," you should not paint with such a broad brush. You'll find the 95 percent or better of all companies are attempting to do as honest a job in this area as possibly can be done. It's only the few sharpsters that occasionally get notoriety that have abused accounting principles.

Q: The board's concern, then, has been with these marginal companies?

A: Yes. We've been most concerned about it, because it creates a credibility gap that is unwarranted. The profession is accused of aiding and abetting this practice, and yet in reality we're attempting to do just the reverse.

Q: Along this same line, how would you define the basic role of the Accounting Principles Board?

A: Well, let me further expand the previous comment. We have not applied ourselves exclusively to this area [of accounting abuse]. Equity accounting, for example, is one. I don't think there was any tremendous abuse there. In fact, it's going to help more companies than it's going to hurt.

Our intent was to get a better recognition of the economic facts. Companies that had substantial interests in other companies, but not a controlling interest,

---

[†]Excerpts from an interview of Mr. Defliese by members of the financial and business news staff of *The New York Times* on the work of the Accounting Principles Board. Reprinted from *The New York Times*, May 9, 1971, pp. 1, 9. Copyright © 1971 by the New York Times Co. Reprinted by permission.

frequently did not receive a rate of return on that investment equivalent to the actual result.

Q: How does this work in practice?

A: This permits companies to give recognition to the earning capacity of their investees—we've invented a new term in that respect—without the actual flow of cash.

It's a recognition of departing from historical costs and reflecting economic results a little bit more closely, even though no transaction actually takes place. The difficulty with accounting is that it started off as a transaction-oriented art, and has now moved over into an economic reflection type of art. We're making entries when actually no transaction has taken place. This is a new concept for a lot of people. Some people resist it considerably.

Q: Where is this leading?

A: We are moving toward a better reflection of the economic facts as best we can. And as slowly as we can. We can't do this overnight because, first of all, there isn't complete agreement within the profession as to what needs to be reflected, or how it needs to be reflected. We have to reach that stage first.

Then we have to deal with the implementation, and that's going to take longer. In many respects, perhaps, the implementation, or the inability to implement, will hold back the development of our theories.

Q: Would you assign a higher priority in the board's work to reflecting economic realities than to trying to reduce areas of difference in accounting?

A: The two go hand in hand. Because as part of the operation of eliminating alternatives, you have to get closer to the economic facts. For example, right now we're dealing with the premature retirement of debt by the repurchase of bonds that may be selling at a discount or a premium. Accounting has recognized several methods of dealing with the discount or premium as a result of the repurchase.

Well, in attempting to narrow that into one method, we have to get at the economic facts of life. In other words, does the company really have a gain or loss from this refunding operation? And, if so, when is it earned? Is it earned at the time of the refunding, or is it earned over the period of time of the original life of the bond?

Q: But given the complexity of business life today, doesn't there have to be some leeway in accounting methods?

A: Yes. I don't want to give the impression that varying treatments aren't necessary. It's only when the facts—the identical facts exist in the identical circumstances—that there should be only one answer.

Q: So the board has no desire to create a uniform set of accounts for American business?

A: No, absolutely not. This is the misconception that many people have when the word uniformity is used—that everything is going to fit into a particular mold. And of course when you do that—like the [Internal] Revenue Code—you immediately open all kinds of loopholes for circumstances that vary, that really shouldn't fit into that mold.

Well, accounting will never do that. If the circumstances are such as to call for a different answer than that which is given by an opinion, the accountant is free to use that other answer. There is not the straightjacket approach. I'm merely saying that we're not going to sponsor varying treatments for the same set of facts.

Q: Some accounting authorities—for example, A. Carl Tietjen, partner in Price Waterhouse & Co.—have accused the APB of creating an accounting cookbook that grows like Topsy and is an open invitation to the loophole finder.

A: There is no question that the more cookbookish we become, the more prone we are to the loophole finder. But we have found that our pronouncements in the past have been too general, enunciating broad principles with very few guidelines, or very general guidelines.

Because of this, practice has become so varied that the basic principle erodes. We had to go back and set out specific guidelines to be followed, hopefully setting out enough to minimize or avoid the loophole problem. We're never going to overcome that completely, but I do believe by this method we minimized the number of opportunities that people may have to use the loopholes, and that when they do they are limited to rather inconsequential areas rather than to the broad basic principles.

Q: Paul Grady, retired director of research of the American Institute of Certified Public Accountants and retired partner of Price Waterhouse, has charged that "dictatorial tendencies on the part of the APB have been in evidence for the last 10 years." How do you answer that charge?

A: Well, if that is what they are, I wish they'd been in evidence for the 10 years. Because it's only from about Opinion 7 and 8 [the board has now issued 19 opinions] on that there has been this tendency toward definitizing our approach. And we feel that we're running upstream in this area, and that we should have started sooner.

Q: Does Mr. Grady represent the old guard of the accounting profession?

A: Yes, I think he does in that respect. This is to be expected from people who have, shall we say, lived during the era when broad statements were sufficient for our purpose. But because of the speed with which things have moved in the last 10 years, this is now obsolete. We have to move faster, we have to move more definitively.

I would say that the younger generation is convinced that this approach we're taking now is the only way out. We're more concerned about the public and the credibility question than we are about flexibility and choosing among alternatives. The question shouldn't leave that much leeway.

Q: On one particular issue, there has been a great deal of criticism among bankers and security analysts of the board's Opinion No. 13, which defined net income for banks as including gains or losses on transactions in investment securities. What is your opinion?

A: [Opinion 13] finally placed bank accounting in the 20th century and required that loan losses be reflected as part of the determination of current operating income. Securities gains and losses also were included in income as a separate item, but it is probably not the best answer at the moment because they're based entirely on realized gains and losses and do not recognize unrealized gains and losses.

There ought to be some smoothing [of profits and losses on security transactions] in that it [the present method of taking actual profits or losses into account when they occur] does provide for a certain amount of manipulation. [Bankers] can pick and choose in order to influence their net income, and that's not good.

(Mr. Defliese explained that spreading the results of bank security transactions over a five-year period had been the original choice of the accountants, but that differences of opinion among the bankers, bank regulatory agencies and the accountants had led to the adoption of the present method of reflecting the entire result in net income at once.)

Q: Many accountants believe that no one is really happy with the board's decision on merger accounting. Isn't there something wrong with a system that would permit a rule that nobody is happy with?

A: Well, it's just like legislation. I'm sure that there are very few laws passed today that you could say that every legislator is happy about.

Q: But the point is that no legislator is happy with this thing.

A: Let's put it this way—they're happy to get an opinion out. What they're saying is that they don't agree fully with what's there.

We had to move and this is a move in the right direction.

Q: Would it be better if the Accounting Principles Board, rather than being composed largely, as it is now, of active accountants who are subject to pressure from their clients, were made up of elder statesmen who were no longer responsive to clients, no matter how subtle their pressure might be?

A: Well, the answer to that, of course, usually is that we have clients on all sides of issues, and consequently we are in a better position to be impartial in this respect. We hear them very patiently, and make up our own minds which way we should go.

They [the present board members] have their fingers on the pulse of practice, and deal with them, with each other, in a better fashion than any group that might be isolated. I think I'm concerned considerably about isolation because we have found that things move too fast in practice, and it's better to be close to the heat of the kitchen than farther away from it.

Furthermore, elder statesmen, so-called, would nevertheless be subject to the same biases that they may have had while they were in practice.*

**Editors' Note: An addendum following this article notes that, at the time of the interview, the APB had issued 19 opinions on topics as diverse as accounting for taxes, leases, pensions, mergers and banks not to mention a voluminous set of guidelines for presenting earnings per share, rules for accounting for convertible bonds, and the requirement for a statement of the sources and applications of funds. In addition, the addendum reported that Mr. Defliese had a detailed timetable stretching through mid-1973 for the Board's opinions, most dealing with new issues including accounting for the insurance industry, "phantom stock" executive compensation plans, and additional work on accounting for leases. It is also noted that in the month following the interview, the Board held its first public hearing on the issue of accounting for marketable securities and was in the midst of several hearings concerning accounting in the oil industry.*

APB CHAIRMAN IN LONDON†

An Interview of Philip L. Defliese

MR. Defliese, what exactly is the purpose of your visit?
I am here as a guest of Sir Ronald Leach to sit in on one of the meetings of your Accounting Standards Steering Committee [ASSC] and to observe the way in which the British Institutes are attempting to formulate accounting principles, so that I can make a comparison with how we do it. I also want to discuss some of the technical questions that are now before them.

You are the Chairman of the Accounting Principles Board. Tell me more about the APB and accounting principles.
That's right. I am managing partner of Lybrand, Ross Bros. & Montgomery, and I'm the Chairman of the APB.

Accounting principles are very necessary; without them we could not formulate or prepare public accounts. The term 'principle,' is an inaccurate one, because it embraces many concepts, mechanisms, conventions, methods and the like, which we broadly term 'principles.' Sometimes it is questioned whether we have fundamental principles. We believe we do, though we know that there is a need for a constant re-evaluation of those basic principles.

In the United States you refer to 'generally accepted principles'—What are they?
We have two types of principle: those which have been formalized through APB opinions and pronouncements, and those which have been adopted informally through practice.

APB Opinions are binding on AICPA members?
That's right. Since the APB was created we have written 19 Opinions, and these are binding upon our members. The APB has 18 members, 14 of whom are practitioners, two accounting professors, one an industrialist, and one a financial analyst. All, however, are CPAs.

The practitioners cover a wide spectrum of the profession; as all major firms and many medium sized firms are represented; we also have a small practitioner, to complete the range.

The APB is the successor to what was originally the Committee on Accounting Procedure—notice that it didn't use the term 'principles' at that time—which was formed back in 1938, soon after the Securities Acts were

†An interview of Philip L. Defliese, Chariman of the American Institutes' Accounting, Principles Board (APB), by *Accountancy* when he was in London in June, 1971. Reprinted with permission from *Accountancy*, July 1971, pp. 411-414.

passed, and the SEC formed; this was at a time when it was becoming apparent that there was a need for developing more formalized accounting principles. That Committee operated from 1938 until 1959, and it was then succeeded by the Accounting Principles Board. The objective of the APB was, again, to have a more formal organization than the previous Committee, a more effective charter, and a more effective research organism attached to it. That's where we are now.

How does the APB impose its pronouncements?
In certifying accounts, members of the Institute must follow the principles pronounced by the Opinions. If management departs from the principles, they are obliged either to qualify their opinion, or, if they feel that there is justification for the departure because there is substantial authoritative support for the other treatment, they are permitted to give an unqualified opinion, provided they make full disclosure of the departure and its effect.

Not all CPAs are members of the AICPA, so how does the APB control other CPAs?
That is correct: a CPA need not be a member of the Institute. We have no control over the other CPAs, but there is *effective* control by virtue of the existence of the SEC. Companies that trade publicly are required to register with the SEC, and file annual statements certified by CPAs or public accountants. In the event that a qualified opinion, or a circumstance which should qualify an opinion exists, the SEC has the right to require the accountant to alter his filing, or the company to alter its filing; this means that there is some control over the non-member CPA.

How are relations between the APB and the SEC ?
The SEC and the AICPA have established very good rapport; we are in constant touch with them in all our efforts to produce uniform accounting principles. They advise us of the trouble areas as they see them, and we attempt to deal with them as they arise. Before we issue an opinion we obtain their comments, and give close consideration to their views on any proposal we make, so that while we don't necessarily agree with them on all points, they generally agree with us. They have taken the public posture that they prefer that the principles be formulated by the APB, and also that they will support the opinions as they are issued, so that companies that are registered with the SEC are well aware of the fact that they need to comply with these opinions in order to have their statements accepted.

It is sometimes suggested that Britain should have an SEC; would you advocate this?
That is difficult for me to answer, because I am not that familiar with the mechanisms that you have. You have a Board of Trade, and a Stock Exchange and the City Panel and a number of other instrumentalities which I think are in a position to exercise the same kind of restraint, even though it may not be as legislative bodies; but I do believe that your Parliament (which is somewhat more informal than our Congress) supports—or would support—any actions taken by these groups and to that extent they have the authority to move in this area. The

real question is whether or not they would voluntarily exercise this authority if the need arose. That's difficult for me to answer.

I think that this is more a difference of form than of substance. You have many of the mechanisms that we have; they may be somewhat dispersed, but whether you need to formalize these into some instrumentality is difficult for me to say.

How does the SEC work?

In the United States the filings are scrutinized rather carefully by staff of the SEC, and should the need arise the SEC comments to the company concerning the filings and their inadequacy or inaccuracy, and requires that the filings be amended wherever they feel there is a need for it.

The SEC has taken the position that it can't accept a qualified opinion from an auditor. When I say 'qualified'—and I want to make sure that I clear this up—I mean that there are some qualifications that they will accept where it is possible for the auditor to make an evaluation (such as the realizability of research development costs); but the SEC will not accept a qualification based on an error, or one where there were inaccuracies in the application of a principle; it will require the company to amend and correct the error or misapplication. To that extent, therefore, the auditor has a more powerful weapon to achieve compliance with his opinions. In other words, he takes the position that he has to qualify his opinion, and if the company is willing to accept the qualification and take it to the SEC it is then a matter between the company and the SEC; usually it is resolved in favor of the accountant, because the SEC, generally speaking, has approved of the principles the accountant is applying. Unless the accountant is wrong, therefore, the company is in a position to be required to amend.

What exactly is the status of the APB? Who created it?

The APB is an instrumentality of the AICPA. It is created by a charter which the Institute designed, and which was approved by the Council of the AICPA. Members are elected to the APB for a three-year term, and are eligible for re-election for another three years by the Board of Directors of the American Institute. Purely on the surface I have the view that the APB's opinions have a somewhat stronger authority in our country than in yours, because the spectre of the SEC lurking in the background requires compliance.

To what extent is there co-operation between the APB and the ASSC?

The Secretariats of the two Institutes exchange exposure drafts. We are in a position to observe theirs, and they ours, and we try to minimize differences as much as we possibly can. We recognize that we cannot always achieve this, but certainly want to do so to the extent that we can. I am hopeful that the British attitude will be the same.

It seems to me that APB opinions get more complicated year by year. Is this just imagination or are they really getting more difficult?

You are absolutely right, and this is a matter that has been under some discussion among our members. They too are concerned about the complexity of recent APB opinions. If you examine some of the early pronouncements of the Committee on Accounting Procedure—and even some of the APB's earlier pronouncements—you will find that they were written in broad generalities, and consequently, have proved to be somewhat inadequate for the purpose. We have found through experience that unless we become quite definitive in our criteria practice begins to diverge and this divergency ultimately erodes the principles to the point here they need rebuttressing. In order to prevent this divergency from taking place at the outset we are becoming more and more definitive in our opinions: you might say, a more cookbook approach toward setting out guidelines for practice, and this, we hope, will prevent the erosion of principles. I believe that this is going to continue to be the case as long as business continues to become more complex. We have to compare the complexity of our opinions with the complexity of business. This is becoming much more difficult to deal with simply.

The financial architects have become more imaginative as time has gone on, and we have to be in a position to deal with them effectively, in order to make certain that our statements are as understandable as they can possibly be. This is not to make them simpler, but merely to cope with the many different things which arise. This is particularly true in the investment banking field, where the number of different types of shares is constantly being increased—in fact, I was reading in yesterday's paper that the Border and Southern Stockholders Trust company had introduced a new twist, that of an ordinary convertible share which is automatically converted on a two for one basis in seven years, on which no dividend is going to be paid, and on which there is also a subscription right to another share at the end of the seven years at a certain fixed price. Now, here is a new type of share which needs to be dealt with in calculating earnings, and net asset values, and the like. We attempted to anticipate all the possibilities which there are in our earnings per share opinion, which is why it is so complicated.

Is this process inevitable? So far, British accounting standards have been fairly straightforward; are they too going to become more complex as time goes by?
I have noticed that your opinions are condensed and simple, and quite straightforward. As I said, we have been along this road, and we find that things drop out between the paragraphs when a particular point is not covered, and of course the financial architects are constantly scrutinizing these in order to find the loopholes.

Do you have any difficulty in persuading small practitioners to follow APB opinions?
We have received some commentary from small practitioners who feel, perhaps, that what we are doing is not applicable to them, and perhaps some of the positions we take have an adverse effect on their practices. They feel that we make them go through an unnecessary exercise; for example, when earnings per share was pronounced, and it was required that the per share figure be placed at the bottom of the income statement in all cases, many small practitioners objected

to being required to put this on a close company statement, where it was felt that it served no useful purpose. That sort of thing we recognize as being somewhat of a burden, but it is a simple calculation in those cases, so that it doesn't create any real hardship. We have consequently seen fit not to succumb to that criticism.

Up until, say, about five or six years ago there were some pockets of opposition to uniformity. I think that most of them are disappearing, because it has been seen that without some uniformity things can go in all different directions, and this is not in the public interest. Consequently, as I say, most practitioners today are behind the movement to standardize as much as possible. Uniformity is a very desirable objective to the extent to which it can be applied. Now, judgment always has to be used in applying a principle to a set of facts, and it is only where the same set of facts and the same set of circumstances exist that there should be one answer to the accounting treatment. This is what we mean by uniformity: we are not trying to create a code of accounts, or a straitjacket, into which everything must be forced. We just don't feel that there should be two or more alternatives for identical facts.

It is sometimes suggested that the APB went about things in the wrong order: it spent too much time putting out 'bush fires' and too little in thinking about basic accounting theory.

I agree that there is a need for re-evaluation of basic accounting theory, but I don't believe that we need to delay the issuance of opinions which have as their purpose the elimination of alternatives. In the meantime, there are so many different theories available that for us to reach a consensus before we move would delay things interminably. Accountants are no different from economists in this respect. As I have pointed out frequently, there are as many different theories on how to cure inflation as there are economists to talk about them, and this is equally true of accountants. The big issue on an accountancy course is whether or not historical-cost accounting should continue to be the basic premise, or whether we should move to price level or to fair value accounting, either in one step or in two steps. What the ultimate is it is difficult to determine. We all recognize that accounting principles today do not reflect the economic facts of life as properly as they should, but that doesn't mean that we cannot strive to achieve that objective, and everything we are doing is moving in that direction.

Prices have increased very rapidly in Britain during the last 12-18 months. Is this also a problem in the United States? And is anything being done on the accounting front?

Inflation varies from year to year, but it has been in the past two or three years reaching the point where it is causing everyone concern, and I would venture a guess that if it is not controlled we will probably have to do something. We have already taken a step in that direction by issuing a statement on price level accounting, so that we have the mechanism available. However, this is a non-binding statement: it is a recommendation, and, of course, many companies have not seen fit to adopt it. It is quite possible that it won't be adopted very much unless it becomes binding. We are not yet at the stage where we would insist on its application.

Right now, we recommend that there be two statements, that the primary statement be on a historical-cost basis, so that a proper comparison can be made with those companies which are not yet furnishing two sets. The supplementary statement is on price level basis, and is intended to give an indication of the effect of inflation on the results, and I don't think that we are going to be able to move in the direction of price level or fair value accounting until taxation changes come about in this area.

Some other countries which have had rapid inflation have given recognition to the problem by altering their tax codes and providing relief. We see no indication that this is going to happen in the United States or in Britain.

Is the APB strong enough to influence the tax code and call for relief?
That's a good question. I don't think it will be strong enough until the conditions are such as to make it necessary.

That is a gray area right now—which way it goes depends on developments. If we can control inflation in the United States there will be a strong tendency not to move in that direction. There's a tremendous resistance towards departure from historical-cost, particularly in the taxation area, and there is quite obviously going to have to be a need before there is a move.

In our basic statements depreciation is always based on historical-cost. There have been only a very few companies (maybe one or two) that have attempted to issue price level statements. There is really no trend in that direction at all.

Revaluation of freehold properties, which is quite common over here, is unusual in the United States, is it not?
Yes, though this is not to say that accountants are basically opposed to it. I think that we could very easily move in that direction, provided the SEC would let us. This is one area where the SEC has taken a rather firm stand, simply because of its early history; there were many abuses in this area, and it had to come down rather hard and take the position that revaluations should not be permitted. That has carried through to this day.

As time goes on, and particularly as accountants move further into the area of price level and fair value accounting, the SEC attitude may change, provided that we can demonstrate to them that we can set up rather rigid guidelines and controls so that abuses would not arise.

Another difference between the two countries is that buildings are always depreciated in the United States, whereas in Britain freehold land and buildings are often retained 'at cost.'
At the present time we insist on depreciating all tangible assets other than land, so that ultimately the cost of the property is allocated over the period of its use. This we consider to be not so much a question of valuation as an allocation of costs. This is where the difference in theory lies. However, as you say, it does

create anomalies, particularly in the real estate investment area: companies that are organized solely for the purpose of owning and operating real estate as such (apartment houses, hotels, buildings, etc.) are obligated under our accounting principles to depreciate those buildings, and yet, from an economic standpoint, they are appreciating. The true economic fact does not come through in those cases. The situation is less compelling (although certainly as serious in fact) in industrial companies, where plant and equipment are depreciated, and where to a large extent the values are in the equipment rather than in the structure itself. In these cases there is a constant need for replacement through obsolescence, and consequently I think it is a better approach. But where you are dealing purely with income-producing real estate the value of the property is tied directly to the income it can produce, and as long as its ability to produce income is such as not to deteriorate through the years, then depreciation becomes somewhat of an anomaly, and I think that your approach is, perhaps, a bit more realistic in certain areas, though I think it could be less realistic in others, where the obsolescence factor might be very important.

What about the sinking fund method? A number of Canadian companies are using this.
At the moment we will not allow the sinking fund method, generally speaking. That's not a written rule; it is one that has evolved through SEC practice, because the SEC won't accept it. Many accountants, however, do feel that this is a good idea simply because it levels cost where the interest on a mortgage or a debenture issue that supports the structure is high in the early years. You therefore counterbalance the high interest with the low depreciation in the early years, and *vice versa* in the later years, and you achieve a level cost very similar to a lease rental. In fact, the leasing movement in the United States (apart from the question of off balance sheet financing) has been greatly stimulated by the objective of leveling the cost of maintaining property in terms of interest and depreciation. In re-examining the question of leases (which is now on the APB's agenda) we are concerned about the fact that if we require leases to be capitalized and depreciated, and interest charged, we create these higher early charges and lower later charges which disturb the level costing that we have attempted to achieve through the leasing mechanism. So we are somewhat deeply involved in this right now, and I don't know where we are going to come out.

Is there any appeal against an APB opinion or an SEC ruling?
Under our judicial system a company always has the right to appeal to the Court any time it feels that there has been some inequity or injustice by Federal or State agency. Where there is a departure from an opinion the SEC is in a position to require an amendment enforcing the opinion. If a company decides to challenge this it must do so in the Courts, and the Courts will decide whether or not there is a basic inequity. There has been a challenge of this sort in the past. It is not exactly to the point, because the SEC did not become directly involved inasmuch as it never reached that stage, but the American Electric Power did challenge the Institute's authority to issue a pronouncement, and that challenge was taken to the

Supreme Court where it was ruled that the Institute was qualified to issue these pronouncements, since it was directing itself to its membership as such. The quasi-governmental status of the Institute was lurking in the background, in as much as it was clear that the SEC would not accept anything that was not an unqualified opinion on the part of the auditor.

APB opinion 16 (on pooling of interests) and the British exposure draft on acquisitions and mergers cover much the same ground, with one fundamental difference: APB opinion 16 bolts the stable door after the horse has gone, whereas the British exposure draft gets the horse under a tight rein from the start. Are you happy with APB opinion 16, or is it still a stop-gap measure?
We are satisfied with 16 to the extent that we believe that it has eliminated all the abuse areas. The earlier pronouncement on poolings was rather broad; it had no specific guidelines, and as a result practice diverged considerably in its application. We believe that APB opinion 16 brings it back to what was the basic principle and to the extent to which it has done that we are satisfied. Of course, the debate is going to continue within the profession as to whether or not poolings should be permitted at all. There is a segment of theorists who believe that poolings should not be permitted, but that everything should be a purchase, and that assets acquired through merger or amalgamation should be reflected at current values. This, of course, is again the accounting theorists grasping for greater recognition of economic fact, a step to fair value accounting, so to speak. What these theorists ignore is the fact that the acquiring company has assets which have appreciated also, and to require that one side of a merger be stated at current value and not the other is a disparity that should not be permitted.

That is why the pooling instrument has been used as a principle to avoid the write-up on either side, and to preserve the original bases when stock is used as a mechanism for bringing companies together when in reality no resources of a company are being used. The purchase assumption—particularly if it is a cash purchase or one through debt—is that there is a resource of the company being used, and consequently the basis of accounting ought to follow the usage of any other purchase. This is a theoretical debate which I think will continue for some time: it is locked into the goodwill issue.

What about goodwill? APB opinion 17 considers this, does it not?
Goodwill has been an enigma to accountants for close to a century, and we are not going to solve the problems it creates that quickly. All we are doing at this point is providing uniformity, so that people are able to evaluate the effects of a purchase more readily. We are applying a uniform approach of a maximum forty-year amortization.

Do you think that uniformity itself is a desirable aim?
Yes, I think that the thrust of our operation is something which I want your people to be thoroughly aware of. We are moving rapidly towards the elimination of alternatives in the pubic interest because we feel that analysts, and particularly the public shareholder, the unsophisticated shareholder, are unable to cope with

the complexities of accounting well enough to be able to deal with it effectively. Even with full disclosure the nuances of accounting are very difficult to deal with.

I suggest that your Institute should concern itself with the same problem —I know they are—and recognize the need to deal with this as effectively as possible within time limitations in order to be ahead with the operation. We in the United States were unable to deal with it as effectively as we should have. As things began to move in our country the use of exotic types of securities was so rapid and so complex that it took us a considerable time to formulate in our own minds what needed to be done, and to establish the guidelines and principles to cope with it, or to provide this information.

ACCOUNTING PRINCIPLES BOARD'S CONCLUSIONS DESERVE TIME TO OPERATE†

by
Phillip L. Defliese

MR. Spacek's recent condemnation of the Accounting Principles Board's two new opinions on business combinations (mergers) and intangible assets (goodwill) is not unexpected. He can usually be counted on to speak out on matters before the board—particularly when the board's views differ from his. He no doubt is right much of the time, but this time I earnestly believe he is dead wrong. He is simply too pessimistic about the effect of the opinions on financial reporting.

Certainly the board is a long way from eliminating all the alternatives in accounting. Many open items still call for resolution. And the term "generally accepted accounting principles" needs further clarification. Just now these are to be done is a matter of concern within the profession; opinions are wide and varied. Indeed, opinions vary within Mr. Spacek's own firm, since their chief technical partner, a member of the APB, assented to the opinion on business combinations. And polls of financial analysts show that they, too, are widely split on this issue. All of this simply emphasizes the fact that accounting is not the exact science some analysts and writers would have us believe. It is neither exact nor a science, and it certainly doesn't derive from divine edict.

There is no doubt that the attempt to prescribe accounting principles in the areas of business combinations and goodwill was the most difficult job the board had undertaken to date. Perhaps the board should have taken more time and done more experimenting before attempting to reach a conclusion, for the research study upon which the board's deliberations were based in part, and which was authored by two of Mr. Spacek's partners, made no attempt to relate its theories to actual situations.

For 30 years the pooling method of accounting worked well. But in recent years the original criteria, which were spelled out in general terms were indirectly eroded by the growing use in mergers of exotic securities and unusual conditions spawned by imaginative financial architects. The old criteria were silent on such matters and there arose by necessity a case-by-case consideration by the SEC and the accounting profession until matters became so chaotic that something had to be done in a hurry.

---

†This article was written in response to a "point-of-view" article in *The New York Times* of August 30, 1970 by Leonard Spacek of Arthur Andersen & Co. Reprinted from *The New York Times*, September 13, 1970, p. 10. Copyright © 1970 by the New York Times Co. Reprinted by permission.

APB No. 15 and its predecessor No. 9 on earnings per share put an end to the "funny preferred stock" game that pumped up earnings whenever such securities were used in mergers. And the new opinion on business combinations supplies well-rationalized criteria that will make pooling purer by eliminating all the devices formerly used to achieve bizarre results within the pooling concept. Had these criteria existed all along (although it would have been impossible to anticipate all the devices ultimately used), we might never have had the abuses that led to such serious questions concerning pooling.

Mr. Spacek says that the heart of the problem is accounting for goodwill. In his view, goodwill, no matter how much was paid therefore in cash or otherwise, should be written off immediately. I call this non-accounting for goodwill. I would respect his point more if it were not accompanied by his charge that the board's new merger accounting opinion is primarily an attempt "to avoid goodwill problems." Certainly the new opinion will force more combinations to take the merger route rather than the purchase form—and goodwill will not arise. But this is no more "sweeping an undesirable situation under the rug" than is the immediate arbitrary writeoff urged by Mr. Spacek.

Actually, there is no single heart of the problem. In addition to the goodwill aspect, there is the basic question as to whether accounting balance sheets should reflect current values. Mr. Spacek criticizes the October 31, 1970, cutoff for the differing treatment of assets acquired before and after that date. This is nothing new in accounting. There are many who would like to eliminate the present hodgepodge of historical costs that results from recording in terms of dollars originally paid, properties of equal current value but acquired at different times. Others deplore the non-recognition of certain types of assets—such as oil reserves in the ground. But the adoption of "fair value" accounting will not come overnight. We cannot tear down the temple of historical costs and still expect meaningful earnings-per-share reports to be issued next quarter.

Mr. Spacek's proposal would "fair value" all assets and liabilities of the merged company in any business combination. But what about those of the continuing company? Until this question can be resolved, the board has wisely clung to the pooling principle under which historical costs are retained on both sides whenever there is a true pooling of risks and benefits, as evidenced by an exchange of common stock for common stock only.

On this latter point, Mr. Spacek criticized the Board for not allowing common stock equivalents to qualify for pooling—i.e., a low-rate convertible preferred stock that must be deemed as converted in any calculation of earnings per share. This prohibition was established because, as the opinion carefully points out, the exchange of preferred stock for common in fact results in a change of relative risks and thus destroys the theoretical basis for pooling.

Furthermore, under present rules, assented to by the Arthur Andersen representative, common stock equivalents are not permitted to receive accounting recognition until converted. Those who oppose pooling in principle should be happy about this restriction since it limits its applicability.

Mr. Spacek's logic is at its best when he criticizes the different accounting required when cash, instead of stock, is used in a combination. Certainly the recipient considers them the same—except that cash may result in income tax—provided there is an active market in the stock. But is it the same to the issuer? When cash is used, a resource is given in exchange for new resources and no increase in equity results. But when stock is issued, no resource is given—if it is agreed that a company's own unissued stock is not a resource—but equity is increased. The counter argument, of course, follows: Sure, but since a company can sell its own stock and then buy the other company for cash, shouldn't the same treatment be given in either case? But ask any investment banker whether this is possible on precisely the same terms and with the same results. He'll tell you it can't be done—especially in this market.

Another point frequently downplayed in considering whether stock is the equivalent of cash is the fact that when common stock is exchanged for common stock, the "seller" is receiving back a portion of what he is giving to the "buyer." in addition to receiving a portion of the "buyer." This is a form of "self-dealing" in which the seller never completely parts with his company and thus does not constitute a sufficiently sound base for establishing new values.

Now what is Mr. Spacek's major concern? He says that accounting is not presenting the economic facts of life. Philosophically he is right. I feel the same way. And I recognize the urgency with which we must continue to strive to achieve that goal. It will not be easy because even the economists and financial analysts can't agree on what constitutes an appropriate measurement for the economic facts of life. Certainly our fundamentals needs re-examination and there should be exhaustive experimentation before we move ahead—lest we flush the baby with the bath.

Meantime, these opinions deserve a chance to operate. They ought not to be condemned on the basis of ill-conceived judgments or undue pessimism. They have the support of the SEC and I am sure they will have the exemplary effects intended by the two-thirds majority of the Accounting Principles Board. As long as we can produce financial statements moving towards greater comparability by narrowing the alternatives, we will be moving toward our goal. The two new opinions admittedly are compromises, but in my opinion they are viable compromises that correct abuses of the past and certainly provide for greater uniformity.

I do not agree that the APB's directives will "further pollute financial reporting to the public." If I did, I would stop practicing.

THE APB AND ITS RECENT AND PENDING OPINIONS†

by
Philip L. Defliese

IT is always easier, and often more exciting, to destroy than to build. Churchill put it: "There are men who derive as stern an exultation from the proximity of disaster and ruin, as others from success." The Accounting Principles Board is engaged in building—methodically, persistently, relentlessly, but building nevertheless.

In eleven years the Board has hammered out seventeen Opinions, Drafts and redrafts, reversals of some Opinions, the solicitation of a broad spectrum of viewpoints, and thousands of hours of research, discussions, arguments, and, yes, compromises—all this was the stuff of these Opinions. The fact is that we were—and are—dealing with complex issues that resist simple solutions. These matters are the substance of enterprise, of economics during a time of dynamic change. These matters are complex and not reducible to a few broad generalities. And they are not matters that can be settled by fiat or decree. Nor are they matters that should be settled on the basis of the loudest shout.

That the APB is presently under a barrage of criticism is probably salutary when one considers the diversity of its sources and its often conflicting and, indeed, illiberal nature. It confirms the independence of the Board—independence from desires of would-be tsars wishing to impose their pet theories, and independence from the shortsighted demands of those businesses that fear an immediately negative effect. In this atmosphere—and with seventeen Opinions put forth (several of the more recent ones already profoundly affecting the nature of financial reporting)—I want to state unequivocally as chairman-elect of the APB that you will be hearing more shouting, more wounded yells in the years, and even months, ahead. We intend to deal with the realities, and deal with them now. Our docket calls for the issuance of no less than six, perhaps as many as eight, additional Opinions in the next twenty-four mouths.

In the most recent debate over business combination, the one issue against which industry was united in its opposition—the amortization of goodwill—was never relaxed. And if the Board members are pawns of industry, they have a

†Presented at a seminar sponsored by the Conference Institute on November 19, 1970 in New York. Reprinted with permission from *The Journal of Accountancy*, February 1971, pp. 66-69, copyright © 1971 by American Institute of CPAs. Opinions of the authors are their own and do not necessarily reflect policies of the AICPA. Also published, in a slightly abridged version, under the title, "The Accounting Principles Board and Its Recent and Pending Opinions," in *The New York Certified Public Accountant*, April 1971, pp. 279-283, 314.

peculiar way of demonstrating it. The record shows that over the years the members from the major accounting firms split differently on different issues, and even members from the universities and industry were sometimes divided.

The fact is that business, and the vehicles of business, and finance are certainly not becoming simpler. Accounting's response must be equally sophisticated and deep. And, perhaps more important, our actions must be responsive to the whole economy—not to any particular group.

Perhaps the crux of the problem lies in the unconscious tendency many of us have to expect all fundamental principles to be of divine origin—much like the Ten Commandments. The truth is that accounting principles are man-made; they've evolved from a rudimentary double-entry system which gradually embraced formalized concepts of realization and matching of historical costs with current and future revenue. In reality these are accounting conventions which have been buttressed, gradually, by selective touches designed to eliminate abuses and preserve an essentially conservative approach. And gaps have developed, some of which have resulted in confusion and misuse while we went about the job of minimizing alternatives. During all this time there has been developing, understandably, a cry for a better basic structure for this edifice. The only problem is that some of the critics speak as self-appointed prophets newly returned from a long visit on Mount Sinai. Most of us know it is not that simple.

A LOOK AT THE RECORD

That the Board's progress so far has been substantial, and its accomplishments great, is evidenced by the record. The record is, of course, not complete—it never will be, for the economic phenomena with which the Board deals are changing, and will continue to change as long as human ingenuity is applied in exploiting man's economic environment.

Many have said that the Board did nothing during its first five years. In reality it accomplished two basic tasks through a traumatic process, which, in retrospect, considering the small segment of our history this period represents, seem monumental in effect.

First, the genuine philosophical conflict that long existed within the profession as to whether accounting principles should be construed broadly or narrowly was resolved. At the time the Board was formed, there were at one pole those who favored the freedom to select any of several rational alternatives for the treatment of a particular transaction. At the other pole were those who would eliminate the areas of difference and inconsistency by selecting, defining, and promulgating the single best of several alternatives—the "best" to be determined through study, research and exposure.

The profession is now agreed on the need for specifics in defining accounting principles and reporting practices and is rapidly moving in that direction. The alternatives are being reduced and abuses eliminated. Flexibility, as a basic concept, is dead.

Second, in the early years the authority of the Board's Opinions rested only upon their general acceptance. Then the major firms not only differed sharply on the Opinions issued, but, in one notable instance, some disregarded it in practice. This was abetted by the SEC, which accepted the conflicting alternatives. By action of the Council of the AICPA in 1964, APB Opinions were made more authoritative. All of this is now behind us. The profession is not only united in its intention to follow APB Opinions, but both the SEC and the major stock exchanges have also indicated their intent to back us with the full strength of their regulatory powers.

Since that time, 12 Opinions have been issued that, however inadequate in the minds of some, and despite some minor setbacks, have eliminated many abuses and improved financial reporting and, indeed, improved it dramatically.

- Opinions 5 and 7 on leases, while admittedly inconsistent, have eliminated the major abuse of the time—the building up of unrecorded equities in properties by charging excess rent to income—and they have set guidelines for distinguishing a financing lease from an operating lease as well as broadening disclosure requirements.
- Opinion 8 eliminated a hodgepodge of practices and manipulations in the pension cost area.
- Opinion 9 brought back the all-inclusive income statement and eliminated short-circuiting income charges to surplus.
- Opinion 11 standardized tax allocation practices, except for certain areas still under study.
- Opinion 13 for the first time made banks include loan losses and security transactions in determining their net income, and
- Opinion 14 standardized practices on convertible debt and debt with warrants.

THE SIGNIFICANCE OF CRITICISM

Accusations of vacillation and compromise stem from the simple fact that there are as many concepts of accounting theory as there are economic theories to solve inflation. Fortunately for the economists, they don't have to express opinions on individual financial statements—opinions upon which they can be sued if someone thinks they are wrong. But accountants recognize the need to narrow the differences in accounting methods and to set precise rules as quickly as possible. Accordingly, the Board members are often willing to adjust their own views. In this approach we follow the example set by our democratic and representative government—and I haven't heard any serious suggestions that we scrap *that* process. This approach rests on assumptions that no one man has all the answers—that many viewpoints must be heard and, if possible, accommodated. It was Churchill, I believe, who suggested that representative government was a terribly wasteful system, given to compromises and inefficiencies, but that every other system was far worse. I hope that government by the consent of the governed never succumbs to far worse military juntas or intellectual elites.

The criticism of the Board's Opinions by industry certainly proves that we are not yes men for industry. The criticism emanating from the profession itself is usually spasmodic, expressed most violently by those whose pet theories are rejected by the Board, and subsiding when those theories are accepted. Different firms have criticized Tax Allocation, Earnings Per Share, Business Combinations and Intangible Assets. When it suits their convenience, they criticize the complexity of the rules in Opinions they dislike, and praise the detailed requirements of those they espouse. All of this makes for publicity, but does not advance the concept of meaningful reporting one iota.

Most businessmen and laymen are now learning that accounting is not a simple art or an exact science, and it cannot run ahead of the complexities that arise daily. This has been a revelation to many analysts and writers, and much of the storm is a necessary step in an educational process. The limitations of accounting in trying to determine the precise income of far-flung complicated business empires for as short a period of time as a quarter of a year are becoming increasingly appreciated.

Some criticism of the Board is valid. We have not yet agreed on what basic accounting principles should be for the future. We are now in the process of publishing a statement of what basic accounting concepts and principles *are* presently. We can now proceed to make basic revisions. We are generally agreed that present accounting must, for a time, rest on historical costs and the concept of matching those costs with current and future revenues plus rather conclusive evidence of realization. The future points toward price level and fair value accounting, with more liberal concepts of realization. Because theory and practice are sometimes hard to reconcile, agreement in this area will not come easily.

The Board has also been criticized for its research efforts. Some of these efforts have, of course, been too little and too late, but some allowance must be made for the pioneering efforts involved. The Board has made some mistakes in selecting authors and advisory board members.*

THE BOARD'S FUTURE OPERATIONS

Review of the Board's operations is now under way. The basic question is whether there is a better way to determine accounting principles. The Board has an open mind concerning these inquiries; we welcome changes that would improve performance. Both a smaller Board of full-time distinguished accountants divorced from practice, and a court of independent accounting jurists have been suggested. Many feel that a smaller group would be just as divided, and if divorced from practice and if not representative of the entire profession, would not receive the support of practitioners. Professional self-regulation is our democratic heritage, and we feel there is no better way. A court brings with it all of the drawbacks of the legal system, particularly the slowness and conflicts in

---

**Editors' Note: The Journal of Accountancy text indicates the omission of material at this point for the sake of brevity.*

rulings. An appeals court, to which APB Opinions and other regulatory rulings could be appealed, would certainly add confusion to our present complicated system.

Over the years the Board has sharpened its procedures. All interested parties are now invited to submit viewpoints and appear before special committee meetings and symposiums designed to give everyone an opportunity to be heard. This process will soon be expanded into more formalized open hearings.

EFFECT OF RECENT OPINIONS

Now let me briefly review recent and pending Opinions. Opinion 15—Earnings Per Share—has generally been hailed by the profession and financial analysts, and, while it was condemned by the financial community when it was issued, business is learning to live with it. It has effectively taken all the fun out of what was the funny money game—a game never envisioned beforehand, but which emerged out of the "go-go era" to swamp us. Opinion 15 is criticized for being arbitrary and complex. But the industrial and security fields have become too complex to deal with simply. And if we are to approach uniformity, there are times when we have to be arbitrary and draw lines.

In issuing Opinion 15, the Board had to recognize that while one faction said "give us more facts and guidelines to work with," the other said "you are confusing us with too many earnings-per-share figures; make it simple." By compromise and our two-thirds' majority rule, we came up with a workable answer, although complex. I can assure you that accounting will never get simpler.

The Opinions on Business Combinations and Intangibles (goodwill), despite the criticism and trauma that surrounded their issuance, *do* eliminate most of the abuses of the pooling and purchasing methods of accounting for mergers and, for the first time, provide uniformity in the treatment of goodwill.

The problems which faced the Board in dealing with these Opinions, in the view of many, were basic. The APB was not ready to alter the basic concepts of historical cost and matching costs and revenue. The retention of historical cost on both sides of a merger is basic to the pooling concept. And the matching concept has a large bearing on the question of whether goodwill should be capitalized indefinitely, amortized or written off immediately. During the first 25 years of pooling, the old principle stood up well; it was only when the abuses of the past five years came to the fore that an urgent need for action developed. There simply wasn't time to reach agreement on the restructuring of all basic accounting theory, so we settled for the elimination of abuses.

The Business Combination Opinion re-establishes the original pooling concept in which two or more groups of shareholders exchange, on a continuing basis, risks and benefits through a straight common-stock-for-common-stock exchange, without preferences or contingent payments on either side. Only under these criteria is there justification for a continuation of historical cost bases on both sides. In this respect, the pooling concept was well named.

To achieve their objectives, these Opinions had to set up some rigid (and occasionally arbitrary) guidelines. This is always an easy target for those who disagree with an Opinion in principle. Ironically, those who are most opposed to pooling are now attacking the guidelines that would limit pooling.

Goodwill has been an accounting enigma for decades. Purchased goodwill, when amortized, creates a form of double charge when expenditures for its regeneration are made simultaneously. Since goodwill cannot be assumed to be perpetual, some method of eliminating the cost of goodwill had to be devised; at the same time, most accountants refuse to defer the regeneration charges to the future because there is no objective way to do it. The use of a long period of amortization—a maximum of 40 years—therefore was the most practical and objective solution.

Naturally, reactions are still mixed on these Opinions, but they must be given time to prove themselves. The size test created the most furor, but no abuses, in fact, were ever ascribed to disparity in size—except that there were too many mergers! If there is one point accountants agree on, it is that accounting principles should not be designed to prevent or restrict business transactions; this is a matter for antitrust legislation or regulation.

PENDING OPINIONS

As I noted, our schedule calls for the issuance of six to eight new Opinions in the next two years or so. While many of these will be designed to put out brushfires, some may also begin to depart from basic concepts used today. Please recognize that any trends I indicate are strictly tentative. They include:

Accounting Changes. This Opinion will attempt to standardize the disclosures required when a company changes from one accepted accounting method to another accepted accounting method. Without permitting charges to be buried in the past, it will nevertheless provide restated data to disclose proper trends. It is hoped that accounting changes will become fewer as we continue to reduce the alternatives.

Intercorporate Investments (50% and Under). This Opinion will change the present accounting for holdings of sizable minority interests in other companies. It probably will involve a departure from historical costs.

Marketable Securities. Here we will set uniform standards for the valuation of securities held by all types of companies and prescribe the accounting for gains and losses, both realized and unrealized. Once again, there probably will be a significant departure from cost.

Premium and Discount on *Retirement of Convertible Debt*. The repurchase of convertible debt is becoming a prevalent practice, and uniformity of treatment of the premium or discount is needed.

The Funds Statement. This Opinion probably will require a funds statement as a basic financial statement to accompany all balance sheets and income statements. Most listed companies are already following this practice.

Diversified Companies. This Opinion will set proper guidelines for fair presentation of operations of companies in many lines of business. It may very well follow closely the new SEC requirements.

Components of an Enterprise. This is a bit different from diversified companies, since it sets guidelines for reporting on legal components rather than product lines; the two are not always the same.

Extractive Industries. This is an area where less diversity of accounting practice is greatly needed—particularly in the oil and gas industry.

In addition, special committees of the Institute are now working toward solving industry problems related to land development companies, insurance companies, savings and loan associations and others. I expect that these will be resolved within the next year or so. Unsettled questions on income tax allocation will also be resolved.

FOR THE FUTURE: CHANGES IN FUNDAMENTALS

Some of the more fundamental questions centering on depreciation methods, inventory valuation and fair value vs. historical cost accounting are also under study. It may appear that we are putting the cart before the horse in dealing with the other questions without first settling the more fundamental issues. We all recognize that the principles of accounting do not presently reflect the economic facts of life, but we dare not undertake revolutionary change without the careful analysis which leads to valid conclusions and without adequate experimentation with live cases to be sure of the result. This will take time. Financial analysts tell us that they recognize our problem, and they are content with smaller changes that lead to greater uniformity in financial statements, so that they can better analyze trends—pending our ultimate resolution of the basic fundamentals.

I can assure you that the Board will diligently pursue the solution to the many problems that face us today. The alternatives need to be reduced. We cannot divert all of our attention to studying the basic structure while pressing problems need solution. But we will not delay the consideration of these fundamentals. Now that we have issued a statement on the basic concepts as they exist today (which statement, by the way, was passed with only one dissent), we can examine our fundamental structure and progress more quickly. I feel sure we can do this while we are working on the burning issues, some of which will point the way for the ultimate change. Our changes must be evolutionary rather than revolutionary. Our capitalistic structure cannot stand radical changes; accounting principles must recognize the part they play in our economy and be responsive to this environment. But it is certain that the interests of the ultimate user of financial statements, the investor, will be served.

IN THE MEANTIME: FULL DISCLOSURE

In the meantime, you can rely on the disclosure requirements of the profession to "tell it like it is." These requirements are constantly being expanded.

Except for a few isolated cases, the integrity of disclosure in financial statements has not been at issue. On the question of adequacy, we are criticized, on the one hand, for not telling enough, and, on the other, for having six pages of footnotes to three pages of financial statements. The problems are complex, and excessive disclosure should be hailed rather than criticized. We cannot boil down many figures to one figure, no matter what magic we attempt, and investors must be educated to realize that earnings per share do not represent cash in the bank. If we ever adopt fair value accounting when we report earnings per share we will probably need to specify those portions attributable to production, price-level changes, inherent appreciation, and a host of other matters. Then many may say, "Give us the good old days!"

I have confidence in the course we are taking, and I am sure that accounting will be on a firmer footing at the end of the Seventies than it is at the beginning.

BUSINESS COMBINATIONS REVISITED: A Temporary Defense of the Status Quo[†]

by
Philip L. Defliese

HERE WE GO AGAIN!

BOWING to the demands of a small number of long-standing critics of the pooling-of-interests method of business combinations, the Financial Accounting Standards Board (FASB) has placed on its growing agenda the entire subject of business combinations for reconsideration. In addition to the requests stemming from conceptual disagreement, a considerable number of requests had also been received for clarification and interpretation of specific minor issues that had arisen in the area. Thus, the decision to reopen the subject was taken in lieu of handling these matters separately.

It is now more than three years since the Accounting Principles Board of the American Institute of CPAs approved Opinion No. 16, *Business Combinations*, and No. 17, *Intangible Assets*.

The issuance of these Opinions came after a two-year open struggle of unprecedented intensity. (At various times, lawsuits were even threatened by members of industry and Board members.) Then, this writer supported, and still does support, a strengthened pooling concept. This position rests on the conviction that the concept provides the only viable method within an historical cost framework for many types of combinations and that no other method will be feasible until fundamental changes in accounting are agreed on.

This is not to suggest that present accounting methods for business combinations should never be changed. It is merely a question of not having found the right answer to a difficult problem. This writer has always considered APB Opinions to be transitionary—a view whose validity many former Board members now freely concede, even though they were extremely reluctant to express it when the Board was alive, for fear of detracting from the authority of the Opinions. (Only once did the Board admit this point—in Opinion No. 8, *Pension Costs*.) When accounting theory provides results closer to economic

---

[†]An elaboration of a paper presented at the DR Scott Memorial Lectures in Accountancy at the University of Missouri–Columbia in February 1974. (New York: Coopers & Lybrand, 1974), 22 pages. Reprinted with permission of PricewaterhouseCoopers LLP. Also published with slight variations as "Business Combinations Revisted," in *DR Scott Memorial Lectures in Accountancy*, Volume VI, Alfred R. Roberts, ed. (Columbia, MO: Department of Accountancy, College of Administration and Public Affairs, University of Missouri–Columbia, 1974), pp. 46-65; and "Business Combinations Revisted: A Temporary Defense of the Status Quo," in *Ohio State Law Journal* (1974), pp. 393-411. Portions reprinted under the title "Business Combinations Revisted," *Financial Executive*, September 1975, pp. 42-47.

facts than it now does, we may be able to develop superior approaches to the most difficult issues of business combinations and goodwill.

It is well-known that Opinions 16 and 17 were derived from a single proposed opinion that could not gain the necessary two-thirds vote of the Board needed for approval, such was the diversity of views among the 18 members. Many members (including this writer) accepted Opinion No. 17 only because it was necessary for compromise, and because they believed that the effect upon business of the 40-year amortization requirement would be minimal (and, in many cases, avoidable, by carefully subscribing to the new pooling criteria). The drawbacks were a small price to pay for the overall gain, principally the restoration of pooling to its original posture.

If the FASB is to do justice to the question of poolings, its re-examination must explore:

1. The accounting and business environments that existed at the time Opinions 16 and 17 were under consideration, which substantially influenced their conclusion, and the extent to which these environments have, or have not, changed since.
2. The compromises that were made at the time—not only their nature but also their immediate and long-term effects.

THE ACCOUNTING ENVIRONMENT THEN AND NOW

In the early nineteen-sixties, just as it was getting under way, the APB suffered a serious reverse that for a time threatened to destroy its effectiveness. One of its first Opinions, concerned with the investment tax credit, was overruled by the SEC. The profession had split on the issue and, after a traumatic struggle, the AICPA Council ultimately pronounced APB Opinions binding on its membership. The SEC, moreover, consented to an understanding that would preclude such disagreements. At the same time, however, the Commission urged haste in getting on with the job of narrowing accounting alternatives.

During this disturbed period, the APB was considering the possibility of issuing a pronouncement on the basic concepts underlying financial statements. As the subcommittee studying the question struggled to reach agreement on a recommendation, it became apparent that no progress in that direction would be made unless the project was divided in two: one to deal with the concepts as they were known to exist, and the other to deal with what they should be for the future. A pronouncement on the former subject was finally issued, as a Statement rather than as an Opinion, in October 1970—at the same time as Opinions 16 and 17. The project dealing with future concepts was chaired by the most vocal critic of present concepts, but it never got off the ground. The immensity of this task was demonstrated when the AICPA in 1971 commissioned the special Study Group on Objectives of Financial Statements, whose report was released in the fall of 1973.

In 1968, about the time the APB began its stormy discussions on business combinations, the AICPA published a research study on goodwill (ARS No. 10),[1] a follow-up of an earlier study on business combinations. The authors, two partners of Arthur Andersen, recommended that all business combinations be recorded on the purchase method and that goodwill be written off against stockholders' equity as of the date of acquisition—a proposal that very few agreed with. This recommendation required the acquired company's assets to be valued at current values while the acquiring company's assets remained at cost, since historical cost was to remain as the basic framework. Mergers were viewed as exchange transactions on which a new cost basis would be established for the acquired companies; this is the basic theory behind the purchase method.

When the Board began discussions on the subject of business combinations and goodwill, it was found that poolings vs. purchases and goodwill amortization vs. no amortization represented only two positions out of many prevailing among Board members. Some felt that a better approach to fair value was needed; others clung tenaciously to historical cost, and there were many positions and variations in between.

At the same time, there were many thorny accounting questions that were troubling the Board, not confined to the subject of business combinations but certainly relevant to it. A few of the many examples include:

1. Accounting methods for certain industries

Oil and gas. A wide variety of generally accepted accounting principles were (and are) in use, producing considerable disparity in income results.

Investment real estate. Accounting practices are far behind economic realities.

2. Treatment of certain items

Marketable securities. Many institutions, pension funds, insurance companies, and conglomerates managing portfolios were using varying accounting principles for the timing of capital gains as income and the valuation of affiliated companies. Accounting in this area was often, and still is[2] arbitrary.

Research and development. Costs can be, and are, either capitalized or expensed, or partly so.

Depreciation and inventory valuation. A large number and variety of methods are in use.

3. Financial reporting policies

Price-level financial statements. The use of these statements to supplement the historical cost statement was recommended, but not required, by the APB.

---

[1]G.R. Catlett and N.O. Olson, *Accounting for Goodwill*, AICPA Accounting Research Study No. 10, 1968.

[2]However, APB Opinion No. 18, *Investments in Affiliated Companies* (1971), has considerably standardized practice in this narrow area.

Although price-level statements represent a first step toward fair value, the recommendation has been virtually ignored.

This situation was further complicated by the fact that there was as yet no way of establishing uniform approaches toward the implementation of AICPA pronouncements. The value of such uniformity was generally understood, but practicing accountants had not yet grasped the necessity of working together to achieve it. Thus, AICPA pronouncements were usually couched in general terms, allowing for the application of judgment in their use. This was before the Institute adopted the practice of issuing "unofficial" or "official" interpretations. As a consequence, the SEC became the interpreter of AICPA pronouncements (without publishing its interpretations) and "precedent" accounting became the vogue.

While all this was going on, a subtle and important change was taking place in the public mind. The public, which was heavily involved in a fluctuating bull market, was beginning to view accounting as a measurement of management performance; earnings per share (EPS), a statistic invented by the financial analysts and adopted by the SEC, became more important than absolute results. The public stockholder was not interested in the details, assuming that he could understand them. At first, the accountants resisted a concept alien to their practice; later they gave in and accepted responsibility for calculating EPS, albeit in general terms. Methods of calculating EPS were rather loose, and the situation was chaotic until APB Opinion No. 15 (just before 16!) provided a definitive "cookbook," with over 100 interpretations.

Pooling as a means of accounting for a merger evolved in the early fifties, principally in response to the desire to avoid recording unrealistic amounts of goodwill and otherwise inflating the balance sheet values when high-priced stock was used as the merger vehicle. The SEC, historically allergic to inflating values, embraced it. Its underlying principle, concerned with a pooling of common equity interests involving no expenditure of resources (cash or debt), was certainly sound at the time. The criteria for qualifying as a pooling were spelled out in general terms in ARB No. 48 (*Business Combinations*, 1957). But the absence of official interpretation on matters arising in connection with pooling (the SEC provided day-to-day determination of which combinations qualified) paved the way for the spread of certain dubious practices, many of which were aimed at immediately creating unrealistic EPS results. Examples include:

- Convertible preferred stock with nominal dividends, and other unusual stock issues, were employed in mergers in lieu of common stock at a time when disclosure of potential dilution by common stock equivalents was not required.
- Merger terms often provided for future issuances of stock contingent on profitability of subsequent operations.
- Shareholders of acquired companies were often guaranteed cash prices for their new stock (from the company's resources) if certain values were not ultimately realizable by the new shareholders. These raised the question of whether purchasing was taking place.

• Assets of pooled companies with low-cost bases were occasionally sold off immediately by the acquiring companies for instant earnings of sizable amounts.

• When sizable amounts of cash or debt were employed in addition to stock, a part-purchase, part-pooling accounting for one transaction was allowed.

THE BUSINESS ENVIRONMENT THEN AND NOW

It is not surprising that, in these circumstances, pooling fell into disrepute. Nevertheless, these practices might have been tolerated for longer than they were had it not been for the special market conditions that prevailed in the late nineteen-sixties. During this period, a continually rising stock market created a growth-oriented mentality spurred by the price/earnings multiple cult. One result was an unprecedented number of mergers, motivated to a large extent by the ability to achieve the results referred to above; the movement, in fact, reached its peak at this time.

It was only to be expected that the intensification of merger activity would be reflected in an increase in the objectionable pooling practices described above. Boom periods are usually characterized by a discernible lapse in financial responsibility, and the late sixties were no exception. Abuses were rife: The creation of instant EPS by means of "funny preferreds" is a notable example. Another example, bearing directly on our subject, was the widespread failure to make proper comparison with prior-year pooled results in annual reports, a laxity that produced distorted presentations until the SEC finally cracked down on the practice.

Under the circumstances, a reaction was inevitable. Leading authorities, among them A.J. Briloff (of "dirty pooling" fame), called for changes,[3] and the SEC pressed the APB for action. The result was the issuance of Opinions 16 and 17, re-establishing the ground rules for the use of pooling.

It should be noted that Dr. Briloff did not advocate the absolute abolition of pooling (his alternatives are not too clear), an attitude shared by many authorities, including Professor Snavely, who defended pooling,[4] and the SEC itself. After studying ARS No. 10 (on goodwill), the then chief accountant of the SEC (Andrew Barr) wrote, as follows (March 1969), to the AICPA on the subject of pooling:

> There is no expenditure or disbursement of resources when stock is issued. The company issues a fractional interest in its net equity and earnings potential for which it receives a capital contribution....

---

[3]A. J. Briloff, "Dirty Pooling." *Accounting Review*, July 1967, pp. 489-496.

[4]H. J. Snavely, "Pooling Is Good Accounting," *Financial Analysts Journal*, November/December 1968, pp. 85-89.

In periods of high market price levels, purchase accounting tends to introduce inflationary values into the balance sheet when the assets and intangibles of the acquired companies are valued at the market price of the stock issued. These amounts usually cannot reasonably be expected to be recovered from the earnings of the acquired companies. The financial abuses arisings from such practices were an important consideration in the passage of the Securities Acts and the Public Utility Holding Company Act.

An acquisition for common stock is a capital transaction which increases both total assets and equity, and the acquisition of a profitable business increases the earnings of the enterprise.

We would have to agree that in most business combinations, one company is acquiring the other, but we do not agree that an acquisition for stock is the same as an acquisition for cash or necessarily should be accounted for in a manner similar to a cash purchase.

Since 1970, the merger movement has subsided considerably. The indications are that recent mergers have been undertaken with greater caution than generally prevailed before 1970. Of course, the bear markets we have been experiencing have had something to do with this, but there is good reason to accord Opinions 16 and 17 much of the credit. Another mayor change is the elimination of abuses in the EPS area, thanks largely to APB Opinion No. 15, which, among other things, put the spotlight on dilution caused by common stock equivalents. More recently, the bear market has stimulated a considerable number of transactions in treasury stock, an activity that has a bearing on future pooling. (Treasury stock transactions will be discussed later.) These post-1970 developments suggest that reopening the pooling issue at this time is premature. At most, what is called for is a tune-up, not a major overhaul.

THE COMPROMISES OF OPINION 16 AND THEIR EFFECTS

In evolving its opinions on business combinations, the APB was confronted with some fundamental premises of a conflicting nature. If a corporation buys a building for $1 million cash, or for $1 million worth of stock (market value), it records a value of $1 million. If it buys a corporation whose sole asset is a building worth $1 million (which is recorded on the acquired corporation's books for $100,000), issuing stock instead of cash, shouldn't it also record a value of $1 million? Most members said yes; it seemed so simple. But most poolings are *not* that simple.

Corporations are more than buildings—they involve people, products, processes, know-how, and customers, an aggregation that engenders an intangible earning power usually called "goodwill." This aggregation produces an accounting result based on historical cost concepts, EPS, which ultimately is reflected in a company's stock values, values determined by the market, not by the company. And when companies combine, these elements also combine, but in a fashion that is not always arithmetical. Given the many other areas of accounting that relate to this subject, it is easy to understand how dissension arose, and why the Board membership broke into factions according to whether they advocated pooling as then practiced, pooling reform, size-test pooling, or purchase accounting.

After a period of deadlock, the Board decided that the best it could do was to "reform" pooling. In addition, the Board agreed, in deference to an SEC request, to require amortization of goodwill (over 40 years) when purchase accounting is used. The Board's rationale in its explicit acceptance of the validity of pooling is attested to in the following passage from Opinion 16:

> *Validity of the concept.* Those who support the pooling of interests method believe that a business combination effected by issuing common stock is different from a purchase in that no corporate assets are disbursed to stockholders and the net assets of the issuing corporation are enlarged by the net assets of the corporation whose stockholders accept common stock of the combined corporation. There is no newly invested capital nor have owners withdrawn assets from the group since the stock of a corporation is not one of its assets. Accordingly, the net assets of the constituents remain intact but combined; the stockholder groups remain intact but combined. Aggregate income is not changed since the total resources are not changed. Consequently, the historical costs and earnings of the separate corporations are appropriately combined. In a business combination effected by exchanging stock, groups of stockholders combine their resources, talents, and risks to form a new entity to carry on in combination the previous business and to continue their earnings streams. The sharing of risks by the constituent stockholder groups is an important element in a business combination effected by exchanging stock. By pooling equity interests, each group continues to maintain risk elements of its former investment and they mutually exchange risks and benefits....The fractional interests in the common enterprise are reallocated—risks are rearranged among the stockholder groups outside the corporate entity.... Each stockholder group in a pooling of interests gives up its interests in assets formerly held in addition to an interest in the assets of the other. The clearest example of this type of combination is one in which both groups surrender their stock and receive in exchange stock of a new corporation. *The fact that one of the corporations usually issues its stock in exchange for that of the other does not alter the substance of the transaction.... [emphasis supplied]*

Implementing the Board's decision to reform pooling, Opinion 16 set forth a number of requirements that combinations would have to meet to qualify as poolings of interest. Perhaps because they resulted from compromise, heavily influenced by the antipoolers who were anxious to restrict poolings at any cost and mindful of the alleged abuses (on which there was not complete agreement), these criteria are not always as simple as might be expected:

1. The parties combining must be entirely independent companies merged through an exchange of voting common stock for voting common stock (in uniform proportion) in a single transaction with no strings or contingencies (future payments or stock issuances).
2. The equity interests of the companies must not have changed within two years prior to combination and no treasury shares can be acquired between initiation and completion of the combination (to prevent restructuring of capitalization and bail-outs by means of large treasury stock acquisitions).
3. No cash may be involved, and no plan may be entered into for reacquiring the shares or otherwise assuring a cash realization to the shareholders of the acquired company.
4. No significant assets may be sold within two years after the combination. (If so, the resultant gain or loss is treated as an extraordinary item, a condition

that remains in effect even though extraordinary items are now severely limited under APB Opinion No. 30.)

5. Combinations entered into shortly after year-end date cannot be reflected retroactively. This prevents a company from papering over its losses by pooling with a profitable company after its year-end.

In addition, disclosure requirements were strengthened in order to avoid any misleading implications.

Opinion 16 eliminated or modified certain requirements for qualifying as a pooling that the Board, or its predecessor, had previously supported in various pronouncements. One of these requirements concerned the relative size of the constituent companies. As proposed in ARB 48, this so-called size test would be based on a ratio of no more than 20 to 1. This proved a feeble restraint in the nineteen-fifties, and eroded quickly; the reformers were soon calling for limits of 3 to 1 and even 2 to 1. The same view was gaining ground in the United Kingdom. Nevertheless, after considerable and often acrimonious debate, the Board agreed—by a bare two-thirds majority—that the relative-size criterion simply could not support an accounting principle, and the size test was dropped. Even the then chief accountant of the SEC concurred with this view, although his opinion, expressed some time before Opinion 16, was his own and did not reflect the Commission's view.

The requirement for continuity of ownership interest was clarified. Previously, continuity of interest had been interpreted to mean that shareholders (of the acquired company) could not dispose of their new shares immediately. (Practice at that time had, however, allowed dispositions of about 25 percent.) But shares of stock are as fungible as grains of wheat, and a shareholder should be entitled to sell his shares (or buy shares) before or after a business combination. Such a transaction, moreover, does not alter the continued existence of ownership interest (one shareholder merely replaces another), unless the shares are redeemed by the company since it is the *shares* that represent the ownership interest rather than the *holders*. Then, too, there is no justification in accounting theory for restricting such sales on the acquired side of a combination and not on the acquiring side. Reflecting these considerations, Opinion 16 permitted the shareholders of both constituents to trade shares in the open market before and after the combination. However, the *companies* were prohibited from the following actions in the two-year period before pooling: (a) buying shares from shareholders so as to shrink capitalization in anticipation of a pooling, and (b) using company resources (or guarantees) in subsequent trades of the "selling" stockholders.

This position cleared the air considerably. In the past, it had been common practice to partially liquidate a company (for cash) prior to pooling to enable certain controlling shareholders to obtain cash, or for the acquiring company to limit its acquisition to that portion of the company it wished to continue operating by arranging for the acquired company to declare a liquidating dividend to the old shareholders beforehand.

Antipoolers often cite the purchase of treasury shares as a particularly objectionable pooling practice. They hold that since the shares can then be used by the company in poolings, such purchases are equivalent to using cash for a business combination, which calls for purchase accounting. This is irrelevant to poolers if the purchases are made on the open market or from persons unrelated to a prospective combination; a company is always entitled to shrink its capital, or trade its shares, if the trades do not involve constituents to a pooling or a proposed pooling. The antipoolers were persuaded to accept purchase of treasury shares when clearly undertaken not for pooling but for other purposes such as stock options and stock-purchase plans. Reference was made to a "systematic pattern" of treasury purchasing as a criterion for these purposes. This compromise was not satisfactory to either party, and the controversy has continued.

In an attempt to resolve the question, the SEC issued ASR No. 146, which went beyond Opinion 16 and proposed severe restrictions on the purchase of treasury shares to provide stock for stock options, purchase plans, or for the conversion of convertible preferreds and debt. In the present bear market, companies have considered their own stock an exceptional investment, and have made substantial treasury stock purchases, which they hope to use to redeem outstanding convertible stocks and bonds at a later date when prices recover. The SEC now contemplates placing severe limitations on treasury share purchases of this type. Under pressure from the profession, however, the SEC has suspended the effectiveness of ASR No. 146, pending further study.

This writer is forced to admit his total inability to perceive the relevance of treasury share purchases in the open market to a pooling that is not contemplated at the time. If a company can shrink its capitalization in the open market *after* a pooling (as is permitted), why can't it do it *before* a pooling, if the market is right. Unless the "selling" stockholders in a pooling receive cash for their shares, cash is not involved and the pooling concept is not violated. The continued refusal of antipoolers to accept this argument, principally because they see no difference between the use of cash or stock in a business combination, has burdened us with a compromise that has no basis in logic. Obviously, further reconsideration of this issue is needed.

THE PROBLEMS OF PURCHASE ACCOUNTING

Opinion 16 did away with the freedom to choose between the pooling method and the purchase method. In effect, the method is now dictated by the terms of the exchange. Any combination not meeting the strict criteria for a pooling must be recorded as a purchase. Of course, it is a simple matter to structure the combination as either, if both groups of shareholders are open-minded regarding the manner in which the merger or acquisition is to be effected. When stock is used in a purchase, however, and market values are high, the accounting consequences of the purchase method are awesome, because of the required restatement of asset values of the acquired company to market value and the consequent amortization of goodwill. Under these conditions, pencils are sharpened if the pooling method is not available. In the final analysis, there is every reason to believe that the new rule has made for sounder mergers.

When the purchase method is brought into play by the use of cash or debt, the costs (fair value) ascribed to the assets purchased are presumed to be readily measurable in the aggregate (the total purchase price), and there remains only the task of allocation. Most accountants agree that the excess of such aggregate value over the values ascribed to tangibles and specific intangibles is an indefinite intangible representing many factors—an excess commonly described as "goodwill." But when stock or assets instead of cash or debt are used in the purchase of an operating company, the determination of the purchase price or "cost" as used in accounting is not so easy. Opinion No. 16 says:

> The fair value of an asset received for stock issued may not be reliably determinable, or the fair value of an asset acquired in an exchange may be more reliably determinable than the fair value of a noncash asset given up. Restraints on measurement have led to the practical rule that assets acquired for other than cash, including shares of stock issued, should be stated at 'cost' when they are acquired and 'cost may be determined either by the fair value of the consideration given or by the fair value of the property acquired, whichever is the more clearly evident.'

In practical terms, this means that, since goodwill (in all its facets) is always one of the assets acquired in the purchase of an operating company, the purchased company cannot be specifically valued by reference to values of the assets. Its "purchase price" is therefore determined by the fair value of the securities issued, and, for this purpose, market quotations are generally used. This is the approach being followed today in most business combinations employing the purchase method.

It is no secret that share values may bear little or no relation to the underlying asset values at certain times. In an exchange of stock for stock of two publicly traded stocks, the exchange rates are usually predicated on the relative market quotes (plus a "sweetener"). Using the market values of the shares issued as a basis of valuation, the accounting result can thus be horrendous under the purchase method. If the aggregate market value of the shares issued is less than the book value of the acquired company, a condition common in bear markets, the assets will be written down, producing an increase in earnings (from lower depreciation) that would not reflect economic reality. If the market value of the shares is *greater* than the book value acquired, a condition associated with bull markets, the resultant lower earnings (from increased depreciation and amortization of goodwill) would be equally misleading. In view of the fact that a bear market seems to be the order of the day, this consideration has immediate relevance.

At present, the stocks of many companies are being traded at values far below book value. A good example is American Airlines, which, at December 31, 1972, had a book value of about $21 per share. In December 1973, it was trading in the neighborhood of $8 per share. An aggressive and enterprising company could offer its shares at an exchange value of $10-11 per share (assuming CAB permission is granted) and effect a pooling. Under the purchase method, the net assets of American Airlines would have to be written down approximately 50 percent (about $290 million), and future earnings would be raised by a consequent reduction of about $25 million in depreciation. Thus, a losing company might suddenly become a profitable company! This is unrealistic from either an accounting or an economic standpoint. It should be apparent that depressed market values have no relationship to the value of underlying assets; and the same is true of inflated market values.

To further demonstrate the fallacy of the purchase method, some examples of poolings that took place during the bull market of the late sixties are given in the Appendix. These examples, involving mergers between publicly traded companies, show how the mergers would have been reflected under the purchase method and what they would look like if current stock values were used. The examples were specially selected because it is believed that they conform to the more important pooling criteria contained in Opinion 16—this was rare in the sixties. Thus, they represent exchanges of voting common stock for voting common stock of publicly traded companies at exchange ratios reflecting the relative stock values at the time, plus a small sweetener to induce stockholders to accept the offer.

In each case, it is clear that if the purchase method had been applied and market quotations used as the measurement of underlying asset value, there would have been a need to inflate both tangible and intangible assets by amounts ranging from $12 to $151 million. There is every indication that it would have been impossible to avoid ascribing large portions of these excess amounts to goodwill and amortizing them over a 40-year period in accordance with Opinion 17. The combination of such amortization and the increased depreciation on written-up tangibles would have depressed their earnings severely. If the shares that were originally issued are now valued on the basis of November 30, 1973, stock prices, these same assets would require adjustments ranging from a *deficiency* of $22 million (actual write-down from original book values) to an excess of only $45 million. Of course, this shows what a bear market can do to stock values, but, more to the point, it shows that the use of the purchase method coupled with stock market values that can fluctuate severely can be distorting.

Referring specifically to the first illustration in the Appendix, one can visualize the effect of applying market values in the application of the purchase method. The merger between Litton Industries and Stouffer foods on March 31, 1967, was effected at a time when Litton common was selling at $104 per share, Stouffer was selling at $27 a share, and an exchange ratio of .312 of Litton for 1 of Stouffer was used. If purchase accounting had been applied, the net assets of Stouffer would have had to be written up by $66 million, or 218 percent. At November 30, 1973, Litton was selling for $9 per share (adjusted). While many subsequent factors may have a bearing on this depreciation in market value, it would appear that the Litton value in 1967 was inflated (as was Stouffer's) and that placing such a value on the Stouffer assets would have been unrealistic. When the market values of both constituents are inflated (as was the case in this illustration), pooling preserves some reasonableness in the accounting.

Admittedly there is one major flaw in this exercise: It is doubtful that the mergers would have taken place if purchase accounting had been mandatory. "As if" research in accounting is always subject to this sort of consideration, especially since it is well known that management is unwilling to enter into a transaction if the accounting result proves unrealistic. Unfortunately, the use of stock market values or market sales not involving the company itself is becoming more prevalent in accounting. It has occurred in certain instances where corporate ownership changed hands through substantial public offerings of stock. The SEC is considering the imposition of purchase accounting whenever 50 percent or more of the common stock of a company changes ownership, and recently the Commission asked the FASB for a determination on this question. In one case, where 100 percent ownership of a subsidiary was sold to the public, the SEC insisted on a revaluation of the net assets to conform with the proceeds of the offering.[5]

CONCLUSION—QUO VADIMUS

The pooling method of accounting for business combinations makes it possible to report the results of the constituent companies' operations subsequent to combination on the same historical basis as before it, so that meaningful comparisons may be drawn. The tendency to inject stock market values into accounting valuations of underlying assets should be suppressed for the present. Assuming that the old abuses of pooling have been substantially curtailed by the strict standards laid down in Opinion 16—and many believe this to be a fair assumption—it would seem that, for the time being, pooling will have a place in corporate accounting as long as the accounting profession continues to use the historical cost method as the universal basis for determination of earnings.

Purchase accounting, while it has the advantage of updating the tangible values for one constituent of the combination, has drawbacks that far outweigh this advantage. The most important of these are:

1. *The failure to provide informative comparisons with past results.* The fact that only one constituent of a business combination is "fair valued" hardly makes for a useful comparison with past results (except where the assets comprise a very small part of the total assets of the combined constituents). Furthermore, even if it *were* possible to fair value *both* constituents, it is extremely doubtful that an informative comparison would be feasible, because, thanks to the inadequacy of our present standards of measurement, the accountant's determination of fair value may not even approximate true value. If we cannot agree on the proper accounting for portfolios of marketable securities, oil discovery and development, and investment real estate, how can we agree on the value of a block of stock given in exchange for stock or for the package of assets, tangible and intangible, that the stock represents?

2. *The unrealistic approach to goodwill.* Assuming that meaningful values could be determined for business combinations, we must still face the problem

---

[5]Hughes Tool Company, prospectus dated December 1972.

of goodwill. Today, the concept of goodwill is applied to a wide variety of situations. Accountants can no longer indiscriminately label it with universal descriptions such as "the tendency of customers to continue" or "the purchase of earnings in excess of a return on tangible assets."

Properly speaking, goodwill in business combinations is the excess of a cash purchase price over the fair value of tangibles and intangibles that can be identified. This excess represents an intangible that is attributable to certain factors, some of which are very difficult to pin down. These factors tend to vary between businesses (especially between non-capital-intensive businesses). Consider the following situations: A one-product company manufacturing a gadget presently popular with the adolescent market; a popular soft-drink bottler with a (no-cost) perpetual franchise and established routes; a research organization with a record of scientific discoveries and successful development of scientific products; a multiproduct company engaged in the manufacture and distribution of name-brand foods; and a successful retail chain-store operation.

Is it not reasonable to suppose that in these different business operations, the excess will be attributable to different factors? Careful analysis will probably show that goodwill arising in different transactions possesses different attributes calling for different accounting.

While the varying aspects of goodwill have been recognized in a general way, the problem has not been given the consideration it deserves. This consideration may not be feasible until the objectives of accounting are defined. In the meantime, a number of approaches have been proposed. These vary considerably in validity, but even the best cannot be recommended without major reservations. The most important of these proposed approaches are: Immediate write-off to equity—an evasion rather than a solution; permanent capitalization until loss of value becomes observable; amortization to income—which creates a distortion of income produced by the goodwill; and the creation of separate asset and equity accounts reduced periodically on an arbitrary basis. This last recommendation is associated with the new chief accountant of the SEC, John C. Burton, who advanced it in a Financial Executives Institute study, which, by his admission, cannot be defended on the grounds of absolute truth or even revelation.[6]

3. *The prevalence of mixed bases that would result if purchase or new-entity accounting resting on fair value were permitted at this time*. This mixture of bases would be confusing and meaningless to the readers of financial statement. This writer does not oppose the concept of the ultimate use of fair value basis accounting or valuation bases that depart from present generally accepted accounting principles. But these issues should not be attacked piecemeal; what is needed is a significant research effort to determine what

---

[6]Burton, John C., *Accounting for Business Combinations* (1970), Financial Executives Research Foundation.

valuation bases can best serve the measurement bases of financial statements as a whole. Now that the Study Group on Accounting Objectives has issued its report, the subject needs full exposition, and agreement must be reached on this basic issue. Only then will it be worthwhile to reopen the difficult issues of poolings vs. purchases and goodwill.

A CONCLUDING PLEA

The action of the FASB in reopening consideration of basic combination principles is inappropriate at this time. We have not yet resolved the many burning issues inherent in historical cost accounting—marketable securities, oil and gas accounting, investment real estate, depreciation, inventory valuation, price level, etc. Many, if not most, of these subjects will not be resolved until the fundamental framework of accounting for the future is determined. Despite the precision with which reported results regularly appear, accounting has not yet matured to the point where we can assume that it is measuring performance adequately. To tinker with business combinations, which is perhaps the most sophisticated area of accounting, without resolving these basic issues, would be a repudiation of good sense.

Appendix: Comparison of Accounting for Business Combinations on Pooled Basis, Purchase Basis, and New-Entity Basis (Notes 1 and 2)

Issuing Company Other Combining Company Combination Valution Date	LITTON INDUSTRIES, INC. STOUFFER FOODS CORP. March 31, 1967		TELEDYNE, INC. RODNEY METALS, INC. December 1, 1967	
	No. of Common Shares Outstanding	Market Quotation Per Share	No. of Common Shares Outstanding	Market Quotation Per Share
At combination valuation date (Note 3):				
Issuing company	21,460,100	$ 104.25	8,470,000	$ 134.00
Other combining company	2,956,590	27.00	925,000	36.63
Shares to be issued in combination	922,456		290,000	
Exchange ratio	.312 for 1		.31351 for 1	
Issuing company's market quotation per common share at November 30, 1973 (Note 3)	$9.21		$24.78	
	In Dollars (000 omitted)	%	In Dollars (000 omitted)	%
Net assets acquired on pooled basis (Note 4):				
Issuing company	$ 402,500	93	$ 153,090	94
Other combining company	30,250	7	10,150	6
	$ 432,750	100	$ 163,240	100
If combination accounted for on a purchase basis, excess (deficiency) of cost over carrying basis of other combining company's net assets based on market quotations at (Note 3):				
Combination valuation date	$ 65,920	218	$ 28,710	283
November 30, 1973	(21,750)	(72)	(2,960)	(29)
Net change	($ 87,670)	(290)	($ 31,670)	(312)
If combination accounted for on a "new-entity" basis (Note 5), excess (deficiency) of cost over carrying basis of both constituents' net assets based on market quotations at (Note 3):				
Combination valuation date	$ 1,913,700	442	$1,011,190	619
November 30, 1973	(213,480)	(49)	54,400	33
	Aggregate (000 omitted)	Per Common Share	Aggregate (000 omitted)	Per Common Share
Net assets attributable to common equity (Note 6):				
Pooled basis	$ 302,050	$ 13.49	$ 143,510	$ 16.38
Based on market quotations at combination valuation date (Note 3):				
Purchase basis	367,970	16.44	172,220	19.66
New-entity basis	2,215,750	98.99	1,154,700	131.82

Appendix *(Continued)*: Comparison of Accounting for Business Combinations on Pooled Basis, Purchase Basis, and New-Entity Basis (Notes 1 and 2)

Issuing Company	TRANSAMERICA CORP.		AMFAC, INC.		FOREMOST-McKESSON, INC.	
Other Combining Company	TRANS INTERNATIONAL AIRLINES CORP.		FRED HARVEY		"21" BRANDS, INC.	
Combination Valution Date	January 17, 1968		March 15, 1968		September 2, 1969	
	No. of Common Shares Outstanding	Market Quotation Per Share	No. of Common Shares Outstanding	Market Quotation Per Share	No. of Common Shares Outstanding	Market Quotation Per Share
At combination valuation date (Note 3):						
Issuing company	23,643,663	$ 53.63	2,466,184	$ 39.62	11,033,412	$ 27.12
Other combining company	6,276,768	25.38	484,800	36.00	2,678,275	9.25
Shares to be issued in combination	3,138,384		533,280		1,004,353	
Exchange ratio	1 for 2		1.1 for 1		.375 for 1	
Issuing company's market quotation per common share at November 30, 1973 (Note 3)	$19.97		$28.88		$11.63	
	In Dollars (000 omitted)	%	In Dollars (000 omitted)	%	In Dollars (000 omitted)	%
Net assets acquired on pooled basis (Note 4):						
Issuing company	$ 565,470	97	$ 82,050	90	$ 190,990	94
Other combining company	17,250	3	9,170	10	13,120	6
	$ 582,720	100	$ 91,220	100	$ 204,110	100
If combination accounted for on a purchase basis, excess (deficiency) of cost over carrying basis of other combining company's net assets based on market quotations at (Note 3):						
Combination valuation date	$ 151,050	876	$ 11,960	130	$ 14,120	108
November 30, 1973	45,440	263	6,230	68	(1,440)	(11)
Net change	($ 105,610)	(613)	($ 5,730)	(62)	($ 15,560)	(119)
If combination accounted for on a "new-entity" basis (Note 5), excess (deficiency) of cost over carrying basis of both constituents' net assets based on market quotations at (Note 3):						
Combination valuation date	$ 910,920	156	$ 27,630	30	$ 207,820	102
November 30, 1973	9,680	2	(4,610)	(5)	21,240	10
	Aggregate (000 omitted)	Per Common Share	Aggregate (000 omitted)	Per Common Share	Aggregate (000 omitted)	Per Common Share
Net assets attributable to common equity (Note 6) – Pooled basis	$ 525,270	$ 19.61	$ 91,220	$ 30,41	$ 118,700	$ 9.86
Based on market quotations at combination valuation date (Note 3):						
Purchase basis	676,320	25.25	103,180	34.40	132,820	11.03
New-entity basis	1,436,190	53.63	118,850	39.62	326,520	27.12

Appendix Notes

1. Combinations represent (a) acquisitions involving common for common or common for net assets and business, and (b) constituents both publicly held.

2. Dollars approximated to the nearest ten-thousandths, except for per share amounts.

3. Market quotations represent (a) at combination valuation date, the closing sales price on the day preceding public announcement of the proposed combination or day approximating date of acquisition agreement, and (b) at November 30, 1973, the closing sales price adjusted for stock splits and stock dividends since date of combination.

4. Net assets acquired on pooled basis derived from pro forma financial data included in proxy statement relating to proposed combination.

5. "New-entity" basis, as used here, refers to use of market quote of *each* constituent to a combination as the basis for asset revaluation of the respective constituents (not a generally accepted accounting principle), following the logic that if one constituent is so valued so should the other be. It should not be confused with a new-entity approach sometimes advocated, in which both sides revalue (to current value) all tangible and specific intangible assets, and goodwill is ignored.

6. "Net assets attributable to common equity" gives effect to involuntary liquidation value of preferred stock where applicable.

THE SEARCH FOR STANDARDS: U.S. AND ABROAD†

Transcript of Conference Discussion Involving Philip L. Defliese, Stephen A. Zeff, and Others

REASONS FOR DISCONTINUING APB

[PAUL E.] FERTIG, Moderator: What were the conditions in accounting decision-making in the United States which made it imperative for many to decide to discontinue the Accounting Principles Board (APB) and to develop the Financial Accounting Standards Board (FASB) structure?

DEFLIESE: There was a rather booming stock market which precipitated many mergers. There was the emergence of the conglomerates with their emphasis on earnings per share and the use of alternative accounting principles to achieve operating results. These factors interacted so that accounting and the APB was felt to blame. The APB which was set up to narrow the alternatives in accounting was not doing its job either effectively or rapidly enough. Yet in some instances, certain segments of industry felt the APB was doing too effective a job. So you can make a case that the APB was doing too good a job, as well as for one that they weren't doing well enough. Finally, there was a great deal of agitation over the questions of pooling of interests and the earnings per share, which were not resolved satisfactorily for some.

Change was advocated on the ground that the APB was not independent (because it was made up of practitioners who were presumably serving the interests of their clients) and because it was not a full-time group (and therefore couldn't work at the job enough). The combination of these factors led to the conclusion by the Wheat Committee that there ought to be a change.

ZEFF: Certainly the tripping off mechanism for the setting up of the Wheat Committee were APB Opinions No. 16 and 17. There was a very fractious series of meetings about pooling that began with an exposure draft which disavowed entirely the pooling of interests, in accordance with the view of many academics and practitioners. Industry was wholly opposed to that solution. There was a tremendous amount of pressure brought to bear on the Board both from government and industry frequently arguing different positions. Some of the strongly held views of members of the Board caused it to have real difficulty in

---

†Reprinted with permission from *Accounting in Transition: Oral Histories of Recent U.S. Experience*, Thomas J. Burns, ed. (Columbus, OH: College of Administrative Science, The Ohio State University, 1974), pp. 19-43.

arriving at a majority position. The Board couldn't get 12 votes, which is the necessary two-thirds vote to pass anything—until the subject was eventually divided into two parts. The Board had actually reached a fragile 12-6 agreement on a unified position in June, but a month later, when one member of the majority decided he simply couldn't continue to hold to the view he had earlier supported, the Board was embarrassed. It again lacked a majority. This series of very difficult meetings was completely reported in the press. Moreover, the Financial Executives Institute (FEI) conducted a vociferous media campaign, sending its press releases all over the country. After the issuance of Opinions 16 and 17, which many found disappointing and probably nobody agreed with exactly, there was a widespread belief that the Board was ineffective. Whether or not it was true that the Board was actually ineffective, the appearance of these highly controversial opinions certainly encouraged this conclusion.

Also, there were those who were looking for an Opinion from the Board providing a broad framework of accounting principles. In October of the same year in which Opinions 16 and 17 were issued, they were disappointed when the Board opted for a Statement instead of an Opinion. In the middle of November, the leading partners of three big firms wrote to the President of the AICPA and in effect said that we need to have another look at the APB. This led to a conference chaired by Institute President Marshall Armstrong in Washington, D. C. in January, 1971. The three firms were Arthur Andersen, Arthur Young, and Touche Ross. All three letters were written within one week of each other. I haven't yet found out why they happened to be written in such close time proximity. The viewpoint of Bob Trueblood has subsequently been reported in *The New York Times*. He said in effect that his firm was reconsidering its support of the entire APB program and might in the future consider not accepting some pronouncements. This was a very strong statement and gave rise to alarm within the institute. These three letters were the immediate impetus for setting up the Wheat Committee. The Wheat Committee wasn't asked to say whether the APB had failed but only what could be done to improve the situation, so there was a presupposition that there existed certain defective elements in the APB structure.

But there are other points that could be mentioned. One was the lack of research support for the APB, as emphasized by many critics. After all, the idea behind the APB approach was to provide a research base for the kind of pronouncements which had been issued by the old Committee on Accounting Procedure (CAP). Yet the research base had been hardly more evident in the work of the APB than during the tenure of the CAP. Research was not being utilized. Not much research was even produced. The research that was produced didn't address the questions that the Board seemed to want to answer. The research frequently didn't utilize evidence that the Board would have found persuasive in reaching its conclusions. As the Board went along in years, its reliance on research became less and less.

Since research was an essential element in the APB concept, its absence or ineffectiveness in the APB operation caused many observers to become disenchanted. In particular, the absence of a guiding philosophy or a set of objectives and the issuance of APB Opinions 16 and 17 certainly provoked tremendous criticism. There was also a growing feeling that the FEI presented an insurmountable obstacle, unless this powerful body could be brought within the rule-making process.

DEFLIESE: What you have said is correct. You may have injected a bias concerning the opinions since only the passage of time will determine whether they were effective for the time, and whether some of the research that would be necessary in order to depart from the present historical cost concepts and the pooling concepts could have been accomplished in time to achieve any alternative rules. This subject is going to be reopened by the FASB. The research that may be necessary to achieve the reformulation of accounting concepts and objectives that are necessary as a prelude to getting anything done in that area will be found to be essentially the same for the FASB as it was for the APB. Without it, the FASB is not going to get much done.

I am restudying APB Opinion No. 16. I intend to recast some 68 mergers on a purchase basis rather than on a pooling basis. You can visualize what would have happened if the values under the purchasing concept would have been adopted a few years ago. Most of the share values today are probably a tenth of what they were then. If goodwill or any other intangibles would have been created on the basis of those values, our accounting today would be grossly inflated. So there is a real need for this type of research. We can't really begin to judge the results of those opinions until such research is done. Just as leaders can't always be judged until after they are gone, those opinions can't be judged yet.

THE BRITISH AND OTHER EXPERIENCE

ZEFF: Since 1970, the Accounting Standards Steering Committee (ASSC) in Great Britain has been issuing a series of exposure drafts—it is a body which represents all the major accountancy bodies in that country. In January, 1971, the ASSC issued an exposure draft No. 3 on Mergers and Acquisitions. This draft, which doesn't treat goodwill, is otherwise roughly identical to one of the earlier drafts of the APB on poolings, calling for a three-for-one size test. It is significant that this ASSC draft has still not been converted into an opinion or replaced by another draft, yet it is understood to be dead. Of the 11 that have been issued so far by the ASSC, the exposure draft on mergers and acquisitions has been the object of more criticism than any other draft. By the way, the ASSC did not use the terms "pooling of interest" and "purchase," but substituted "merger" and "acquisition" in order, one assumes, to get away from the stigmas attached to the former terms. But that device didn't seem to solve the problem. Britain simply didn't learn from the U.S. experience. They are discovering that the same fractiousness can occur there as has occurred here. Countries don't always learn from other countries.

FERTIG, Moderator: In the matter of accounting decision-making, how are other countries getting along compared to the United States?

ZEFF: That is a hard question because it is difficult to compare progress in different countries owing to the different institutional settings and social environments which one finds in those countries. For example, no country has such an open political system as we have. There is no country in the world that would have had anything like the Watergate hearings on television, and only few countries would have held hearings at all. The U.S. press is by far the most openly critical of institutions of any press in the world. Certainly the APB was subjected to greater scrutiny in the financial press than has any comparable body abroad.

This country is also the most litigious in the world. Many lawsuits on financial matters which are brought in the U.S. would in Britain be settled out of court through quiet negotiations in some club on London's Pall Mall Street.

In Canada, there has been less professional and public criticism of the rules-making process than in the U.S. even though Canada recently changed its process to follow rather closely the FASB approach. (Canada is much influenced by events in this country.) In Britain, there is not very much open criticism of rule-making. Matters tend to be settled behind the scenes. Nonetheless, when government wants something done, it makes its views known privately and can have tremendous impact on the final outcome. It was only as a result of some public criticism, rather rare in Britain, coupled with private representation by government, that the British changed their rule-making process in the latter part of 1969.

In studying different countries that have had some experience with establishing accounting standards, I find that the most significant single factor which forces the profession to change is public criticism in the financial press—particularly for a profession that conducts most of its affairs in confidential terms and is not accustomed to public scrutiny, let alone public criticism. Public criticism has done much to "move" the accounting profession. This is so in Canada, very much so in Great Britain and also in Australia. Anywhere there has been sustained public criticism, there has been change in the system. This has been perhaps the most pervasive factor that one can discern in the experience of countries which have engaged in rule-making.

The main reason that the CAP was replaced by the APB and the APB was replaced by the FASB was the criticism from within the profession. In the case of the demise of the APB, criticism from within the profession had been fueled by public criticism. This kind of open criticism within the profession does not exist in most other countries. So in this sense it is somewhat hard to draw conclusions on a comparative basis.

DEFLIESE: There is no doubt that the demise of the APB is largely attributable to the criticism within the profession rather than by the press itself. But obviously the one stimulated the other. This is an American characteristic and it is in contrast to what we find in other countries.

EFFECT OF LITIGATION

FERTIG, Moderator: Neither one of you mentioned anything about the lawsuits or concern of the profession over litigation having any bearing on this matter particularly.

DEFLIESE: If you will examine the lawsuits very carefully, you will find that very few hinge upon accounting principles. Most involve a failure in auditing or disclosure or other elements of our profession. That is why the influence of litigation does not bear on the subject of accounting principles.

MANAGEMENT AND OTHER PARTICIPATION

FERTIG, Moderator: Following up Steve Zeff's comment about the participation of management in the formulation of accounting standards, how do you feel about the adequacy of management participation under our new arrangement?

DEFLIESE: There is a limit on how much you can get management to participate in an exercise of this sort. We are fortunate to have at least one industry representative on the FASB. It would be difficult to get very many that would be qualified and would be willing to undertake that type of operation just as it is difficult to get many in the profession to disassociate themselves from firms to undertake the assignment. Also, everyone recognizes that management should participate but that it should be limited to a smaller segment because most standard-setting has to be within the professional area.

ZEFF: Aside from the chairman, the only member of the FASB who took a salary cut was the former financial executive. This suggests one reason why it may be difficult to persuade financial executives to take such a position. The important thing is that the FEI is part of this new operation by having two representatives serving as trustees of the Financial Accounting Foundation (FAF), and a former financial executive on the FASB. The severe test of the FASB will come when some of its pronouncements meet with general industry criticism. Such criticism may affect the continuing willingness of the FEI to be allied with this new program. Two or three former financial executives on the FASB would not necessarily implement this concept any more effectively than simply one. Yet in a number of ways the broader umbrella of the FASB is probably the most important innovative feature of this new approach. The APB, which was formally a part of the AICPA, counted as many as two financial executives among its members, but it did not have a direct link with the FEI. Certainly one man out of seven on the FASB is a larger percentage of representation of financial executives than one man (or even two men) out of eighteen for the APB.

Actually, I favored an economist on the FASB. One of the weaknesses of the APB was that it was unable or unwilling to anticipate the possible dislocations that some pronouncements would have caused in certain sectors of the economy. Possibly an economist on the APB might have sensitized the members to the possible implications of their opinions beyond those simply for investors. Life was very difficult for the APB because it did not appreciate the depth of government or industry interest when it was contemplating pronouncements.

DEFLIESE: It is unfortunate that the original membership of the APB, a 21-member Board which included three members of industry and three members of academia, was not continued. That membership provided a much broader representation. When that membership was reduced, the industry representation was considerably reduced. The results of the APB might have not been so different in the long run with more diffused membership. But the Board might have been better able to refute the charge that the Board was less effective because outside participation was inadequate.

ZEFF: David Norr, the only financial analyst member of the APB, testified before at the Wheat hearings that it is not essential that a financial analyst be represented on the APB. Of course, David Norr is not a typical financial analyst, as he is very knowledgeable about and interested in accounting.

DEFLIESE: Dave Norr is somewhat of a mixture of an accountant and a financial analyst. As a highly knowledgeable CPA, he is greatly influenced by his accounting background in his views on financial analysis; and even within his own fraternity, they recognize that influence. I would much prefer that there be a financial analyst among the seven.

FERTIG, Moderator: Given a seven-member FASB, would you agree that four accountants would be minimum?

DEFLIESE: Yes. At least four practitioners are needed to provide a reasonable cadre because that means there are going to be at least four different viewpoints.

FERTIG, Moderator: That isn't what I meant.

DEFLIESE: That may be a little facetious but I'm not so sure that that's not going to happen.

STATEMENTS STILL REPRESENTATIONS OF MANAGEMENT

FERTIG, Moderator: Is it fair to say that we have finally broken from the tradition that financial statements are the representations of the management?

DEFLIESE: No, I don't think we are ever going to depart from that responsibility which management has for financial representations. Auditors are closely associated with those representations. Periodically there is a need for a reexamination of the auditors' role in financial reporting but the prime responsibility will always be that of management.

ATTEMPTS TO CODIFY STANDARDS

FERTIG, Moderator: For at least 25 years or perhaps longer, there have been attempts to codify accounting standards in writing to try to develop a short statement of concepts that would suffice as a rule book and almost invariably these efforts have fallen into disrepute. Do we now have machinery which you think would be better able to tackle the job than we have ever had or are we still where we have always been? APB Statement No. 4 for example, or ARS No. 7, the inventory? Or the inputs to the Trueblood Committee such as the objectives of financial statements? What about generalized statements of accounting standards?

DEFLIESE: I don't consider APB Statement No. 4 or ARS No. 7 represent failure to codify. I won't accept that because no one has been able to point out to me where they are failures now. They have been criticized for failing to point a direction for the future; that is an invalid criticism because that was not their objective. They were attempting to codify that which is, not that which should be; the objectives group was asked to direct itself to the latter and they have come through, in rather broad terms. Is their report sufficient for us to proceed to what we should design for the future? I don't know, but certainly the exercises we have been through in APB Statement No. 4 and in ARS No. 7 have pointed up all the inconsistencies that we have in our present accounting conventions. These exercises confirmed that we are backing conventions rather than principles. If we look at the evolution of accounting from its bookkeeping origins, we have to acknowledge that our discipline "grew like Topsy." There is a group of concepts that have been put together for a purpose. The important question is: Are they or are they not achieving that purpose or to what extent do they need to be modified in order to achieve that purpose?

About economics, the important thing to recognize is that the last thing a bookkeeper has ever thought about is economics. Bookkeepers are interested in recording the facts of transactions and they are not interested in the economic implications of these facts. Accountants have had a difficult time developing themselves beyond those origins. If we are going to revamp accounting to more closely pattern the economic effects, we have to get some new ideas. Many writers including myself are attempting this. Much more of this needs to be done before we attempt to formulate a pattern that would make it possible for us to depart from our historical cost concept and still produce meaningful financial statements quickly. This is a difficult task and it needs much work.

UTILITY OF GENERAL OBJECTIVES STATEMENT

FERTIG, Moderator: Are generalized statements of objectives of financial statements useful in the promulgation of principles? Are the various firm statements on objectives prepared for the Trueblood Committee helpful in deciding on the difference between a good and a bad accounting principle?

ZEFF: We have had much difficulty in agreeing on particulars, partially because certain precepts and assumptions are simply not expressed. Until we put them in print and discuss what basis there is for one versus the other, we are not going to reach agreement, except by accident, on a number of the final specific questions. To the extent that a determination of the objectives of the financial statements is essential to arriving at agreement on these assumptions, we are not going to make much progress until we agree what we are doing, why we are doing it, and for whom.

For this reason, it is important that the FASB take seriously the Trueblood report and the need for accounting objectives. It is more likely that the FASB will go further with this project than did its predecessors, as it is more removed from the world of industry and accounting practice. It is easier to generalize and deal with abstract questions if each member doesn't have to think of every issue in terms of the problems that his client-partners are currently facing or may soon be facing. The FASB members will be better able to work at the level of generalization which is required when one talks about objectives.

Let me make one side point. There has been an interesting evolution in the way we have used the very important phrase, "generally accepted accounting principles." In the days when that term was first used, in the early and middle 1930's, it was the prevailing belief, as espoused by George O. May, that we were primarily interested in trying to find out what is "best practice." From that, it was suggested we may determine what meets business needs. Who was to say that there is a better practice than those which were actually used in business? It was clearly stated in the Accounting Research Bulletins of the CAP that their authority rested on their general acceptability. One former member of that committee said not too long ago that every Accounting Research Bulletin carried its own apology for intruding on anyone's contrary ideas, in effect providing that readers might take it or leave it depending upon how acceptable the argument was. But as a result of the very difficult agreement reached by AICPA Council in 1964 regarding the authority of APB Opinions, the APB was told that it shouldn't limit its role to codifying extant practice. Yet Accounting Research Study (ARS) No. 7 reflects the older idea that perhaps if we find out what is done we will have a better vision of what we want to do. This conclusion does not necessarily follow. It is one thing to do an empirical study of what is being done, as opposed to prescribing what should be done. The former was ostensibly the basis of ARS No. 7, which was also based on *Montgomery's Auditing* to some extent. But I am not sure we get any necessary vision out of where we ought to go from simply reviewing where we are now. Both functions are important, but we should not assume that a knowledge of what is accepted inevitably leads to an identification of what should be accepted. I suspect that there is a growing realization of this point of view in practitioner circles.

"ACCOUNTING POWER" OR POLITICS

FERTIG, Moderator: The opposing view is that the development of accounting principles are really the result of political forces. The SEC has a regulatory interest and corporate management has other interests in principles which would permit high flexibility and earnings per share that would be acceptable to management. Also accountants themselves constitute a pressure group. Accountants are interested in accounting principles that are capable of being audited. Financial analysts have their own interests. So the formulation of accounting principles is a matter of getting a resultant of a variety of political pressures. Are statements of accounting objectives really useful, if in fact the development of accounting principles is really a matter of what Bob Sterling calls political power or "accounting power," as he calls it?

DEFLIESE: There is a need to give cognizance to the views of all interested parties and this was the major complaint that the FEI and the financial analysts had against the APB. They felt that cognizance was not being given to their views on these matters. Yet in many cases the FEI and the financial analysts were at the extreme opposite ends of the spectrum in terms of position, with the APB somewhat around the middle. The academics were usually somewhere also at one extreme or the other depending on their particular views on the subject, which didn't always coincide. There was no doubt that someone had to referee this. The APB was trying to reconcile the varying views and the result was compromise, in many respects.

This is going to continue. The FASB is not going to suddenly have the light of God descend upon it so as to issue the fundamental truths of accounting that presumably exist someplace. Perhaps someone is going to have to make another trip to the mountain to get the stone tablets and come down in order to find where accounting should be. But these varying forces are going to have to come together and reach agreement. Until they do, we are not going to have anything that makes sense out of accounting. We may not come up with the best answer immediately; but as these things evolve, we may. The objectives, of course, are the framework which will serve as the basis for the refereeing. If we can agree on the objectives, and perhaps agreement could be reached on those more readily than on the specifics, then we can always try to fit the solutions within the framework of the objective.

FERTIG, Moderator: You don't see any conflict between the objectives and what you call refereeing them?

DEFLIESE: No.

ZEFF: The general objectives are necessary to help the Board crystallize its own thinking and perhaps to help the accounting profession and others understand why the Board has reached specific conclusions. The clarification of and an agreement on objectives will make it easier to gain consensus within the profession on certain solutions. The problem will still exist of having to sell specific conclusions to outside parties who may not be bound by the agreement within the profession on objectives. To a large degree, we have entered an era of accounting standards by negotiation. However, if you have a clearer conception of where you are heading and why you want to go there—than if you don't have any conception at all, which would seem to be the current case—it may be easier to sell solutions.

We have reached the point, as a couple of financial analysts wrote recently in *The New York Times*, where accounting has become too political. The SEC was involved at least once, if not twice, in the investment credit. The Treasury Department was involved at least twice, if not three times. Various industry groups have exerted their influence, directly to the APB, directly to the SEC, and even through Congress and the Administration.

We probably are going to have even more of it. I suspect that as soon as the FASB comes up with a recommendation that some individuals don't like, perhaps even some within the accounting profession, they will attempt to appeal their case directly to the SEC. Right now there is an environment of advocacy being generated. The accounting firms are gearing up to make presentations and submissions to the Board on their differing points of view. I am frankly fearful that once the major accounting firms commit themselves publicly to particular positions a pride of authorship will prevent them from acceding to contrary FASB conclusions, even if these conclusions were to be intellectually palatable. I am further afraid that some of them may even carry their arguments right to the SEC, effectively converting the SEC into an accounting court. This is a valid concern. If we develop too much of a climate of advocacy within the accounting profession, by making known our views in such uncompromising terms as we have seen recently, it is going to be very difficult for firms to say publicly that they have changed their position.

BRITISH PRINCIPLES BY NEGOTIATION

The most thoroughgoing example thus far of accounting principles by negotiation is going on right now in Great Britain. The British accounting profession has been trying, through the ASSC, to gain a broad base of acceptance for a pronouncement which essentially embodies the recommendations in APB Statement No. 3 on the general principles of inflation-adjusted accounting. Britain is a country where a ten percent rate of inflation has persisted for several years. In early 1971, the ASSC, which speaks for the profession subject to the final approval by the councils of five participating accountancy bodies, brought together the Department of Trade and Industry (DTI) (similar to, but more powerful than, our Department of Commerce), the Board of Inland Revenue (similar to our Internal Revenue Service), the Confederation of British Industry (CBI) (the spokesman for British Industry), the Stock Exchange, and the Bank of England, hoping to convince them of the merits of inflation-adjusted accounting. The ASSC had some difficulty in eliciting a response. It issued a discussion paper, similar to what the FASB intends to do even before taking a tentative position; it held a number of meetings with security analysts, as well as a series of private conferences with representatives of the DTI, Inland Revenue, the CBI, the Stock Exchange, and the central bank. Finally, in January, 1973, the ASSC felt bold enough to issue an actual exposure draft embodying its price-level recommendation. The ASSC exposure draft, in departing from its American prototype, provided for a *required* supplementary presentation of price-level financial statements in companies' annual reports to stockholders. In the same month, perhaps by pre-arrangement, an influential committee of the CBI largely endorsed the ASSC's proposed solution. (Eight months later, the CBI Council adopted this view as its own.) The Stock Exchange and Bank of England also signified a favorable reaction. Indeed, a few companies began to adopt the recommended accounting, anticipating that the draft would be enacted. The government hadn't said anything publicly up to this point. The ASSC had not been able to secure any kind of position from the government.

The exposure period was set at six months. During this time, the accounting profession was working behind the scenes, as only in England they can, with various groups that might be affected by such a pronouncement. A bare five days before the close of the six-month exposure period, on the last day of Parliament prior to the Summer recess, the Secretary of State for Trade and Industry announced that his department was going to inaugurate a major inquiry into the entire question of inflation-adjusted accounts. Since this was the last day of the Parliamentary session, no questions could be asked the next day. Nobody had any idea how extensive the study would be or whether the government was *a priori* favorably or unfavorably disposed toward the ASSC exposure draft. No one had any idea of the terms of reference of the study or of its likely membership. There was no opportunity to ask any questions, as Parliament had adjourned for the summer. The accounting profession was made to look foolish because it had taken steps which were suggestive of success in negotiating an acceptable solution with all affected parties. Now the government abruptly announced that it was going to look into the matter and possibly delay the final issuance of an opinion for perhaps as long as two years. The accounting profession didn't know what to do. The ASSC finally resolved to push ahead with a recommendation to the various councils of the participating accountancy bodies for a pronouncement along the lines of the exposure draft, owing to the government inquiry, the profession will probably delay the effective date of any pronouncement for two years. They will get an opinion out which will not take effect until the government has finally completed its inquiry. So here is a case where the accounting profession went to tremendous lengths, including behind-the-scenes meetings, a discussion paper and fact sheet, educational sessions, a six-month exposure draft, and other documents that were issued to educate all parties involved. They reached the threshold of finally taking the decisive step and were thwarted. This experience could as easily happen here, although probably with much more public posturing and bluster than in Great Britain.

DEFLIESE: Welcome to the club!

SAFEGUARD OF FASB FROM SPECIAL INTERESTS AND THE AICPA

[*THOMAS L.*] *STOBER, Moderator:* What safeguards exist to keep the FASB from being controlled in the formulation of accounting standards by special interest groups?

DEFLIESE: The safeguard is that the FASB members are under contract, highly paid, and completely disassociated from all prior interests; and thus they are presumably independent. This is the main safeguard.

FERTIG, Moderator: Do you think the FASB separation from the AICPA will be effective?

DEFLIESE: Since the Institute does dominate in the selection of the board members, the FASB does have an umbilical cord to some extent to the Institute. But that is not a sufficient association to in any way detract from the independent aspect of these board members once they are selected.

INTERDISCIPLINARY EFFORTS

STOBER, Moderator: What about the historical evolution of accounting principles bodies with respect to interdisciplinary efforts?

ZEFF: The question about the historical evolution of interdisciplinary efforts is a good one. But there hasn't been any on a world basis. Most countries look to what has happened in this country—they try to pattern the U.S. experience against their own environment—so really the principal experience is that of the U.S.A. It is interesting that less than four months after the Wheat Committee report was accepted by the AICPA Board of Directors and Council there was already on the agenda of the Board of Governors of the Canadian Institute of Chartered Accountants (CICA) a proposal for a Canadian Accounting Foundation drawn along the lines of the Wheat Report recommendations, except that only the chairman of the proposed standards committee would have been full-time. The latter was one of Philip Defliese's recommendations, namely that the chairman, at least, should be full-time.

It would take a great deal of time to trace the evolution of the process by which accounting principles are established in this country, but the experience in the United States has not been very long. It was not until 1959 that the AICPA finally had a senior technical committee making recommendations on accounting principles which had financial executives as members. The predecessor CAP was composed of only academics and practitioners. Such committees have always had members from the Big Eight firms; they have also had a small minority of academics as members.

Unfortunately, academics are often unable to do the required research to support their positions and seldom have practical experience with the particular problem areas facing the profession. Now, for the first time, there should be effective academic input. There have been excellent academic members but their participation has been impeded by not having the same kind of research and staff support within their universities as the partner-members, particularly those from the large firms, have had from within their firms. Each FASB member, however, enjoys the same research and staff support as his colleagues. In summary, except for the composition of the Wheat and Trueblood study groups, there hasn't yet been any significant interdisciplinary history in either this country or abroad.

INFLUENCE OF THE SEC

FERTIG, Moderator: Is the influence of the SEC on accounting principles over the years good or bad?

DEFLIESE: Well, it's good. It's had its good points and its bad points. Without the support of the SEC, there is no doubt, particularly in the latter stages of the APB, nothing would have been accomplished. From about 1965 on, the SEC largely supported the APB pronouncements once they saw the light of day. It was a great help and certainly it buttressed the 1964 council that made the APB pronouncements effective. On the other hand, in the early stages of the APB, the investment credit debacle with the SEC considerably diminished the influence of the APB as a result. This took a long time to overcome.

Unfortunately, too, in the latter stages, where the SEC would not go along with some of the things that the APB was doing, the APB attempting to avoid a confrontation compromised some of its views. Opinions Nos. 16 and 17 are good examples of the interaction of the views of the SEC, industry, and everybody else; the interaction resulted in the compromises reached in those opinions. For many years, the SEC was highly in favor of pooling. The SEC felt that the purchase method would create highly inflated balance sheets in many instances by recording intangibles which didn't exist. If in the poolings the share values had been used to apply the purchase method, the values generated were inflated in many cases. Since this was not good accounting, they espoused pooling to a large extent. But at the same time, the SEC insisted on amortization of goodwill. Therein lies the problem that the APB had in getting something out that was meaningful because many board members were not particularly disposed toward the concept that all goodwill had to be amortized over a maximum of forty years. So the SEC influence has been both good and bad. The FASB may find itself very much in the same posture as the APB did with the SEC.

STOBER, Moderator: Is the SEC working towards eliminating pooling of interest at the current time?

DEFLIESE: Well, there has been a change of personnel there and as a result, you get different views.

Usually the SEC view comes down to the view of the latest chief accountant for the SEC. At the moment, there is an anti-pooling feeling at the SEC because its present chief accountant is against pooling. Unfortunately, the general implications of extensive application of the purchase method have not been fully appreciated. Therefore, the research, particularly the applied research that is necessary in these instances, has to be done very carefully. Pooling is easy to criticize but when the purchase method is applied to what would otherwise be a pooling and that method is followed to its bitter end, sometimes you recognize that the pooling concept isn't that bad.

ZEFF: In the light of what Phil Defliese has said, it is ironic that the present chief accountant, prior to taking that post, was the author of a research study published by the Financial Executives Research Foundation which was intended to support the FEI position on poolings.

DEFLIESE: Yes, but don't overlook the author's personal views which were included in the study which were obviously anti-pooling; these views were very much to the chagrin of the FEI at the time.

ZEFF: If it were not for the SEC, the AICPA would not have started issuing pronouncements—at least not as early as 1939. This decision by the Institute was the result of an explicit message from the SEC to the accounting profession in 1937-38 that if the accounting profession did not provide the SEC with what it called substantial authoritative support, it would utilize its full statutory authority to decide what was proper accounting practice. This message was communicated to the AICPA, which gave the Committee on Accounting Procedure this new authority without any great enthusiasm. The AICPA has since warmed to the task.

I would agree with Phil Defliese that the SEC had both favorable and unfavorable influences on the development of financial reporting. For many years, the SEC had been a very reactionary body regarding any major innovation in accounting principle. The SEC has chiefly been preoccupied with closing loopholes and preventing abuses. It hasn't given constructive thought to fundamental changes in the nature and scope of accounting, including, for example, departures from traditional historical cost. In this latter regard, it has always been undeviatingly opposed to all departures from traditional historical cost.

To illustrate how negative the SEC has been, back in 1950 the CAP unanimously approved a bulletin authorizing quasi-reorganizations applied to instances where current values were higher than recorded values. But the issuance of this 1950 bulletin was delayed until the SEC chief accountant, who was present at the committee meeting, could find out from the SEC commission whether the SEC would go along with it. The message came back they would not, and the bulletin never was issued. So when one is criticizing the CAP for not going further in the 1950's, the object of the criticism might better be the SEC.

Sometimes the SEC experiences difficulty in assessing the political aspects of an issue, taking the form of pressure from the Treasury, from other regulatory agencies, or from the Congress which the SEC is not able to withstand.

Furthermore, continuity in the SEC's policies cannot always be assured, as its membership changes and the chief accountants change.

THE CANADIAN SITUATION

The situation in Canada is superior to that in the U.S. in that the Canadian profession is in a potentially stronger position to influence the future course of accounting practice than is the FASB in this country. (Of course, it must be conceded that the momentum and impetus for improvement in Canadian accounting practice would be measurably less in the absence of the U.S. example.) In December, 1972, for the first time, the ten provincial securities commissions[1] in Canada made it known through National Policy No. 27 that henceforth the generally accepted accounting principles which they accept in reports filed under the provincial securities acts will be those contained in the CICA Handbook, namely those that are recommended by the Canadian Institute's Accounting Research Committee (formerly the Accounting and Auditing Research Committee.) In this way, the CICA committee can ordinarily be assured in advance of the support of the ten provincial securities commissions. In the U.S., the FASB has the word of the SEC chief accountant that it is the intent of the SEC to support to every degree possible the pronouncements of the FASB. But this is not the assurance that the Canadian profession has been given by their provincial securities commissions. The FASB and the SEC must engage in a continuing dialogue in order that each can feel out the other on priorities and on the range within which compromise is feasible. This process is dangerously susceptible to mistaken and misunderstood signals, leading, perhaps, to an open rebuke.

DEFLIESE: We have seen in this country that when a pronouncement is ready to come out which may not be fully acceptable to the government or industry, there will be rumblings; this is likely to happen in Canada, too, once they reach one that may be so highly sensitive to provide the pressure groups to exert their influence. This is more readily to happen in Canada than Britain.

THE BRITISH SITUATION AND NATIONALISM

ZEFF: It is more likely to happen in Canada. The Canadians are a canny lot; they frequently don't embark on a project that is controversial until they see what has happened in the U.S.A. first. Once they begin to sense the strengths and weaknesses of the U.S. solution, as well as the forces tending toward and against change in Canada, they will start to turn the wheels. They watch the experience in the U.S.A. very closely, while the British clearly haven't done this. Of course, the industrial and financial makeup of British society is very unlike ours, whereas

---

[1]No national securities commission exists in Canada.

one finds considerable similarity in institutional environment between the U.S. and Canada.

DEFLIESE: The British have been operating their institutional arrangements with a combination of naivete and smugness. But now with their inflation pronouncement, they have one that is going to give them trouble.

ZEFF: It is sometimes hard to compare the U.S. and Canada or the U.S. and Mexico, because the economic influence of the U.S A. in both of those countries is enormous. As a result of subsidiaries of U.S. corporations operating in those countries, and the resulting work done for purposes of eventual consolidation with parent-company accounts by Canadian chartered accountants and Mexican *contadores publicos*, U.S. accounting practice has considerable impact. One can discern a flow of accounting recommendations from the U.S. to both Canada and Mexico. This is not to suggest, however, that the Canadian and Mexican professions slavishly follow U.S. precedent.

One result of the nationalistic drive that exists in any country is the belief that the country is in some sense distinctive or different so that on some accounting questions they will attempt to be different just to be different or to preserve a national identity. This national sensitivity permeates accounting no less than other subjects having international policy implications. For example, the Mexican Institute recently formally recommended the acceptance of direct costing for inventory accounting. The Mexicans are the first to have an accountancy body formally recommend direct costing for financial accounting purposes. The fact that the U.S. hadn't done so was more a source of pride than of concern to Mexico; here was an area where the Mexicans were able to affect accounting practice without simply following an American initiative.

DEFLIESE: They did it because they knew we wouldn't do it.

ZEFF: Yes, there is the natural desire to be different, but one also finds instances in which these countries are inescapably influenced by U.S. practice. Such an example is the Canadian oil and gas industry, which is effectively controlled in the U.S. In 1967 when both the Canadian Institute and the American Institute were considering pronouncements on income tax allocation, the APB, since it had a research study then in progress on extractive industries, decided to exclude, at least temporarily, the possible tax-allocation implications of intangible development costs. Since the Canadians had no such study in progress, they decided to cover intangible development costs in their pronouncement which, like APB Opinion No. 11, favored comprehensive tax allocation. But the oil and gas industry in Canada simply refused to comply; the companies were told, apparently by their home offices in the U.S.A., that "we're not subject to it and therefore you will not be subject to it." Canadian chartered accountants were told by the companies that they could issue all the qualified reports they liked, because there is no Canadian securities commission, unlike the case in the U.S.A., that insists upon unqualified reports in Canada. The large accounting firms in Canada got together and decided that it would be unwise to assure qualified reports for the entire industry. So they tacitly agreed that they wouldn't enforce the section of the Canadian pronouncement having to do with intangible development costs, as long as the companies gave full disclosure, until the Americans enact the same requirement.

DISCLOSURE—MEASUREMENT CONTROVERSY WITH SEC

FERTIG, Moderator: In recent years we have had some division of responsibility perhaps between the SEC and the accounting profession with regard to accounting principles, namely that the SEC would have primary responsibility for disclosure and the FASB would have primary responsibility for accounting measurement. Is there any possibility that you can see any redivision of duties there that would be along different lines?

DEFLIESE: I am afraid that I have difficulty disassociating disclosure from measurement. The two go hand-in-hand, and to say that the FASB will deal with measurement if the SEC will deal with disclosure just won't work. The FASB is going to have to deal with both.

ZEFF: Well, I don't have as much difficulty accepting this division of responsibility. The SEC chief accountant has said in a number of speeches recently that the SEC is attempting to enforce its primary preserve of authority, which is disclosure, while leaving measurement largely to the FASB. The SEC has traditionally acted unilaterally, sometimes not even consulting the accounting profession or, when it does, not necessarily accepting the profession's view, in matters of disclosure. After all, disclosure is what Regulation S-X is all about. There was a big battle in 1950 over whether all of the accounting series releases, some of which dealt with asset and income measurement, should be incorporated in that document. On the strength of forceful reorientations from the accounting profession to the contrary, the SEC implemented a compromise solution. Until now, no one has questioned the SEC primacy in questions of disclosure. It is due to the nature of the SEC's recent aggressiveness in this sphere that this dichotomy has come under attack. The companies act legislation found in British Commonwealth countries, such as Canada, the United Kingdom, New Zealand, and Australia, deals almost entirely with disclosure. The companies acts do not become involved with measurement questions.

The SEC chief accountant is historically correct when he says that the primary preserve of the SEC is disclosure. But he has recently gone into areas where the APB has had difficulty resolving measurement questions, apparently with the aim of utilizing disclosure as an interim solution. This is what has been different about his actions. In the past, disclosure issues haven't been as close to measurement issues as they have been, for example, in the area of leases.

DEFLIESE: The entire province of the SEC emanating from the 1933 and 1934 acts might be said to be disclosure. In other words everything they do is in the area of disclosure. They are really not attempting to regulate what companies can do and cannot do; the SEC is specifying what disclosures may be made in order to permit them to do what they want to do about issuing securities. But the disclosure of what is necessary to prepare a complete set of financial statements is still the province of the rule-making body of the accounting profession. Of course, there may be differences of opinion concerning the appropriate statements and the disclosure of those differences would be in the province of the SEC to specify. That has happened frequently where there might be an application of an accounting convention that is questioned by the SEC. The SEC has frequently satisfied itself by disclosure of a difference of opinion concerning the accounting treatment rather than the actual correction or changing of the financial statement. In that area, disclosure is their province and they could set up the determination of the degree of disclosure in order to satisfy their requirements. But basic disclosure is something you can't separate from the measurement process.

ZEFF: That lawsuit brings up the sensitivity of the profession to the recent aggressiveness of the SEC not only in disclosure but also in other areas, like SEC Accounting Release No. 146. This would not have occurred a few years ago.

It is also ironic that the suit, brought by Arthur Andersen & Co., was withdrawn when the SEC said it would hold hearings, because one of the firm's arguments was that the SEC had not held any hearings. But in 1965, the matter of dealing with the tax-allocation implications of using one method of recognizing the income from installment revenues for financial accounting purposes and another method for Federal income tax purposes was presented in a paragraph of an exposure draft, the one which eventually led to APB Opinion No. 6. It had to do with the "deferred tax credit" account, whether it should be a current or noncurrent liability where you have a current installment receivable. It finally was removed prior to issuance of the resulting opinion. Once the opinion was issued without the paragraph, Arthur Andersen & Co., which felt very strongly that the credit should be a current liability, as had been stated in the exposure draft, petitioned the SEC to take the action anyway. The SEC, in its Accounting Series Release No. 102, did so. Yet there were no public hearings, and Arthur Andersen & Co. did not complain that there were no public hearings on that particular matter. Moreover it was a matter of disclosure.

APPREHENSION ABOUT CASB

STOBER, Moderator: What about the CASB [Cost Accounting Standards Board]? Is it possibly going to be taking over some formulation of financial accounting standards?

DEFLIESE: That is a good question and I don't know the answer. There is a great deal of speculation going on at the moment as to the impact of the CASB's influence on the FASB. Particularly inasmuch as the CASB has legislative authority far and beyond that which is available to the FASB and everyone is watching that development with a great deal of apprehension.

ZEFF: The chief accountant of the SEC and the staff of the CASB are both aware of the possible overlapping of their two spheres of authority. There have been a number of consultations between the two bodies to the point where the CASB was considering a couple of issues which the SEC thought more properly fell within the purview of the FASB, and the CASB was going to consider and has now deferred at the request of the SEC, awaiting some kind of advice from the FASB. So there is an attempt between the two to avoid conflict, but the CASB has undoubted statutory authority. The CASB can recommend something, and if Congress doesn't overrule it within 60 days, which in itself would be quite an event, it becomes law. The SEC could not interfere, and there is nothing anybody can do about it. So the implications for financial accounting of the work of the CASB are there; it all depends upon the CASB's intentions and patience.

DEFLIESE: The basic authority of the CASB only relates to government contracts and the pricing and such, and need not directly affect financial reporting. Obviously, there will be an influence just as in the regulated utility area, where the actions of commissions do ultimately affect the accounting.

THE FUTURE OF THE FASB AND THE INVESTMENT CREDIT

STOBER, Moderator: Would you anticipate the same history for the FASB as the APB had?

ZEFF: In the sense that the APB finally concluded its history, the FASB will someday wind up its history. An interesting question is who would declare the FASB a failure. In the past it has been committees or officers of the AICPA. In the case of the FASB, the role of the AICPA is more remote. What factors might eventually lead to failure of the FASB? Is it simply that there would be bad research? Would it result from badly drafted and conceived pronouncements? If more than a few FASB pronouncements were opposed and overturned by the SEC? Will there be continual pressure on the FASB from Congress as a result of the initiatives of financial executives? Supposedly a declaration of failure would be up to the Financial Accounting Foundation (FAF). In effect, the FAF would have to declare itself out of business unless it were to replace the FASB with something else. The FASB is its only reason for existence, and if the FASB is not to be replaced, the trustees of the FAF must conclude that there is no longer any need for the FAF to continue in being. That has been a difficult decision for institutions to make. It will have to be fairly obvious that the FASB has failed or that the SEC consistently refuses to implement its recommendations or that the recommendations are palpably bad. I don't quite know who would have the courage to make that kind of statement. Also, it is not inevitable that, should the FASB be generally conceded to be a failure, that this outcome will be followed by governmental regulations, as some have suggested. This could, of course, be; it could have been true after the APB. It depends very much upon what the cause of the failure was, who is the SEC Chairman, and who is the SEC Chief Accountant.

FERTIG, Moderator: Do you think the FASB will be any more successful than the APB in responding to criticisms?

DEFLIESE: It depends upon which criticism you are talking about.

FERTIG, Moderator: With regard to narrowing financial statement alternatives.

DEFLIESE: It is bound to do that. It will be successful because it is going to have to come out and narrow some alternatives. It will do that. Whether it will do a good job of it or not depends on your own viewpoint. There are going to be differing views on just that point and as Steve Zeff has pointed out, the crucial test will be acceptance on the part of the SEC. If the SEC accepts what comes out, the FASB will be successful in narrowing the alternatives. It takes two to tango in this exercise. As the past has indicated, you can't tell which one is going to be the culprit and whether the FASB will be the culprit or the SEC. Also, Congress is another element. Industry need not be injected because industry will be in the influencing area, whether it is going to influence the SEC or Congress or the FASB.

I don't feel as pessimistic as some may feel about the FASB. The FASB will be as successful as the APB in doing some of its job. I believe the APB was successful in some areas although I may have a biased view along those lines. But the FASB will be in many respects even more successful. But it will have the same troubles in accomplishing its objectives as the APB had. They are not going to be able to solve them any more readily than the APB did. I just hope they survive their troubles.

ZEFF: While the FEI is formally allied with this new program, there is nothing that prevents individual companies or industries from stoutly disagreeing with anything the FASB wants to do. In this regard, there is nothing inherent in the FASB structure that makes the FASB any more likely to be successful than the APB in negotiating with its critics. They still have the old political pressures to deal with. They must try to resolve problems in the oil and gas industry with respect to full costing with the same pressures that fell upon the APB. If the FASB tries to move ahead in marketable securities, it will encounter the same resistance as did the APB. If it tries to urge the capitalization of leases on a larger scale by lessees, it may face another letter-writing campaign to Congress which was waged so successfully two years ago.

DEFLIESE: How about the Investment Credit?

ZEFF: The Investment Credit is unique. It came up three times, not twice. It first arose in 1962, when the behind-the-scenes efforts of a number of Federal agencies, including the Treasury, obliged the SEC to reflect views of those who were trying to persuade it rather than the genuine opinion of the chief accountant and perhaps even the view of the commission itself. It came up again in 1967 as part of the exposure draft that led to Opinion No. 11. It didn't appear in the final opinion because Stanley Surrey of the Treasury Department made known his views publicly that he was opposed to the allocation of the investment credit following which the SEC advised the APB it could no longer provide support. In 1971, it was enshrined in legislation. I have suggested that the next time this comes up, as I suspect it will, it will be made an amendment to the Constitution! This is the only step higher than Congressional legislation, for each time the matter has arisen it has escalated from before.

NEED FOR PATIENCE AND STUDY OF RECORD

DEFLIESE: In summary, I make a plea for patience As exhibited in this discussion, there should be recognition that solutions to our accounting problems are not going to come readily, or out of a hopper. These problems require a great deal of further research, a great deal of thought, and a great deal of exposure. All of this is going to take time.

Therefore, the FASB cannot immediately grind out pronouncement after pronouncement which can serve as a panacea for our problems. It will not happen and it should not happen because the FASB should take the time necessary to do the job. That should be recognized and everyone should not be impatient. The major problems of accounting and the auditing process exist in the judgmental selection of the accounting principles that are appropriate. Here the profession is going to have to take a greater responsibility than it has taken in the past concerning appropriate accounting by virtue of exercising the profession's auditing power.

ZEFF: One of the sloppiest portions of our accounting literature is that which comments on how accounting principles are established. There have been altogether too many speeches and articles, and perhaps even monographs and books, containing ostensibly empirical statements which have not been adequately researched, and recollections that have not been verified and checked against the record, which *is* available. As a result, inferences have been drawn and conclusions have been reached which would not emerge from a fair reading of the available evidence. Too many individuals believe that in this area one can simply stand up and say whatever he thinks, regardless of what has occurred or what appears in the record. In discussions of the development of accounting principles, a subject which is so important to the profession, while content is important, process is no less important, and at times even more important than content.

Occasionally I am astonished when I read articles that have been written as often by academics as by practitioners, financial executives, or security analysts to find statements that are palpably untrue when compared to the historical record. In writing about APB opinions, some writers indulge themselves by referring in vague terms to arguments for or against an abandoned proposition, without specifying who advanced such arguments, and when during the course of evolution of the opinion. I frequently can find no evidence whatever that such arguments were made. These writers are simply setting up "straw men" in order to propagandize their own argument. Until we compile a record, we are in a vulnerable position to assess the achievements of either the CAP or the APB. We haven't yet agreed on the criteria for evaluating these organizations. We should eschew that kind of contrived argument, where a certain conclusion is wanted and any available means is used to dignify that result. In recent years, we have become more careful of logical analysis and empirical validity both in our literature and in our discussion of most accounting topics; we should be more willing now to discipline ourselves when commenting on the process by which accounting principles are developed.

THE ACCOUNTANT'S ROLE IN THE NEW WORLD ORDER†

by

Philip L. Defliese

THE accountant of today must lift his sights. While ours is a comparatively new profession, too many accountants regard themselves as mere 'bean counters.' It is also my impression that this reflects the attitudes of young people on the brink of choosing careers.

Curiously, though, young persons having the vision to see beyond the concept of 'bean counters' are the ones entering our profession. In fact, one survey published in the magazine, *Psychology Today* indicated that as a group, accountants lead all other professionals in terms of IQ measurements.

Intelligence, though important, is not as important to our profession as vision. It is the ability not only to perceive the workings of the company that lives and breathes behind the cold figures of financial statements; it is the vision that takes into account the rapid march of events—social, political, and economic. It is the vision of seeing business and economic trends emerging so that we can not only report what is happening, but act as sophisticated financial advisers to help businessmen everywhere bring progress and order to what is today a chaotic and troubled market place.

CAPITAL CRISIS

Right now, we must come to grips with the fact that the world appears headed for a period of continued uncertainty and instability. The question of how the economic pie is to be divided and enlarged will touch all of our lives. Just the other day the developing nations won concessions and commitments from the developed countries. These, essentially, called for capital infusions to help them lift themselves to develop their economics and their level of living for the masses.

But as we know from painful experience, it is not only the developing nations that are seeking the capital to develop. The capital crisis affects us all: the big multinational corporation, the conglomerate, and the small business. It crosses borders and ideological lines. The problems of the American aerospace industry, for instance, in raising money are not particularly different from major industries in Japan.

---

†The substance of an address at a luncheon meeting of the London Chartered Accountants on October 2, 1975. *The Accountant*, October 9, 1975, pp. 413-414. Reprinted with permission from Lafferty Publications. Also reprinted with minor modification in *The Journal of Accountancy*, December 1975, pp. 71-73.

In its edition of September 22nd, *Business Week* noted that the US business establishment needs to raise $4.5 trillion in new capital in the next 10 years or face a ruinous money shortage that could make the nation's economy—and I quote—'a miserable place for anyone.' The article went on to predict that unless this unprecedented sum was raised, the nation could be plunged into 'social unrest and class conflict.' It saw, too, the gobbling up of small businesses by large companies. It saw high unemployment as a chronic condition. It saw chronic shortages of goods and bottlenecks. It saw a business cycle whose attempts at recovery would sputter out.

But no less important was the recognition that in Eastern Europe, state bankers and governments are stepping up their borrowing from the West. The fact is that the Soviet Union has raised $350 million from western banks, and hopes to borrow another $200 million by the end of this year. When I was in Russia, last year, a Soviet leader stated to Western businessmen that their greatest need was capital.

WASTEFUL ARMS RACE

Now, for the fist time, the terrible consequences of the capital shortage is coming home to all nations, regardless of ideology. With growing populations and industries to nurture, the capital must somehow be created, and it can only be created through profits and saving. Or capital being misspent, and I mean misspent, could be diverted from unproductive enterprises to pursuits that would, in turn, generate new wealth for investors. I refer, of course, to the armaments race.

Now that thc United States and the Soviet Union can jointly pioneer the heavens they should surely be able to make a new concerted effort to slash arms budgets on earth. The cost of stockpiling and maintaining nuclear arms and largely unproductive armies cannot be tolerated in modern times.

I am not a politician and have no such aspirations. But as a businessman who has traveled widely I find the prevailing sentiment of other businessmen to be at one with my own thoughts. We need political stability. We need world order. We need conditions in which business can flourish. We need to see the politicians dampen inflammatory rhetoric and work toward lessening thc arms burden. We need to point out that the burden of international armaments on a grand scale—the cost of Russian, American, British, French, and other weaponry—could be substantially lifted, and the funds diverted into the proper work of providing capital which in turn will result in the feeding, housing, clothing, and educating of future generations.

SPEEDING THE CHANGE

But first the world needs to be made safe for business; and the businessman, the accountant—the humble 'bean counter' if you will—can have an important role in speeding the change from a climate of fear and suspicion to an era of progress. Accountants, increasingly, are crossing borders and following the path of thc international and multinational corporations as they create goods and services on a wide scale.

The rapid international expansion of international trade since the termination of the Second World War—and it is accelerating as never before—means that nations are drawing closer together. Yet, despite this, the critical factor of capital investment remains the outstanding problem.

As you are well aware, an international movement is under way by accountants of leading nations to set up internationally acceptable standards for our profession. This body—the International Accounting Standards Committee—seeks to reconcile the differences in accounting methods that are, literally, impeding the free flow of international capital and holding back investment, trade and progress.

IMPORTANT GOAL

I want to recall, for just a moment, the words of Sir Henry Benson, the first Chairman of IASC, who said, "The most important goal is to set down international standards that will be applied world-wide and, above all, enforced if necessary by disciplinary proceedings by the professional bodies concerned."

Sir Henry was correct when he further expressed the view that the public, and particularly the non-conservative political parties and trade unions, regard all financial statements with some degree of suspicion; that people of one nation tend to be critical of accounting records produced in other countries. Until the public comes to trust the accounting statements presented to it, progress will be slower than necessary in a time when urgency is the order of the day.

For example, since 1948, consolidated accounts have been compulsory in Great Britain, and British accountants have long held that they cannot present a fair picture of corporate developments without them. In the US, the Securities and Exchange Commission has generally required consolidated statements since the late thirties. Even so, complete consolidation of all subsidiaries is not yet absolute in the US and UK. But other nations do not find consolidated accounts necessary for presentations to stockholders, or as a condition of listing on the local Stock Exchange.

Many of the technical tasks taken on by the IASC will sound dull and routine to the general public. Most people will not comprehend their urgency whatsoever. But the issues of stock valuation, depreciation of fixed assets, the translation of foreign accounts, the very need for the disclosure of accounting policies, the issue of consolidated financial statements and inflation accounting, are absolutely vital to business, and their swift resolution may be a pre-requisite to the job of stabilizing world trade and the free flow of capital.

Instant communication and almost instant transportation have shrunk the globe. World business on a massive scale with the gradual elimination of trade barriers and the free market of current exchange is the new frontier unfolding before us. All nations have common needs as their peoples have common hopes and common dreams. As for accountants, the time has come for us to quit counting beans. We have work to do.

It is mind-boggling to consider that two countries with as extremely diverse political, economic and social ideologies as the USA and Russia can agree upon and coordinate two diverse space technologies so as to link vehicles in outer space with split-second precision, while we accountants cannot agree whether LIFO or FIFO is the appropriate method of costing sales.

TRUE AND FAIR?

Certainly within the UK and the US there is finally a widespread awareness that historical cost financial statements do not fairly present financial position and results of operations. In the US we have not been so bold as to call our accounts 'true and fair'; instead we use 'present fairly in conformity with generally accepted accounting principles.'

In the US we have had our Wheat Commission Report, which led to the formation of the Financial Accounting Standards Board bringing industry into the rule-making process—a salutary development. Then we had the Trueblood Report giving us basic objectives which will now be elaborated upon by the FASB in December. CPP was recommended by the Accounting Principles Board in 1969, and in 1974 by the FASB; the outcome will be available by December. Your SSAP [Statement of Standard Accounting Practice] 7 precipitated Sandilands, and I suspect it and Trueblood precipitated *The Corporate Report.* Australia has two exposure drafts—CPP and current value; take your choice! The diversity of these proposals demonstrates the fact that we are far from achieving agreement on so urgent an issue.

The fact remains we have not agreed on basic concepts of accounting: we have not agreed on whether profit determination should provide for cost of capital production and capital maintenance, and the other aspects of inflation. We have not realized that a distinction must be made between propriety accounting and corporate accounting.

We must move quickly before others move for us. The broad scale indexing in Brazil which has turned around its capital drain, was put in by the Government—not the accountants. In the US the House of Representatives of Congress has just passed an energy Bill which requires the SEC to establish uniform accounting standards for oil and gas companies and at the request of a Congressman requires the Comptroller-General of the United States to audit any and all oil companies and submit findings to Congress.

The plain fact is that Representative Moss who sponsored the amendment to the Bill discovered that diverse methods were used and wanted to do something now. The SEC has also recently proposed that replacement cost accounting results be disclosed in footnote. If we move rapidly now we may yet save the day, and hopefully, since as accountants we have more expertise in this area than many other professions, we will lead government rather than be led.

In the US unfortunately only the FASB can set accounting standards, and so an international standard, promulgated by IASC, must suffer through any 'due process' procedures. So it is in many other countries.

Nevertheless, our objectives are the same, and I predict that we will have world uniform accounting standards long before we eliminate warfare, and perhaps the achievement of the former will help bring about achievement of the latter. Meanwhile, let us accelerate our activities in this sphere.

THE CREDIBILITY PROBLEM

But uniform accounting standards alone will not solve the credibility problem. Users of financial statements must also have confidence in the reliability of the figures. Although agreement in the accounting area is a necessary first step, unless there is universal understanding of the meaning of an audited statement, our capital markets will not be justified in ascribing to those statements the credibility they deserve. Some of the multinational accountancy firms have established uniform approaches to auditing, although much progress has been made and in this respect the differences are probably not significant. Nevertheless, substantial differences in auditing standards do exist among many countries, all these can be resolved more quickly by the establishment of an International Auditing Standards Committee along the same lines as IASC.

One further development of international proportion requires note. It is expected that in Munich in 1977 there will finally be formed an International Federation of Accountants, perhaps the first world-wide professional organization of any type. It will be a federation of accounting bodies of all countries and will include industry groups as well as professional groups.

Accordingly, let us understand our own importance and let us draw into our circle the brightest and most visionary of our youth to join us in the shaping of a better world order.

While much of our work may always remain tedious and detailed, let us lift our eyes and sights to the grand design of what we can do in the business community that is emerging around the world, and what we can do for world prosperity through better economic understanding, upon which the future peace of mankind will ultimately depend.

ACCOUNTING FOR LEASES

SHOULD ACCOUNTANTS CAPITALIZE LEASES?
The Economic Case Against It at Present†

by

Philip L. Defliese

PREFACE

THE question of capitalization of leases by lessees has long been a smoldering issue for the accounting profession. Recently the debate intensified sharply with the following developments:

- The new Financial Accounting Standards Board (FASB) has designated "accounting for leases by lessees and lessors" as one of the seven items given priority on its initial technical agenda.
- The Civil Aeronautics Board (CAB) announced that it is considering a rule-making proposal[1] for airlines under its jurisdiction by which rental payments under certain long-term leases would have to be accounted for as depreciation and interest. This feature is significant because interest is not an allowable cost for rate-making purposes, and it is not clear whether the "deferred charges" resulting from the capitalization would be added to the rate base for determining allowable return on investment. Other regulatory agencies have occasionally informally expressed similar intentions.
- The Securities and Exchange Commission (SEC) exposed for comment proposed rule-making, amending Regulation S-X,[2] that would require all registrants to disclose, among other matters concerning leases, the alternative net income resulting from the imputation of straight-line depreciation and interest in lieu of rent "as if" financing leases (as defined) were capitalized by lessees. Such

---

†An elaboration of a paper presented at Accounting Colloquium III at the University of Kansas in May 1973. (New York: Coopers & Lybrand, 1973), 24 pages. Reprinted with permission of PricewaterhouseCoopers LLP. Portions also published under the title, "Accounting for Leases: A Broader Perspective," in *Financial Executive*, July 1974, pp. 14-23; and under the title "The Economic Case Against Capitalization of Leases—A New Look at Facility Accounting," in *Institutional Issues in Public Accounting*, Chapter 10, Robert R. Sterling, ed. (Lawrence, KS: Scholars Book Co., 1974), pp. 345-361, which also contains related commentary by Ross M. Skinner, pp. 362-369, and the transcript of a conference discussion involving Defliese, Skinner and others, pp. 370-373.

[1]Letter of W. Fletcher Lutz, Director, Bureau of Accounts and Statistics, CAB, dated April 20, 1973.

[2]Release 5401, Securities Act of 1933, June 6, 1973.

disclosure could imply that the alternative net income is more appropriate than the reported net income or that there is at least an appropriate alternative determination of net income.

This paper makes the case for delay. It is this author's opinion that the actions of the CAB and the SEC are precipitate. Before many leases are treated as the equivalent of ownership, full consideration must be given to all related accounting matters, a time-consuming exercise, perhaps, but one for which there is no substitute. The FASB project is expected to be an in-depth study, and the results of that study should not be prejudged. This paper will be submitted to the FASB, the CAB and the SEC in partial response to requests for comments.

THE ISSUE IS JOINED

One of the most controversial of the many unresolved issues in accounting today is that of capitalization of leases. For many reasons, leasing has become a popular alternative to the purchasing of productive facilities, and good managements go through a "lease or buy" exercise before committing themselves to capital replacement or expansion programs. From all indications, it appears that the trend toward leasing will continue.

The considerations that enter into the "lease or buy" decision may be classified as economic (operational and financial), legal and accounting. Certainly, the economic reasons should dominate, and the legal and accounting reasons should he secondary. Because accounting as a communicative art is still so far removed from a reflection of true economic facts, care must he taken to avoid radical changes in lease accounting (for lessees) that may create distortions—the tail should not wag the dog.

Nevertheless, the pressures for such changes are building up. At the time the FASB was proposed as the successor to the Accounting Principles Board (APB), the latter was conducting a full-scale inquiry into lease accounting with a view to making vital changes. When the succession became a reality, the FASB inherited the project and has recently accorded it priority. Meanwhile, the SEC has proposed new disclosure requirements, broader even than the broadened requirements set forth in the recently adopted APB Opinion on this subject.[3] In effect, the SEC proposal calls for the disclosure of (a) the discounted present value of the lease commitments and (b) alternative net income amounts based on the imputed capitalization of financing leases (as defined in the proposal). This proposal represents a prejudgment of the FASB project, an action which the APB judiciously avoided. The confusion that will result from the presentation of alternative net income figures to investors—before either the FASB or SEC decides the major question of lease capitalization—can scarcely be imagined. Disclosures are not always meaningful, and sometimes they can be misleading—a fact well known to all accountants. The time to stand back and view with

---

[3]APB Opinion No. 31, *Disclosure of Lease Commitments of Lessees*, June 1973.

perspective the consequences of such precipitous action is now—before the damage is done.

It is axiomatic that all leases are a means of obtaining the use of business facilities. Some are tantamount to financing the purchase of a facility, but many are not. When a lease results in a lessee's ownership of an equity interest in the property, the APB requires that it be reflected as a purchase. This stand, expressed in its Opinion No. 5, *Reporting of Leases in Financial Statements of Lessees* (1964), failed to please many who considered it far short of the mark. The APB has hesitated to go beyond this point, although, in Opinion No. 7, *Reporting of Leases in Financial Statements of Lessors* (1966), the Board permitted lessors to use the "financing" method of accounting for many leases that lessees were not necessarily required to capitalize. At that time, the Board recognized how strongly some felt about this inconsistency and promised a reconciliation of the conflicting views; because of the complexity of the subject and the priority of other issues, the promise was never fulfilled. In the meantime, major facility leases of the "off-balance-sheet financing" type have proliferated, and the controversy rages.

CONFLICTING THEORIES

Many leases that do not meet the APB's requirement for capitalization may still be classified as "financing" (as opposed to "operating") leases because they provide for essentially full recovery of the lessor's cost (plus interest) through the lease payments and recovery of an estimated fair value of the residual. Consequently, it is possible to structure a lease in such a way that the lessee will not have to capitalize the property under Opinion No. 5, while the lessor may treat it as financing under Opinion No. 7. In fact, this is the prevalent practice today. In particular, companies whose tax posture prevents their obtaining the full tax benefits of accelerated depreciation and the investment tax credit associated with ownership, find it cheaper to lease, because lessors who can utilize these benefits are able to pass them on to the lessees in the form of reduced financing costs.

The inconsistency between Opinions 5 and 7 has irked many accountants for years; it certainly gives the appearance of letting something slip through the crack—hence, the term "off-balance-sheet financing." The solution seems relatively simple until one (a) attempts to define precisely the characteristics that call for capitalization and (b) views the result of capitalization as it affects the income statement, in the light of all the economic facts surrounding the use of business facilities.

Extremists have a ready answer to the first problem—capitalize *all* leases. They see no need to distinguish between circumstances and characteristics, reasoning that a lease provides the same utility as ownership. They ignore the factor of risks and rewards of ownership or relegate it to the element of estimation inherent in the cost allocation process. Among other accountants, there is little agreement as to how to distinguish the "financing" leases that should he capitalized. The SEC proposal uses a purely arbitrary approach, suggesting imputed capitalization of leases whose terms (including renewal options) cover 75 percent of the "economic" life of the property.

Many who advocate lease capitalization—whether entirely or on a selective basis—seem to agree on the effect of capitalization on the income statement. They would replace rental expense with depreciation (usually straight-line) and interest on debt, and thus create higher charges in the earlier years—an effect quite different from the usual level rental payment.

"Off-balance-sheet financing" has been growing rapidly since World War II; prior to that time, the term was rarely used. The motivation was to minimize debt on the balance sheet, thereby retaining a debt/equity ratio that would facilitate future borrowing and avoid violation of existing or future indenture restrictions against additional debt. This is still a prime consideration.

It is interesting to note that a recently published research study sponsored by the Financial Executives Institute[4] devoted 129 pages to the balance sheet question and only *one* page to the income statement. Obviously, the balance sheet question still predominates in the thinking on this subject. However, the current SEC proposal providing for alternative net income figures will undoubtedly focus more attention on the income statement effect. With the widening of lease commitment disclosure requirements and the growth in creditor and investor sophistication, the balance-sheet motive will probably become less important.

The income statement question. Today most "off-balance-sheet financing" is designed to level the cost of a facility over its useful life. This makes it possible to avoid the impact of the combination of straight-line depreciation and higher interest (on a large, gradually declining debt) in the earlier years. The theory holds that (all other things being equal) if a facility's ability to generate revenues in its earlier years is no greater than its ability in later years, the leveling makes possible a better matching of costs and revenues. To put it another way, without such leveling, the determination of periodic income (the net income results over the years) would be distorted.

Proponents of capitalization of leases by lessees frequently argue that such leveling overstates income in the early years because of the omission of the heavier charges that result when interest and depreciation are substituted for level rental payments.[5] Interest has traditionally been considered a financial cost (as opposed to an operating cost) and treated as a period cost, despite the fact that the practice of capitalizing it during construction periods has long been prevalent in the public utility field and has spread to other businesses as well. Nevertheless, the notion of delaying the expensing of interest, once the related facility is operative, would ordinarily shock most accountants. But isn't the lessee's accounting for rental expense on the right economic track when it results in a

---

[4]*Accounting for Leases*, Hawkins, David M., and Wehle, Mary M., Financial Executives Research Foundation, 1973.

[5]"Reporting of Leases—Comment on APB Opinion No. 5," Graham, Willard J., and Langenderfer, Harold Q., *Journal of Accountancy*, March 1965, page 60.

level cost (which includes finance charges) of a facility that provides the same service year after year? If so, the better approach is to capitalize the aggregate holding cost of the facility, including interest on both debt and equity money involved in it, and to allocate this total holding cost over the facility's useful life on a level basis. This is the major premise to be developed by this paper.

The balance sheet question. Just what a balance sheet is intended to portray is now under study. Certainly there is general agreement that (a) it does not today "present fairly" financial position in the sense that a layman thinks of that term and that (b) the term "financial position" has yet to he defined adequately for accounting purposes. If we retain the present narrow concepts of "assets" and "liabilities," we must resolve the esoteric question of how to determine which leases can be classified under these headings and therefore qualify for capitalization. If, however, we aim for a more accurate reflection of resources and commitments and worry less about balancing and debt/equity ratios (substituting some other measures of viability), as I have previously proposed,[6] the issue of balance-sheet treatment becomes less relevant, and we can focus instead on the income statement.

There are, of course, legal differences between lease and debt commitments; but normally, they become effective only on bankruptcy. Many believe the legal distinction is enough to require different accounting treatment; others feel legal form should be ignored. If, for argument's sake, we disregard the residual, the value of a property at the end of a lease, there seems to be little difference, substantively or economically, between "a full-pay-out" lease[7] covering the entire economic life of a facility and ownership financed with 100 percent (or nearly 100 percent) debt. Consequently, it seems reasonable that, except for interest rate differentials, accounting for these two arrangements should produce essentially the same annual net income result. But the real question is: Which result is more appropriate? This paper will concentrate on the income statement question and leave the capitalization debate to those who propose that solution, who must obviously first decide what a "balance sheet" is intended to show and what "financial position" means—if those terms are to be retained.

THE ANALYTIC APPROACH FOLLOWED

Before we can properly extend to leases the application of "generally accepted" conventions for facility accounting, we should first determine whether the application of those conventions truly reflects the economic facts. To do that, we must resolve certain questions relating to depreciation, major maintenance and renovation, income tax allocation (particularly the discounting of deferred

---

[6]*The Objective of Financial Accounting*, Defliese, Philip L., Coopers & Lybrand, 1973, page 18.

[7]A "full-pay-out" lease is one in which the terms assure the lessor of the recovery of his investment plus a reasonable return for the use of money, subject only to the usual credit risks and realizability of the residual.

taxes), and capitalization of interest, all of which bear on the economics of leasing *and* owning property.

While most accountants will probably agree that those issues are of as great or greater significance than the question of capitalization vs. expensing of leases, many overlook the fact that these issues are all *interrelated* and *cannot be resolved independently*. This paper will demonstrate that effect. Because of this interrelationship, the true economic effect of facility usage is better reflected in the accounting for level lease rentals than that resulting from capitalization or ownership accounting under present conventions. Until this problem is resolved, capitalization on a blanket basis is ill-advised; the distortion must not be compounded!

Background considerations. Serious questions concerning the objectives of financial statements have been raised. An AICPA Study Group[8] is researching the matter and will soon issue recommendations covering the whole future development of the art of accounting. That effort may result in major changes in accounting, hopefully toward formats that more accurately portray a company's operations and its financial resources and commitments. Perhaps the old concepts of balance sheet and income statement will give way ultimately to something more meaningful. If so, the process will take time.

For the immediate future, the retention of historical cost accounting, with a possible requirement for some supplementary data based on price levels or fair values to provide perspective, seems to be inevitable. Historical cost still provides the framework within which to resolve some of the more pressing issues currently facing the accounting profession. Certainly, the effort to reduce alternatives in many areas or to establish appropriate criteria for the use of alternatives can, with limitations, be sustained within this framework. Once agreement to continue with historical accounting is reached and reasonable progress is made in reducing the alternatives, the stage can be set for the larger debate that must precede the contemplation of such a far-reaching change as the adoption of fair value. This paper is predicated upon two assumptions: first, that within this historical cost framework, accounting can be made to reflect the underlying economic facts more closely (but not completely) than at present; second, that until more fundamental changes in accounting theory are made, the pervasive principles that are summarized under the heading, "matching of costs and revenues,"[9] will dominate periodic income determination concepts.

The attempts to bring the accounting concept of annual income more into line with economic facts are accelerating, representing a trend long overdue. In analyzing the factors that seem to deter this process, we find a resistance to the commingling of two types of economic cost—operating and financial—which presumably are considered to be different. Some feel that only operating costs

---

[8]Study Group on Objectives of Financial Statements formed by AICPA in 1971. A report is expected in the Fall of 1973.

[9]APB Statement No. 4, *Basic Concepts and Accounting Principles Underlying Financial Statements of Business Enterprises*, 1970, par. 147.

should influence operating income and that financial costs (those costs arising from the manner in which an enterprise finances its operation, such as by debt, common or preferred equity capital) should otherwise find their way into the accounting process, depending on their nature. This may be logical from a theoretical standpoint, but from a practical standpoint it is not. In setting meaningful standards for the determination of periodic income, accounting cannot ignore either operating or financial costs nor can it allow one to dominate the other. In the final analysis, both elements must be given due consideration to determine true economic cost—and this will be developed more fully in the later discussions on interest capitalization. A good illustration of the current trend toward a recognition of both costs is the greater use of the earnings-per-common-share statistic (which gives recognition to the financial cost of preferred stock, by deducting the preferred dividend) rather than the absolute net income amount (which does not recognize the cost of preferred stock financing).

THE INTERRELATED ISSUES

As has been previously stated, there are four interrelated accounting areas that are closely tied in with the question of appropriate accounting for facilities, whether owned or leased. These are:

• *Depreciation.* The equal acceptability (for financial accounting purposes) of accelerated methods and the straight-line methods of depreciation scarcely makes for comparability. In general, accountants do not challenge use of the straight-line method by a company even though other companies in the same industry may use accelerated methods. In theory, a company should select a method in accordance with valid accounting and operating criteria, but unfortunately acceptable criteria have not been agreed upon. The problem is further complicated by the existence in some industries of substantial variations in the estimated useful lives of major facilities and the fact that the SEC has banned the use of sinking-fund and annuity depreciation.[10]

• *Major Maintenance and Renovation.* Repair and maintenance costs that recur annually are currently expensed, and this is as it should be. But items that recur on a longer cycle—such as major engine overhauls, repainting and redecorating of apartments, remodeling of kitchens, etc.—are usually ignored until they occur. Then some are expensed and others are capitalized. Failure to accrue or defer these items appropriately (giving due recognition to the incidence of the cash outlay and the related tax effects) is to ignore the economic facts inherent in wasting assets—hardly a way of achieving a proper matching for the determination of periodic income.

[10]The SEC, on an informal basis, will not accept sinking-fund or annuity method depreciation. They are acceptable in certain situations in other countries, such as Canada and the United Kingdom.

• *Discounting of Deferred Taxes.* Even before the APB adopted comprehensive tax allocation,[11] it provisionally outlawed the discounting of deferred taxes[12] on the assumption that prior consideration should be given to the broader subject of discounting as it relates to all items in financial statements. Subsequently, the Board continued the ban on discounting, largely because it deemed deferred taxes to be a deferred credit account and not a liability account.[13] Nevertheless, the issue keeps cropping up. Furthermore, some feel that the issue of whether deferred tax accounts are deferred credits, liabilities, or valuation accounts (net of tax concept) should be reopened as well.

• *Capitalization of Interest.* The practice of capitalizing an allowance for interest on plant construction in progress has a substantial theoretical and practical basis. Not only has it been accepted by regulatory agencies in the public utility field, but it has also spread among other industries. The AICPA has formally accepted capitalization of interest on land inventory for the retail land sales industry.[14] Questions have also arisen as to the appropriateness of capitalizing interest on all long-term holdings of inventory—such as stocks of tobacco and liquor—and facilities—such as equipment, timber, oil and mineral deposits. Thus the trend toward recognizing interest as a holding cost seems to be accelerating. Recently, the cost of money has also received increased recognition in accounting thought,[15] so that a thorough review of this basic question is now clearly in order.

Accountants have a propensity toward over-segmenting their problems, particularly as they attempt to apply theory to practice; this is, no doubt, a carryover from their transaction oriented heritage. As previously suggested, there are probably few who would acknowledge the fact that the four foregoing issues, together with the question of capitalization of leases, cannot be resolved separately without due consideration being given to their interrelationship. However, this is precisely the case, as can be seen by examining each issue more closely.

DEPRECIATION

Today, we readily accept the distinction between "book" and "tax" depreciation. In the early days of the Internal Revenue Code (IRC), the distinction barely existed. Only when the federal government, recognizing the role that tax

---

[11]APB Opinion No. 11, *Accounting for Income Taxes* (1967).

[12]APB Opinion No. 10, *Omnibus Opinion* (1966), par. 6.

[13]See note 11, pars. 35 and 6.

[14]*Accounting for Retail Land Sales*, AICPA, 1973, page 19.

[15]APB Opinion No. 21, *Interest on Receivables and Payables* (1971).

depreciation policy can play in stimulating and fine-tuning the economy of the country, began to stretch accounting rationale in the depreciation provisions of the IRC did a separate theory of tax depreciation begin to evolve. This made possible the development of various methods of facilitating quick recovery of invested capital—accelerated depreciation methods, extremely short lives, minimal salvage values, as well as the granting of investment tax credits—thereby encouraging reinvestment and quicker replacement; to minimize abuses, recapture rules were developed. Thus it can be said that the divergence between book and tax depreciation is no longer an accident; it is a policy. For this reason, tax depreciation must be disregarded in any discussion of financial accounting,—except as it relates to the question of deferred taxes (discussed later), or to certain situations extant in the regulated utility industry, because many regulatory agencies have elected to ignore deferred tax accounting in favor of current "flow through" of book/tax timing differences relating to depreciation.

But what about book depreciation? Existing methods of allocating a facility's cost to the periods benefitted are inadequate, and little progress has been made in finding better methods. Depreciation is looked upon strictly as cost allocation in determining periodic income. This is fine, except that, operationally and financially, it should also be looked upon as a means by which the cost of a facility is recovered through the revenue produced by operations (with the government returning its share through income tax deductions). Note that when the funds statement attempts to reflect cash now it adds back depreciation to net income. The current trend toward a greater emphasis on the cash realization aspect of net income, or cash flow, is quite evident.

Depreciation practice is still fettered by the influence of tax depreciation practices and by conservatism—e.g., in some instances, salvage values have been kept down and estimated lives have been arbitrarily set low. At the other end of the spectrum, companies under tight regulation, such as public utilities and railroads, are frequently required to spread facility costs over long periods without adequate regard for the obsolescence that might reasonably be anticipated or without any allowance for a sensible economic replacement policy. Also, a typical victim of the straight-line depreciation requirement is the investment real estate company that must report losses in the early (high interest) years despite full occupancy and a property that may be appreciating instead of depreciating. Commercial properties that are properly maintained and periodically renovated can frequently be resold many years after purchase at prices approximating their cost or more than cost because of price level changes and other factors. Present depreciation methods usually ignore these factors, and perhaps properly so within our current framework.[16]

Thus current practices in depreciation accounting fail in many cases to produce results that adequately reflect economic fact. This is perhaps most evident in attempting to arrive at a proper allocation of maintenance and

---

[16]This paper does not attempt to deal with the effect of changes in the level of prices of assets and the manner in which those effects should be reflected in financial statements of their owners.

expiration costs over a useful life determined by realistic replacement policy. New approaches giving recognition to the interrelationship of the foregoing factors (including interest and taxes) must be developed in this area, industry by industry, in order to achieve a proper matching of costs and revenues. This will require a virtual overhaul of accounting depreciation practices, which can only be undertaken if certain long-standing concepts, attitudes and prejudices are set aside. Consideration might even be given to replacing the term "depreciation" (which connotes loss of value), since the accounting concept has outgrown that narrow connotation of the word.

MAJOR MAINTENANCE AND RENOVATION

As mentioned above, the question of proper handling of major maintenance and renovation costs is closely allied to the depreciation issue. Policy in this area should receive equal consideration with obsolescence in setting a depreciation policy. Ignoring obsolescence can unduly lengthen lives (at the risk of uneconomic production), and omitting major maintenance and renovation can shorten lives. The interrelationship should be apparent, and accounting must give attention to developing a methodology that reflects a coordinated policy in this area. When a policy of systematic maintenance and renovation exists, it should be general practice to accrue and defer the related costs (recognizing the cash and tax consequences) and to give recognition to such policy in deciding on the appropriate depreciation policy to be followed. This is not often done at present.

DISCOUNTING OF DEFERRED TAXES

As previously indicated, accountants divide into three camps on the subject of deferred taxes (excepting, of course, those who would ignore some or all tax timing differences under a complete or selective flow-through theory—a diminishing lot). Those who espouse the liability theory reason that one must assume profitability, without which a company cannot long survive; consequently, the tax benefit must eventually be paid back, perhaps even at a higher rate. Essentially, they look upon deferred taxes as an obligation whose payment has been deferred for perhaps a long period without concomitant obligation to pay interest. They recognize that there is always a cost of money and they make a good case for discounting such a long-term liability.[17] Others, who object to the "front ending" of income that results from discounting, hold that the benefits of such a loan should flow into income only as the "borrowed" funds are utilized in operations.

Those who reject the liability theory entirely point out that no liability exists until future profits are earned, hence discounting is improper. They insist that the deferred tax is only an advance recognition of the tax benefit of depreciation, and this benefit must he deferred and matched with the future book depreciation that

---

[17]See note 15.

receives a lesser tax benefit. Still others view deferred taxes in the same light as they do other tax benefits—a sharing of the cost of every expenditure with the government. And if the government thus elects to return its share earlier, a smaller net investment exists in the meantime. These accountants advocate the net-of-tax, or valuation account, concept. This net-of-tax approach, considered in conjunction with the interest effect of allocation of the unrecovered investment on a rational (preferably level) basis, produces a result which is very similar to discounting.

Each of these theories has merit, and there are those who switch from one to another according to how they wish to proceed in particular instances. (Similar dilemmas exist in theology and must be resolved by faith.) About the only point on which all deferred-tax people agree is that there should be a proper matching of cost and revenue. But what is cost in this case?

Today, discounted cash flow has become the yardstick of comparison of all values; recognition of interest as a yield factor is inherent in that exercise. Accounting has already recognized this with long-term receivables and payables that may or may not carry appropriate interest rates.[18]

A business that owns a productive facility has an investment at risk at any time equal to the net unrecovered investment (net of tax benefits realized and the portions assumed to be previously recovered through depreciation charges to operations) plus the net holding costs (interest, maintenance and renovation) necessary to maintain the facility until its estimated salvage is realized. The interrelationship of the foregoing factors (including yield) recognized in determining the level cost to be allocated (recovered) makes further consideration of discounting deferred taxes unnecessary.

CAPITALIZATION OF INTEREST

This brings us to the last link in the chain—interest cost. The cost of money—whether equity or borrowed—invested in a facility is a basic element of the cost of holding or operating that facility.[19] This is not a new idea. The arguments for interest as a cost, rather than as an element of profit, were summarized almost 50 years ago,[20] and rejected as far back as 1918 by the AICPA;[21] recently the National Association of Accountants also rejected the

---

[18]See note 15.

[19]The same theory is applicable to all current assets and unamortized deferred charges.

[20]*Interest as a Cost* (1924), Scovell, Clinton H. (CPA), Ronald Press. (Mr. Scovell was co-founder of the firm Scovell, Wellington & Co., Accountants and Engineers, subsequently merged with Coopers & Lybrand.)

[21]*Report of Special Committee on Interest in Relation to Cost* (September 14, 1918), American Institute of Accountants Year-Book, 1918. See note 19.

idea.[22] From an economic standpoint, there is no justification for reflecting differing costs for rented facilities and purchased facilities (using borrowed money) because essentially the same costs (assuming identical rates) are incurred. The problem is further complicated when equity money is employed because the cost of such money is not allocated to the investment. The real problem lies with the traditional accounting concept of net income. True net income should first recognize a cost equivalent to ***interest*** on capital investment—the return which would be earned if invested elsewhere.

Accordingly, interest holding costs, whether imputed or real, on unrecovered investment should be added to the cost of a facility[23] to determine its overall cost to be spread over the accounting periods benefitted. This concept, in part, is related to what economists call "opportunity cost" of equity capital. To quote from a recent economics text,[24] "every factor of production is paid at least its opportunity cost (what it might earn in the next best alternative employment)." In regard to opportunity cost of capital, the same authority states, "The opportunity cost of capital to the firm is the same whether it uses its own funds or borrows them in the free market if lending and borrowing interest rates are equal." Thus, the interest rate is the bridge used in "converting the [holding] cost of a physical asset into the cost of the services of that asset." Management is well aware of this economic (and financial) effect and gives it prime consideration in the lease or buy (and borrow) exercise.

Inevitably the question will arise: Is it necessary to impute an interest cost to all investments in facilities since equity capital provides some or all of the necessary funds? Why not capitalize only the actual interest paid and apply it to the facilities for which the debt was created? This is simple and direct, but it is also arbitrary and unrealistic—a facility financed out of equity money is no different in its revenue-producing capacity from one financed out of debt.

To overcome this objection, we could propose that capitalized interest paid be allocated to all assets in proportion to the debt/equity ratio. This would seem more equitable than an arbitrary allocation, but it would provide only a partial recognition of the cost of holding a facility. Consequently, the only solution is to apply an interest charge (net of tax) for equity funds as well as debt funds to all assets during their holding period. To the extent such charges exceed interest actually paid, a credit will appear separately in the income statement as a nonoperating return on investment, and operations will bear an appropriate charge as the holding costs (which include the interest factor) are expensed or amortized. This will be amplified later.

---

[22]*Fixed Asset Accounting: The Capitalization of Costs*, Position Paper of Committee on Management Accounting Practices, NAA Management Accounting, January 1973.

[23]See note 19.

[24]*Principles of Economics*, Nichols & Reynolds; Holt, Rinehard & Winston, Inc. 1971, pp. 185-186, 253.

LEVEL COST ALLOCATION THEORY OF FACILITY ACCOUNTING

The interrelationship of the four foregoing problem areas should become apparent when one considers that the cost of holding a facility consists of:

(a) All construction and acquisition costs, *plus*

(b) All costs of major maintenance and renovation during the holding period to point of disposition (net of income tax benefit), giving due recognition to the incidence of cash expenditure, *less*

(c) All recoveries of total investment in the form of tax benefits of depreciation (including accelerated depreciation) and investment tax credits, *plus*

(d) Interest (real and imputed)—net of income tax benefits—on the resultant unrecovered net investment over the holding period.

Oncc this aggregate and net cost is determined, it should be considered to be recovered through operational revenue (less the expected residual or salvage) over the realistically estimated holding period on a logical, or at least a systematic, basis. The accounting technique to reflect this recovery is cost allocation or depreciation. In the absence of strong evidence in favor of a different approach, the allocation would be level over the years held. Obviously, the holding period should give due consideration to obsolescence and the replacement policy of the company.

Essential to this theory of facility accounting is the concept of depreciation as a means by which a company recovers its net unrecovered investment (as defined earlier) through operations. Put another way, the cost incurred by the loss in value of the net investment in the facility must be charged to operations over the period of use in a rational manner. But by the same process, the cost of the investment is recovered over its holding period through the revenues generated by its use. This involves some attempt to match such cost with projected revenue. (When revenues differ from projections, the gain or loss from over or under-utilization is operational in character and not attributable to the facility.) Since interest on the unrecovered investment—giving due regard to the tax recoveries—is an element of cost, it, too, must be spread in the same manner.

To allocate this newly defined depreciation to the periods of use requires the exercise of logic and judgment. The arguments for accelerated methods are no better (in the ordinary case) than for straight-line, especially if matching is the pervasive motivation. All the methods rest on arbitrary premises; in the final analysis, only by making logical assumptions can accountants determine periodic income.

The fact that interest (whether from debt or equity) is included as a cost should not alter the basic theory. Nor should it upset those who consider "historical cost" as including only cash costs. Obviously, new definitions are in order. In fact, *because* interest is a factor in determining the net cost to be allocated, it need not be considered a factor in determining methodology. Similarly, if interest is assumed to be a holding cost, the fact that unamortized interest (whether real or imputed) resides in the balance sheet amount of the unrecovered investment in the facility should not disturb the theory (as long as that balance is not in excess of net realizable value on a going-concern basis).[25] It should be remembered that the determination of the balance sheet amount of unamortized investment rests entirely on the *assumptions* the accountant makes. Acceptance of this view depends, of course, on a willingness to accept a new concept of unamortized historical cost *and* a new concept of net income that more closely reflects the economic facts.

The level cost allocation theory solves many of the problems that arise in connection with the capitalizing of interest and the discounting of deferred taxes. This achievement is largely attributable to the following three features: (a) inclusion in the computation of interest on unrecovered investment; (b) treatment of the actual tax benefits as a recovery of investment as received—thereby reducing the interest on *unrecovered* investment (a closer conformity with cash-flow); and (c) allocation of the balance on a level basis. In essence a form of discounting takes place. The theory puts all holding costs on a realistic basis and better matches these costs with expected revenues from a potentially level capacity.

Disregarding for the moment the question of balance sheet presentation, this theory also makes academic the issue of capitalizing leases because, except for the element of major maintenance and renovation—a cost the lessee usually bears anyway, most financing lease terms produce approximately the same results described above, i.e., the level rental payments are predicated upon the same expected revenues and costs. Consequently, if finance-type leases were capitalized, and the accounting suggested here followed, the annual net income results would be about the same.

In structuring a lease, most financing lessors use essentially the same model, making certain that their yield on unrecovered investment (giving due consideration to investment credits and tax depreciation recovery) is a constant predetermined percentage. What this really amounts to is that accounting for lease payments as rents today produces a result more in accordance with the economic facts than does ownership accounting. Is it any wonder that many companies would rather lease today than buy? A skewed accounting result is certainly something to be avoided and bears importantly on every business decision.

THE OPPOSING ARGUMENTS

To sustain the validity of this new concept of facility accounting, it is necessary to demonstrate that the economics of leasing are presently receiving more realistic accounting treatment than the economics of ownership. Unfortunately, it will be some time before all the elements entering into the latter can be clarified from an accounting standpoint. With this handicap in mind, we must now address ourselves to the most important arguments against new facility

---

[25]Facilities that are operating profitably and are expected to continue to do so for their anticipated useful life are usually not given a net realizable value test.

accounting. These are of two types: those that relate to the basic concept and those that relate to implementation; they are often difficult to separate.

INTEREST

Perhaps the greatest resistance will arise in connection with the interest factor. Capitalization of interest, or deferment of interest to other periods, will be opposed on the ground that it is a period financing cost. Traditionally considered a cost of borrowing money, it is accrued and expensed on the basis of the debt balance during the period and excluded from the determination of operating profit. To the recipient, interest income must always relate to the unrecovered investment, although opinions may vary as to what constitutes unrecovered investment at any given time. But why is interest holding cost different from any other cost for which there are continuing benefits in the form of future revenue? The same accountants who might object to deferral would probably have no hesitation in deferring appropriate start-up costs and valuable R & D, and in amortizing them on some basis designed to match expenses and revenues. The continuing benefits of a tangible facility investment are usually far more predictable than are those of many deferred costs.

The inclusion in accounting costs of an imputed return on invested capital (a portion of which is capitalized) is a revolutionary idea for most tradition-minded accountants. This approach goes to the heart of the concept of net income. Under present accounting practice, it is assumed that net income includes a return equivalent to interest on invested capital, and no attempt is made to determine that portion of net income attributable solely to operational elements of profitability. Implementation of the concept advocated here would require a breakdown of income into its two elements—capital income and entrepreneurial income. The capital portion would represent the *interest* that should be earned on invested capital (a new accounting standard approaching opportunity cost), and the entrepreneurial portion would represent the excess or deficiency arising from the entrepreneur's operations; in other words, the additional return on equity compensating for the risks assumed beyond that of a creditor.

This can be illustrated by the following (somewhat simplified) version of the lower section of a hypothetical income statement:

Income from operations (after taxes)*		xxxxxxxxxx
Add, Interest on capital investment:		
Imputed interest on net investment in facilities and operating assets (capitalized or charged to operations)	xxxxxxxxxx	
Less, Interest paid to creditors and lessors (after taxes)	xxxxxxxxxx	
		xxxxxxxxxx
Net income		xxxxxxxxxx

*Net operating income after charges for all holding cost of facilities including interest and depreciation.

Such a presentation would be more revealing to an investor than that under present practice. Moreover the effect on public utility accounting could be revolutionary. Regulatory agencies do not presently allow interest as a cost, except that portion capitalized on construction in progress. Instead they allow a return on utility investment base (rate base) giving some consideration to the proportion of capital that is borrowed in setting an allowable rate of return.[26]

One stumbling block to the implementation of the concept of interest capitalization is the determination of the rate of interest to be capitalized. If debt is created specifically to acquire a facility, choice of rate appears to pose no problem. The rate for equity capital, however, might be difficult to determine. Some might argue that the current rate of return being earned on invested capital should be employed rather than the debt rate currently obtainable. However, if income is to be segmented, as previously discussed, use of the debt rate is more appropriate, since the income from operations should properly include only a charge for the interest cost equivalent to debt, because the enterprise usually has the option (with limitations) of using debt capital in lieu of equity capital. Returns on equity that are greater than the debt rate obtainable are considered to be rewards for the greater risks assumed and are entrepreneurial profits. The rewards for those risks should be reflected in operations.

There is the further question: Should the rates change as interest rates fluctuate? Economists would probably prefer a constantly changing rate of return on equity, on the assumption that an enterprise has a new option each year as to how it will invest its capital. This is not realistic, and would conflict with the notion of historical cost, as redefined herein. The option to use borrowed money or equity money arises at the time the commitment is made and is rarely changed later.

ASSUMPTIONS REGARDING DEFERRED TAXES

Those who feel that deferred taxes should be discounted at all times will probably welcome the interest on unrecovered investment aspects of this approach; the differences in effect are minor. On the other hand, some discounters, and some who feel that no discounting should take place (the deferred credit people), may take issue with the following assumptions inherent in that approach:

• *The cash flows from accelerated tax depreciation are assured.* This assumption, in turn, hinges on annual profitability throughout the holding period sufficient to utilize the tax deductions thus provided. Some accountants are reluctant to anticipate tax benefits based on future profits.

---

[26]This is not the only aspect of public utility accounting that would be affected by the thesis presented in this paper. The elimination of flow-through to income of the tax benefits of the excess of accelerated depreciation over straight-line depreciation, as now required in many jurisdictions, would be far more consequential.

• *The cash flows in excess of debt repayment requirements can earn the same rate of interest.*

• *The same tax rate will prevail throughout the holding period.*

Admittedly these assumptions are a bit beyond those adopted by accountants when they determine traditional results on a going-concern basis. Nevertheless they are as reasonable as most assumptions made in estimating the useful life and salvage value of a facility for depreciation purposes. It is presently customary to make a recomputation whenever the elements entering into the determination of the annual depreciation charge change, and, in such cases, the unamortized balance is spread over the remaining useful life. Such a recomputation would he made under the proposed concept whenever any of the basic assumptions were changed. And there is always net realizable value as the ultimate safeguard.[27]

METHODS OF DEPRECIATION

Some of the oldest theories in accounting concern depreciation. Arguments for and against the various methods are well known and need not be repeated here; similarly, the evolution of the various acceptable tax methods is not relevant (though we have discussed their origins earlier in another context).

As previously discussed, except for the SEC ban on interest methods of depreciation, financial accounting presently permits the recording of depreciation under any of several methods without much regard to circumstances. It might appear that the simplest course would be to establish criteria for these various methods rather than replace them by the level cost allocation method proposed here. In fact, when analyzed carefully, few situations (within a historical cost framework) will be found to justify methods other than straight-line. In theory, projected revenues could serve as a basis, but in practice the difficulties would be insurmountable. Who could predict the revenues of a lathe or the president's office furniture? It seems that level costing is always appropriate if the revenue *potential* is equal throughout the holding period.

Accelerated methods have been recommended in situations involving a high risk of obsolescence, principally as a means of implementing a conservative approach. Unless there is good reason to expect revenues produced by the facility to diminish over time, the better approach is to shorten the estimated useful life. The counter-balancing of higher maintenance costs in the later years of a facility's life with declining balance depreciation (in order to level cost—sic!) is generally more of an assumption than a reality. Except in those cases where excessive use will speed replacement (trucks, dies), the unit-of-production (or use) method carries the matching of costs and revenues too far (for example, the holding cost of an idle machine can't be ignored).

---

[27]See note 19.

Interest methods. The sinking fund, annuity, and similar interest methods[28] of depreciation attempt to allow for the interest return on unrecovered investment. These methods have few adherents today because of concern about smaller charges in the earlier years; obviously the impact on the income statement of the cost of the unrecovered investment is ignored in their thinking. But years ago, these methods were recommended for investment real estate property as a means of offsetting higher interest on debt in the earlier years, thereby achieving a form of level costing. Such results would be laudatory if they were not so difficult to support without close consideration of the interest on unrecovered investment concept developed here, but not otherwise sponsored. Except for the inclusion of tax effects (a factor that has become more prominent in recent years), the approach advocated in this paper has a remarkable kinship to the annuity concept.

Use of the annuity method of depreciation as a means of reflecting the economics of leasing and ownership has recently been suggested. In November, 1960, W. Barry Coutts, writing on "Interest and Depreciation Methods" in the *Canadian Chartered Accountants*, stated:

> Rental payments under a typical long-term lease represent normally both a charge for interest on the funds invested in the asset and a provision for depreciation, that is, for the return of the amount invested over the useful life of the asset. When funds are borrowed and used to acquire a similar asset, similar provisions are required to reflect the interest paid on the borrowed money and to record the expiration of the cost of the asset over its useful life. Under conventional accounting, however, these two methods will produce widely varying results in the accounts even if all the terms of the lease are exactly equivalent to those involved in ownership.
>
> Further analysis suggests that it is the failure of the conventional straight-line depreciation method to take the time value of money into account that is at the base of the trouble. The basic fallacy in the conventional approach can readily be demonstrated by pointing out that no business enterprise would be willing to compute future rentals at face value. No enterprise, to be more specific, would pay $1,000 in order to discharge in advance ten years' rent at $100 per year. It is equally illogical to assume that a price of $1,000 would be paid for the use of an asset which is estimated to be worth $100 in each year of its ten-year life.
>
> A simple illustration (see next page) will demonstrate the application of this technique in the procedure usually referred to as the 'annuity method' of computing depreciation. In the accompanying table the amounts involved in applying the method to an asset with an original cost of $1,000, a life of 10 years, and an assumed average cost of money of 10 percent is illustrated.

---

[28]See note 10.

ANNUITY METHOD OF COMPUTING DEPRECIATION

Year	Balance of Cost	Annual Depreciation	Accumulated Annual	Depreciation Accumulated	Interest Income
(1)	(2)	(3)	(4)	(5)	(6)
1	$1,000	$ 163	$ 63	$ 63	$100
2	937	163	69	132	94
3	867	163	76	208	87
4	792	163	84	292	79
5	709	163	92	384	71
6	617	163	101	485	62
7	516	163	111	596	52
8	405	163	122	718	4
9	282	163	134	852	29
10	148	163	148	1,000	15
		$1,630	$1,000		$630

It will be noted that the net effect of this procedure on the income account will be the difference between the depreciation charge and the interest credit. This amount will actually be the same as the annual addition to the depreciation account shown in column 4, and will accordingly increase from year to year as the interest credit declines. The annuity method thus produces a constant depreciation charge but an increasing net total cost over the asset life.

The usefulness for many purposes of a depreciation cost which is exactly comparable with rent seems hard to deny. Even the 'interest credit' by reflecting the theoretical return which should be received from investments in fixed assets is useful as a measure of the extent to which the desired return has actually been earned.

More will be said about this approach later.

ILLUSTRATIVE EXHIBITS

To illustrate the similarity of ownership and lease accounting espoused in this paper, three exhibits are attached. They are over-simplified in order to demonstrate the principle more clearly.

Exhibit I assumes purchase of a facility for $1,000,000 using entirely money borrowed at 10 percent interest. Exhibit II assumes lease of the same facility from a financing lessor who borrows the entire amount at 10 percent interest. As a further simplification, no use of equity money is assumed and all net cash flows, including the net charge to operations for holding costs (or rentals), are considered reduction of the debt (or investment) after payment of interest to date. (An equivalent result is obtained if the lessor's equity money is used and a before-tax return of 10 percent is imputed on unrecovered investment.) Again, for simplification, major maintenance and renovation are assumed to be zero.

Under use of the level costing technique proposed herein, Exhibit I produces an annual depreciation charge (net of 50 percent income tax) of $43,069 over a 16-year productive life. Depending on how the income statement is ultimately restructured, as it relates to the presentation of income taxes (a controversial subject itself), this charge can he shown as a gross charge of $86,137, or as a net charge of $43,069. The same set of facts structured as a lease, Exhibit II, produces an annual rental payment of $86,137, before taxes, which results in a net charge to income of $43,069 (the net after-tax cash cost to the company). Thus it can he seen that in each case the only net charge to income (after consideration of all interest and tax effects) is a constant $43,069 over the 16-year period. Not only are the accounting results the same, but they more clearly reflect thc economic facts of the circumstances.

ANNUITY DEPRECIATION AS AN INTERIM ALTERNATIVE

Although many accountants who recognize the profession's failure to conform accounting more closely with economics will agree with the basic premise of this proposal, few will want to take the bold steps necessary. Redefining annual net income (the segmenting previously suggested), and including real and imputed interest in total facility cost (a new concept of historical cost) to be leveled over productive life, involves drastic changes. Obviously these should not be undertaken without considerable empirical research and experimentation.

As was suggested earlier, the annuity method of depreciation is accepted in some other countries and certainly merits consideration as an alternative in this country. Straight-line amortization of the deferred investment tax credit is, of course, acceptable here. The combination of these two generally accepted methods, when applied to the same set of facts as in Exhibits I and II, produce in Exhibit III an annual net charge to income (when a return is imputed on the amount of tax payment deferred that is similar to a loan) almost equivalent to that of leasing. Note that the book entries for depreciation and loan interest produce annual charges that are essentially level, and that the net effect on income, considering all factors, is almost equal. The combination of the interest factor inherent in the annuity method, the declining interest on borrowing, and the imputed interest earned on deferred taxes serve to portray an economic result closer to that of the facility costing previously proposed. This is a further argument against any disclosure, for the present, of an alternative net income figure based on imputed straight-line depreciation and declining interest for leases. A reconsideration of the annuity method as an acceptable, and perhaps the universal, method, could serve as the first step in the process of unraveling this problem.

CONCLUSION

Unless there are compelling reasons to spread all holding costs on a basis other than evenly over the holding period, level costing of all such costs (including interest on unrecovered investment) is the appropriate accounting for facilities. Except for the element of major maintenance and renovation (which should be appropriately spread in any event), such accounting closely approximates the charges under finance-type leasing as practiced today; Exhibits I and II clearly demonstrate this.

Thus, from an economic standpoint, lessee accounting provides a better form of accounting than is presently permitted for ownership accounting. Disregarding, for the present, the question of balance sheet disclosure (a major issue not to be taken lightly under present conventions), it would seem inadvisable to require the capitalization of finance-type leases by lessees, explicitly or implicitly, until thorough review and redefinition of interest capitalization, discounting of deferred taxes, depreciation, and major maintenance and renovation, and their interrelationships are accomplished. This is particularly so, since the objectives of financial accounting—that is what the balance sheet and the income statement should portray—are still in question. Thus it appears most inadvisable to require disclosure of an alternative net income amount on an "as if" capitalized basis, with conventional straight-line depreciation and interest accounting, because the reader will automatically infer that this is either the more appropriate amount or an alternative amount that an investor should give serious consideration to. It is far better to tolerate the lack of comparability that exists between companies following different facility acquisition policies until an accounting methodology for facility usage which produces a result more reflective of the economic facts can be agreed upon, especially since many companies are today both buying *and* leasing.

Exhibit I. Proposed Ownership Accounting Using Level-Cost Allocation Method

A facility is purchased for $1 million, having a 16-year useful life, residual value of $150,000 (tax salvage value of $50,000). The purchase is financed with a loan of $930,000 ($1 million less $70,000 assumed immediate investment tax credit) with 10% interest payable at year-end. Productivity and revenues are assumed level throughout this period; all net cash flows, including level holding cost, are assumed recovered from revenues and available at year-end and applied to payment of interest and reduction of the debt.

Year	(1) Unrecovered Net Investment at Beginning of Year	(2) Add Interest on Net Investment (after tax) [1]	(3) Depreciation for Tax Purposes [2]	(4) Tax Benefit of Depreciation (at 50% rate)	(5) Investment Tax Credit at 7% [3]	(6) Sale of Residual (net of tax on excess over tax salvage value)	(7) Allocation of Net Holding Cost [4] (net of tax)	(8) Unrecovered Net Investment at End of Year (1+2)-(4+5+7)
0	$ 1,000,000				$ 70,000			$ 930,000
1	930,000	$ 46,500	$ 285,714	$ 142,857			$ 43,069	790,574
2	790,574	39,529	204,082	102,041			43,069	684,993
3	684,993	34,250	170,068	85,034			43,069	591,140
4	591,140	29,557	136,054	68,027			43,069	509,601
5	509,601	25,480	102,041	51,021			43,069	440,991
6	440,991	22,050	52,041	26,020			43,069	393,952
7	393,952	19,698	0	0			43,069	370,581
8	370,581	18,529	0	0			43,069	346,041
9	346,041	17,302	0	0			43,069	320,274
10	320,274	16,014	0	0			43,069	293,219
11	293,219	14,661	0	0			43,069	264,811
12	264,811	13,241	0	0			43,069	234,983
13	234,983	11,749	0	0			43,069	203,663
14	203,663	10,183	0	0			43,069	170,777
15	170,777	8,539	0	0			43,069	136,247
16	136,247	6,812	0	0		$ 100,000	43,059	0
Total		$ 334,094	$ 950,000	$ 475,000	$ 70,000	$ 100,000	$ 689,094	

Notes:

[1] Equivalent to after-tax cost of interest on debt, which is capitalized rather than charged to income.

[2] Seven years; ADR, double-declining balance for the first two years and sum-of-the-years-digits for the remaining life; salvage $50,000.

[3] Credit assumed obtainable at time of investment (year 0).

[4] Computed as Investment ($1,000,000) plus interest net of tax benefit ($334,094), less tax benefit of depreciation ($475,000), less investment tax credit ($70,000), and less sale of residual, net of tax ($100,000), which equals the net cost of holding the facility ($689,094).

Exhibit II. Present Lessee Accounting with Level Rental Payments

A financing lessor purchases facility under the same condition described in Exhibit 1 with a loan of $930,000 ($1 mi lion less $70,000 assumed immediate investment credit) and leases it to a lessee for level annual rentals over the 16-year useful life.[1]

Year	(1) Required Annual Rental	(2) 10% Interest on Unpaid Loan Balance (col. 7) (before taxes)	(3) Depreciation for Tax Purposes	(4) Tax Gain (Loss) 1 - (2 + 3)	(5) Net Tax Benefits (expenses)	(6) Net Cash Flow (after taxes) (reduces loan balance) (1 - 2 + 5)	(7) Unpaid Loan Balance at End of Year (7 - 6)
0							$ 930,000
1	$ 86,137	$ 93,000	$ 285,714	($ 292,577)	$ 146,289	$ 139,426	790,574
2	86,137	79,057	204,082	(197,022)	98,501	105,581	684,993
3	86,137	68,500	170,068	(152,431)	76,216	93,853	591,140
4	86,137	59,114	136,054	(109,031)	54,516	81,539	509,601
5	86,137	50,960	102,041	(66,864)	33,433	68,610	440,991
6	86,137	44,099	52,041	(10,003)	5,001	47,039	393,952
7	86,137	39,395	0	46,742	(23,371)	23,371	370,581
8	86,137	37,058	0	49,079	(24,539)	24,540	346,041
9	86,137	34,604	0	51,533	(25,766)	25,767	320,274
10	86,137	32,027	0	54,110	(27,055)	27,055	293,219
11	86,137	29,322	0	56,815	(28,408)	28,408	264,811
12	86,137	26,481	0	59,656	(29,828)	29,828	234,983
13	86,137	23,498	0	62,639	(31,319)	31,320	203,663
14	86,137	20,366	0	65,771	(32,885)	32,886	170,777
15	86,137	17,078	0	69,059	(34,529)	34,530	136,247
16	86,137	13,625	0	72,492	(36,245)	36,247	100,000[2]
	$ 1,378,172	$ 668,184	$ 950,000	($ 240,012)	$ 120,012	$ 830,000	

Notes:

[1] See notes to Exhibit I.

[2] Loan balance at end of year 16 is paid from proceeds of sale of residual , $150,000 less 50% tax ($50,000) on excess of proceeds over tax salvage value of $50,000.

Exhibit III. Alternative Ownership Accounting Application of Annuity Method of Depreciation and Assumed Return on Deferred Taxes

A facility is purchased under the same conditions described in Exhibit 1 with a 10% loan of $930,000 ($1 million less $70,000 assumed immediate investment tax credit) requiring level annual repayments (interest and principal) each year-end and a balance of $100,000 at end of year 16 (equivalent to net cash value of residual).[1]

($000's omitted)

Year	Net Book Basis of Investment at Beginning of Year	(1) Book[2] Deprec-iation (annuity method)	(2) Book Deprec-iation (net of tax) (1) x 50%	(3) Tax Deprec-iation (net of tax)	(4) Deferred Tax (3) - (2)	(5) Cumulative Deferred Tax	(6) Interest on Loan (net of tax)	(7) Straight-Line Amortization of Investment Tax Credit	(8) Book Net Charges to Income (2)+(6)+(7)	(9) Assumed[3] Interest Earned on Deferred Tax at 5% (5) x 5%	(10) Net Effect on Income (8) + (9)	Unpaid Loan Balance at End of Year
0												930.0
1	1,000.0	23.6	11.8	(142.9)	(131.1)	(131.1)	46.5	(4.4)	53.9	(6.6)	47.3	906.9
2	976.4	26.0	13.0	(102.0)	(89.0)	(220.1)	45.3	(4.4)	53.9	(11.0)	42.9	881.5
3	950.4	28.6	14.3	(85.0)	(70.7)	(290.8)	44.1	(4.4)	54.0	(14.5)	39.5	853.6
4	921.8	31.5	15.8	(68.1)	(52.3)	(343.1)	42.7	(4.3)	54.2	(17.1)	37.1	822.9
5	890.3	34.6	17.3	(51.0)	(33.7)	(376.8)	41.1	(4.4)	54.0	(18.8)	35.2	789.1
6	855.7	38.1	19.0	(26.0)	(7.0)	(383.8)	39.5	(4.4)	54.1	(19.2)	34.9	751.9
7	817.6	41.9	21.0	0	21.0	(362.8)	37.6	(4.4)	54.2	(18.1)	36.1	711.0
8	775.7	46.1	23.1	0	23.1	(339.7)	35.6	(4.3)	54.4	(16.9)	37.5	666.0
9	729.6	50.7	25.3	0	25.3	(314.4)	33.3	(4.4)	54.2	(15.7)	38.5	616.5
10	678.9	55.8	27.9	0	27.9	(286.5)	30.8	(4.4)	54.3	(14.3)	40.0	562.0
11	623.1	61.3	30.7	0	30.7	(255.8)	28.1	(4.4)	54.4	(12.8)	41.6	502.2
12	561.8	67.5	33.7	0	33.7	(222.1)	25.1	(4.3)	54.5	(11.1)	43.4	436.3
13	494.6	74.2	37.1	0	37.1	(185.0)	21.8	(4.4)	54.5	(9.2)	45.3	363.8
14	420.1	81.6	40.8	0	40.8	(144.2)	18.2	(4.4)	54.6	(7.2)	47.4	284.1
15	338.5	89.8	44.9	0	44.9	(99.3)	14.2	(4.4)	54.7	(4.9)	49.8	196.4
16	248.7	98.7	49.3	0	49.3	(50.0)	9.8	(4.3)	54.8	(2.5)	52.3	100.0
17	150.0											
		850.0	425.0	(475.0)	(50.0)	–	513.7	(70.0)	868.7	(199.9)	668.8	

Notes:

[1] See notes to Exhibit I. [2] Book depreciation is at 10% using annuity method. The starting basis is $1 million and the residual is $150,000.

[3] The deferred taxes will earn 10% (5% net of tax) through operations or interest, and will benefit the income statement accordingly. For simplicity, it is assumed that the tax benefit is obtainable at beginning of year through reduced estimated payments. A more precise calculation would be to assume a half-year benefit.

CAPITALIZATION AND AMORTIZATION OF LEASES†

by
Philip L. Defliese

NATURE OF THE PROBLEM

LEASE accounting has been surrounded by controversy for many years, particularly during the postwar period and the 60's when leasing became more popular. It is estimated that $100 billion of assets are on lease in 1975. The issues involved have settled into a gray zone between economic reality and fundamental accounting rules—*substance versus form*. Business decisions concerning the use of assets to produce revenue are founded on economic reality. How the assets are obtained would appear to be of lesser significance. One might suppose that two companies using similar assets to produce similar revenue would report results that look alike. However, this is not true when one acquires its assets through purchase and the other through leasing. Present accounting rules prescribe a meticulous examination of the rights involved in and the form of transactions. While authoritative pronouncements attempt to recognize substance, accounting practice has emphasized form, and has created a motive for basing economic decisions, in part, on how accounting rules will make transactions appear.

At present, an Exposure Draft of a proposed accounting standard on *Accounting for Leases* issued by the Financial Accounting Standards Board (FASB) is under consideration. Much comment was elicited by the FASB from the accounting profession, regulatory bodies, and the financial and investing community, and a public hearing was held on the subject before the draft was issued. While significant changes in existing accounting rules for leasing may result from its adoption, the present status leaves management with considerable leeway. This results in part from the nature of leasing itself and in part from the somewhat inconclusive state of present accounting rules. This chapter will deal with the status quo (with appropriate caveats), but will also provide an outline of the proposed new standard.

A *lease* is a legal instrument that transfers certain property rights and obligations from lessor to lessee. It resembles a sale-and-purchase agreement in the kind of rights and obligations that change hands, but differs in the extent to which control is transferred. Because the lessor retains some *control* (e.g., title),

---

†Reprinted from *The Modern Accountant's Handbook*, Chapter 10, James Don Edwards and Homer A. Black, eds. (Homewood, IL: Dow Jones-Irwin, 1976), pp. 175-200. Reprinted with permission of the McGraw-Hill Companies.

accounting for leases as sales is often not appropriate. Further, *performance*, that is, delivery and payment, required for a sale is not completed at the time a lease transacted, as the lessor continues to make the property available and the lessee pays only as the property is used. Yet many leases do give the lessee the same effective use of property as would be obtained in a purchase.

The effective use of property without ownership and a reduced initial cash demand are the economic bases for leasing. While these economic realities have been given proper legal form, the accounting transition from simple sales reporting to a reflection of this new package of rights and obligations remains incomplete at present.

The development of more definitive accounting rules has lagged behind the economic use of leases. Leasing was originally confined primarily to land, but its use has expanded substantially in the last 20 years to other types of assets. Since business attitudes towards ownership of machinery are different from attitudes towards ownership of land, business has been able to sidestep the legal strictures of ownership in its pursuit of the economic benefits of leasing. Economics and law have helped to create a gap, and accountants are still in the middle.

The impact on financial statements of the distinction between owning and leasing is significant. "Accounting" assets appear on the balance sheet along with the debt obligations incurred to obtain those assets. If leased property is judged not to be an accounting asset, the balance sheet of a lessee is not directly affected. That decision will also create different costs in the income statement and different disclosure requirements in the notes. Thus, two companies doing the same work, with the same physical plant, will seem to perform quite differently if one capitalizes property and the other does not. Some would agree that they are in fact not exactly alike and should therefore not appear to be; others disagree. The dispute centers around measuring the similarities and differences accurately and reflecting the economic substance appropriately within the present conceptual framework of accounting[1] and the needs of financial statement users.

Since the lessee's degree of control over assets need not always be absolute or for their entire physical life, leasing is an attractive way to produce the same revenue as by purchasing assets and simultaneously to advance other goals. These goals include the exercise of some influence over the following: the income statement, by allowing a choice as to the pace of cost recognition; the balance sheet, through options for the recording of assets and liabilities; tax planning; and impact on performance ratios.

Uniform lease/purchase accounting treatment, however, will not necessarily cause two companies using similar assets to produce similar revenue to report results that look alike. Among factors, other than lease accounting, that produce these differences are: (1) ancillary accounting issues, such as deferral of preopening costs (a major retailer who primarily leases charges off preopening costs as incurred, while a very similar retailer who owns stores capitalizes such

---

[1]The FASB has on its agenda a proposed standard on the *Conceptual Framework of Accounting*.

costs); (2) timing of acquisitions (although indexing of costs can mitigate this problem); and (3) operating philosophy (one supermarket chain leases stores on a 15- or 20-year term in order to sell its groceries, while another chain sells groceries in order to acquire real estate under long-term leases which it believes will appreciate in value).

Accounting rules have also affected the financial statements of *lessors*. These rules determine whether a lease is a *financing arrangement* (where a lending institution is involved) or a *sale* (in the case of a manufacturer or dealer). Still other leases, in which the lessor will reacquire the property to be leased again, are strictly of an *operating* nature. Each type of lease requires different accounting treatment, and a careful examination of the contract terms and circumstances must be made to determine which treatment is appropriate. The outcome of this analysis is critical to the pace at which manufacturing profit, if any, is recognized, and to the timing and nature of income items for financing institutions.

OVERVIEW

This chapter will explore the economic issues that affect leasing decisions, as well as the pertinent present and proposed authoritative accounting pronouncements. The impact that the alternative decisions have on financial statements will be discussed. The principal accounting questions involve the determination of which leases are to be capitalized by the lessee, and how income is to be recognized by the lessor. Corollary issues are symmetry, that is, whether the accounting determinations of lessee and lessor should be consistent with one another, and whether certain types of leases, such as leveraged leases, leases between related parties, and leases by manufacturer or dealer lessors, require special rules.

The economic decision to acquire assets occurs before the decision as to the method of obtaining them. The "lease or buy" decision, viewed from the point of economic alternatives, focuses on the pragmatic questions of the tax impact of accelerated depreciation and the investment tax credit, possible obsolescence, asset life and period of need, available credit, and, of course, cost measured by the discounted cash flow technique. These questions concern the substance of real needs and available resources, as well as the impact that the alternative decisions will have on daily operations and efficiency. To the extent that no universally accepted technique for measuring cost is available and subjective judgment is a very important feature (such as in determining an appropriate discount rate), the determination of economic impact in arriving at a lease or buy decision can be very difficult.

Authoritative accounting pronouncements have sought to eliminate the advantages that have arisen due solely to choice of *form*. While allowing "true" leases to be accounted for as such, accounting rules have attempted to require transactions that are in substance purchases or sales, but take the form of leases, to be recorded as purchases or sales. The first of these pronouncements, still in effect, *Accounting Principles Board (APB) Opinion No. 5*, "Reporting of Leases in Financial Statements of Lessee" (September 1964), set criteria for a lessee's recognition of a purchase where the substance of the transaction so indicates. *APB Opinion No. 7*, "Accounting for Leases in Financial Statements of Lessors" (May 1966), prescribed somewhat different criteria for a financing arrangement or sale recognition by a lessor. *APB Opinion No. 27*, "Accounting for Lease Transactions by Manufacturer or Dealer Lessors" (November 1972), deals with the special circumstances of manufacturer-dealer lessors, as contrasted with financing institutions. *APB Opinion No. 31*, "Disclosure of Lease Commitments by Lessees" (July 1973), is the profession's most recent pronouncement on the subject, and deals exclusively with disclosure requirements for lessees. The Securities and Exchange Commission (SEC), in *Accounting Series Release (ASR) No. 147* (October 1973), set SEC disclosure requirements. These extend considerably beyond, and effectively supersede, *APB Opinion No. 31* for public companies. The proposed FASB standard, if adopted in present or slightly modified form, would supersede all previous AICPA pronouncements, and may supersede the SEC's[2] as well.

THE LEASE OR BUY DECISION

Leasing has distinct advantages and disadvantages, which can be identified and evaluated in specific circumstances. Some aspects of the question of whether to lease are subjective, leaving room for more than one answer. Most importantly, leasing is an alternative worth considering even if it is ultimately rejected.

Advantages of leasing

To the lessee

Economic issues:

1. *Limited commitment in case of property obsolescence.*
2. *Entire cost of property is financed* (including interest during and after construction).
3. *Restrictive loan provisions* barring new debt may be overcome in some instances.
4. *Period of need* may be considerably shorter than property's useful life.
5. *Tax deductibility* even for property that is not normally depreciable (e.g., land).
6. *Possible avoidance of some local taxes* where these are based on property values.
7. *Ability to share tax advantages* of ownership where these cannot be used directly by the lessee (see later section, "The Economic Issues").

---

[2]Full texts of all pronouncements should be consulted.

Accounting issues:

1. *Off-balance sheet accounting treatment*: no recorded assets or liabilities provided the transaction meets certain accounting requirements (see later section, "Criteria for Capitalization").
2. *Improved income statement performance in early years*: level lease payments will generally be less than the combined interest and depreciationexpense resulting from ownership accounting (this reverses in later years).

To the lessor

Economic issues:

1. *Secured interest in property* (but limited general creditor rights in bankruptcy as to rentals for remaining lease term).
2. *Right to residual value of property at end of lease.*
3. *Rate of return greater* than on the loan of an equivalent sum.

Accounting issues:

1. *Sales accounting* may be available under certain conditions.

Disadvantages of leasing

To the lessee

Economic issues:

1. *Higher total cost of discounted cash flows* (see Exhibit 1).
2. *No interest in residual property value* where recovery is reasonably certain.
3. *Loss of tax advantages* of investment tax credit and accelerated depreciation. Exhibit 1 does not give recognition to the investment tax credit the purchaser could obtain in the first year. This effect would be neutralized if the lessor arranges either to pass through the credit to the lessee or appropriately reduce the rental payments.

To the lessor

Economic issues:

1. *Obsolescence* may impair recovery of residual value or ability to re-lease after first lease term.
2. *Profit is dependent* on viability of lessee.
3. *Reversal of tax advantages* in later years of lease.

Exhibit 1. Buying versus Leasing: Comparison of Cash Flows ($100,000 asset)

	Buy								Lease			
Period	Debt Service [1]	Principal Repay-ment	Interest Pay-ment	Deprec-iation [2]	Interest plus Deprec-iation	Tax Benefit at 50%	After-Tax Cash Cost	Present Value	Rental [3]	Benefit at 50%	After-Tax Cash Cost	Present Value
1	$ 11,507	$ 3,614	$ 7,893	$ 12,500	$ 20,393	$ 10,197	$ 1,310	$ 1,213	$ 10,990	$ 5,495	$ 5,495	$ 5,088
2	11,507	3,912	7,595	11,667	19,262	9,631	1,876	1,608	10,990	5,495	5,495	4,711
3	11,507	4,234	7,273	10,833	18,106	9,053	2,454	1,948	10,990	5,495	5,495	4,362
4	11,507	4,583	6,924	10,000	16,924	8,462	3,045	2,238	10,990	5,495	5,495	4,038
5	11,507	4,961	6,546	9,167	15,713	7,856	3,651	2,485	10,990	5,495	5,495	3,740
6	11,507	5,370	6,137	8,333	14,470	7,235	4,272	2,692	10,990	5,495	5,495	3,463
7	11,507	5,813	5,694	7,500	13,194	6,597	4,910	2,865	10,990	5,495	5,495	3,206
8	11,507	6,292	5,215	6,667	11,882	5,941	5,566	3,007	10,990	5,495	5,495	2,969
9	11,507	6,810	4,697	5,833	10,530	5,265	5,242	2,622	10,990	5,495	5,495	2,749
10	11,507	7,372	4,135	5,000	9,135	4,567	6,940	3,214	10,990	5,495	5,495	2,545
11	11,507	7,979	3,528	4,167	7,695	3,848	7,659	3,285	10,990	5,495	5,495	2,358
12	11,507	8,637	2,870	3,333	6,203	3,101	8,406	3,338	10,990	5,495	5,495	2,182
13	11,507	9,349	2,158	2,500	4,658	2,329	9,178	3,375	10,990	5,495	5,495	2,020
14	11,507	10,120	1,387	1,667	3,054	1,527	9,980	3,398	10,990	5,495	5,495	1,871
15	11,507	10,954	553	833	1,386	693	10,814	3,409	10,990	5,495	5,495	1,732
	$ 172,605	$100,000	$ 72,605	$ 100,000	$ 172,605	$ 86,302	$ 86,303 [4]	$ 40,697	$ 164,850	$ 82,425	$ 82,425 [5]	$ 47,034

[1] $100,000 of debt borrowed at 8 percent. The debt service, payable quarterly in arrears, will be sufficient to amortize the loan fully over 15 years.

[2] Asset cost of $100,000 will be depreciated over 15 years using the sum-of-the-years'-digits method. It was assumed that the asset had no salvage value.

[3] Rental on a 15-year lease will be payable quarterly in arrears. The rental was based on an interest factor of 7¼ percent. It was assumed that the lessee's credit would require 8 percent interest. Since the lessor retains the depreciation benefits of the asset, he or she can charge a rent based on 7¼ percent even though the acquisition has been financed at 8 percent.

[4] Present worth of $86,303 cost of buying, at 8 percent, is $40,697.

[5] Present worth of $82,425 cost of leasing, at 8 percent, is $47,034.

Comment on Notes 4 and 5: When comparing the cumulative after-tax cash costs, buying is the more expensive alternative by about $4,000. However, present valuing the annual outflows results in buying being the more economical alternative by approximately $6,000.

THE ECONOMIC ISSUES

Answering the substantive question, should a company lease or buy, involves several factors:

Cost: The costs related to each alternative may be compared on the basis of their associated cash flows, discounted to present values at an appropriate rate. Generally the rate that measures the *opportunity cost*[3] of funds is used. The tax effects that attend these choices are critical elements in this comparison and are discussed below.

Tax impact: For the lessee, lease payments for business purposes are tax deductible even though the asset might not be depreciable if bought, for example, land. Accelerated depreciation and the investment tax credit are major considerations in the cash flows used to determine relative cost. If these cannot be used by a would-be purchaser (e.g., because of insufficient taxable income), their use in the analysis must be adjusted accordingly. For the lessor, positive cash flows are generated from these tax advantages when he retains them. Alternatively, if a lessor cannot use the investment tax credit, he or she may under certain conditions pass it through to the lessee.

The foregoing tax impact must be tempered with the caution that the Internal Revenue Service, upon examining the terms of lease transactions, may require that a lease be treated as a purchase and sale, with the concomitant tax changes. Its rules of thumb for issuance of an advance ruling that a lessor (particularly in a leveraged lease transaction) may use the operating method are set forth in Rev. Proc. 75.21 and are generally as follows:

1. The lessor's minimum investment in the property must be equal to 20 percent of the property's cost, and this minimum must be maintained throughout the life of the lease. At the end of the lease, the value of the property must be at least 20 percent of the original property cost. (Compliance with this condition is difficult to establish where the property, at the expiration of the lease, is of the special-purpose type—that is, usable only by the lessee. The Revenue Service has not yet determined whether it will issue rulings in this circumstance.) Only the amount of consideration paid or personal liability incurred by the lessor to buy the property will count toward this minimum. The lessor's net worth must be sufficient to satisfy any personal liability the lessor assumes.
2. The lessor must show that at the end of the lease term, the useful life remaining to the property is one year, or 20 percent of the originally estimated useful life, whichever is greater. In applying these conditions,

---

[3]The rate of return obtainable from equivalent funds in investments of the same risk.

the IRS will deem the lease term to include all renewals and extensions except when they are negotiated (1) at the option of the lessee and (2) for fair rental value at the time of the renewal or extension.

3. Where the lessee has an option to purchase the property, he or she cannot also have a contractual right to pay less than the value of the property as determined at the time the option is exercised. There cannot be a contractual agreement whereby the lessor can compel the lessee or any other party to buy the property, nor can the lessor have any intention to negotiate such an agreement. This prohibition applies to provisions allowing the lessor to abandon the property to any party.
4. The lessee may not furnish any part of the cost of the property (with minor exceptions), or make loans to, or guarantee loans on behalf of, the lessor to enable the latter to acquire the property. However, loans or loan guarantees may be permissible under certain conditions if repaid or rescinded before the property is placed in service.
5. The lessor must show a reasonable expectation of profit from the transaction, apart from tax deductions, allowances, credits, and other tax benefits.
6. If rent payments fluctuate more than 10 percent above or below the level calculated evenly over the lease term, the Service has the right to determine what, if any, part of the excess or deficiency is prepaid or deferred rent, respectively.

Failure to meet the tax ruling criteria does not automatically result in capitalization for tax purposes. Subjective criteria similar to the accounting criteria are considered for this purpose.

It should be noted that some lessees prefer capitalization for tax purposes (but not necessarily for accounting purposes), and so elect if they can justify the result in accordance with the applicable accounting and tax criteria.

Period of need: If the asset is not needed for a major portion of its economic life, leasing is a convenient way to obtain its use only for the period needed.

Obsolescence: Where flexibility to replace existing assets quickly and easily is important—for example, because of changing technology or erratic competition—leasing may be preferred.

Existing debenture or other covenants: If a company is specifically precluded from incurring additional debt to purchase assets, a lease may provide asset use without indenture violation; however, many lenders are now restricting lease obligations.

Available credit: Purchase requires larger credit at inception, and may be more difficult to finance, than a lease.

Accounting effect: Leasing that provides off-balance sheet financing of the facility to the lessee and level lease charges to income that are generally lower than combined depreciation and interest charges in the early years may result in economic advantages in the capital market. In addition to a better debt-equity ratio, a young growing company will show better earnings during this period.

At one extreme, if the need for an asset is quite short and the asset's useful life is relatively long, a lease provides use without ownership, financing of debt, risk of recovery of residual value, or expense of selling when the asset is no longer needed. (The use of a car for two months for a visiting executive is an example.) At the other extreme, a company with cash or available credit facilities (at a low rate) can buy more inexpensively than lease, assuming that it can use the cash flow benefits of accelerated depreciation and the investment tax credit. Even in those circumstances, however, more subjective factors, such as obsolescence, may result in a decision to lease.

Clear-cut examples make good textbook reading, but rarely seem to fit business reality. Among the elements affecting the decision are some having a subjective impact whose importance may vary from situation to situation. In addition, not all quantifiable data can be relied on to remain static, so today's correct decision may become incorrect in tomorrow's world. Nonetheless, decisions must be made on the basis of available facts.

The most interesting examples from the business executive's point of view are those where alternatives are available and an optimum answer is required. Weighing the impact of a substantial asset acquisition in terms of a lease or buy decision can be reduced to a simple economic model of discounted cash flows. But if the asset has a high obsolescence potential (e.g., a computer, or heavy equipment for a product in a volatile market, such as double-knit fabric machinery), a decision that purchasing is less expensive, based on discounted cash flows, will be disregarded for a way to minimize losses if conditions change. Potential obsolescence is one of the most cogent reasons to incur a higher total lease cost. To the extent that possible business reversals can be anticipated, this higher cost can be predetermined and identified as a form of insurance.

In most cases, the asset will cost the lessor who buys and then leases it a sum equivalent to what a would-be lessee would pay for it. Since the lessor's cost of financing the purchase is included in the lease payments, the lessee can usually be assured that he or she will be paying the lessor at least what would have been paid had the lessee bought the asset, assuming the lessor cannot obtain credit at a lower cost than the lessee. Should the prospective lessee not be able to make use of the tax advantages of ownership, especially accelerated depreciation and the investment tax credit, leasing may provide a vehicle whereby those benefits may be at least partially passed through to the lessee in the form of reduced lease payments.

In summary, dollar cost will generally be lower in buying provided that full use of tax advantages (depending on effective tax rate) can be made. However, the individual circumstances of each situation should be weighed carefully in reaching a decision.

THE ACCOUNTING ISSUES

The accounting treatments for purchases and sales, and for financing and operating leases, are clear-cut. Unfortunately, many lease transactions do not fit neatly into these categories. In theory, if a lease transaction is in substance a sale or purchase, then the lessee is required to capitalize the asset and to record the related debt. The lessee depreciates the asset and pays off the debt; the lessor removes the asset from the plant or inventory accounts and replaces it with a receivable. For a financing institution, the excess of total payments to be received over the asset cost represents income to be recognized in decreasing amounts over the term of the lease (generally as a percentage of the remaining investment). Where a manufacturer or dealer profit is involved, accounting for a lease as equivalent to a sale will also allow early recognition of the manufacturing profit. If there is no sale or purchase, the accounting is even simpler: the lessee pays and records lease costs as they come due, making appropriate accruals when payments and accounting periods do not coincide the lessor records an operating lease, taking rent revenue into income as it accrues and depreciating the asset, which stays on the books.

The lessee

Criteria for capitalization. *APB Opinion No. 5* requires capitalization if the transaction is "clearly in substance" a purchase. It expressed this concept by utilizing the term "material equity." If a lessee has such an interest in the leased property or the lease payments create one, capitalization is called for. Evidence of material equity, discussed at length in the next section includes the following:

1. The lease is noncancelable by either party, except upon a remote contingency, and
2. The initial term and renewal options cover the property's useful life, and the rental at renewal is substantially less than the fair rental value (bargain renewal option), or
3. A purchase option exists at a price that appears to be at the inception of the lease substantially less than the probable fair value at the time of exercise of the option (bargain purchase option).

The following circumstances are indicative of a purchase in all circumstances, *except where it is clear that no material equity exists*:

1. The property is for special-purpose use of the lessee.
2. The lease term is substantially equal to the life of the property, and lessee pays costs incidental to ownership, for example, taxes, insurance.
3. The lessee guarantees the lessor's obligations.
4. The lease is capitalized for tax purposes.

The practical effect of the application of *APB Opinion No. 5* has been to require capitalization of few long-term leases. Most lessees have been able to structure their leases so that no "material equity" builds up. Generally, a level payment lease with fair value options to purchase or renew, even though the lease term is substantially equivalent to economic life, will not result in the buildup of equity, and will hence be treated as a lease.

The above criteria do not apply, however, if the parties are related (discussed below). Recently, the SEC has invoked this section of *APB Opinion No. 5* where an intermediary lessor has been created for the purpose of holding and financing a lease, and such lessor is in the nature of a sham or of no economic substance.

Effectively, *APB Opinion No. 5* requires capitalization of all leases between related parties. Paragraph 12 states as follows:

> 12. In cases in which the lessee and the lessor are related, leases should often be treated as purchases even though they do not meet the criteria set forth [above], i.e., even though no direct equity is being built up by the lessee. In these cases, a lease should be recorded as a purchase if a primary purpose of ownership of the property by the lessor is to lease it to the lessee and (1) the lease payments are pledged to secure the debts of the lessor or (2) the lessee is able, directly or indirectly, to control or influence significantly the actions of the lessor with respect to the lease. The following illustrate situations in which these conditions are frequently present:
>
> a. The lessor is an unconsolidated subsidiary of the lessee, or the lessee and the lessor are subsidiaries of the same parent and either is unconsolidated.
> b. The lessee and the lessor have common officers, directors, or shareholders to a significant degree.
> c. The lessor has been created, directly or indirectly, by the lessee and is substantially dependent on the lessee for its operations.
> d. The lessee (or its parent) has the right, through options or otherwise, to acquire control of the lessor.

Disclosure. As the leasing movement grew, increased emphasis was given to greater disclosure of the terms of noncapitalized long-term leases so that users could draw therefrom any conclusions they considered pertinent. *APB Opinion No. 31*, Disclosure of Lease Commitments by Lessees (1973), superseded previous requirements. It requires the following disclosures (paragraphs 8, 9, and 10) as an integral part of the financial statements:

Total Rental Expense

> 8. Total rental expense (reduced by rentals from subleases, with disclosure of such amounts) entering into the determination of results of operations for each period for which an income statement is presented should be disclosed. Rental payments under short-term leases for a month or less which are not expected to be renewed need not be included. Contingent rentals, such as those based upon usage or sales, should be reported separately from the basic or minimum rentals.

Minimum Rental Commitments

9. The minimum rental commitments[4] under all noncancelable leases[5] should be disclosed, as of the date of the latest balance sheet presented, in the aggregate for:

a. Each of the five succeeding fiscal years,
b. Each of the next three five-year periods, and
c. The remainder as a single amount.

The amounts so determined should be reduced by rentals to be received from existing noncancelable subleases (with disclosure of the amounts of such rentals). The total of the amounts included in (a), (b), and (c) should also be classified by major categories of properties, such as real estate, aircraft, truck fleets, and other equipment.

Additional Disclosures

10. Additional disclosures should be made to report in general terms:

a. The basis for calculating rental payments if dependent upon factors other than the lapse of time.
b. Existence and terms of renewal or purchase options, escalation clauses, etc.
c. The nature and amount of related guarantees made or obligations assumed.
d. Restrictions on paying dividends, incurring additional debt, further leasing, etc.
e. Any other information necessary to assess the effect of lease commitments upon the financial position, results of operations, and changes in financial position of the lessee. (For example, in instances where significant changes in lease arrangements are likely it may be desirable to state that the information given is for existing leases only and is not a forecast of future rental expense. A statement could also be made that the amounts given may not necessarily represent the amounts payable in the event of default.)

The *Opinion* recommended, but did not require, disclosure of the present value of net fixed minimum rentals (by major categories of asset), based on interest rates implicit when negotiated.

---

[4]The minimum rental commitments are not necessarily indicative of the values of the property rights vested in the lessee.

[5]For purposes of this Opinion a noncancelable lease is defined as one that has an initial or remaining term of more than one year and is noncancelable, or is cancelable only upon the occurrence of some remote contingency or upon the payment of a substantial penalty.

The SEC's disclosure requirements set forth in *Accounting Series Release No. 147* are more extensive and more stringent. Specific measures of materiality are set forth for the disclosures enumerated above (i.e., 1 percent of revenue). If other measures of materiality are met (5 percent of total long-term debt and equity, 3 percent effect on net income), then disclosure is required of present value of minimum lease commitments, average interest rate used, and the impact on net income of capitalizing all financing leases and recording straight-line depreciation and interest expense. For this purpose, "financing leases" are defined as those with noncancelable terms equal to 75 percent or more of the property's economic life, or those that assure the lessor of a recovery of his or her investment plus a reasonable return. The data collection and computation required for those disclosures can be extensive.

The lessor[6]

Capitalization does not pose the same problems for lessors. The lease is always recorded—as property if it is an operating lease or as a receivable (or investment) if it is a financing lease. The main difference is in the manner of recording income. Under the "operating method" rent revenue is recognized as it is received; if a lease is accounted for as having the substance of financing the sale of the leased property, the "financing method" is used. A simple example shows the major characteristics of the two different methods. The assumed facts illustrated are:

Company A manufactures a piece of equipment at a cost of $35,000 and has it available for sale or lease at January 1, 19xl.
The equipment has an estimated useful life of five years and has no scrap value.

Operating method. On January 1, 19xl, Company A leases the equipment to Company B for five years, beginning January 1, 19xl, and ending December 31, 19x5, for $10,000 annually payable each year in advance. Company A uses the operating method; it recognizes revenue as the rent is earned and depreciates the asset by a straight-line method based on the five-year estimated life, resulting in a profit in each of the five years as follows:

Rent revenue	$10,000
Depreciation of equipment	7,000
Income from Leased Property	$ 3,000

Company A's profit for the five years totals $15,000.

Financing method. Company A uses the financing method, which accounts for the lease as equivalent to the sale of the property, resulting in a long-term

[6]Portions of this section have been extracted from Philip L. Defliese, Kenneth P. Johnson, and Roderick K. Macleod, *Montgomery's Auditing*, 9th ed. (New York: The Ronald Press Co., 1975), with permission.

receivable from Company B. Company A recognizes an immediate gross profit of $6,700, representing the difference between cost ($35,000) and the present value of the five payments ($41,700) using a rate of 10 percent as the rate of discount. This is equivalent to the normal selling price. Interest on the receivable is then recorded as follows:

Year	*Uncollected receivable at December 31*	*Interest Earned*
19x1	$34,870	$3,170
19x2	27,356	2,486
19x3	19,019	1,735
19x4	10,000	909
19x5	-0-	-0-
Total Interest		$8,300

The total income is the same under the financing (sales) method ($6,700 plus $8,300 interest = $15,000) as under the operating method, but it is recognized in a different pattern—more in the earlier and less in the later years of the lease period.

Lease transaction variations. The preceding example illustrates the two basic methods. However, they may appear in combination depending upon possible variations in the transactions. For example:

1. Company A might have leased the equipment to Company B and then assigned the lease (not the property) to Company C for $41,700. Company A could recognize the gross profit immediately by treating the transactions as a sale and an assignment of a receivable. Company C would recognize the interest earned from the long-term receivable as it is earned.
2. Company A might have sold the equipment for $41,700 to Company C (a finance or leasing company), which in turn would lease the equipment to Company B under the same terms, producing the same aggregate accounting result.
3. If Company C borrowed the purchase price (or a portion of it) at an effective rate of less than 10 percent, a transaction known as a "leveraged lease" would result (see below).

Choice of method. The methods of accounting for lease revenue and their combinations cannot be applied indiscriminately. *APB Opinions Nos. 7* and *27* describe the circumstances in which each type of accounting is appropriate.

In general, revenue should be recognized by the operating method if a lessor retains significant risks or rewards of ownership or is unable to estimate reasonably the collectibility of amounts due or amounts of future costs under the terms of the lease. Many leases obligate the lessor to service the equipment. Accounting for leases as equivalent to sales, that is, by the financing method, is an example of accounting for the substance of a transaction rather than its form when it appears that a sale by a manufacturer or dealer has really taken place, or when the manufacturer is assured the receipt of normal selling price under the terms of the lease, appropriately discounted. That often requires dividing a transaction into its elements—an element of sale and an element of long-term financing—and accounting for the elements separately. Banks and financing and leasing companies that purchase property for the purpose of financing a long-term lessee normally use the financing method for accounting purposes, but might use the operating method for income tax purposes (including accelerated depreciation). That combination would give rise to deferred income taxes.

The *APB Opinions* referred to above are complicated; and a reader should consult them, particularly to understand fully the accounting for leases as financing or sale transactions. For example, a manufacturer- or dealer-lessor must account for a lease transaction with an independent lessee as a sale if at the time of entering into the transaction (1) collectibility of the payments required from the lessee is reasonably assured, (2) no important uncertainties exist concerning the amount of costs yet to be incurred under the lease, and (3) any *one* of the following conditions is present:

a. The lease transfers title to the property to the lessee by the end of its fixed, noncancelable term; or

b. The lease gives the lessee the option to obtain title to the property without cost or at a nominal cost by the end of the fixed, noncancelable term of the lease; or

c. The leased property, or like property, is available for sale, and the sum of (1) the present value of the required rental payments by the lessee under the lease during the fixed, noncancelable term of the lease (excluding any renewal or other option) and (2) any related investment tax credit retained by the lessor (if realization of such credit is assured beyond any reasonable doubt) is equal to or greater than the normal selling price or, in the absence thereof, the fair value (either of which may be less than cost) of the leased property or like property; or

d. The fixed, noncancelable term of the lease (excluding any renewal option) is substantially equal to the remaining economic life of the property. (This test cannot be complied with (1) by estimating an economic life substantially equal to the noncancelable term if this is unrealistic or (2) if material contingent residual interest is retained in the property.) [*APB Opinion No. 27,* par. 4.]

Leveraged leases

A leveraged lease is a refinement of the leasing vehicle in which three parties instead of two play a role. The lessor, often referred to as the *equity participant*, is the owner of the property but may have contributed as little as 20 percent or less toward its acquisition. A lender provides long-term credit on a nonrecourse (mortgage) basis for the bulk of the acquisition cost. The leveraged lease is a carefully balanced package of cash flows and tax benefits for the lessor. They result in a return of his or her initial investment very quickly, followed by cash accumulation, net outflow, and finally net proceeds from sale of the asset. The ultimate profitability of such an arrangement to the lessor is heavily dependent on the effective use of the temporarily excess funds arising from the investment tax credit and accelerated depreciation. The availability of the anticipated tax benefits must be substantially assured before the actual yield rate can be safely computed.

The accounting for this seemingly precarious balance is very much at issue. The long-term lender has recourse only through the leased property and the lessee; consequently, it is acceptable (in this case only) to record the investment on a net basis, with excess tax credits accounted for as deferred credits. The real issue is the allocation of overall income to proper periods. Some would apply existing (*APB Opinion No. 7*) standards to leveraged leases, while others propose that new standards be developed. It is argued that the lessor should recognize revenue from the transaction by applying an overall yield percentage, mathematically computed, in proportion to the unrecovered net investment, since that investment is the lessor's only economic contribution to the transaction and there is no direct liability. In many cases, however, that theory must be substantially qualified or negated by the test of collectibility, because sometimes full utilization of the tax benefits and the projected cash flow sufficient to completely recover the investment cannot be considered reasonably assured in the early years of a lease.

The question of overall yield is also at issue. Some believe that an imputed yield during the period of the negative investment (when realized tax benefits exceed net investment) should be anticipated in determining overall yield. Many variations are found in practice, and there are no authoritative pronouncements on the subject at present. The standard proposed by the FASB's Exposure Draft requires calculating the overall yield without any yield imputation on negative investment and spreading income over only those periods in which a positive investment exists. (Earnings on the excess cash during the negative years would flow through to income on a realized basis.) Exhibit 2, taken from the FASB's Exposure Draft (with permission) and modified slightly, demonstrates this method. (It should be noted that the investment tax credit is spread over all positive periods—the preferred method. Alternatively, it may be taken into income immediately when realized as provided by the Revenue Act of 1971.)

Third parties

Lessors are motivated by, among other things, the need to secure financing and the desire to promote the early recognition of profit. Where a manufacturer—or dealer—lessor can transfer all the risks and rewards of ownership to a financing institution and receive a full payout of the investment, both objectives may be acomplished. *APB Opinion No. 27* addresses this area and basically prescribes that if the original lease agreement between lessor and lessee is not a sale, then the subsequent transfer of the lease to a third party is also not a sale unless the risk/reward/payment criteria noted above are met.

EXHIBIT 2

Leveraged lease example—terms and assumptions

Cost of leased asset (equipment)..	$1,000,000
Lease term....................................	15 years, dating from December 31, 1974
Lease rental payments	$90,000 per year (payable last day of each year)
Residual value..............................	$200,000 estimated to be realized one year after lease termination
Financing:	
Equity investment by lessor......	$400,000
Long-term nonrecourse debt.....	$600,000,bearing interest at 9% and repayable in annual installments (on last day of each year) of $74,435.30
Depreciation allowable to lessor for income tax purposes............	7-year ADR life using double-declining balance method for the first two years; sum-of-the-years'-digits method for remaining life, depreciated to $100,000 salvage value
Lessor's income tax rate (federal and state)	50.4% (assumed to continue in existence throughout the term of the lease)
Investment tax credit.....................	7% of equipment cost or $70,000 (realized by the lessor on last day of first year of lease)

Symmetry

The symmetry issue arises from the inconsistent accounting definitions and standards set for lessees vis-à-vis those for lessors. *APB Opinion No. 5* set narrow, though sometimes difficult, criteria for lessees, while *APB Opinion No. 7* set comparatively broad standards for lessors. Further, the thrust of the lessee requirements is toward balance sheet recognition (capitalization) and the resultant effect on income, while the lessor standards are mainly concerned with income recognition. As applied to lease accounting, symmetry would require that what is a sale for the lessor is a purchase for the lessee. Conversely, what is not sold by the lessor cannot have been bought by the lessee. The problem has been that because of the unequal criteria set for lessees and lessors, property considered as sold by a lessor has been viewed by a lessee as an operating lease and has not been capitalized on the balance sheet. Some feel strongly that as a matter of pure theoretical substance symmetry is essential. Others disagree on the basis that each company must account for transactions in accordance with its own circumstances. The proposed standard in the FASB's Exposure Draft (discussed below) implicitly requires symmetry.

Exhibit 2 *(Continued)*. Cash Flow Analysis by Years

Year	(1) Gross Lease Rentals and Residual Value	(2) Depreciation (for Income Tax Purposes) *	(3) Loan Interest Payments	(4) Taxable Income (Loss) (Col. 1 - 2 - 3)	(5) Income Tax Credits (Charges) (Col. 4 x 50.4%)	(6) Loan Principal Payments	(7) Investment Tax Credit Realized	(8) Annual Cash Flow (Col. 1 - 3 + 5 - 6 + 7)	(9) Cumulative Cash Flow
Initial Investment								($ 400,000)	($ 400,000)
1	$ 90,000	$ 137,222	$ 54,000	($ 101,222)	$ 51,016	$ 20,435	$ 70,000	136,581	(263,419)
2	90,000	243,628	52,161	(205,789)	103,717	22,274		119,282	(144,137)
3	90,000	203,303	50,156	(163,459)	82,383	24,279		97,948	(46,189)
4	90,000	162,978	47,971	(120,949)	60,959	26,464		76,524	30,335
5	90,000	122,654	45,589	(78,243)	39,435	28,846		55,000	85,335
6	90,000	30,215	42,993	16,792	(8,463)	31,442		7,102	92,437
7	90,000		40,163	49,837	(25,118)	34,272		(9,553)	82,884
8	90,000		37,079	52,921	(26,672)	37,357		(11,108)	71,776
9	90,000		33,717	56,283	(28,367)	40,719		(12,803)	58,973
10	90,000		30,052	59,948	(30,214)	44,383		(14,649)	44,324
11	90,000		26,058	63,942	(32,227)	48,378		(16,663)	27,661
12	90,000		21,704	68,296	(34,421)	52,732		(18,857)	8,804
13	90,000		16,957	73,043	(36,813)	57,478		(21,248)	(12,444)
14	90,000		11,785	78,215	(39,421)	62,651		(23,857)	(36,301)
15	90,000		6,145	83,855	(42,262)	68,290		(26,697)	(62,998)
16	200,000	100,000		100,000	(50,400)			149,600	86,602
Totals	$ 1,550,000	$1,000,000	$516,530	$ 33,470	($ 16,868)	$ 600,000	$ 70,000	$ 86,602	

* Due to computer error, the annual depreciation amounts vary from those that would have appeared on the tax return.

Exhibit 2 *(Concluded)*. Allocation of Annual Cash Flow to Investment and Income

	Annual Cash Flow				Components of Income *		
Year	(1) Lessor's Net Investment at Beginning of Year	(2) Total (from cash flow analysis, Col. 8)	(3) Allocated to Investment	(4) Allocated to Income †	(5) Pretax Income	(6) Tax Effect of Pretax income	(7) Investment Tax Credit
1	$ 400,000	$ 136,581	$ 112,436	$ 24,145	$ 9,331	($ 4,703)	$ 19,517
2	287,564	119,282	101,924	17,358	6,709	(3,381)	14,030
3	185,640	97,948	86,742	11,206	4,331	(2,183)	9,058
4	98,898	76,524	70,554	5,970	2,307	(1,163)	4,826
5	28,344	55,000	53,288	1,712	662	(334)	1,384
6	(24,944)	7,102	7,102				
7	(32,046)	(9,553)	(9,553)				
8	(22,493)	(11,108)	(11,108)				
9	(11,385)	(12,803)	(12,803)				
10	1,418	(14,649)	(14,735)	86	33	(16)	69
11	16,153	(16,663)	(17,637)	974	377	(190)	787
12	33,790	(18,857)	(20,896)	2,039	788	(397)	1,648
13	54,686	(21,248)	(24,550)	3,302	1,276	(643)	2,669
14	79,236	(23,857)	(28,639)	4,782	1,848	(931)	3,865
15	107,875	(26,697)	(33,209)	6,512	2,517	(1,268)	5,263
16	141,084	149,600	141,084	8,516	3,291	(1,659)	6,884
Totals		$ 486,602	$ 400,000	$ 86,602	$ 33,470	($ 16,868)	$ 70,000

* Each component is allocated among the years of positive net investment in proportion to the allocation of net income in Column 4.

† Lease income is recognized as 6.036 percent of the unrecovered investment at the beginning of each year in which the net investment is positive. The rate is the implicit rate which when applied to the net investment in the years in which the net investment is positive will distribute the net income to those years.

Sale and leaseback

There is generally no dispute concerning the proper accounting for sales of property with a concurrent long-term lease of the property from the purchaser back to the original owner. *APB Opinion No. 5* (paragraphs 21 and 22) settled the matter. All profits and losses (after taxes) on such transactions must ordinarily be *deferred and amortized* proportionally over the lease term as a modification of rent (or depreciation if the lease is required to be capitalized). One exception was granted to construction companies that both build and operate commercial properties, permitting them to reflect a reasonable profit on completion of construction. Losses must be recognized immediately if the fair value of the property at the time of the sale and leaseback is less than the depreciated cost.

The proposed standard in the FASB's Exposure Draft adheres to this general concept, with the following modifications:

1. The exemption for construction companies is eliminated.
2. The deferment of profit is not required if the lease does not qualify as a "capital" lease (as defined below) that is required to be capitalized, and the rental is equal to or greater than a "fair rental" determined for the property.

This proposal appears to be a liberalization of the current rule to the extent that some profits may be recognized immediately.

Proposed FASB standard on accounting for leases

The Exposure Draft issued by the FASB on August 26, 1975, has previously been referred to. While its adoption in present form cannot be assured, readers should be aware of the indicated trend, recognizing that the proposed standard, which is the most comprehensive ever issued on the subject by an authoritative body, comes after long study and research and a history of considerable controversy over the issue of lease capitalization.

Some aspects of the proposal have been referred to in previous sections on "Leveraged Leases" and "Sale and Leaseback." The other major points, including changes from present standards (*APB Opinions Nos. 5, 7, 27,* and *31*), would be as discussed in the following paragraphs.

From the lessee's standpoint. Leases must be capitalized if they qualify as "capital leases" (a new term for financing leases). A *capital lease* is one meeting any *one* of the following criteria:

1. Title passes to lessee at end of lease term (no change).
2. The lease contains bargain purchase options (no change).
3. The lease term (which includes bargain renewal option periods) is equal to 75 percent or more of the estimated economic life of the property (new).
4. The estimated residual value at the end of lease term is less than 25 percent of the property's fair value at the inception of the lease (new).

5. The property is special purpose to the lessee, that is, it cannot be used by others except with excessive (uneconomic) cost (new).

All other leases are classified as *operating leases*.

As at present, capitalization results in recording debt at its present value and allocating rental payments to interest and principal. Depreciation of the resultant asset is required "consistent with the lessee's normal depreciation policy." The meaning of the latter term is unclear; as a minimum, straight-line depreciation would be required.

From the standpoint of the lessor. The financing method currently in use by lessors qualifying under *APB Opinion Nos. 7* and *27* would generally remain in effect. Such leases would be classified as "sales type" when held by a manufacturer or dealer and "direct financing" when held by others (usually financial institutions), and (as at present) unearned income would be amortized to income over the lease term in proportion to the remaining balance of the receivable. However, the proposal does liberalize the criteria to some extent. Whereas *APB Opinion No. 27* requires that the discounted payments must equal normal selling price or fair value, the proposed standard requires only that the lease qualify as a "capital lease," as defined above.

Disclosure. Since the capitalization criteria would be effective only for leases entered into after December 31, 1975, the proposal provides for disclosing the present value of all existing and subsequently transacted noncapitalized leases (including operating leases) in the balance sheet (on both sides), with the amounts shown short, that is, not included in the totals. With respect to both capitalized and noncapitalized leases, the disclosures presently required by *APB Opinion No. 31*, previously discussed, are generally retained and somewhat expanded. The SEC requirement of providing an alternative net income figure "as if" all noncapitalized finance-type (capital) leases were capitalized retrospectively has not been proposed.

There are many other finer point variations of disclosure between the proposed standard and present practice which need not be covered here since they may be changed before final adoption. The entire text of the Exposure Draft should be consulted.[7]

SUMMARY

The objective of accounting in general, and lease accounting in particular, is to enable users of financial data to better understand events and their impact on the condition of a business entity. Users necessarily view lease accounting not as an argument about technicalities, but rather as a pragmatic decision-making vehicle. This much is elementary; however, the identity of these would-be users, the information they are seeking, and the decisions they want to make are often unclear and sometimes unknown. Nevertheless, users have a common interest in

---

[7]As of April 1, 1976 the FASB has not yet acted on the proposed standard.

the events that take place and their effects, but the different uses to which they would put this information require that accounting not allow misleading inferences. The data that appear in the financial statements must be correct, identifiable, and complete. It is often argued that at some point more information adds no more to understanding and may actually be counterproductive. Since there is no way to anticipate the use to which any accounting data may be put, the balance of reporting swings toward more complete disclosure.

As leasing continues to be discussed and the alternatives in lease accounting continue to be studied, we approach a consensus position on what presentation of the facts is most appropriate. Adoption of the FASB Exposure Draft in present or modified form may put an end to much of this discussion. But use of a facility to generate revenue is acknowledged to be an economic cornerstone. The costs associated with the use of a facility over its useful life can be estimated and matched with revenue as it is earned. One of the most pervasive disputes concerns the speed and regularity with which costs are charged against revenue. Alternatives vary from that of conservatives who would accelerate the charges, claiming that future revenue production is uncertain, to concepts that combine total anticipated costs (including interest on unrecovered capital employed) and tax benefits and allocate them over the life of the facilities on a level basis.[8] The leveling bears witness to the widespread desirability of a level income impact. There is certainly a good argument for using the sinking-fund depreciation method (not permitted in the United States by the SEC) to counterbalance high interest costs in early years and achieve this leveling.

The possibility of implementing a far-reaching change to present accounting practice by bringing several problem areas together for simultaneous resolution has been addressed before and will continue to receive the attention of the accounting profession.

---

[8]Philip L. Defliese, *Should Accountants Capitalize Leases?* (Coopers & Lybrand, 1973).

FUNDAMENTAL ACCOUNTING CONCEPTS AND OBJECTIVES

THE OBJECTIVES OF FINANCIAL ACCOUNTING†

by

Philip L. Defliese

PREFACE

MOST users of financial statements believe that they understand the objectives of those statements. They accept the attestation of the auditor to a fair presentation of "financial position" and "results of operations" as if these objectives were precisely formulated, and a standard methodology available to achieve them. Few investors realize how much disagreement exists not only on the methodology but on the objectives themselves. Even fewer, perhaps, grasp the implications of this disagreement for the value of the document on which they are relying.

For many years accounting practice has been governed by a body of outworn conventions loosely denominated "generally accepted accounting principles." The imprecision of these conventions allows for a latitude of interpretation in accounting practice that is no longer tolerable. Until this frayed and inadequate standard is replaced by something more meaningful, accounting will be unable to keep pace with the growing demands being placed on it.

Recognizing this need, the American Institute of CPAs has convened a Study Group on the Objectives of Financial Statements. The Group is re-examining the entire theory of accounting, treating the formulation of objectives and their implementation as different aspects of the same problem. From the diversity of ideas that has already been aired in hearings before the Group it is clear that the dimensions of that problem are as yet unfathomed.

Evolving and implementing a grand design for change in the practice of a profession can hardly be done overnight—especially when the theoretical basis of the profession's discipline is a subject of disagreement. It is not only a question of the research, an immense project in itself, but also of the logistical burden of

---

†An elaboration of the oral recommendations made in May 1972 to the AICPA's Study Group on Objectives of Financial Statements. (New York: Coopers & Lybrand, 1973), 22 pages. Reprinted with permission of PricewaterhouseCoopers LLP. The preface was also reprinted under the title, "The State of the Accounting Art," in *The CPA Journal*, April 1974, p. 25; and portions of the paper were published under the title, "Accounting Practice—Design for Change," in *Financial Executive*, January 1974, pp. 14-18, 23.

maintaining consensus. At every step, a new working agreement of compromise must be achieved between many disparate interests, otherwise the applicability of the final results will be limited. There are no alternatives to this deliberative method, because there is virtually no margin for error. The risk of creating chaos in what is still—despite the skepticism of many—a dynamic, well-ordered capital market is too great to permit the implementation of untested procedures.

The document that follows offers no shortcuts to the epic task facing the accounting profession. It is designed to survey the scope of that task and to set forth guidelines for a pragmatic approach. The setting of accounting principles is an ongoing project, one that cannot and should not be finished as long as the economic system itself displays vigor.

ACCOUNTING AT THE CROSSROADS

Demand both from within and without the accounting profession is for progress. Abuses in corporate reporting must be corrected and, beyond that, a new, comprehensive framework must be developed. Accounting is a valuable art; the success of our capital market system depends ultimately on the effective reporting of results.

There is no question but that public accounting is now at a crossroad. The choice is simply one of retaining its conservative, individualistic ways or of streamlining its practices and outlooks to meet the demands of the twenty-first century.

At the heart of the issue is the question of the diversity of accounting methods available to report results and the concomitant question of comparability. The fabulous growth of the U.S. capital market has been spurred on by both the highly sophisticated and the unsophisticated. Ours is truly a broad-based market whose participants include the most knowledgeable institutional investor as well as everyone's "Aunt Minnie" or "Uncle Harry." Financial reporting must serve both—and the wide spectrum of professionals in between. We need now to recommit ourselves fully to enhance the credibility of financial reporting, to develop a methodology that will assure more reliable results.

The start has been made by the Accounting Principles Board—and that effort must be continued by the new Financial Accounting Standards Board. Over the last five years, the APB has made progress toward reducing the number of alternatives and establishing uniform guidelines.

But it has not been enough, and the profession is wisely aware of the need to gear for future demands upon it while it also attempts to cure past and present abuses. The need to re-examine basic objectives is paramount, and that is what this Study is all about. However, a review of the lapses of the recent past will show that the need is not so much for *new objectives* as for *objective guidelines* for *applying* accounting principles and a better understanding of the attest function of auditing.

EXPERIENCE OF THE ACCOUNTING PRINCIPLES BOARD

When the Accounting Principles Board was created in 1959, research was seen as the foundation upon which badly needed new principles would be established; emphasis was to be given to the re-examination of objectives and proposed broad principles. Unfortunately, research was slow in coming, and, to a great extent, its fruits were dissipated by a tendency to recommend untried theories couched in generalities. (The need for *applied* research in accounting still escapes many researchers.) Meanwhile, the APB had to abandon the search for new principles to contend with a series of brushfire issues that arose in the fast-moving Sixties—pension costs, extraordinary items, convertible debt, earnings per share, poolings, and goodwill. The opinions issued on these problems are admittedly stopgaps, but they do provide a degree of uniformity not previously attained. In this context they thus represent an important measure of progress.

GENESIS OF THE PRESENT CRISIS

To understand the present crisis in the accounting profession, one must go back to the early postwar era. Twenty-five years ago, we had only 6 million public shareholders in this country; now there are almost 32 million, not counting those who have an indirect interest, through insurance, pensions, etc., truly a tribute to the vitality of our people's capitalism. In 1947, the average daily turnover on the New York Stock Exchange was less than 1 million shares; in 1971, it was well over 15 million. Thus, the public as a whole is more investment-conscious than it was, and the number of financial analysts available to aid investors has proliferated.

The heavy influx of investors underlies the persistence of the price-earnings fetish. The price-earnings multiple is a beautifully simple concept with an almost irresistible appeal to the uninformed. Granted that this ratio is valid within certain limits, it is still merely the result of market action that, in turn, often arises from an earnings report or estimate. The earnings-per-share figure, moreover, which all accountants acknowledge as an imprecise statistical formulation, has been no less than deified as the ultimate denomination of all the imprecise estimates and determinations made in accounting to arrive at operating results.

Thanks in great measure to the large number of investors who use EPS as a sole analytical touchstone (even dividends, once an important price determinant, have taken a back seat to this indicator), the responsiveness of the market to reported earnings is acute. As a result, management—including fund management—is expected to perform for its principals by constantly reporting improved results, and the accountants have not been excluded from this pressure. *Trends* of earnings have become more important than the earnings themselves, and only those capable of deep analysis are interested in the makeup of the earnings per se. The accounting profession, which never wanted to be involved with EPS—simply because it never considered it an accounting result—was plainly not ready for this shift in emphasis.

Accounting is essentially transaction-oriented, a heritage of its bookkeeping past. With few exceptions, it uses a historical cost framework, never current value (except to recognize apparent losses in value). It was not until the regulatory commissions were created and the income tax law enacted, in 1913, that refined concepts of accrual accounting (not dependent on transactions)—and, particularly, depreciation—were put into general practice. Depreciation did not become "required" until about 1930, and some companies even then wrote their plants down to one dollar to avoid it. The controversy over whether income tax was an expense or a sharing of profits with the government (surplus charge) raged for many years, and deferred tax concepts became imperative only during the war and postwar period when tax rates rose and rapid depreciation for tax purposes was permitted. Consequently, many of our accounting "theories" evolved out of a need to deal with circumstances as they came up.

ACCOUNTANCY TODAY: SOME KEY CHARACTERISTICS

• Despite all the efforts to develop a logical theory, accountancy still remains a collection of artificial conventions. These provide a recognizable framework for making basic operating approaches intelligible. But these conventions are far from having the status of "revealed truth." The profession, in fact, has yet to concur on their definition. It took the APB years to agree on the substance of its Statement No. 4: "Basic Concepts and Accounting Principles Underlying Financial Statements of Business Enterprises." The Board recognized that it could not examine the future objectives of financial reporting until it defined the function's present status. Critics of the Board point out that it failed because it did not provide a chart for the future. But that APB Statement actually represents the first logical step towards the goal: before setting a course, we must first know where we are.

• Practicing accountants have a bent for thinking in terms of analogy and clinging to precedent. As far back as 1932, the profession adopted the term "generally accepted accounting principles" as the premise on which auditors' opinions should rest. The use of this convenient formula (which was never defined) reflects to some extent the notion that a principle, once established by usage, can be applied in any situation where a reasonable case could he made for an analogy. The trouble is that analogies can be stretched. (They can also become confining and retard progress.) And they have been stretched, leading to a host of alternatives that have sprung up over the years in financial reporting. It is this erosion of standards that the APB has tried to combat.

• Accounting theory labors under the curse of balancing, as exemplified by the balance sheet (and its rigid presentation rules) and the need for relating the income statement to the balance sheet. We cannot scrap the double-entry system, but we should open our minds to the acceptance of a less formal format, one designed to give the user more meaningful information. It is useless to argue whether deferred income taxes are liabilities, deferred credits, or valuation accounts. In the final analysis, all that matters is the effect of the widening gap between tax accounting and financial accounting on present and future income and the ability of a company to meet its obligations. Unfortunately, the aggregate on the debit side is still occasionally labeled "total assets." Deferred charges included on the asset side cannot be equated with cash, and it's about time the practice of adding them together ceased entirely.

• The path of progress in accounting theory is obstructed by a number of seemingly inviolate notions, which vary in nuisance value. One of the most pernicious is the idea that the ultimate objective of accounting is to give an accurate picture of financial position. The auditor's familiar imprimatur of the balance sheet: that it "presents fairly the financial position" would be a flagrant lie if it were not for the added reassuring qualifier, "in conformity with generally accepted accounting principles."

The concept of financial position, which would not even be particularly useful if it could be effectively presented—and it cannot—must be dethroned. (Earlier versions of the auditors' opinion did not even use the word "financial.") Something more meaningful must be found, even though the quest will doubtless be a long one. And the debt-equity ratio must go the same way as financial position; the amounts taken from the balance sheet represent neither the entire debt (because of off-balance-sheet financing) nor the true equity in an economic sense.

THE PROMISE OF FASB

Awesome as the present crisis is, there is no question but that it can be surmounted. Creation of the independent Financial Accounting Standards Board to replace the APB is a sign that the profession is alert to the need for a major effort. The constituency of the new Board removes any doubt as to the rulemakers' independence. The ultimate report of the Study Group, to which this statement is addressed, should set a clear direction for the new FASB to follow. Additional work by the AICPA on sorely needed provisions covering auditing procedures and self-disciplinary measures will buttress this effort.

One should not expect too much, however, from the Study Group on Objectives of Financial Statements. Without applied research to support its recommendations, it cannot presume to have all the answers. No part-time group with limited research capacity can produce a comprehensive, highly structured plan to replace the present system within such a short time.

THE ROLE OF THE STUDY GROUP

The Study Group should, however, be able to agree on the assigning of objectives to one of three categories according to the time estimated for accomplishment: long term, short term, and intermediate. The short-term goals will generally involve no earth-shaking departures from present-day principles. The long-range goals will require not only considerable research but also time-consuming deliberation by industry and the profession to determine together exactly what the goals are. The intermediate goals are those on which less research and faster agreement are anticipated than in the long-term case. In its report, the Group should indicate the problems associated with each objective and recommend the research necessary to evaluate the objective's feasibility.

The Group should be able to provide a master plan for fulfilling the long-term objectives. Greater emphasis, however, should be on the precise definition of the short-range goals and on the means of implementing them; in-depth consideration of the other two classes can be deferred. More will be achieved this way than by attempting to cover all three areas in greater detail. Physicists may theorize that the time element in relation to human life-span is a major stumbling block to travel in outer space; meanwhile they must, however, concentrate on getting the bugs out of moon travel. The position of accounting, which is far from a precise science, is in many ways the same.

The research backup required by the Study Group's recommendations will be formidable. This research must be carried on as a joint effort. Apart from the fact that no single individual, group, or firm is equal to the task, it is desirable that the research reflect the many points of view now prevalent.

The public hearings the Group has held to solicit the views of all interested parties have produced a diversity of suggestions and recommendations deserving of careful study. Although the Group will be under pressure to issue a report, it should consider delaying any definitive proposal until it gives these same parties the chance to react to tentative proposals now being evaluated. The implications of the ultimate report of this Group are so far-reaching that they warrant this consideration. The public is entitled to understand the nature of the debate, and it should have an opportunity to participate to some degree.

THE IMPORTANCE OF PUBLIC INVESTORS

Because of limited time and research capability, the Study Group should concentrate on the needs of public investors. In this context, "public investor" is defined as a person or institution that purchases debt or equity securities, generally on an open market (or through a public offering of the offerer), relying upon the data made public by the issuer and the advice of those who analyze such data. The needs of private creditors (such as banks, insurance companies, and vendors) and of government agencies and regulatory commissions are secondary. These users are in a position to obtain additional information on request because of the contractual or jurisdictional nature of their relationships.

The 32 million public investors naturally account for a large part of the trading of securities in this country. Yet the number of people who have, or should have, a stake in financial statements is much higher. Even though some of the 32 million do not actively participate in market turnover, their number is more than counterbalanced by the many insurance policyholders, pensioners, and savings bank depositors whose funds are invested in the market. The interests of labor and other segments of the public at large can be readily equated with those of the public investor, and thus no great distinctions are needed.

FUNDAMENTAL PURPOSES OF FINANCIAL STATEMENTS

Simply stated, financial statements should provide one (*and only one*) source of information, which should help the investor or potential investor make a timely decision as to whether to buy, sell, or hold a particular security investment. As will be shown later, it is irrelevant whether the security is a stock or bond; the financial data upon which the decision rests is essentially the same for both, and thus financial statement format has virtually nothing to do with the choice between debt or equity securities.

It must be re-emphasized that financial information is only one factor in investment decision-making. Other factors having equal or greater weight include the state of the art of any activity with which the company is directly concerned, nature of the industry, condition of the economy, competitive position, management and research expertise, labor relations, government regulation, etc.

Although the accountant has been forced to calculate and attest to an earnings-per-share figure, this does not mean that in the preparation of financial statements he is assuming the role of security analyst. Security analysis is a different discipline, with its own special methods of handling financial data—a discipline that, by the way, is virtually terra incognita to a large percentage of the investing public. Instead, many of the do-it-yourself investors rely almost exclusively on financial statements. The fixation on the magic EPS figure, which is supposed to be a digest of operating results, has, of course, accentuated this trend and sharply publicized the accountant's role. (Fortunately, APB Opinion No. 15, "Earnings-Per-Share," has somewhat deflated the EPS boom by requiring several EPS figures, and has also standardized the calculation methods.)

Can financial data be simplified to the point where the man on the street can understand it? The answer is clearly negative. Various levels of sophistication always exist, and any hope of reducing financial statements to the point where they can be understood by the lowest common denominator and still serve their purpose is simply unrealistic. The growing complexity of modern business makes it difficult for accountancy not only to cope with, but also to reflect simply the economic changes brought about by an innovative environment. Of course, much can be done to standardize financial statements and to eliminate superfluous and confusing details, but this is not simplification in the true sense. Confining the discussion to financial data, the public investor needs to know:

• *The prospects for an adequate return on his investment in terms of yield (dividends and interest) and capital appreciation.* This translates into the need for a realistic determination of periodic income, past, present, and, *particularly, future,* presented on a comparable basis. The ultimate need for forecasts of at least one year is paramount because an investor should be more concerned with where his company is going than where it has been. But carefully designed guidelines plus experimentation, and delineation of responsibility will be needed before this requirement can be imposed. Certainly a step in this direction would be to call for more frequent and more meaningful interim reports to shareholders (not just for SEC filings), a requirement surprisingly not now in effect for all publicly held companies. Earnings trends, when fully informative, have traditionally been a sound basis for investment decision; certainly the past often serves as a good indicator for the future of a well-established, stable company. But the accuracy of earnings projections can be considerably improved by providing a more meaningful income statement, as discussed later.

• *The factors on which he can assess the safety of his capital.* The issuer has an obligation to reveal its resources and responsibilities, its liquidity, and its viability in terms of future needs and commitments. Comparability with the data of those who are competing in the same capital market is, of course, essential. To do justice to these factors, traditional concepts of "financial position" should be discarded and the balance sheet and funds statement restructured. Safety and return on capital in this context boil down to the future marketability of a security; reliance on forced liquidation is foolhardy. In today's atmosphere, debt securities are seldom held to maturity. Faced with the need to sell, a bondholder must rely on the ability of his company to earn a profit, because this factor will usually have a greater impact on the bond's price than the company's expected ability to repay the debt in the year 2000. Thus, the safety of his capital is usually largely dependent on the prospective earnings rather than on the proceeds of a possible liquidation.

• *The factors that influence the economic value of an investment so that proper choices can be made.* Some attempt must be made to reflect *current* estimates of values in addition to historical values and to give more recognition to intangible and human resources. When estimates of current values are available, investors can attempt to assess their impact upon future income flows. It should be recognized, however, that accounting can never establish the true "net worth" of a company; the only reliable criterion is the familiar "what a willing buyer will pay" and a "willing seller will take." The accounting profession can only hope to provide more meaningful financial data as a guide.

The above objectives are not startlingly new. They are merely a re-articulation of what most accountants consider present objectives to be. What is really needed is an attempt to direct accounting toward a methodology that will achieve those objectives—implementation is the key!

A MASTER PLAN

LONG RANGE

When accountants say that they are trying to reflect economic facts, they do so with tongue in cheek. For example, because they are better prepared to deal with downside or conservative valuations than upside, they cling to historical costs, knowing that these often do not reflect economic realities. Not until we provide a meaningful framework for current valuation of invested capital will financial accounting truly serve the needs of the investing public. The ultimate development of this framework is the aim of the proposed long-range plan. The liquidation value of a corporation is of little interest to investors who are not hoping to liquidate. Consequently, reported annual income must remain the core of any valuation exercise; thus the nature of income is the central consideration.

Advanced theoreticians hold that the income of a period consists of the difference between the values of the net economic resources of a company at the beginning and at the end of the period. And it is difficult to disagree with this concept. But the realization of income through the use of current values, particularly those that fluctuate, is something else. Any attempt to carry out this noble theory at present would produce chaos. For one thing, even economists can't agree on what economic resources are; for another, valuation measurement techniques are presently very subjective and undeveloped. If accountants cannot agree today on proper costing concepts for historical cost accounting—in such areas as inventories, depreciation, and research and development—how can they be expected to agree on current valuation concepts?

Current values are fine to look at, but one must consider the question of when do the values actually inure to the benefit of the owner. In short, when are these values realized? Anyone who has attempted to manage his own personal portfolio knows what it is like to feel richer or poorer at different times. As the result of market fluctuations, the term "paper profits" is probably better understood by investors than "earnings per share."

The best example of the difficulties encountered in trying to construct a value framework is found in the experience of the APB over the past three years on the problem of marketable equity securities. This became an exercise in frustration. After much study and discussion, a majority of the Board concluded that quoted market values at closing date were the ideal balance sheet values, and that both realized and unrealized gains and losses should flow through the income account. What could be simpler and more objective? The practice of mutual investment companies (who sell and redeem their shares daily on this basis) was used as a model. But the companies that manage huge portfolios of equity securities and whose performances are measured by different market criteria—principally insurance companies and conglomerates—were horrified at this decision. What effect, they asked, would a fluctuating market have upon quarterly and annual earnings? Are market values at closing date a true indication of periodic income when the intent is to obtain long-term appreciation? They pointed to wild fluctuations just prior to and after year-end and showed that liquidating value (in bulk on any given date) would be drastically less than their market quotes.

When the APB backed off (leaving the issue still unresolved), critics blamed the equivocation on the lack of real objectives for financial statements. In actuality, the trouble is that, with all the objectivity of a market quote, there is still disagreement on how the intrinsic values should be determined *and* on the point at which income is *earned* in such cases.

Whatever framework we adopt, the concept of income realization cannot be entirely divorced from the concept of income determination. Transaction-oriented accounting must remain as an underpinning to provide objectivity even if we move toward a current-value framework. Implicit in this view is the need to examine all current values to distinguish those that are expected to be realized ultimately through sale or exchange and those that are destined to enter the earning process through utilization. Has a company whose single-purpose plant appreciated in value for a variety of reasons actually earned the difference between cost and current value?

Certainly such intangibles as social and personnel values have no place in this exercise, no matter how important they may be to society or the well-being of a particular company. Although they may have some significance from the standpoint of investment evaluation, factors of this nature will, for a long time, be virtually impossible to quantify with any useful degree of precision.

Nevertheless, the search for a skeletal structure of accounting, based on current values must go on, but the effort cannot he pursued in a vacuum. No matter how much more useful a balance sheet providing realistic values may be to the investor, the primary tool will remain periodic income—annual income statements. Consequently, a closer analysis of the elements entering into periodic income must be made, with a view toward refining the principles of realization, because, as indicated previously, values are meaningless unless they inure to the owner's benefit.

As the basis for this analysis we should recognize the importance of the following elements affecting income:

- The ability to provide a product or service at a price in excess of cost, using traditional cost accounting concepts (which also need re-examination).
- The effect of economic forces upon our resources—such as market fluctuations—which may be beyond our control (fortuitous) or within our control (premeditated).
- The effect of research and discovery. This is important in the scientific and natural resources field.
- The effect of price-level changes on values entering into the determination of income. These changes, of course, are beyond control, but they can often be anticipated, and they can be quantified to a degree.

Timing of the recognition of these elements becomes the major factor in the *determination* of income.

The strategy in arriving at a value structure must include the formulation of a number of hypotheses and then in testing them for feasibility, first on a theoretical and then on a practical plane. This will require a concentrated research project carried out over at least three years by a sizable full-time team chosen from diverse disciplines and philosophies. Because of its far-reaching implications this project should be approached carefully. No one person or firm has the solutions to these problems nor the resources to pursue them.

SHORT RANGE

In the meantime, auditing techniques must be improved, and concepts of historical cost accounting and the matching of costs with revenues must be retained and refined so that users' needs will, within the confines of this frame of reference, be better satisfied. During the last several years, the APB has given high priority to the narrowing of alternatives. What has been accomplished, however, can only be described as clearing the tip of an iceberg.

In the process, the Board, in many instances, had established rather definitive guidelines for judgment and aroused the ire of critics who believe that the accountant's judgment is sacrosanct and should not be governed by arbitrary rules. (The profession's concern with its freedom is far from dead; it is the chief factor in the refusal to agree on the meaning of materiality in accounting.)

Accounting based on historical costs has sometimes been blamed for failure to recognize hidden losses in the economic values of assets on the traditional balance sheet. These failures, however, are not inherent in the concept; they result from failures to apply it. The APB has already laid down in its objectives a series of precepts designed to minimize these lapses:

> Reductions in the utility of productive facilities caused by obsolescence due to technological, economic, or other change are usually recognized over the remaining productive lives of the assets. If the productive facilities have become worthless the entire loss is then recognized.... The amount at which those facilities are carried is sometimes reduced to recoverable cost and a loss recorded prior to disposition or expiration of the useful life of the facilities. (Statement Number 4, paragraph 183)

Uneconomic plants have been written down (or off) in the past, as has goodwill that has evaporated, and the recoverability of deferred R&D is (or should be) carefully watched. In addition, we have seen over the last few years a tremendous growth in the practice of writing down plants, R&D, undeveloped land held as inventory, and the like, *long before* they were disposed of. Obviously, our present framework not only permits this but also requires it, and it is doubtful that a value concept would have recognized them sooner. Nevertheless, a better understanding of the precepts that underlie historical cost accounting is needed.

While the "going concern" concept of value is valid, better approaches to the problem of dealing with historical cost valuations need to be established until current-value measurement concepts can be developed and implemented.

Alternatives in accounting grew up because of varying industry practices and circumstances, and the misuse of alternatives results from applying irrelevant principles under the guise of analogy and "general acceptability." In our attempts to narrow alternatives we have tried unsuccessfully to find fundamental truths that could be applied across the board. It appears that this Holy Grail will remain forever out of reach. Instead we must concentrate, in the short-range period, on:

• *Refining income realization concepts on an industry-by-industry basis.* It is foolhardy to expect that realization and measurement concepts can be equally applicable to steel, oil and gas, land sales, construction, insurance, and timberlands. In the extractive industries, discovery and natural growth values—an inventory approach—should be considered as a first step toward value accounting without abandoning cost in all other areas. On the other hand, it may still be necessary to recognize differing circumstances within industries. Current efforts of the accounting profession have already led to some progress in the area of developing specialized principles for different industries, and this experience has shown that various approaches to realization determination are mandatory.

• *Expanding the income statement into more meaningful categories.* This will give the investor some important clues concerning those elements that are expected to recur and those that are not. For example, instead of being buried in the traditional major headings, the following items should be separately disclosed (net of related tax effects): (a) the costs attributable to a six-week strike that produced a three-year labor contract; (b) abnormal writedowns of inventories, receivables, and R&D; (c) unusual gains and losses on dispositions of productive facilities and other one-time transactions; (d) costs of abandoning product lines or outlets and of starting new ventures, and (e) the effects of variations in discretionary expenses. Breakdowns by industry lines—already begun—are essential, and this trend should be developed and refined. In the last analysis, the income statement should tell a *story* of operations, not just the "*results* of operations."

Once the income statement has been restructured to its highest degree of usefulness to investors, the need for an "extraordinary item" classification will disappear. This approach will also sound the death knell of the abbreviated functional income statement, with its uninformative "cost of sales" and "general and administrative expenses" captions. In addition, the industry-by-industry refinement of income realization concepts will probably result in varying presentations of the income statement, some of which may differ considerably from present formats.

• *Restructuring balance sheet (without changing basic concepts) into a statement (in single-step narrative form) of resources and commitments designed to demonstrate liquidity and viability.* The balancing aspect and grand totals should be abandoned. Instead, the emphasis should be on telling a story that a reasonably knowledgeable investor can analyze. The result might be shown somewhat on the following order:

Resources

Liquid: Assets and prepayments that will be liquidated in one year, less liabilities payable in one year, should be shown. The one-year rule should be rigid, even when the expected operating cycle is longer. All items should be reduced (with amounts shown) by any related deferred taxes that will be paid or reduced when liquidation takes place. Consideration should be given to a further breakdown between those items that will be quickly liquidated (accounts receivable and accounts payable) and those that will not, i.e., inventories. If tax elements are subject to a rollover effect based on continuing operations, this should be explained.

Investments in Property: Segregated according to operating, nonoperating, held for disposition, etc., net of depreciation, loss reserves, and any related deferred taxes that would indicate the degree to which future tax deductibility has been utilized.

Other Long-Term Assets: (fully described with purpose explained).

Purchased Intangibles: Classified by acquisition and underlying nature (see later comments), with description of the basis on which they will benefit income and, if needed, how they will be charged against income.

Deferred Charges and Credits to Future Income: Shown with clear indication that they are not resources in the same sense as the other assets. They should be broken down according to class and period in which to be charged off or related to income, net of related deferred taxes.

Commitments

Long-Term Debt: Classified according to maturity, with disclosure of individual and embedded interest rates, amounts maturing in each of the next five years, etc.

Contractual Commitments: Long-term leases, by classification of properties, with disclosure of present value of the commitment and annual minimum and current rentals; obligation for pensions, funded and unfunded, vested, etc., with description of the company's approach toward fulfillment.

Shareholder's Equity

Invested Capital: Without distinction between par and additional paid-in capital, and a description of current changes.

Invested Earnings: With a complete reconciliation replacing the traditional retained earnings statement.

• *Restructuring "funds" statement to provide a reconciliation of cash and other changes affecting liquidity.*

SOME UNRESOLVED PROBLEM AREAS

Deferred Taxes. It can be seen from the restructured balance sheet that deferred tax accounts become valuation accounts modifying the carrying values of the resources and commitments to which they relate. Although this "net of tax" concept is not presently accepted, it more closely resembles the economic effect upon the related items when their tax deductibility is either accelerated or decelerated. This should clear up many of the previous misconceptions in this area.

Capitalization of Leases. Leasing rather than buying has become a favorite financing vehicle. Discerning observers have noticed that full-life leasing avoided inflating both sides of the balance sheet (particularly the liability side), and, for a while, creditors who made a fetish of the debt-equity ratio were fooled, or fooled themselves. Now, there is still resistance to the reformers' demands that such leases be capitalized, but mainly because the effect on income is different. If a lease is translated into amortizing debt, the interest factor is heavier in the early years, lighter, later; the benefits of a level-cost lease are lost.

The restructured balance sheet previously discussed eliminates the balance sheet problem (making it more a matter of disclosure), but does not eliminate the income statement problem. There is no doubt that the accounting for capitalized leases and for ownership with mortgage debt should be the same in determining income. The real question is whether *level* costing of facility usage has a place in accounting. And why not?

This boils down to a question of accounting for interest. Tradition classifies interest as a nonoperating period cost, which harks back to the days when equity capital predominated and borrowing was incidental. Today, heavy financing of facilities is commonplace and interest is more a function of maintenance and utilization, as are depreciation and repairs. Level costing of all factors relating to facility usage (including interest) is the only answer to a proper matching of costs and revenues. Obviously, this is a departure from transaction-oriented, period-oriented accounting, but a beginning is needed if economic factors are ever to override mechanics.

Business Combinations and Goodwill. Retention of historical cost accounting concepts over the short haul will require maintaining our present approach to business combinations and goodwill, as outlined by APB Opinions No. 16 and 17. At the same time, the application of the guidelines prescribed by those opinions should be carefully watched in practice to prevent their distortion and erosion and to modify them where experience indicates the need for modification.

The nature of "goodwill" requires further study. Within a cost framework, all costs need to be recovered or run through the income statement at some time; goodwill and similar intangibles are no exception.

Today, the concept of goodwill is applied to a wide variety of situations. In accounting for goodwill, generalizations such as the "tendency of customers to continue" or "the purchase of earnings in excess of a return on tangible assets" cannot be postulated. The type of goodwill acquired in a particular transaction must be realistically analyzed and evaluated to determine whether the "excess" can be attributed to the same characteristics. Consider the following examples: a one-product company engaged in the manufacture of a gadget presently popular with the youth market; a popular soft-drink bottler with a (no-cost) perpetual franchise and established routes; a research organization with a record of successful development of scientific products and discoveries; a multiproduct company engaged in manufacture and distribution of brand-name edibles; and a successful retail chain-store operation.

If the excess is not attributable to the same characteristics, approaches should be taken in dealing with the excess in each activity. Careful analysis will probably show that goodwill arising in different transactions possesses different attributes calling for different accounting. While the varying aspects of goodwill have been recognized in a general way, they have not been given adequate consideration in our accounting.

There is another important question: Do the differing aspects of goodwill suggest that, in some cases, self-developed goodwill arises in the same way as purchased goodwill, that is, from expenditures that may be written off as incurred or after? A careful analysis will show that goodwill may be the result of spending a lot of money or of spending none, of being in the right place at the right time, of cornering the best brains, of stumbling on a product, or of other actions or circumstances. Consequently, generalized analogies cannot be drawn. Each element must be dealt with separately; once analyzed, the accounting should become clear. Costs are amortized because they have a limited life and must be measured against the revenues related thereto, not for the sake of conservatism Do we depreciate land? When values suddenly disappear (as in the case of unsuccessful deferred development costs), they should be written off against earnings.

Research and Development. Research and development costs also require careful re-examination. Appropriate guidelines are needed to establish the extent to which they may be deferred—and many should not—for future amortization. The guidelines should also provide for full identification and disclosure of all projects and the bases upon which realization and amortization will be computed.

INTERMEDIATE RANGE

APB Statement No. 3 recommended the use of price-level financial statements as supplements to historical cost statements. It also gave rather specific guidelines for their preparation and use. Such statements are complicated, and admittedly do not go all the way toward value accounting. (In fact, they serve to demonstrate that accounting will never be able precisely to delineate periodic income in the economic sense.) There is also an unavoidable degree of confusion produced by presenting two different results. But the price-level statements do provide needed perspective, and hence should be required. They will be a constant, useful reminder of the effect of inflation on dollar values. In fact, it may be appropriate to consider such a requirement as more of a short-range rather than an intermediate-range recommendation. Certainly it is not essential that all short-range objectives be achieved before price-level statements are required.

In addition, perspective can be achieved by requiring disclosures of current values alongside the historical costs of those resources whose values are soon expected to flow through the income stream. The practice gained in this exercise should be useful in the ultimate shift to value accounting whenever that implementation becomes feasible in the future.

SUMMARY AND CONCLUSIONS

The disclosure of certain abuses in corporate reporting has spawned public demand for the accounting profession to abolish the present leeway for alternative methods so long tolerated in accounting practice. To achieve this uniformity of approach, it will ultimately be necessary to develop a comprehensive accounting structure. This in turn will necessitate a profound investigation of the fundamental significance of accounting concepts. To accomplish this, the profession must first throw off many confining ideas inherited from the past. Accounting theory must be freed of unnecessary formalism and adherence to meaningless or unattainable concepts.

Although the Accounting Principles Board has made a valuable start, it remains for the Financial Accounting Standards Board to undertake and complete this formidable task. The FASB must assemble a large and broad-based research team, including representatives of a wide range of interests. Objectives must be classified according to time estimated for accomplishment. The long-range objective should be a system of current valuation coupled with a more realistic approach to income. A high priority short-range objective would be the development of better guidelines for historical cost accounting. Intermediate objectives would include procedures for disclosure of price-level changes and current values.

To overhaul the theory and practice of accounting is an enormous logistic exercise that will tax the pooled resources of the entire profession. We must accept, as fact, that there is no alternative to meeting this challenge and mobilize our resources with dispatch. It is not merely the interests of the accounting profession that are at stake but those of business and society as a whole.

WHAT MAKES PROFITS LOOK 'OBSCENE'[†]

by
Philip L. Defliese

PRESENT financial accounting does not reflect economic reality. Worse than that, it creates an illusion of enormous profits where often no true profit exits, thus making some corporations look far better than they really are and exposing others to savage attacks and harsh legislation.

That may sound like heresy from a professional accountant, but it is true. For centuries, profits have been what the accountants have said they were, and for the past half-century, accountants have organized professionally to the point where the new independent Financial Accounting Standards Board has become (at the sufferance of the SEC) the final arbiter. Until the FASB moves (it needs time), financial statements will not "present fairly financial position and results of operations" in any absolute sense; they will do so only "in conformity with generally accepted accounting principles."

Those so-called principles are a hodgepodge of conventions stemming from the double-entry bookkeeping system developed during the Renaissance. Rather than redesign them, accountants have preferred to update them, with the result that they are a patchwork affair. Accountants may have harnessed the computer, but their basic tenets remain Elizabethan—the period just prior to the birth of economics and the evolution of the corporation.

Much is said today of the need for price-level accounting, including discovery (oil) and growth (timber) values. What follows, however, is confined to historical-cost accounting—which needs attention first.

BOTTOM-LINE FIXATION

Accountants' concepts of profit are still dominated by an inbred fixation with the bottom line, buttressed by a completed-transaction orientation designed to provide a proprietor with some idea of how he is doing. This furthers the myth that shareholders are proprietors who consider the bottom line all theirs and think they can therefore properly evaluate it. In reality, most shareholders are temporary investors who have bought shares, usually from others, and who look to dividends and market appreciation in relation to their particular cost as a measure of return. Such an evaluation makes no assessment of the company's return on the capital *it* has invested. To such an investor, the proprietary concept

---

[†]Reprinted from *Business Week*, August 4, 1975, pp. 10-11, with special permission, copyright © 1975 by The McGraw-Hill Companies, Inc..

is irrelevant; he switches into bonds and convertible preferreds when his investment objectives demand it and disregards legal form except to the extent that different kinds of securities (with different risks) pay different returns.

America's problem today is that the word "profit" has become tainted. When Senator Jackson recently called the profits of the oil companies "obscene," he failed, probably through no fault of his own, to recognize the true nature of profits, particularly in an industry employing accounting that does not give adequate recognition to either the cost or the value of capital invested. This attitude towards profits (which is far from unusual) seems all the more incongruous in a society presumably dedicated to the free enterprise system.

The figure that accountants now report as profits omits a major hidden cost: the cost of equity capital. We need an accounting approach that will give this factor the weight it deserves and put present accounting profits in a more realistic light.

Under present accounting, the cost of *borrowed* capital is recorded, and the cost of *equity* is not. Thus, if two enterprises each obtain $1 million capital, one borrowing at 9% and the other issuing common stock, the report on operations will show a $90,000 pretax charge for the borrowing enterprise but no corresponding cost of equity capital for the other. If both companies purchased the same assets and experienced the same operating costs and revenues, their reported profits would differ sharply. The earnings-per-share statistic adjusts for this anomaly, but it is imprecise and sometimes misleading.

The time has come to recognize the fact that the entire cost of capital, whatever its source, must enter into the determination of accounting profit.

THE 'OPPORTUNITY COST' FACTOR

Historically, economists have criticized the accountant's method of determining net incomne, and justifiably so. They maintain that "opportunity cost" must be given full weight in determining profits. Opportunity cost is another term for "cost of capital" and closely approximates "return on investment." It is the approximate return that one would receive if an opportunity existed for the equivalent capital to be invested in the most advantageous alternative income-producing asset of equivalent risk.

Once this and all other costs are covered, the reminder is profit. For convenience, economists use the term "interest" as the wages of all forms of capital. It should not be confused with the narrow commercial or accounting concept of interest.

Even in its treatment of interest in the commercial sense, accounting sticks to form rather than substance. (Our tax laws are equally inconsistent.) Interest on debt is expensed (on a time basis without regard to the properties in which the capital is invested). Dividends on preferred stock—many having approximately the same terms as bonds—are not allowed as an accounting cost. Convertible debt bears a lower interest charge because of its conversion feature, yet the latter's cost goes unrecorded.

There is one important source of capital whose accounting does provide for the capital cost automatically. It needs mentioning because it has become a favorite tool of business—and a controversial subject in accounting. It is the finance-type, long-term lease, which is designed to return the lessor his full cost, plus interest.

The popularity of this sort of lease can be ascribed to two features: (1) In many cases its terms can be constructed to keep it off the balance sheet, and so the debt-equity ratio—the sacred cow of financiers—is unimpaired. (2) It charges level annual costs that embody return of invested capital and interest, thus matching potentially level revenue—the ultimate accounting objective. Disregarding for the moment the balance-sheet problem—which can be easily cured—no better approach to recognizing the cost of capital usage and proper allocation to accounting periods can be found.

But many accountants, including those at the SEC, are horrified by this divergence from conventional accounting. They propose to capitalize the lessee as purchases, record higher interest cost in the early years, and charge straight-line depreciation. This thwarts the level costing that makes so much economic sense. Frustrated temporarily by the reluctance of the accounting profession to accept this proposal, the SEC now requires footnote disclosure of the income effects "as if" so capitalized. It thereby ignores another "as if": The alternative to debt would be to use equity capital for which accounting recognizes cost—except, of course, the unreliable earnings-per-share statistic.

The simple solution is to recognize the cost of sources of capital—including retained earnings—in the determination of profit. Lease costing does this automatically. What remains is the agreement to add on imputed interest cost to the actual coat of all facilities used in operation. The total unrecovered cost would then be charged to operations in some rational and systematic way—preferably level for operating properties. The source of the capital is irrelevant, except in the determination of the over-all rate of interest to be so charged—admittedly, not a simple matter.

CHALLENGING A BIAS

To ask accountants to accept imputation of interest on equity capital, for which cash is never directly expended, is to challenge a deep-rooted professional bias. Unless there is ultimately a cash expenditure, transaction-oriented accountants are reluctant to recognize an economic cost. Fortunately, double-entry bookkeeping is equal to this challenge: For every charge there must be a credit, and the credit in this case falls into the appropriate section of a new form of operating statement—not income statement—designed to show a more realistic economic result.

Take the case of Hypothetical Corp., which last year reported $500-million in sales and costs of $475-million, including interest and taxes. After paying $1-million in preferred dividends, it wound up reporting $24-million net profit for the common shareholders ($2 per share).

At the beginning of the year, Hypo Corp. had $200 million invested in facilities and operating assets. Its capital structure consisted of common stock, preferred stock, and $100-million in 6% debentures. Since interest on debentures was tax-deductible, the net cost of this debt was $3-million (assuming a 50% tax rate).

If we assume 10% is a fair return on invested capital and that all interest allocated is expensed currently (a rare likelihood in actual practice), a realistic though severely oversimplified accounting for Hypo's operations would look like this:

Statement of Operations
(in millions of dollars)

Income operations		
Sales		$500
Less: Costs (including taxes but not including interest)	$ 472	
Cost of capital invested	20	492
Profit from operations ($0.67 per share)		$ 8
Capital operations		
Interest (imputed) on net investment		$ 20
Less: Interest paid creditors (net of tax)	$ 3	
Preferred dividends	1	4
Net return on equity investment ($1.33 per share)		$ 16
Total income and capital operations		$ 24
Less: Dividends on common stock ($1 per share)		12
Current year's capital formed and retained		$ 12

In other words, only $8-million of the $24-million Hypo reported really represents profit. The rest is essentially interest (in the economic sense) on invested capital.

On the surface, this approach represents a radical departure from current practice in reporting income. But how radical is it in substance? Essentially, it only implements a distinction whose validity most economic analysts recognize. Current earnings as we know them would be broken down into cost of capital and true profits from operating under the risks of our free enterprise system. In many cases, profits thought to be exorbitant would turn out to be modest; some regulated utilities would have to use red ink instead of black.

Our economic system is floundering from a severe lack of real profits essential to capital formation and preservation. Profits need enhancement, not trimming. The sooner accounting methodology is modernized to put corporate earnings in perspective and demonstrate that they are not obscene, the better equipped we will be to reverse this situation.

THE SEARCH FOR A NEW CONCEPTUAL FRAMEWORK OF ACCOUNTING[†]

by
Philip L. Defliese

A conceptual framework of accounting, like beauty, is in the eye of the beholder. Some beholders see no rhyme or reason to the present framework—in fact may even doubt its existence. Others believe that it not only exists but also is well documented in Accounting Principles Board Statement no. 4.[1] These opinions are not equally divided. As might be expected, those in the former group constitute a vocal minority; they include many academics and are supported by some practitioners and major firms.

After almost 20 years of heated discussion of this subject, the issue is about to be joined. Last December the Financial Accounting Standards Board published its tentative conclusions about the objectives of financial statements and its long-awaited discussion memorandum (DM)[2] of 360 pages on the elements of financial statements and their measurement. Public hearings on the tentative conclusions and part 1 of the DM—elements—will be held in August. Hearings on parts 2 and 3—qualitative characteristics and measurement—will be held in January 1978. These are postponed dates set by the FASB at the request of many (including the American Institute of CPAs) who thought that the original six-month submission period was inadequate to deal with such a lengthy, complicated and pervasive issue. However, recognizing that some will take the view that measurement cannot be dissociated from objectives and elements, the FASB has indicated that it will hear those arguments in August as well.

An AICPA task force, which was created to respond to this project, has just launched an experimentation program in which it is expected about 30 major companies will, on a voluntary basis, anonymously restate their 1975 and 1976 financial statements to follow four distinct accounting models derived from

---

[†]Reprinted with permission from *The Journal of Accountancy*, July 1977, pp. 59-67, copyright © 1977 by American Institute of CPAs. Opinions of the authors are their own and do not necessarily reflect policies of the AICPA. The following "author's note" appeared at the bottom of the first page: "This is a critical but neutral report. Any biases of the author that may appear—and he has them—are unintentional."

[1]APB Statement no. 4, *Basic Concepts and Accounting Principles Underlying Financial Statements of Business Enterprises* (New York: AICPA, 1970).

[2]FASB Discussion Memorandum, *An Analysis of Issues Related to Conceptual Framework for Financial Accounting and Reporting: Elements of Financial Statements and Their Measurement* (Stamford, Conn.: FASB, December 2, 1976).

various proposed conceptual and measurement alternatives. Results of this project, discussed later in this article, will not be available until later this year.

Arguments on the issues discussed in the DM—particularly in the measurement area—are beginning to warm up. Some parties have expressed the view that the FASB has couched the issues in such terms that a radical change in our present framework is inevitable. In seminars held in a number of locations, Ernst & Ernst has baldly stated

> The bias toward substantive change in generally accepted financial reporting practice is so overwhelming as to negate the asserted neutrality of the discussion memorandum.[3]

Price Waterhouse & Co. has stated

> The U. S. business community should firmly reject any notion of abandoning historical cost based accounting and reporting. Moving to current values/costs would be not only an ineffective response to inflation but also a serious disservice to prepares and users of financial information.
>
> Business reports of publicly held U.S. entities should be supplemented by understandable data that express historical costs in dollars of uniform worth. This is a direct response to inflation, highlighting the extent and the sources of inflation's impact on reported results and on the various classes of invested capital. Price-level techniques are well established. What we urge is simpler application for more useful results.[4]

On the other hand, Touche Ross & Co.[5] and Arthur Andersen & Co.[6] seem inclined toward a current value framework. The other major firms have maintained some sort of open-minded neutrality.[7]

Members of the FASB deny any preconceived bias, and I believe them. Robert Sprouse, vice-chairman, speaking last May at a conference on the subject at the Wharton School, said

> Some reactions to the discussion memorandum suggest a fear that the seven members of the FASB are of a single Machiavellian mind attempting to lead managers and auditors and users down a primrose path to financial accounting disaster. Perhaps it only sounds self-serving for me to attempt to assure you that the discussion memorandum is not a booby trap. If the discussion memorandum is perceived to be other than fair and neutral in presenting issues and alternative resolutions, it is not due to some sinister motive.

---

[3]Ernst & Ernst, *FASB Conceptual Framework—Issues and Implications* (Cleveland, Ohio: Ernst & Ernst, 1977), p. 3.

[4]Price Waterhouse & Co., *Common-Sense Accounting in an Era of Persistent Inflation* (New York: Price Waterhouse & Co., 1977), foreword.

[5]Touche Ross & Co., *Economic Reality in Financial Reporting* (New York: Touche Ross & Co., 1976).

[6]Arthur Andersen & Co., *Accounting Standards for Business Enterprises Throughout the World* (Chicago: Arthur Andersen & Co., 1974).

[7]Coopers & Lybrand sponsored a study by Jack C. Robertson, *Business Income Determination Through Use of Current Cost Accounting*, but is noncommittal on the issues.

Nevertheless, one must acknowledge that some previous actions of the board provide some clues. FASB Statements nos. 2, 5 and 8 seem to point toward a rigid asset/liability concept of earnings. Speaking of credibility, in the preamble to the DM[8] the FASB said

> Some contend that the credibility of corporate financial reporting has eroded in recent years. Among the criticisms that have come to the board's attention are
>
> - Acceptability of two or more methods of accounting for the same facts.
> - Switches to less conservative accounting methods.
> - Front-ending of income.
> - Use of reserves to artificially smooth earnings fluctuations.
> - Failure of financial statements to warn of impending liquidity crunches.
> - Deferrals followed by 'big bath' write-offs.
> - Unjustified optimism in estimates of recoverability.
> - Off-balance-sheet financing.
> - Unwarranted assertion of immateriality to justify nondisclosure of unfavorable information or departures from standards.
> - Elevation of form over substance.

Acknowledging the difficulty in responding effectively to the issues in the DM, Sprouse said

> For many of us [the project] is difficult to come to grips with because the subject matter is abstract and we are accustomed to dealing with specific, concrete accounting problems. In resolving those specific, concrete accounting problems, we may unconsciously rely on our own conceptual framework, but we have not previously been called upon to spell out our framework in systematic, cohesive fashion so that others can understand it and evaluate it.

And there we are.

In sum, the FASB package is a well-documented and scholarly treatise of the issues and choices facing the accounting profession today. It can be faulted less for voluminousness and redundancy in spots, and more for its omissions. It defers for later consideration (presumably on the premise that agreement on concepts and measurement will help provide the answers) the issues of "realization"—when earnings inure to an enterprise—and "allocation"—how costs are allocated. These, in my view, are the essence of the accounting process and cannot be dissociated from the major issues.

As to bias—each reader must reach his own conclusion. The scant acknowledgment in the document of the present framework (generally the revenue/expense view, explained in detail later in this article), and the other clues previously mentioned, could indicate a bias, but I am convinced the FASB will approach the issues with an open mind.

The FASB states in its preamble[9] that no previously published framework, "by itself has come to be universally accepted and relied on in practice," although

---

[8]FASB DM, "Scope and Implications of the Conceptual Framework Project," p. 4.

[9]*Ibid.*, p. 2.

it acknowledges APB Statement no. 4 as a notable effort that "purports primarily to describe the way things are and not to prescribe how they ought to be." Because present accounting practices evolved over the past century without specific guidance on concepts from any authoritative body, we have in recent years been hearing more about the distinction between "what it is" vs. "what it ought to be." The APB statement, acknowledging that there were conflicting concepts, made it clear that it was necessary first to describe the status quo before any attempt could be made to move forward.

Although most of the accounting profession's past failures can more appropriately be classified in the auditing area, there is no doubt that a crescendo of criticism has been leveled against the profession's institutions—first the APB and now the FASB—for not providing on a priority basis an authoritative conceptual framework for accounting. Nevertheless, we must concede that, throughout our recent past, our capital markets—the backbone of our free enterprise system—have flourished on the basis of "what is" in accounting, despite its failings.

It took some time for this crescendo of criticism to build, but events of the past five years have accelerated the buildup—universal rampant inflation, oil cartel embargoes and their effects have for many observers accentuated the inability of accounting to reflect economic realities. On the other hand, others expect accounting to provide a more stable and objective yardstick to serve as a starting point from which to deal with economic realities and the decisions that flow therefrom. For example, it is generally conceded that the decreasing ratio of dividend payout to reported earnings in recent years is management's recognition of the inability of those earnings to provide for replacement.

The actions of the Securities and Exchange Commission in requiring of major companies footnote disclosure of replacement cost depreciation and cost of sales (Accounting Series Release no. 190) and the actions of accounting bodies abroad toward current value concepts—particularly in those countries beset by more vicious inflation, such as the United Kingdom and Australia[10]—have fueled the fires of discontent here.[11] The lower price/earnings ratios generated by our all-knowing stock markets in this decade, compared with the last, is telling us something. All of this points up the fact that the need for definitive pronouncements is now more apparent and that we can expect them to be issued soon.

---

[10]Institute of Chartered Accountants in England and Wales Accounting Standards Committee, Exposure Draft no. 18: *Current Cost Accounting* (London: ICAEW, November 30, 1976). Institute of Chartered Accountants in Australia and Australian Society of Accountants, Statement of Provisional Accounting Standards, *Current Cost Accounting* (Sydney: ICAA, 1976).

[11] "Flaky Figures," *Wall Street Journal*, May 23, 1977.

To this end, the FASB has described its project[12] as follows:

> A conceptual framework is a constitution, a coherent system of interrelated *objectives* and *fundamentals* that can lead to consistent standards and that prescribes the nature, function, and limits of financial accounting and financial statements. The *objectives* identify the goals and purposes of accounting. The *fundamentals* are the underlying concepts of accounting, concepts that guide the selection of events to be accounted for, the measurement of those events, and the means of summarizing and communicating them to interested parties. Concepts of that type are fundamental in the sense that other concepts flow from them and repeated reference to them will be necessary in establishing, interpreting, and applying accounting and reporting standards. (Emphasis supplied.)

THE OBJECTIVES ISSUE

When the Study Group on the Objectives of Financial Statements, chaired by Robert M. Trueblood, was commissioned by the AICPA in 1971, it was believed that if we could reach agreement on the objectives, everything else would fall into place. Almost seven years have gone by, and, while the objectives are still not agreed upon, it is now clear that solving that problem will not accomplish much. The real issue is how to implement the objectives. But let us first see what has been accomplished with respect to objectives.

The FASB's tentative conclusions about objectives (proposed in the DM) are essentially in agreement with the Trueblood study group's report, *Objectives of Financial Statements* (published by the AICPA in 1973), and with most other individuals and groups that have addressed that issue: "Financial statements of business enterprises should provide information, within the limits of financial accounting, that is useful to present and potential investors and creditors in making rational investment and credit decisions."[13]

Some believe that an even more important role of financial statements is to provide information that is useful for an evaluation of how management has discharged its responsibility to stockholders—that is, an evaluation of management's stewardship of enterprise resources entrusted to it. But whether management performance can be separated from enterprise performance is questionable, and it is unclear why information designed primarily to be useful for investment and credit decisions cannot fulfill the stewardship reporting role as well. Those who believe that the management stewardship concept should prevail usually also believe that our present framework—particularly historical cost accounting—should continue to be the dominant measurement tool.

The central FASB tentative objective is broadened by the following (paraphrased): Financial statements of business enterprises should provide information

---

[12]FASB DM, p. 2.

[13]*Ibid.*, p. 10.

• That helps investors and creditors assess the prospects of receiving cash from dividends or interest and from the proceeds from the sale, redemption or maturity of securities or loans. Those prospects are affected

1. By an enterprise's ability to obtain enough cash through its earning and financing activities to meet its obligations when due and its other cash operating needs, to reinvest in earning resources and activities and to pay cash dividends and interest.

2. By perceptions of investors and creditors generally about that ability, which affect market prices of the enterprise's securities relative to those of other enterprises.

• About the economic resources of an enterprise, which are sources of prospective cash inflows to the enterprise; its obligations to transfer economic resources to others, which are causes of prospective cash outflows from the enterprise; and its earnings, which are the financial results of its operations and other events and conditions that affect the enterprise. Since that information is useful to investors and creditors in assessing an enterprise's ability to pay cash dividends and interest and to settle obligations when they mature, it should be the focus of financial accounting and financial statements.

It is interesting to compare these proposals with what the APB believed the objectives were in 1970:

> The basic purpose of financial accounting and financial statements is to provide financial information about individual business enterprises that is useful in making economic decisions.... General and qualitative objectives aid in fulfilling this basic purpose and provide means for evaluating present and proposed accounting principles.
>
> General objectives determine the appropriate content of financial accounting information. These objectives are to present reliable financial information about enterprise resources and obligations, economic progress, and other changes in resources and obligations, to present information helpful in *estimating earnings potential*, and to present other financial information needed by users, particularly owners and creditors.[14] (Emphasis supplied.)

There should not be any great controversy over the objectives issue. However, some does exist. In addition to those who espouse the stewardship issue previously mentioned, there are others who say, "We believe the purpose of financial statements should be stated in broader terms. In our view, the primary purposes of financial statements are to encourage capital formation, to support a capital market that allocates available funds equitably among competing demands, and to identify efficient and inefficient users of capital in order to encourage investment and aid the allocation of resources."[15]

---

[14]APB Statement no. 4, pars. 21 and 22.

[15]Ernst & Ernst, p. 56.

They would prefer to state the objectives as follows:

> The objective of accounting should be to contribute to the successful functioning of the free enterprise system by providing reliable data that will (1) enable investment decision makers and others to distinguish efficient users of capital from inefficient users, (2) encourage capital formation, innovation, and risk taking, (3) minimize interference with managerial action, and (4) do so on as economical a basis as possible consistent with achieving this objective.[16]

Central to these subtle differences is the emphasis on investment and credit-granting decision making. It is not clear whether any really great differences of viewpoint exist. The one new element mentioned is the possibility of accounting's interference with management action and it is certainly true that little analysis has been made of the impact of accounting standards. The accounting effect of contemplated business transactions has in recent years come to the forefront in management deliberations. Is this because accounting has recently succeeded in telling the truth, or have accounting standards in the past succeeded in veiling the truth? Management is acutely aware that the perception of the investor is important—but one must agree that accounting fails if it requires management to make uneconomical decisions in an attempt to look better. Recently the FASB has taken steps to determine the economic consequences of its pronouncements and whether management decisions are affected by them.[17]

IMPLEMENTING THE OBJECTIVES—THE MAJOR ISSUES

Considering the scarcity of disagreement regarding objectives, one wonders why there is such concern over the need for a new conceptual framework. In reality, the major differences lie in the approaches available to implement the objectives. A close look at the objectives—and at the nuances they engender—leads indisputably to the fact that these differences occur because people differ in the way they think periodic earnings should be determined, and frequently they even differ as to the definition of earnings. As the complexity of our economic environment has increased, and as the diversity, and sometimes deviousness, in the structuring of transactions has grown, viewpoints concerning their translation into accounting language have multiplied. Just how much income has been realized, and when, are matters no longer determinable by routine convention. Economists' definitions of earnings vary considerably from those of accountants and businessmen, and even among themselves. Thus it appears that the objectives can be implemented only after earnings have been defined and the mechanics of their determination have been agreed upon.

---

[16]*Ibid.*, p. 59.

[17]The FASB has called for submission of research papers on this subject. See FASB *Status Report*, February 7, 1977.

To achieve this goal, the FASB's DM proposes to determine

- The elements of accounting that enter into the process of income determination, their definition and interaction.
- The measurement criteria to apply to the elements in determining income.

Nine basic issues are presented for discussion and resolution. They may be summarized as follows:

Issue 1: Which of the two most widely espoused views of earnings shoud be adopted? The two views of earnings are referred to as the asset/liability view and the revenue/expense view. According to the asset/liability view, earnings are defined in terms of the net change in assets and liabilities. Thus the definitions of earnings, revenues and expenses depend on the rigid definitions of assets and liabilities. A change in emphasis occurs from "earnings" to a statement of the "changes in net assets (shareholders' equity)."

According to the revenue/expense view, earnings are defined in terms of the difference between revenues and expenses (and gains and losses). The definitions of revenues and expenses, rather than those of assets and liabilities, are critical. The notions of proper "matching" of expenses with revenues and "nondistortion" of earnings are central to the revenue/expense view. Assets and liabilities (including deferred charges and credits) are looked on as residuals (rather than separately realizable items) that must be carried forward to future periods in order to accomplish proper matching and avoid distortion in the determination of income of future periods. (It has also been criticized for its amenability to "abuse" in "smoothing" earnings.) It should be recognized that this is generally the prevailing conceptual framework, although it has been modified to some extent by recent FASB action, notably FASB Statements nos. 2, 5 and 8. APB Statement no. 4 stated this in somewhat loose terms in paragraphs 154 to 160 and modified its apparent leaning to the asset/liability view by including deferrals in its definition of assets and liabilities (par. 132).

The asset/liability view and the revenue/ expense view are likely to produce different earnings figures as well as different balance sheet components. It is important to understand, however, that the question is not whether the balance sheet or the income statement is more important. The proponents of both views generally consider the income statement to be the more important in terms of the primary interest to most users. The question is this: Which view produces the more meaningful measure of earnings?

A third view, about which much less is known and for which there appears little support, is the nonarticulation view: According to this view, the definitions of assets and liabilities are critical in the presentation of balance sheets, and the definitions of revenues and expenses dominate the measurement of earnings. The two financial statements have independent existences and meanings; thus different measurement schemes may be used for them. They do not interlock.

Issues 2 through 7: These issues deal with definitions of assets, liabilities, earnings, revenues, expenses, gains and losses. They provide for a choice of definition, depending largely on which view of earnings is espoused—the asset/liability or revenue/expense view.

Issue 8—capital maintenance: Earnings result only after capital has been maintained or costs have been recovered. Thus, the concept of capital maintenance or cost recovery used separates return *on* capital (earnings) from return *of* capital (capital recovery). Two major concepts of capital maintenance or cost recovery are proposed, both of which can be measured either in money or in units of the same purchasing power: the financial capital concept and the physical capital concept. The principal differences between them involve certain changes in prices or assets during accounting periods that are called "holding gains and losses." In the financial capital concept they are included in earnings because every difference between financial (historical) cost and the amount realized is considered "income." They are called "capital maintenance adjustments" in the physical capital concept and with varying labels are usually included in owners' equity or in a statement of equity changes.

Our present framework deals only with financial capital (in units of money), although the Lifo inventory costing of sales technique excludes from earnings the inflated cost of replacement. To that extent, although the balance sheet does not reflect the new value of the physical capital, the income statement gives recognition to the physical capital recovery concept. Replacement cost depreciation concepts (the SEC's camel's nose under the tent) are a step in the direction of replacing financial capital with physical capital. This gets complicated when applied to monetary items or shareholders' equity, when expressed in units of general purchasing power (GPP), etc., and I can only recommend a careful reading of chapter 6 of the DM. The AICPA task force models B, C and D, which are discussed later, incorporate varying concepts of capital maintenance—in ascending degree.

Issue 9—measurement: Part 3 deals with measurement. Two critical determinations are involved in measuring the elements of financial accounting:

1. The unit in which the measurements are to be made (dollars vs. GPP—referred to under issue 8 above).

2. The particular attribute that is to be measured (sometimes referred to as the measurement basis or the valuation basis). Five choices are available:

Present framework:

Historical cost/historical proceeds.

Possible future framework (current value oriented):

Current cost/current proceeds.

Current exit value.

Expected exit value.

Present value of expected cash flows.

There is an implication that no one attribute would be applicable to all elements and that, in addition, each attribute is susceptible to measurement in either units of money or units of general purchasing power. These attributes, which are essentially quantitative, need to be tempered in their choice by the qualitative attributes (discussed in part 2) of relevance, reliability, comparability, timeliness and understandability (about which little controversy is expected). Trade-offs are anticipated in an attempt to provide compatibility, and the FASB provides a series of complicated matrixes for respondents to decide just how the qualitative attributes affect the determination of the quantitative attributes to be applied.

STATEMENT PRESENTATION AND MODELS

The DM provides two appendixes which are not specifically related to the nine issues presented in the text. Respondents are invited to comment on them if they so desire. They deal with the statement presentation of earnings (which brings in some implications regarding realization and allocation) and provide three sets of financial statements derived from the same data, illustrating historical cost, current cost, and current exit value, with the results shown on the basis of both units of money and GPP. They do not attempt to illustrate the choices proposed by the issues—particularly the pervasive issue 1—and this is unfortunate. The task force models attempt this.

THE AICPA RESPONSE

Members of the FASB's task force on conceptual framework had opportunities to comment on the development of the project as it progressed. As one would expect, diverse views were represented and expressed. As it neared completion—almost on a crash basis—certain members expressed the view that unless some empirical research involving the application of the newer concepts was undertaken, it would be difficult for both respondents and the FASB to come to practical grips with the choices. It was during this period that the SEC issued ASR no. 190 requiring replacement cost disclosure. Although this requirement was not intended to replace historical cost, implications along these lines became uppermost in everyone's mind.

Because of that concern the AICPA created a small task force to study the possibility of developing some alternative accounting models for research application which would incorporate the choices provided by the DM. It was sensed that textual discussion wasn't enough to crystallize the issues for most accounting minds and that the practicability of implementation was an essential ingredient to any change. This concern prompted the inclusion of the appendixes in the DM providing hypothetical illustrations, but it was thought that they were not enough.

Thus the AICPA task force was created to work in tandem with the FASB. It was charged with the job of developing the smallest number of models on which the members could compromise, with the result that four models were created as possible alternatives to present practice—historical cost, revenue/expense view. They are explained and illustrated in the booklet published by the AICPA entitled *Experimentation Program—Financial Accounting Models, April 1977.*[18]

Preparatory to a consideration of the four models, the booklet describes 13 choices of concepts that substantially track and restate the issues of the FASB DM, adding a few, particularly on realization and presentation. Briefly described, the models are as follows:

Model A: Condensed supplementary financial statements based on historical cost but stated in terms of GPP. This follows the FASB and APB price level models with modification, principally in the treatment of gains and losses on monetary items and in the classification of deferred tax items as monetary.

Model B: Historical cost financial statements incorporating inventories based on Lifo and depreciation based on the current cost of depreciable assets. Current cost, however, is preferably determined by the application of appropriate indexes to historical cost; it is not to be confused with replacement cost.

Model C: Financial statements based partially on historical cost and partially on current costs and values (generally relying on replacement costs), distinguishing between operating income and value changes, and further distinguishing between realized and unrealized value changes. This model has many elements of the Australian and U.K. models.

Model D: Current value financial statements, applying either replacement cost or current value concepts to all resources and obligations as well as recognizing the effect of changes in the general level of prices on shareholders' equity.

The first three models retain the revenue/expense approach—providing for matching of costs and revenues and permitting the use of deferred costs and credits. Model D incorporates the asset/liability approach, which excludes the deferment of charges or credits (and goodwill) that do not represent separable resources or obligations.

The four models are composites of several alternative concepts and measurement bases and cannot be identified precisely with specific proposals previously publicized. The number of variations and permutations available could have produced a larger number of models, but the task force thought that the experimentation should be limited to those four basic models. Consequently, within these four, variations are possible and perhaps desirable. The treatment of goodwill, deferred taxes and market values of monetary liabilities, to name a few, could vary within each model. Rather than increase the number of models, the task force decided that experimenters should be asked to suggest variations of each model, as they believe appropriate.

Models C and D introduce considerable departure from current presentation. Model C segments the varying facets of income into separate statements, and

---

[18]Copies can be obtained from the AICPA's New York office. Requests should be directed to Paul Rosenfield, director of the AICPA's accounting standards division.

Model D presents one all-inclusive statement of changes in shareholders' equity, subdividing those changes into results of ordinary operations, unusual transactions and events, and value changes (plus the price level effect on equity), providing supplementary statements expanding on various segments.

The task force takes no position on the desirability of any of the models and emphasizes the experimental nature of the project. Furthermore, it takes no position on whether the financial statements contemplated by the models would be supplementary to the present conventional statements (parallel presentation) or would (perhaps only ultimately) replace them. That is a difficult issue which the task force believes should be addressed by the FASB only after experimentation and study of the views of the experimenters as to the practicability, desirability and usability of any new concepts or framework.

The task force recognizes that there are no undisputed criteria for evaluation of the results of the experiment. The companies participating will probably be in the best position to make a judgment once they see their results for 1975 and 1976 presented in five different ways. These comparisons, which should be far more useful than any company-by-company comparison (even within an industry), should be meaningful to all observers, and particularly to the FASB. (It is expected that some of the results will be published on a no-name basis.) In addition, the experimenters' observations of the implementation problems and alternatives that may be relevant—which will be elicited by a comprehensive questionnaire at the conclusion of the project—should be helpful. In fact, this input will probably be the most valuable aspect of the experiment. The price level research conducted by the FASB[19] was a great forward step for empirical research in accounting, but its limitations are obvious. The current experiment is the next step forward.

CONCLUSION

The pervasiveness of the search for a new conceptual framework of accounting, and its implications for the profession's future ability to provide meaningful data to a fast changing economy, are obvious. While the clamor for immediate change to accommodate a world beset by inflation seems reasonable and urgent, we should not cast aside a well-understood framework that—despite its deficiencies—has served our expansive capital markets so well. Change in accounting has in the past been slow, perhaps too slow, so we call it evolutionary. The question now is this: Are we ready for a revolutionary change?

---

[19]Financial Accounting Standards Board, Research Report, Field Tests of Financial Reporting in Units of General Purchasing Power (Stamford, Conn.: FASB, May 1977).

UPDATE ON THE NEW CONCEPTUAL FRAMEWORK PROJECT[†]

by
Philip L. Defliese

ON December 29, 1977, the FASB issued an Exposure Draft for comment entitled "Objectives of Financial Reporting and Elements of Financial Statements of Business Enterprises."[1] In issuing this Exposure Draft—and hopefully ultimately adopting it as the first in a new series of *Statements of Concepts*—the Board is attempting to take the first step in its search for a new conceptual framework of accounting. The Board is also attempting to delineate the issues in such a fashion as to eliminate or minimize the confusion that has been generated over the subject in the past. Not only has the Board put off for future consideration the issue of "measurement"—as previously announced—but it now has also indicated the need for the application of "accounting rules and conventions" in determining accounting results. These, too, will come later. The Exposure Draft is consequently severely limited. Here are the telling quotes:

> 43. ... Determining the elements that should be included in financial statements and when they should be included depends not only on the definitions in this Statement *but also on accounting rules and conventions*. [Emphasis added.]
>
> 44. ... This Statement is limited to the more fundamental aspects of definitions of elements that are less subject to change over time. Other phases of the conceptual framework project will be concerned with measurement *and with rules and conventions for accounting recognition*. [Emphasis added.]

From this we can deduce that the Board is attempting to fragment its project further, presumably to inch up on the thornier issues. A new term is introduced, called "rules and conventions for accounting recognition" and one can only guess that it is somewhat akin to our old friends, "realization" and "allocation." Although previously hinted at in the Discussion Memorandum, it now seems clear that it takes more than definitions to determine accounting results (i.e., income), and this is a good sign.

[†]Presented at the ITT Key Issues Lecture Series sponsored by California State University at Northridge on January 14, 1978. Reprinted from *Contemporary Issues in Accounting*, Dhia D. AlHashim and James W. Robertson, eds. (Indianapolis, IN: Bobbs-Merrill Company, Inc., 1979), pp. 37-54. Reprinted with permission of Dhia D. AlHashim and James W. Robertson. A nearly identical article was published in *The Journal of Accountancy*, March 1978, pp. 74-79.

[1]Financial Accounting Standards Board, *Objectives of Financial Reporting and Elements of Financial Statements of Business Enterprises*, Exposure Draft (Stamford, Conn.: FASB, December 29, 1977).

Prior standard-setting bodies—notably the APB—struggled long, hard, and in vain to separate "realized income" from "unrealized income." That failure was best demonstrated (and has since been repeated by the FASB in Statement No. 12) in the APB's inability to reach agreement on the "marketable securities" issue. Here is a case where there never was much of a question regarding the objectivity of measurement—cost and market are always available—and the problem existed long before inflation became significant. The issue always was *when* do you give *accounting recognition* to the change in value, and that goes inevitably to the heart of the measurement issue. With the new semantics, perhaps we will need to shift our terminology from "realized" and "unrealized" to "recognized" and "unrecognized" income.

Essentially, this Exposure Draft attempts to accomplish three objectives: (1) to establish a new series of Statements known as "Statements of Financial Accounting Concepts," of which this will be the first; (2) to establish the "Objectives of Financial Reporting;" and (3) to define the "Elements of Financial Statements of Business Enterprises." Presumably, the Board has decided to publish the results of its deliberations on conceptual framework of financial accounting on a piecemeal basis—a matter which is controversial.

Because the "measurement" and "capital maintenance" issues were beclouding the thinking on the major conceptual issues—and, I suspect, because the matters involved were too voluminous to deal with in one hearing, the Board had previously announced the split-up of the subject matter into two public hearings, the one this past August and the other on January 16.

A mixed reaction on the part of respondents followed that announcement, particularly when it was hinted that the Board might proceed with a statement on "objectives" and possibly on "elements" in the interim. (The Board had already departed from its earlier practice of not taking a position until an exposure draft was published by issuing its tentative conclusions on objectives; consequently an Exposure Draft on Objectives now would certainly not be out of order.) Some respondents felt that the Board should not attempt to fragment the project on the theory that until all the pieces were in place and workable, it would be better not to issue a standard that might severely constrain all the rest that followed.

Now the Board has gone one step further: in addition to a proposed statement on objectives, it is offering definitions of the elements of financial statements which, presumably, should underlie the remaining considerations of measurement, capital maintenance, and—now for the first time—"accounting recognition." There is much to be said for the argument that no official pronouncements should be made until all aspects of the conceptual framework are resolved and found workable. However, most will agree that a lesser concern need be had about the objectives. Professional objectives are usually very general and abstract, and this is quite true for financial reporting. The U.S. Government had an announced objective to put a man on the moon long before it had the wherewithal to implement that objective. Of course, objectives need to be reasonably feasible, and only that criterion needs to be applied here.

We do not know whether the Board intends to issue the proposed statement before or after it concludes its deliberations and issues exposure drafts on the remaining issues. Comments on this draft must be submitted by April 18, 1978—three months after the public hearings on the remaining issues—principally on capital maintenance and measurement. We can only presume that the comments must be submitted before we know how the Board intends to deal with those remaining issues. In taking this first step, the Board is obviously responding to criticism about the excessive delay in getting on with this project. Nevertheless, some enlightenment regarding its intentions in this area would be helpful.[2]

Let us now analyze the three parts of this Exposure Draft.

THE NEW SERIES

Creation of this new series of pronouncements should not arouse any great controversy. Essentially, this step results from a technicality and a circumstance in which the profession finds itself. The attempt is to remove one technicality with another—a pragmatic solution with which only the purest of the pure will argue.

The Board, in establishing a new framework of accounting—by its own terms "constitution"—will not have the time to reexamine binding past pronouncements which it and its predecessors have issued. Those will remain in effect until amended or rescinded—a later project. Under the AICPA Rules of Conduct, members must adhere to principles promulgated by the FASB and its predecessors; departures create problems. Consequently, since the Board's pronouncements in the conceptual framework area may be inconsistent with the concepts underlying some prior pronouncement—thus creating a dilemma, *the Statements of Financial Accounting Concepts* are deemed *not* to be the establishment of accounting principles within the meaning of the AICPA Rules of Conduct. Thus, while the new series will provide guidance to both the Board and profession in resolving new problems and developing new standards (and later in reexamining old standards), they will not create immediate problems of inconsistency.

THE NEW OBJECTIVES

One cannot help but feel gratified that some ultimate authoritative determination of the objectives of financial reporting will soon be forthcoming. (For convenience, the term *financial reporting* is used in place of *general purposes external financial reporting by business enterprises*; it is a broader term than *financial statements.*[3]) The search for objectives began with the

---

[2]Since the presentation of this paper, the FASB has announced its intention to issue the Statement in final form in the fourth quarter of 1978, before the issuance of an exposure draft on measurement is expected.

[3]In future statements, the FASB will need to distinguish carefully between *financial statements* and *financial reporting*; the responsibilities of management and independent auditors regarding their contents will need to be defined. (See note 4.)

creation of the AICPA Study Group on Objectives in 1971, headed by Robert Trueblood, and with the report of that group in 1973. A final decision on this issue has been too long in coming, and most accountants will agree that it can be dealt with apart from the remainder of the project on conceptual framework.

The objectives proposed do not depart substantially from those previously published as tentative conclusions. They have been rewritten and expressed in fourteen paragraphs of equal standing—which flow from a preamble of eleven paragraphs—and these are all written without summary or emphasis. No one paragraph or comment should be taken out of context; all must be considered in their entirety. (The Tentative conclusions had certain paragraphs italicized which gave them a presumption of greater importance.) Having said that, let me violate this implicit caveat by quoting a few excerpts which give the general thrust of the statement:

> 23. ... Financial reporting should provide information that is useful to present and potential investors and creditors in making rational investment and credit decisions.
>
> 24. ... The major group of *investors* are equity security holders and debt security holders. The major group of *creditors* are suppliers of goods and services which extend credit, lending institutions, individual lenders, and debt security holders. [Notice that debt security holders are considered both investors and creditors.] The terms also include security analysts and advisors, brokers, lawyers, regulatory agencies and others who advise, represent, or protect the interests of investors and creditors.
>
> 33. ... The primary focus of financial reporting is information about the performance of an enterprise's earning activities . . .
>
> 34. ... Information about enterprise earnings (often called net income or net profit) and its components measured by accrual accounting generally provides a better measure of enterprise performance than information about current cash receipts and payments.... Earnings information is also considered to be a good basis for assessing management's stewardship.
>
> 35. ... Although periodic financial measures of enterprise performance provided by accrual accounting may tend to fluctuate less than measures of net cash receipts for the same accounting periods, the purpose of accrual accounting is to measure and report changes in resources and obligations and to relate the corresponding sacrifices and benefits—efforts and accomplishments—to accounting periods rather than to reduce fluctuations in reported results by averaging the results of several periods....
>
> 33. ... Financial accounting cannot directly measure the value of a business enterprise—the present value of its expected net cash receipts—because of the uncertainty of the amount and timing of expected cash receipts and payments, particularly those expected far in the future, and the uncertainty of the proper discount rate . . .

Most of the foregoing will probably be found to be noncontroversial. Semantical differences will be found between the proposed objectives and those contained in the Tentative Conclusions, but these are more in the nature of editorial changes than substantive changes.

Adherents of all the alternative measurement bases of historical cost, current cost, current value, et cetera—whether or not they're in the asset-liability or revenue-expense concept of income camps—will find a home in these objectives. Most accountants will agree that this is what accounting is all about;

where they usually disagree is on *how* to achieve these objectives. That leads us to the elements.

ELEMENTS OF FINANCIAL STATEMENTS

Before proceeding with a definition of the elements of financial statements, the draft once again places great emphasis upon the fact that the determination of periodic earnings serves as the primary purpose behind all that follows. This is well illustrated in the following two paragraphs:

> 37. ... For reasons noted in earlier paragraphs, investors, creditors, and others who are concerned with assessing the prospects for enterprise net cash inflows are especially interested in information about the performance of the enterprise's earning activities provided by measures of earnings and its components. Investors, creditors, and others often use reported earnings and information about the components of earnings to help assess management's performance apart from enterprise performance, "earning power" or other amounts perceived as "representative" of long-term earning ability of an enterprise, prospective cash flows to an enterprise, or the risk of investing in or lending to an enterprise, although earnings information usually does not directly reflect any of those characteristics.
>
> 38. ... Earnings and its components relate to earning activities of an individual enterprise during a particular period. Over the life of an enterprise (or other very long period), reported earnings equal the net cash receipts excluding transactions with owners (subject to the observation in footnote 8) but that relationship between earnings and cash flows rarely, if ever, holds for periods as short as a year. Thus, the major difference between periodic earnings measured by accrual accounting and statements of cash receipts and outlays is timing of recognition of the components of earnings.

The Draft then proceeds to define the eight elements of financial statements—assets, liabilities, owners' equity, revenues, expenses, gains, losses, and earnings, but first it introduces a caveat:

> 43. ... The definitions in this Statement are a fundamental and necessary step, but they will need to be supplemented in two ways to become fully operational. First,[4] the definitions of elements in this Statement describe the distinguishing characteristics of the things and events that qualify for inclusion in the class defined *but they do not dictate which of the things and events that have those distinguishing characteristics should be included in a particular set of financial statements or when they should be included.* Determining the elements that should be included in financial statements and when they should be included depends *not only on the definitions in this Statement but also on accounting rules and conventions.* [Emphasis added.]
>
> 44. ... This statement is limited to the more fundamental aspects of definitions of elements that are less subject to change over time. Other phases of the conceptual framework project will be concerned with measurement and with rules and conventions for accounting recognition.

---

[4]The second step concerns itself with the need to distinguish between revenues and gains, and expenses and losses, all of which goes back to the issue of presentation of earnings statements to be considered by the FASB later. The FASB has placed this issue on its agenda.

Thus we are told that the definitions must be accepted before we are told how they will be applied. Most will agree that definitions are helpful in any exercise of logic. However, Mautz has said:

> ..... Philosophers and logicians and semanticists for years have wrestled with the meaning of words. The problem with a definition is that one definition leads to another definition. Words are needed to explain the words that explain the meaning of other words. I just don't know how we're going to get definitions that meet the purposes for which the Board intends to use them.
>
> There is a real appeal to the definitional approach. In most cases when we face a problem, our thought is: if we only knew what it was. Is it really an asset? Is it really a liability? If we had good definitions, we wouldn't face that problem and our worst decisions would go away. The difficulty with that is that accounting is rich with shades of meanings, with contingencies, with changes in circumstances that have a very real impact upon the way we understand whether an item has slipped over from the asset category to the loss category or not, whether it's a liability or something else. How do we define assets in such a way that contingent interests and other payments contingent upon agreements are cared for in all circumstances? There is a tremendous variety of circumstances and situations in which businesses find themselves. The problem, of course, is not to define assets or liabilities for the usual situation. The problem is to prepare a definition that will serve in the unusual situations. That's when the tests come....[5]

The problem with the use of definitions in the design of a new conceptual framework is that we are now attempting to create anew a framework which has its origins in antiquity. Most accountants find it difficult to make this shift in thinking. It is well known that modern accounting evolved from double entry bookkeeping created in the fourteenth century. Pacioli articulated it in the fifteenth century (he didn't create it) and, as the need for periodic income determinations became more important, the matching concept evolved. Originally, definitions of the type now under discussion were not relevant, and a "balance sheet" was just that—account balances remaining after annual income was determined; it was not considered a determinant of net worth.[6]

Early writings on the subject restricted themselves to the mechanical aspects of bookkeeping; no theories were expounded. The authors were chiefly engaged in solving practical problems and in demonstrating how specific transactions were translated into entries made on the books.[7] This was true until the beginning of the nineteenth century when writers began to concern themselves with the theory of accounts. Since that time authors have attempted to formulate—basically by a process of inductive reasoning from the rules and conventions that had been developed and generally accepted up to that time—the

---

[5]Comments of Robert K. Mautz at Wharton School of the University of Pennsylvania, May 4, 1977 on "The Conceptual Framework of Accounting."

[6]The draft still recognizes this limitation: "Financial accounting cannot directly measure the value of a business enterprise...." (par. 33; see previous Mautz quote).

[7]An excellent treaties on this subject is contained in *Origin and Evolution of Double Entry Bookkeeping* by Edward Peragallo (N.Y.: American Institute Publishing Co., 1938). See particularly p. 92 and Chapter VII.

underlying concepts and definitions of the accounting process. Naturally, it is difficult to do this while at the same time accepting—for the most part—the framework inherited. Separating the economic concepts upon which pure definitions must rest from the conventions that influence their derivation is an almost impossible task.

Considering this background, attempts at articulation inevitably become confused and encumbered with such interrelationships. A good example is the most recent attempt, APB Statement No 4, "Basic Concepts and Accounting Principles Underlying Financial Statements of Business Enterprises," which defined an asset as follows: "Assets—economic resources of an enterprise that are recognized and measured in conformity with generally accepted accounting principles. *"Assets also include certain deferred charges that are not resources but that are recognized and measured in conformity with generally accepted accounting principles."*[8] [Emphasis added. The definition of liabilities included deferred credits.] This demonstrates the influence of rules and conventions in determining definitions of elements entering into the accounting process; it seems that the FASB may find itself in the same position. It should be emphasized that the APB made it clear that its Statement was a codification of status quo and *not* what it felt the concepts should be. (It never got around to that. That was when the FASB took over.)

Nevertheless, we are now asked to hold in abeyance the use to which the definitions will be put. Presumably, this is to help reach agreement on them without the clutter of their effect. Or could it be a march down the primrose path to the inevitable hardline asset-liability concept of earnings which comes through loud and clear from the rest of the statement? (More about this later.) Here again we are told that accounting rules and conventions are needed before we can make use of our definitions. Can a conceptual framework be built on accounting rules and conventions? Are we in a chicken or egg dilemma? Perhaps we are, and it may be best to recognize it forthrightly.

The draft gives a good illustration of the need to apply "rules" as well as definitions in deciding the content of financial statements:

> 44. ... An example drawn from present practice illustrates how rules and conventions affect what is included in financial statements. Two enterprises possess valuable licenses that are no longer issued. One enterprise includes its license as an asset in its financial statements because it acquired the license from another enterprise at a measurable cost; the other does not include its license in its assets because it obtained it without cost when the license was originally issued. Since both licenses are resources of the respective enterprises, to include one assets while excluding the other reflects a difference caused by an accounting rule or convention rather than a difference in basic characteristics of the two resources. Different rules or conventions might include both licenses as assets or exclude both. Rules or conventions tend to change with conditions and circumstances....

---

[8]American Institute of Certified Public Accountants, "Basic Concepts and Accounting Principles Underlying Financial Statements of Business Enterprises," APB Statement No. 4 (New York: AICPA, October 1970), par. 132.

In reading the definitions of assets and liabilities one gets the distinct impression that they have been drafted in sufficiently broad terms to accommodate (but not completely) the adherents of the revenue-expense view of earnings, or at least to minimize the dichotomy that has been articulated between them and the asset-liability viewers. For example:

> 48. ... The resources represented as assets may have various characteristics. For example, they may be natural or man-made, tangible or intangible, exchangeable or usable only by the enterprise to produce other resources; they may have been acquired by purchase, production, investment by owners, discovery, or other nonreciprocal transfer. Although the ability of an enterprise to obtain the benefit from a resource and to exclude others from obtaining it generally rests on a foundation of legal rights, legal enforceability of a right is not essential if the enterprise is otherwise reasonably assured of obtaining the benefit. Similarly, although characteristics such as tangibility and exchangeability of a resource may affect whether its attributes are measurable,[16] *the absence of tangible substance or exchangeability (or both)* of a resource is not sufficient, by itself, to *preclude* the resource from being *represented* in a financial statement *as an asset.* [Emphasis added.]

> 50. ... Although many obligations rest generally on a foundation of legal rights, legal enforceability of a claim is not prerequisite to representing it as a liability in financial statements if the future transfer is *probable*—discharging an obligation *based on custom or moral responsibility has the same effect* on an enterprise's resources as discharging an enforceable claim. [Emphasis added.]

However, to make certain that there is no misunderstanding about where it stands on the basic issue:

> 66. ... there is no place in articulated financial statements for items that do not fit the definitions in this Statement but are sometimes said to be "required to match costs and revenues properly to measure periodic earnings" or "required to avoid distorting periodic earnings."

It is interesting to note, however, that throughout the document (including the appendices where explanations are expected) no mention is made of the major issue (Issue No. 1 in the Discussion Memorandum)—the asset-liability versus revenue-expense view of earnings determination, nor the reasoning behind the Board's conclusion in this respect.

CRITIQUE

Where does this leave us? As the public hearings begin (January 16-20, 1978), the discussions on capital maintenance and measurement, which in turn introduce the purchasing power and current value issues, we are asked to focus on the proposed objectives and definitions of the elements of financial statements. This can be done only if all readers will deal with these issues in terms of the present conventional (historical cost) framework. Just as the issuance of this Exposure Draft will enter into next week's public hearing discussions, so will issues of capital maintenance, measurement and, now, accounting rules or conventions of recognition enter into the commentary on this draft unless we put on the necessary blinders. Although the Board has said the other issues will be considered later, it is unfortunate that the Board did not clearly indicate the premises under which the draft should be considered.

As time goes on, those of use who have been close to the conceptual framework project—and those similarly involved in the U.K. and Australia—have found that it is not easy to break away from historical cost. There is no doubt that—whatever we need to do about inflation—we will need to continue to use historical cost for some time. Consequently, we had best fix up the old car first. Trying to do the ultimate in one leap is like overhauling an old car by painting it first without looking under the hood.

Despite the more expansive definitions of the elements, the Board has come down rather hard in opting for the asset-liability view of earnings. Over 200 commentaries on elements were received, with a vast majority in favor of the revenue-expense view of earnings. Some of those were concerned about the implication that an asset-liability view would lead to a current value concept, but many were more concerned that strict definitions of assets and liabilities would eliminate deferred charges and credits—as we know them—which they consider essential to the matching process. The Board has not told us why this vast majority was ignored, but instead has provided some clues to a possible compromise.

The first clue is the promise of the acknowledgement of some "rules and conventions of recognition" which need to be considered in applying the definitions (as previously discussed). Most people will want to see what these are before agreeing with the definitions—so there will probably be another reason for waiting for a complete package instead of a piecemeal approach.

The other clues reside in the definitions themselves. Notice that a "resource" does not need to be "tangible or exchangeable" to be an asset. The license illustration is fine as far as it goes, but it doesn't tell us how the unexpressed rule will make it come out. The definition adroitly omits "separability"—an attempt to avoid the goodwill issue. Since goodwill is generally recognized as a resource and the draft is silent on the criterion of separability, I can only assume that goodwill can be reflected as an asset, but we will need the rules to tell us how.

Likewise, since preoperational crew training, start-up costs, definitive product development, and the like, can be construed to be resources that benefit the future, they can qualify as assets. (We do not know whether the Board will soften, modify, or amplify its Statement No. 2.) Obviously, before we can accept these definitions, we will need to have more specific illustrations.

Liabilities need only to be probable and measurable, and not necessarily legally enforceable. Here again we need to have some good examples.

The major crux of the asset-liability-revenue-expense dichotomy is deferred taxes. APB No. 11 declared deferred taxes not to be a liability, but called it a deferred credit to provide proper interperiod matching. It disavowed the "net of tax" concept (although APB No. 11 acknowledged it) largely because it wanted to avoid complicated statement presentation. But from a conceptual standpoint, deferred tax credits (e.g., from accelerated depreciation) are—under a historical cost framework—a reduction of the cost of the related asset. This should be obvious because the value of a resource whose tax base is abnormally impaired is lower than an equivalent resource with a higher tax base. Tax depreciation is essentially a partial cost recovery.[9] This concept of deferred taxes (no matter how it might be recorded on the books) would, in my view, be compatible with the definitions contained in this Exposure Draft. If we could get the Board to acknowledge this and provide some other illustrations of how the definitions would work in practice, we might have the basis for a compromise between the two opposing viewpoints and be able to overcome one major stumbling block to progress.

There is an implicit attempt in this Draft to soften this dichotomy. Its rather strong articulation in the Discussion Memorandum has forced people to opt for one side or the other, and this is unfortunate. Most people are not entirely in one camp or the other. For example, many revenue-expense people—who emphasize that proper matching is their main concern—do not agree with a reserve for self-insurance, which is an obvious case of smoothing or averaging earnings. Many revenue-expense adherents assert that there is a big difference between matching and smoothing; they do not believe that charges should be deferred unless it can be shown that a future benefit will be obtained to match the later charge. Nor do they believe in arbitrary reserves to cover future costs that have no bearing on the present period. Likewise, many asset-liability people steadfastly believe in the need for deferred taxes to achieve proper income matching; they also agree that it is not a liability.[10] If this Draft will serve as a basis for the elimination of the need for two rigid camps, it will serve a very useful purpose.

MEASUREMENT: THE MAJOR HURDLE

While the resolution of the issues regarding the elements of financial statements will not be easy, by far the more difficult aspect of the conceptual framework project deals with *measurement*. This is an all-inclusive term, including the issues regarding capital maintenance and the qualitative aspects of the accounting elements.

If we were to assume, for hypothetical purposes, that inflation did not exist, we would still have to deal with the issue of measurement in the conceptual framework exercise. Holding gains and losses of an intrinsic nature occurs without the influence of inflation or deflation, and it is unfortunate that the present period of high inflation has accentuated the concern over the inadequacies of the historical cost basis. Chairman Williams of the SEC has urged that there be

---

[9]This view was taken in the earliest pronouncements on deferred taxes. See "Amortization of Emergency War Facilities" in ARB No. 23, *Accounting for Income Taxes* (December 1944); pars.12, 13 of Chapter 9C, ARB No. 43 (June 1953); and par. 5 of ARB No. 44, *Declining-Balance Depreciation* (Revised, July 1958).

[10]It is interesting to note that par. 40 of the draft, together with fn. 12, acknowledges the need for a proper "matching" to achieve the best measure of periodic earnings.

mandatory disclosure of the impact of inflation on a company and its financial statements.[11]

However, without inflation the issues of measurement become less compelling since inflation influences inventories and plant assets most—inventories turn over rapidly and therefore basic measurement (in a noninflating period) is not a factor in earnings; plant assets are not usually sold but held to the end of their useful lives (requiring only cost allocation in a noninflationary period). Nevertheless, because inflation seems to be ever present, it is difficult to separate the value changes that are due to inflation from those that are intrinsic. Consequently, we must deal with the question of measurement and recognize that it may not always be possible to segregate the causes of value changes.

Public hearings will address themselves to three remaining issues, starting with capital maintenance. Two major concepts of capital maintenance or cost recovery are to be considered, both of which can be measured either in money or in units of the same purchasing power: the financial capital concept and the physical capital concept. The principal differences between them involve certain changes in prices or assets during accounting periods, the so-called "holding gains and losses." In the financial capital concept, they are included in earnings (usually not until realized) because every difference between financial (historical) cost and the amount realized is considered income. They are called "capital maintenance adjustments" in the physical capital concept and, with varying labels, are usually included in owners' equity or in an equity-changes statement.

Our present framework deals only with financial capital (in units of money), although the LIFO inventory costing of sales techniques excludes the inflated cost of replacement from earnings. To that extent, although the balance sheet does not reflect the new value of the physical capital, the income statement gives recognition to the physical capital recovery concept. Replacement cost depreciation concepts (the SEC's camel's nose under the tent) are another example of an attempt to replace financial capital with physical capital. This gets complicated when applied to monetary items or shareholders' equity, when expressed in units of general purchasing power (GPP), et cetera, and I can only recommend a careful reading of Chapter 6 of the Discussion Memorandum. The AICPA task force models, which are discussed later, incorporate varying concepts of capital maintenance in ascending degree.

Two critical determinations are involved in measuring the elements of financial accounting:

1. The unit in which the measurements are to be made (dollars vs. GPP).
2. The particular attribute that is to be measured (sometimes referred to as the measurement basis or the valuation basis). The five choices available include: (*a*) historical cost-historical proceeds [present framework], (*b*) current

---

[11]Harold M. Williams in an address before the AICPA Fifth National Conference on Current SEC Developments, Washington, D.C., January 4, 1978.

cost-current proceeds, (*c*) current exit value, (*d*) expected exit value, and (*e*) present value of expected cash flows.

There is an implication that no one attribute would be applicable to all elements and that, in addition, each attribute is susceptible to measurement in either units of money or units of general purchasing power. These attributes, which are essentially quantitative, need to be tempered in their choice by the qualitative attributes of relevance, reliability, comparability, timeliness, and understandability (about which little controversy is expected). Trade-offs are anticipated in an attempt to provide compatibility.

The AICPA Task Force has an experiment underway in which twenty-three major companies are restating their 1975 and 1976 statements on the basis of four accounting models, in addition to the historical cost (conventional) model. These models run the gamut from price level to current value, and it is hoped that the results will provide some insight into the theoretical and implementary problems that they would encounter. Any one of these models (or modifications thereof) could ultimately replace the present model, or—as is more likely—provide a supplement to our present model in order to place historical results in perspective. We believe the FASB deliberations on measurement will be benefited from the results of this experiment.

SUMMARY

The pervasiveness of the search for a new conceptual framework of accounting and its implications for the profession's future ability to provide meaningful data to a fast-changing economy, are obvious. While the clamor for immediate change to accommodate a world beset by inflation seems reasonable and urgent, we should not cast aside a well-understood framework that—despite its deficiencies—has served our expansive capital markets so well. Change in accounting has in the past been slow, perhaps too slow. We now seem on the brink of a definitive conclusion to this project. Exposure Drafts have a way of crystalizing thought and the one just published, plus what is to come, will demand the close scrutiny of the best accounting thinkers of the world.

ACCOUNTING FOR CHANGING PRICES

A PRACTITIONER'S VIEW OF THE REALIZATION CONCEPT†

by
Philip L. Defliese

I have been asked to discuss how the practitioner looks at the Concepts and Standards Research Study Committee's report on "The Realization Concept," appearing in the April 1965 issue of *The Review*. This report, of course, developed out of *Supplementary Statements No. 1* and *2* to the 1957 Revision of the Association's statement on *Accounting and Reporting Standards for Corporate Financial Statements*. Any discussion will naturally include the three documents, and I shall make no serious attempt to distinguish among them in my remarks. Since I am to speak as a practitioner, you may expect that what I shall say will be largely influenced by considerations of practicality. Despite this, I want you to realize that, personally, I believe the only way in which we ever achieve advancement in what may be termed practical accounting is by first developing and setting forth concepts toward which practice should strive.

As you are well aware, the practitioner must operate within his own frame of reference—that is, he can give recognition only to those economic changes which affect financial position and results of operations *as determined by generally accepted accounting principles*. Thus, he cannot stray far beyond the concepts that are presently understood and accepted by the business community or those that he believes could become acceptable. This does not mean that he cannot look forward to the day when the balance sheet and income statement will present financial position and results of operations in an absolute or economic sense. He must realize, however, that the latter is a different frame of reference which is far from attainment. (The Accounting Principles Board must also recognize the difference between these two frames of references; I believe some of its past problems may have resulted from confusing the two.) We must all realize that, at present, in some respects the balance sheet is nothing more than a vestige of double-entry bookkeeping which acts as a respository for the results of our income statement maneuvers; the best example of this is the use of Lifo inventory valuation, which gives a very meaningful income statement but results in a miserable balance sheet. Our income statement, despite its limitations, however, is more meaningful today than it ever was.

I have heard the Association *Statements Nos. 1* and *2* referred to by some accountants as an attempt to resurrect the proposition that financial progress

---

†Paper presented at Northeast Regional meeting of the American Accounting Association, Babson Institute of Business Administration, April 24, 1965. Reprinted from *The Accounting Review*, July 1965, pp. 517-521, with permission of the American Accounting Association.

should be measured in terms of annual valuations of assets. This proposition was, as many of you undoubtedly know, examined by a special committee of the American Institute of Certified Public Accountants in 1932 and was then rejected on the grounds that it was neither practical nor desirable. While many of the problems which troubled the 1932 committee would, I am afraid, be present in implementing this report, I think that this view of *Statements Nos. 1* and *2* is somewhat superficial.

Under the recommendations of the report, the amount referred to as "net income" is based upon realization through exchange transactions or the occurrence of a "crucial event" in the revenue process, not simply the accretion in net worth. Thus, net income would not differ significantly from what is now conventional. (Bear in mind that for the purpose of this discussion, I am ignoring the difference between those disposal gains and losses which are reflected in income and those which are often reflected as retained-earnings items under present accounting principles.)

OPERATING INCOME

The report on the realization concept and the supplementary statements also appear to stress an objective of recognizing "holding" gains and losses resulting from increments and decrements in the value of assets (other than regular depreciation) as they occur, rather than postponing their recognition and inclusion in the measurement of income only at the time the asset is disposed of.

I believe that the most significant aspect of the report's conclusions stems from its recommendation that the determination of net income be made up of two components:

(a) that resulting from operations; and

(b) that arising from the changes in the value of assets sold, exchanged or utilized during the period (e.g., difference between depreciation computed on historical cost basis and depreciation based on current replacement cost).

In this respect, the Committee has taken a salutary and notable first step. The resulting income statement would provide, I believe, a determination of net results of operations (not "net income") unaffected by price-level and other value changes not related to operations. In addition, effects of latter type of changes—to the extent they are realized or utilized—would be shown separately.

I am sure that you appreciate that many practitioners will have considerable difficulty in accepting the theory that unrealized holding gains, particularly as they relate to plant assets, should be recognized at all. In the practitioner's mind, if two companies of equal size and operations differ only to the extent that one completed its plant ten years ago and the other only recently, the older should have a higher net income because depreciation is an actual cost-allocation device and not an economic equalizer. They may, however, accept an adjustment to *operating* income brought about by the use of current costs, provided that its effect is neutralized by the time net income is determined.

Because of this, and, more especially, since *operating* income would be measured in terms of current values (generally, replacement costs) of assets consumed in operations, it seems to me that the report may be viewed as an approach to the problems of the shortcomings of historical-dollar accounting under conditions where the purchasing power of the dollar is changing. In this sense, its objective and the objective of price-level accounting are the same. Actually, this result could be achieved within our present structure—that is, without recognizing unrealized holding gains at all—because final net income is unchanged from its present meaning. Thus, it becomes a matter of presentation. As a transitional step, this may be appealing to some practitioners. Of course, the approach recommended is different from price-level accounting. The determination of current values by references to replacement costs, as recommended in the report, will naturally recognize changes in the relative value of specific assets other than those related to price-level changes—for, obviously, replacement costs may change even though the price-level is constant.

Management who lean toward price-level accounting have another problem. They are caught in a dilemma between their desire to improve their balance sheets by reflecting some part of their holding gains on the one hand and their repugnance of charging income with more than historical-cost depreciation on the other. I do not intend to imply that practitioners are averse to any recognition of holding gains. Their attitude is pragmatic and is influenced by the purpose to be served by the adjustment. They prefer to allow the nature and objective of the enterprise to be the determining influence. Thus, they have already accepted market value as the proper basis for the holdings of investment companies; and the recording of investments in subsidiaries at equity value rather than at cost is becoming more popular. This evolution will continue.

It must be evident, from these last few remarks, that I am dwelling on the report's impact from the standpoint of how the consumption of long-lived assets is to be reflected in the statement of income. Operating income would be determined with reference to their current value rather than historical acquisition costs. As a matter of presentation alone, this would be an improvement and, as I inferred previously, might aid in the ultimate general acceptance of price-level accounting.

I am not inclined to believe, however, that (except in times of severe price fluctuations) the use of replacement costs of inventories, rather than historical costs, would have a substantial bearing on the determination of operating income. In most companies, the rate of inventory turnover is such that acquisition costs entering into cost of sales would be about the same as replacement costs. If Lifo values are used, then results under current practice should be the same, in all material respects, as would be obtained under the Committee's recommendations. Of course, Lifo leaves us in the untenable position of using current costs in the income statement while reflecting "vintage" costs in the balance sheet. Whether or not this can be overcome remains to be seen. Except for this, I foresee no considerable problem with the Committee's recommendation regarding inventories.

REVENUE TRANSACTIONS

As a practitioner I have very little difficulty with the Committee's views on realization as they affect revenue transactions. As time goes on, the small pockets of "cash-basis accounting" are gradually being eliminated; so the day is not far off when the Committee's views will be widely accepted. Sophisticated application of the concept of matching costs and revenues has already met the Committee's views part way; for example, the costs related to obtaining business are more frequently being viewed as deserving of some revenue allocation.

I believe the Committee's report relating to revenue realization implicitly adopts the percentage-of-completion method of accounting for contract construction and other services on a contract basis, as well as the full recognition of losses inherent in some contracts. It would seem to me that a fuller discussion of this problem is warranted in any treatise of the realization concept. For example, contractual arrangements provide objectively measurable revenue; a market transaction has taken place; and the extent of services performed is usually also determinable. Thus, all three criteria for realization are met. Under the concepts of the AAA report, accounting for revenue in contract situations on a shipment basis or completed contract basis—which is still widely followed—would be unacceptable. As a practitioner, I can agree with this conclusion heartily in cases where the periods of time for contract fulfillment are long and/or performance is either spasmodic or erratic. The present permissiveness of the shipment or completed contract basis in such situations produces a wild distortion of periodic income that is nothing short of an outrage. It is supportable only for income tax purposes. Its acceptability, coupled with the requirement that anticipated losses be also reflected (Paragraphs 11 and 15 of *ARB 45*), should be repealed as quickly as possible.

With respect to loss-type contracts, I am assuming that the replacement-cost principle supported by the Committee's report must give way to the principle of net realizable value. The latter was rejected in *Supplementary Statement No. 2* simply because the first two criteria for realization—(1) the nature of the asset received (definitive contract price) and (2) the presence of a market transaction (definitive contract)—impose a limit upon realization that can not be ignored. Thus, all anticipated losses to completion of a contract must be provided for in the period when the "crucial event" of loss estimation occurs.

REPLACEMENT COSTS VS. PRICE-LEVEL ACCOUNTING

Let me now proceed to some basic observations about the Committee's recommendations, particularly as they relate to the use of replacement costs. At the outset, I shall say that, as a practitioner, I am perhaps both timid and impatient. My timidity causes me to view with some alarm the practical problems involved in determining replacement costs in the case of a large and complex business entity. My impatience wants me to see the admitted inadequacies of historical-cost accounting cured and to see that a cure is adopted that can be generally adopted in this country as quickly as possible.

As to these practical problems in the determination of replacement costs, let me cite some of the statements made by the 1932 American Institute committee to which I previously referred. That committee said in part:

> Any consideration of the accounts of a large business enterprise today must start from the premise that annual valuation of the assets is neither practical nor desirable.[1]

These considerations are, in large part equally applicable today.

I realize that *Supplementary Statement No. 1* fully recognized the problems involved in arriving at replacement costs. As a possible solution, it suggested that "adjustment of historical cost by the use of specific indexes may provide acceptable approximations of current costs." However, in view of the highly specialized nature of equipment needed for today's automated operations and evidence of increasing use of such equipment, I have serious doubts that specific price indexes could be developed that would be capable of being applied on any wide-scale basis.

My present view—and I must emphasize *present*—is that the most practical course to follow in order to correct the shortcomings of historical-dollar account *is the adoption of price-level accounting with the use of a general price index.* This will obviate the need for the multitudinous terminations that would be required to arrive at replacement costs. It will also avoid another problem that I see in an attempt to use replacement costs. This is that their determination is apt to be largely influenced by subjective considerations. As a consequence, at the least, comparability of financial statements of different companies would be impaired, and, at the worst, opportunities for manipulation might be encouraged. However, as a practitioner, I must predict that the adoption of price-level accounting is a long way off.

NON-INCOME ADJUSTMENTS OF STOCK EQUITY

In addition to the practical problems involved, adoption of the recommendations in the report would carry with it what I consider to be a theoretical drawback. To the extent that "holding" gains or losses represent only changes in monetary values resulting from price-level changes, I have considerable question that they should be reported as such periodically in any part of the statement of income. I appreciate, of course, that the effect of these changes would have to be adjusted for in any monetary expression of stockholders' equity.

The Concepts Committee has been aware of this problem. It stated in *Supplementary Statement No. 1*:

> If adjustments for changes in the general price level are not made, the effects of inflation and deflation are necessarily included in the measurement of holding gains or losses. In

---

[1]Special Committee on Cooperation with Stock Exchanges, Letter to Committee on Stock Lists of the New York Stock Exchange, September 22,1932 (reprinted in *Audits of Corporate Accounts*, New York, 1934).

> this case, accounting for long-lived assets assumes implicitly that the effects of price-level changes are not sufficiently important to justify separate recognition.[2]

It then went on to say that it felt precluded from making a recommendation on the important subject of price-level changes and their impact on accounting.

Nevertheless, I do not believe that we can deal with the report's recommendations unless we also deal with the problem of price-level changes. Further, as I inferred previously, I am inclined toward the view expressed by Professor Dixon in his dissent to *Supplementary Statement No. 1* to the effect that changes in asset values due solely to changes in the price level should not be included in holding gains. We all know that price-level changes do not result in gains or losses; rather, it is the monetary unit that has changed. Hence, I would like to emphasize that meaningful statements would result if this type of effect were separately categorized.

Despite the fact that some of what I have said may have appeared to be in the nature of criticism, let me repeat that I think the report on the "The Realization Concept" and *Supplementary Statements Nos. 1* and *2* represent substantial contributions to the advancement of the art of accounting.

---

[2]*The Accounting Review*, July 1964, p. 698.

THE CHANGING BUSINESS SCENE†

by
Warren Chippindale and Philip L. Defliese

> "The cause of lightning," Alice said very decidedly, for she felt quite certain about it, "is the thunder. No! No!" she hastily corrected herself. "I meant the other way about."
>
> "It's too late to correct it!" shouted the Red Queen. "When you have once said a thing, that fixes it, and you must take the consequences."

BUSINESSPEOPLE—whether they be owners, managers, or investors—have been hearing thunder and feeling the lightening strike for several years now. Rapid general inflation has raised many questions and led to considerable discussion about inflated or illusory profits, overcontrol of prices, overtaxation, dividend payments out of capital, a shortage of capital, and the true nature of a company's worth and profitability. In such a situation it is natural that the businessperson should turn to accounting, as the language of business, for explanations and solutions.

Measurement and analysis must precede any explanations, and the principal accounting tools and standards available to the business world for the interpretation of operating results have been those of historical cost accounting.

Historical cost accounting, founded on the premise that an asset should be stated at the actual amount paid for it (less depreciation and amortization), has traditionally not attempted to reflect rising prices due to inflation. While the rise was slow, the effect was rarely significant, and little concern was expressed over any disregard of inflation. Most analysts preferred to deal with the generally accepted accounting principles based on the familiar concept of historical costs. They feared that the judgments of managers and accountants required by current value concepts would lead to inconsistency of public financial reporting. As the rate of inflation increased, however, it became apparent that the distortions were growing too marked to be ignored, and concern arose over the adequacy of the allowances made for the effects of inflation.

---

†Introduction in *Current Value Accounting: A Practical Guide for Business*, Warren Chippindale and Philip L. Defliese, eds. (New York: AMACOM: A Division of American Management Association, 1977), pp. 1-4. The remainder of the book contains chapters on various aspects of current value accounting written by various authors.

In the balance sheet, the value to the business of assets purchased today must be reconciled with those purchased last year, or ten years ago, for far less money. Under historical cost, all are valued at their depreciated original cost. Similarly, liabilities are recorded in the amounts at which they were incurred. The ensuing confusion makes it difficult to judge the true financial position of a company, although it has been recognized for some time now that balance sheets cannot portray the worth of a company as a whole.

As for profits, these are traditionally measured, taxed, and distributed to shareholders by matching lower past costs against income from prices that have been forced rapidly upward by rising replacement costs. As a result, users of operating statements have difficulty in distinguishing between true and inflated profits.

Unlike Alice's abrupt change of mind, the initial accounting response has not been to turn the business world on its ear but rather to look for a solution within the framework of historical cost accounting. For instance, LIFO costing for inventories and general price level accounting, otherwise known as current purchasing power accounting, were introduced. Although each of these concepts has been able in some way to put the data derived from the historical cost framework into a better perspective, neither has been successful in providing a comprehensive solution. The anomalies remain.

Current value accounting is seen by many as the next logical step down the road. As Sir Francis Sandilands, chairman of the British government's Inflation Accounting Committee, has said, the process has been "evolutionary rather than revolutionary: no more than an extension in degree of principles already established in modern accounting conventions."

Yet, current value accounting attempts to tackle directly the crucial problems of gauging the value of a business and measuring profits during times of inflation (or deflation). In current value accounts, the balance sheet shows assets and liabilities at up-to-date values instead of historical costs. The single yardstick is what they are all worth now. Profit is calculated by charging against income not out-of-date historical costs but replacement costs for inventories or capital assets consumed.

The principles, although not yet completely settled, are relatively simple, but their application is bound to be complex and difficult. The purpose of this book is to examine in greater detail the reasons for considering current value accounting, evaluate its advantages and disadvantages, explain the practical problems of implementation, and look at the current status of inflation accounting in all the major industrial countries of the world.

In any business in any country, the important thing is that the system in use provide the information that is needed, whether by management, by investors, by employees, or by the public at large. Good management, as well as sound investment decisions, demands accurate, consistent, and pertinent information. Many accountants, analysts, and managers now believe that in times of even moderate inflation (or deflation), current value accounting is the best way of providing such information.

Nevertheless, businesspeople are understandably reluctant to cast off the lines from the steady mooring that historical cost accounting has provided and embark on a voyage in an uncharted sea. They contend, with good reason, that they can make the necessary adjustments for management decisions and that analysts and the efficient market do the same. In the United States, the recent requirement of the Securities and Exchange Commission for piecemeal replacement cost disclosure has added to the concern. It seems clear that in the United States, no move to displace the present framework (as is presently recommended in the United Kingdom and Australia) should proceed until current value accounting is understood and tried and the results are carefully evaluated as to their soundness, relevancy, and compatibility with present means of measurement. A step-by-step approach of this type has been adopted in Canada. The editors and authors of this book take no position in this regard, except to call for caution and understanding before proceeding.

Precisely where the future will take us is impossible to say with certainty. Current value accounting may present one answer to today's problems, but new problems will demand fresh solutions. Undoubtedly the dialogue, of which this book is a part, will continue.

For today's managers and accountants the Red Queen's strictures are, fortunately, misplaced: it is not too late for change. In some instances, in fact, the culprits may turn out to be not those who change their minds but those who will not consider that possibility.

INFLATION ACCOUNTING: PURSUING THE ELUSIVE†

by

Philip L. Defliese

DESPITE anticipated record-year 1978 earnings of over $12 per share, General Motors last November declared a smaller year-end extra dividend than in 1977 ($6 total for 1978 vs. $6.80 for 1977). The question must be asked: Did GM know what it was doing? GM stock sold off immediately and took the entire market with it for several days, as Wall Street interpreted the action as bellwether GM's concern over a dim outlook for 1979. Yes, GM did know what it was doing, and why, but it failed to communicate adequately its motives. Hence the market reaction. Responsibility for the inadequate communication must, however, be shared by the accounting profession. And soon, if hopes are realized, something will be done about it—the comment period on the Financial Accounting Standards Board's exposure draft, *Financial Reporting and Changing Prices*, has just ended.

Blue-chip companies generally follow the policy of declaring a sustainable percentage of earnings as cash dividends, plowing back the remainder for growth. Inflation has impacted this practice considerably as companies have learned that a greater portion of earnings must be retained to cover the excess of replacement cost over original cost of consumed inventory, plant and machinery (in GM's case, tools, dies, jigs, etc.) to permit them to maintain their existing level of operations without adding heavy debt.

Buried in the GM communiques, inadequately emphasized, was the fact that GM expects to spend $5 billion for capital expenditures in 1979 vs. records of $4.5 billion and $3.6 billion in 1978 and 1977, respectively. In 1978, depreciation provided only $3.04 billion, a shortfall of $5.11 per share. Unfortunately, we cannot determine what portion of these expenditures relates to replacement and what portion to growth. Nevertheless, GM knows that its historical cost determined earnings are inflated, in an economic sense, and that the dividend must be smaller to make up for excess replacement costs—its 1978 payout ratio was the lowest in recent history.[1]

How this message can be conveyed in a more quantified and objective fashion has confounded accounting standard setters around the world for some

---

†Reprinted with permission from *The Journal of Accountancy*, May 1979, pp. 50, 52, 54, 58-63, copyright © 1979 by American Institute of CPAs. Opinions of the authors are their own and do not necessarily reflect policies of the AICPA.

[1]In its 1978 report to shareholders, GM for the first time restated operations on a constant dollar basis for the years 1973-1978, using the consumer price index for 1973 as a base.

time.[2] In 1976, the impatient Securities and Exchange Commission created a hornet's nest when it issued Accounting Series Release no. 190 requiring disclosure of replacement cost depreciation and cost of sales. Businessmen generally dislike any disclosure that disparages historical cost generated earnings. Many companies (including GM) understandably buried the data in the Form 10-K report rather than include it in their annual reports to shareholders. Some considered the implications misleading and said so in no uncertain terms. Even finance-trained GM Chief Executive Thomas Murphy has said that few, if any, businessmen viewed ASR no. 190 with any kindness. He accused the SEC of having opened "a Pandora's box providing the unscrupulous with the opportunity to present and manipulate hypothetical data which can only serve to confuse those it should inform." True, ASR no. 190 has its drawbacks. It was hastily rammed through without research and was premised on a hypothetical future replacement rather than on equipment in use. More on that later.

The SEC cautioned that such replacement data should not be used to reconstruct net income. I shall disregard this caveat—with poetic license—only to illustrate that some adjustment of earnings must be made to communicate the need for an additional dividend limitation which, I believe, GM undertook subconsciously, if not overtly. Based on GM's 1978 10-K disclosure of replacement costs, which it said was hypothetical and probably not useful for this purpose, its $12.24 per share earnings would be reduced by between $3.17 and $3.66, depending on which theory (described later) you subscribe to for the effect of net monetary liabilities (see figure 1).

Now comes the FASB's proposed solution. The exposure draft issued in December (for comments by May 1 with the possibility of public hearings thereafter) fulfills the board's promise to require disclosure of the effect of changing prices as supplementary data, leaving undisturbed the traditional historical cost accounting model as the basic reporting vehicle. Almost all accounting standard-setting bodies throughout the world have now seen the wisdom of this conclusion and are proceeding along these lines. Unless the monetary unit is regularly officially restructured, as in Brazil, a dollar is a dollar is a dollar—historical cost earnings are objectively determined earnings (within present limitations), and the results are in actual dollars. Thus, a company could distribute those dollars if it intended to liquidate and all other things remained equal. The fact that those dollars can no longer buy what they once did is another matter, but more a matter of economics than of accounting. Nevertheless, it is a matter that calls for *interpretation* of the reported historical dollar results by those best qualified to do so. And this is where we now are. It should be noted, of course, that inflation is just one element of the broader concept of "changing prices." The recent severe erosion of purchasing power by inflation has emphasized the need for action but has also served to confuse the issues.

---

[2]The confusion over whether the objective is to redetermine past income on some better economic basis or to predict future cash flows to the investor adds to this problem.

Figure 1: Illustration of Suggested First Approach to the Problem of Changing Prices

Supplemental earnings data—1978* (in millions of dollars)

		Amount	*Per common share*
Net income per income statement (historical cost)		$ 3,508.0	$ 12.24
Earnings reserved to cover estimated excess of current cost over historical cost of			
Depreciation and amortization	$ 862.1		
Cost of Sales	180.9		
	$ 1,043.0		
Less: Portion attributable to net monetary debt capital (12.4%)	139.3		
Portion attributable to shareholders' capital		903.7	3.17
Earnings available for expansion and distribution		$ 2,604.3	$ 9.07

* Amounts based, for illustration only, on General Motors' 1978 10-K disclosures of replacement cost in compliance with ASR no. 190. Replacement cost is not the exact equivalent of current cost. The adjustment for depreciation and amortization is not precise because ASR no. 190 requires straight-line and GM uses accelerated methods for historical cost. As a matter of interest, it should be noted that the GM 1978 annual report showed $2,390.8 million and $8.34 as the constant (1973) dollar equivalents of net income and earnings per share, respectively. See footnote 1.

Opinions among accountants and businessmen differ widely on how to interpret reported earnings in an inflationary environment—the FASB itself is undecided and offers two ways (see figure 2) of doing it. Not even the much maligned Accounting Principles Board had the temerity to offer a choice on an important issue, except when forced to by the SEC (remember the investment credit debacle[3]). No doubt this is a sop to the opposing current cost and constant dollar (price level) factions, a Solomonic decision that may, or may not, temper the fierce controversy between them.

In fairness, it must be reported that the FASB says it is attempting to encourage experimentation that "would help to develop techniques for accumulating, reporting, and analyzing data on the effects of price changes." Thus, we will now have mandatory experimentation. Previous experimentation was voluntary[4] and was understandably conducted under the cloak of secrecy because companies, on a selective basis, didn't want to publicize any but their official results. Now everybody will have to let it all hang out, one way or the other. The proposed standard will apply only to publicly held companies with over $125 million of inventory and plant, or assets over $1 billion. It is estimated that 1,000 U. S. companies will be affected. If experimentation is needed (and it is), one wonders why companies shouldn't report the data both ways so users may make relevant comparisons. As it is, if GM chooses the constant dollar model (as it did in its 1978 report) and Ford chooses the current cost model, how can comparisons be made? It's not clear whether the choice is that optional, as explained below.

This proposal is another step in the board's quest for a conceptual framework for financial reporting, following its issuance, also last December, of its long-awaited Statement on Financial Accounting Concepts no. 1, *Objectives of Financial Reporting*. That statement, in line with previous proposals, affirmed the objective of providing users with information "on the relative standing and performance of a business enterprise . . . *on which to base estimates required for investment and lending decisions*." (Emphasis supplied.) Most preparers, and perhaps many users, will be happy to see that the board acceded to the almost universal clamor to avoid injecting price-change concepts into the basic model, i.e., it did not tinker with historical cost. On the other hand, it's never been made clear just what analysts want or need as supplemental information in this area. We can only surmise, but the emphasis given to "future cash flows of the enterprise" in the objectives statement leads directly to one conclusion—an investor needs to know what to expect in terms of cash dividends and stock price

---

[3]The first APB opinion (no. 2) required one uniform method; when the SEC permitted two methods, the APB amended its opinion (issued as Opinion no. 4) to permit two also.

[4]In 1975 the FASB conducted a voluntary field test of the general purchasing power exposure draft on 101 companies (report issued in 1977). In 1977 the AICPA conducted a test of four types of accounting models designed to reflect changing prices; 23 companies participated voluntarily (report issued 1979). Both tests were on a confidential basis.

Figure 2: Annual Supplemental Statements: Choose Either One.*

(a) Current cost model

Condensed statement of current cost income from continuing operations and other data pertaining to changing prices

For the year ended December 31, 1978

Net sales and other operating revenues	$	50,000
Cost of goods sold at current cost		21,900
Depreciation and amortization expense at current cost		12,100
Other operating expenses		9,000
Interest expense		1,000
Provision for income taxes		3,000
Current cost income from continuing operations	$	3,000
Net holding loss on inventories and property, plant and equipment resulting from a holding gain ($4,500) less inflation component ($4,000) and less income tax ($2,000) on amounts realized	$	(1,500)
Inflation gain on net monetary items	$	575
Foreign exchange loss net of tax	$	(500)

(b) Historical cost/constant dollar model

Condensed statement of constant dollar income from continuing operations in December 31, 1978, dollars and other data pertaining to changing prices

For the year ended December 31, 1978

Net sales and other operating revenues	$**	52,000
Cost of goods sold at restated historical cost		21,200
Depreciation and amortization expense at restated historical cost		11,800
Other operating expenses		9,360
Interest expense		1,040
Provision for income taxes		5,200
Constant dollar income from continuing operations	$**	3,400
Inflation gain on net monetary items	$**	600
Foreign exchange loss net of tax***	$**	500

$** December 31, 1978, dollars.

*** It is assumed that the foreign exchange loss is stated at the same amount as in the basic income statement.

* These illustrations of alternative presentations of supplemental data are from the FASB Exposure Draft, *Financial Reporting and Changing Prices.*

appreciation. The relationship to the need for a better interpretation of reported earnings is obvious.

The present low price-earnings ratios tell us that the efficient market has discounted most reported historical cost earnings as inflated. The constant lowering of the percentages of earnings distributed during the current decade (despite the absolute increases in earnings) tells us that managements have also seen the need to retard distributions to cover excess replacement costs. Presumably, what users need is some better indication of earnings available for distribution and growth, after allowing for excess replacement cost. On the other hand, as a consumer, the shareholder has his problems with the declining purchasing power of the dollar he receives as dividends and his share price on resale; perhaps he also needs something to put his cash flow in perspective. The FASB proposal for a five-year summary provides data that go a long way in this direction.

The proposal appears to provide something for everybody—shareholders, analysts, theoreticians (all camps) and management. It would require a plethora of data from every affected company from which presumably the most useful data (to whom?) will ultimately be chosen or plucked. Presumably, the marketplace will choose, but will Gresham's law operate? Will the useless data drive out the useful? The proposal also has the capability of creating considerable confusion, because only the most sophisticated will understand the implications of each disclosure, especially since the disclosures are discrete, ostensibly incapable of being consolidated into a useful new indicator of earnings available for distribution and growth.

Somehow the FASB cannot resist mixing apples and oranges. Yes, every choice but one provides, more or less, a mixture of current or historical cost with constant dollar (price level) concepts (see figure 2). The one exception is the brief statement of asset values at year-end (see figure 3), which compares historical cost amounts of inventory and plant with their related current cost (not necessarily current value). This statement is required only for those choosing the current cost format. Presumably it is needed to provide some idea of the asset values used to derive current cost income. It is hoped that the Internal Revenue Service will give LIFO companies permission to make this disclosure, as it did for the ASR no. 190 disclosures. Also, we can only hope that users will not add the difference to equity to reconstruct the debt-equity ratio; on this point, however, views will differ.

Now, let us look at the choices, their premises, their advantages and their drawbacks. While the draft seems to permit a free choice between the two different bases, it provides guidelines that "shall be considered" in making the choice. These specify that the current cost format should be used "unless . . . constant dollar . . . better reflects the effects of changing prices . . .," i.e., the constant dollar basis "may be sufficient . . . if cost of sales and depreciation are not significant" (paragraph 25) or when specific price changes follow the general price level (then why not use specific prices?). Does this mean that those choosing the constant dollar model must defend their choice? This vague permissiveness in the guidelines must be clarified. Financial institutions will need to use the constant dollar basis. With the dollar as its commodity, does a bank worry about the dollar's purchasing power? It simply adjusts the interest rate, and its investors look for a different rate of return.

Figure 3 *(Current cost model)*

Statement of asset values at December 31, 1978

	Net historical cost per balance sheet	*Net current cost*
Inventory	$ 5,435	$ 6,920
Property, plant and equipment	40,000	50,000
	$ 45,435	$ 56,920

* These illustrations of alternative presentations of supplemental data are from the FASB Exposure Draft, *Financial Reporting and Changing Prices*.

CURRENT COST MODEL

This model (see figure 2[a]) attempts to determine income from continuing operations using current costs for cost of sales and depreciation.[5] Current cost is defined as the "current cost of acquiring the same service potential (that is, the same operating costs and output capacity) as embodied by the asset owned." This assumption may be made when the asset can be replaced in its present mode (used condition). Much latitude is allowed, including the use of indexes, in setting current cost values. The methodology differs considerably from that of the SEC's release on replacement cost, especially since the FASB model would permit operating cost differentials to be considered when the only available measure embodies replacement with new technology.

Income from continuing operations—the draft's new concept of recurring net income—excludes holding gains and losses, both realized and unrealized (adjusted for inflation), and foreign exchange loss (net of tax) computed in the same manner as in the historical cost income statement. Considering the flack the FASB has been getting on Statement no. 8, *Accounting for the Translation of Foreign Currency Transactions and Foreign Currency Financial Statements,* it is understandable that it would want to segregate these translation effects.[6]

It is unfortunate that the term "holding gain" has entered our literature in this area, since in many instances there is no "gain" at all in an economic sense. Price

[5]An alternative presentation (also illustrated in the FASB draft) reconciles current cost income with historical cost income. A similar option is given for the constant dollar model.

[6]The FASB has announced that it intends to modify Statement no. 8.

changes of inventories and plant assets reflect the combination of a change in the purchasing power of the dollar and in the intrinsic value of the item itself. Often there is only a new monetary denomination without an intrinsic gain, as most homeowners today realize. This model attempts to squeeze out the inflation factor to determine the true holding gains (or losses—especially since the related actual income tax is deducted from those realized). Much debate will center on whether this item should include unrealized gains or losses. (The consumer price index is used to measure inflation, as discussed later.)

The most controversial item in this model will be "inflation gain on net monetary items." This is the same item that created so much controversy in previously proposed constant dollar (price level) models—both the APB's and the FASB's. Many companies operate with a net monetary liability, because heavy long- and short-term debt usually outweigh inventory. (Even the colossus GM had a net monetary liability of about $2.5 billion in 1978.) There is a presumption that, because of this phenomenon, each year's inflation results in a gain from the fact that cheaper dollars will ultimately be used to repay the debt. This can cause a sizable gain for a highly leveraged company.

In the past, the prime controversy was whether this gain (if it exists) should be included in income immediately, as it was in the original price level model, or spread over the periods during which the offset—higher annual replacement cost depreciation of the assets financed—takes place. The FASB model begs the question by presenting the amount as a discrete item for the reader to interpret as he wishes. A few theorists believe no real gain takes place—they say the gain resides in the assets purchased by the debt.[7] One can also take the position that backlog depreciation (inflation's effect on prior years' original cost depreciation) more than offsets any such gains on net monetary liabilities.

A simple example will illustrate: Assume a plant with a 30-year life built 10 years ago for $10 million and financed entirely with 30-year debt has a current replacement cost of $20 million. The current year's inflation rate is 10 percent, resulting in an assumed net monetary gain on the debt of $1 million. The excess of current cost depreciation over historical cost depreciation for the year is only $666,667 ($20,000,000 ÷ 20 – $10,000,000 ÷ 30).

The British have proposed, in their Hyde guidelines,[8] that only those excess current cost adjustments financed by shareholders' equity should be taken into account; those financed by debt are omitted. This is accomplished by applying a net monetary debt-to-total-capital ratio to the adjustment. Thus, if the plant in the above example was financed 50 percent from debt and 50 percent from equity (an oversimplification), the current cost adjustment would be $333,333, with no reference made to a net monetary gain. The theory behind this is that only the

---

[7]Jack C. Robertson, *Business Income Determination Through Use of Current Cost Accounting* (New York: Coopers & Lybrand, 1977), p. 7.

[8]*Interim Recommendation* of the Inflation Accounting Steering Group, U.K. Accounting Standards Committee, November 1977, following rejection of ED 18, the so-called Morpeth response to the Sandilands report (1975).

shareholders' portion of employed capital needs inflation protection (creditors must rely on their interest rates) and that bondholders will later refinance their portion of the higher replacement cost.

Of course, the British are interested in arriving at a surrogate net income figure, based on current costs, that represents an amount available for distribution and growth, after allowance for the added replacement cost applicable to the shareholders' portion of the investment. The FASB's model does not do this; the reader is given various data (some of which are interrelated, as described earlier), and he must reach his own conclusions. Certainly, the items in the current cost model should not be added together, although—unlike the SEC in ASR no. 190—the FASB does not caution against this.

CONSTANT DOLLAR MODEL

This is our old friend, price level accounting or historical cost restated in current dollars—current purchasing power, with some variations.[9] Removed from current income are the controversial "inflation gain on net monetary items," discussed above, and "foreign exchange loss net of tax" (on a historical cost basis), resulting in "constant dollar income from continuing operations." Only realized holding gains (adjusted for inflation) flow through into continuing income; the old price level model included all these items in net income. Here they are pulled apart and separately disclosed for obvious, or perhaps not so obvious, reasons. Unrealized holding gains are ignored; the old model carried them directly to equity.

Another new twist is the index used. Instead of the gross national product implicit price deflator, the consumer price index for all urban consumers is used on the assumption that shareholders can relate to this index: their dividends and share prices are affected in relation to the consumer dollar. But it is also assumed that shareholders must be concerned about preserving the purchasing power of their corporate assets—a negation of the entity theory. No doubt this will stir some controversy. Those who oppose price level accounting conceptually will point out that the CPI—heavily influenced by the market basket of the consumer (food, health care, rent)—has absolutely no relevance to a company in the copper fabricating business, for example. In their view, it was bad enough to use the GNP deflator rather than specific indexes. Even some price level believers will have trouble with CPI. Of course, the availability and reliability of CPI over other indexes is an advantage.

---

[9]A supplement to the exposure draft entitled *Constant Dollar Accounting*, was issued for comment last March. In addition to the differences referred to above, the draft differs principally from the old price level model in the following ways: (1) foreign currency on hand and foreign currency claims and obligations are classified as monetary items, and (2) deferred income tax items are classified as monetary items.

FIVE-YEAR COMPARISON DATA

This summary is by far the most impressive new creation. At first blush, considering the illustrations presented (see figure 4[a], [b]), it appears that the choice between the current cost and constant dollar frameworks must follow the choice made for the supplemental income determinations. Actually, a third choice is available—those choosing current cost may present the five-year summary on a current cost/constant dollar basis (not illustrated in the draft). One's views concerning current cost vs. constant dollar concepts must necessarily carry over into this summary.

Current cost model. In this model the CPI is presented first for each of the five years. The CPI is relevant here because actual cash dividends per share and market prices per share are shown for the five-year period (users must make their own conversions), and we can presume that shareholders (including millions of pensioners) can relate those cash flows, when adjusted, to their needs.

Actual net sales for the five years are given in this model; presumably one should interpret them in the light of the changes shown in the CPI. However, an index tuned to the product being sold would provide a better indicator of volume trends. The other items—notably income from continuing operations—are the adjusted figures from the current cost supplemental income statement. As indicated previously, the CPI index may instead be applied to all the current cost data to produce the current cost/constant dollar format (the unillustrated third choice).

Constant dollar model. This summary requires all items to be presented in either current dollars or dollars of a base period, such as 1967 = 100. The latter choice—proposed officially for the first time—is designed to avoid the confusion of constantly restating prior years' figures. This model facilitates trend analysis because all years presented are on the same selected wavelength. Shareholders will be interested, and perhaps astonished, to see past dividends, earnings per share and market prices restated in current dollars. Managements will understandably be concerned about such disclosures and may opt for the current cost model instead.

BASES FOR CONCLUSIONS

The draft includes a 43-paragraph appendix stating the board's bases for the conclusions reached. Here emphatic support is given to its two-pronged approach, intended to provide flexibility during an experimental period. There is a reassessment and restatement of all the classic arguments for and against each methodology. Several themes come through that are worthy of mention.

Preservation of the investor's purchasing power is the overriding rationale for the need for supplemental information and for the relevance of the CPI whenever an index is used; the shareholder presumably can personally relate to that index when evaluating his investment. The company's cash flows are presumed to be the same as the shareholders'. One cannot deny that dividend and appreciation expectations are dependent on a company's cash flows, but neither

Figure 4: Five-Year Summaries: Choose One of Three *

(a) *Current cost model*

Five-year comparison of selected financial data

	Years ended December 31				
	1974	1975	1976	1977	1978
Consumer price index average for year	XX	XX	XX	XX	XX
Net sales and other operating revenues	$ XX	$ XX	$ XX	$ XX	$ XX
Current cost income from continuing operations	XX	XX	XX	XX	XX
Holding gain (loss) on inventories and plant assets net of inflation and tax	XX	XX	XX	XX	XX
Inflation gain (loss) on net monetary items	XX	XX	XX	XX	XX
Foreign exchange gain (loss) net of tax	XX	XX	XX	XX	XX
Net assets at year-end	XX	XX	XX	XX	XX
Current cost income from continuing operations per common share	XX	XX	XX	XX	XX
Cash dividends declared per common share	XX	XX	XX	XX	XX
Market price per common share at year-end	XX	XX	XX	XX	XX

(b) *Historical cost/constant dollar model*

Five-year comparison of selected financial data in December 31, 1978, dollars

	Years ended December 31				
	1974	1975	1976	1977	1978
Net sales and other operating revenues	$** XX	$** XX	$** XX	$** XX	$** XX
Constant dollar income from continuing operations	XX	XX	XX	XX	XX
Inflation gain (loss) on net monetary items	XX	XX	XX	XX	XX
Foreign exchange gain (loss) net of tax	XX	XX	XX	XX	XX
Net assets at year-end	XX	XX	XX	XX	XX
Constant dollar income from continuing operations per common share	XX	XX	XX	XX	XX
Cash dividends declared per common share	XX	XX	XX	XX	XX
Market price per common share at year-end	XX	XX	XX	XX	XX

$** December 31, 1978, dollars.

(c) *Current cost/constant dollar model* (not illustrated in the draft)

* These illustrations of alternative presentations of supplemental data are from the FASB Exposure Draft, *Financial Reporting and Changing Prices*.

can one deny the irrelevance of the CPI to those flows. Shareholders own an enterprise, but not its assets. On this issue, I suppose, disputants will always agree to disagree.

One also senses a mild preference for the current cost/constant dollar option. This is evidenced by the board's permitting the use of the current cost/constant dollar presentation in the five-year summary even though the current cost method is used in the annual supplemental report, as previously discussed.

The major flaw in this section may be found in paragraphs 59 and 60, entitled "Adherence to the Financial Concept of Capital." Repeating in condensed form the arguments for the financial concept and against the physical capital maintenance concept[10] contained in its conceptual framework discussion memorandum, the changing prices draft concludes in no uncertain terms that the financial concept should prevail. This certainly supports the board's conclusion that the historical cost framework should continue to be used for the basic financial statements. The separate disclosure of holding gains in the current cost model also conforms to this concept. But if the term "current cost income from continuing operations" is to have meaning for the current cost model, the financial capital concept certainly appears incompatible. The board finesses this inconsistency by characterizing current cost as "value to the business" or "current cost of acquiring the same service potential," which on careful analysis boils down to current replacement cost for many of the items—undeniably a physical capital maintenance concept. This will need some sorting out.

AUDITOR'S INVOLVEMENT

The proposal specifies that the required information "is to be presented in supplementary statements, schedules, or notes in financial reports." Interim reporting is not required. The natural question is: Must the data be audited and covered by the auditor's opinion? There is no answer and since the location of the data in the report often has a bearing, the auditing standards board of the American Institute of CPAs will have to grapple with the issue. My guess is that the same approach taken with ASR no. 190 will be followed. Thus, initially the information will be labeled "unaudited" and auditors will "review" the material but not opine thereon. In the long run, once the experimentation period is over and methodologies are shaken down, I believe the material will be required to be audited.*

---

[10]The draft defines the two concepts as

"a. The financial concept of capital: Capital is maintained when the money value of net assets (measured either in nominal dollars or in units of purchasing power) remains constant.

"b. The physical productive capacity concept of capital: Capital is maintained when the net assets remain sufficient to produce a fixed quantity of goods and services."

*Ed. note: See article entitled "Standards for Financial Reporting," by D. R. Carmichael, p. 76.

OVERVIEW

The pressures placed on the FASB to get something out on inflation accounting are understandable. SEC Chairman Harold M. Williams has been harping on the need, and the board wants to show progress. Thus, the current draft shows the effect of hasty action. Nevertheless, it is the culmination of the board's long consideration of the issues, and only because views on the subject are so diverse does the outcome seem flawed and loaded with options. A good consensus in this area is almost impossible because the introduction of elusive economic theory and subjective measurements into an accounting model does not please objective accountants.

The draft will be criticized—justifiably—for being too complicated, understandable by only the most sophisticated accountants and analysts. But so is the subject. Attempts at simplification, such as mine, below, will be criticized for not recognizing all facets of the problem.

As one who has gone up the hill and down again in attempting to devise a framework for accounting that will more closely approximate economic income (whatever that is) and reflect changing prices and values caused by inflation or otherwise, I know that this is a never-ending quest for the impossible dream. Once we leave the solid mooring of objective historical (actual) cost accounting and introduce macroeconomic measurements, such as consumer price indexes and hypothetical replacement cost measurements into the complexities of accounting, we enter a never-never land reminiscent of medieval doctoral dissertations. Financial analysts are expected to make subjective judgments, and differences of opinion among them are commonplace; accountants, accustomed to the tenets of their discipline, will disagree sharply when asked to enter this realm. And the public won't tolerate such disagreements for the same reason—it expects preciseness and objectivity from accountants. Can we safely overcome these hurdles? Perhaps, but only if we walk before we run.

Nevertheless, users today—shareholders and their analysts—need better indications of future cash flows from an investment. If nothing else, the FASB draft will help everyone zero in on that need and the ways of satisfying it. I am sure that something useful will come out of this effort when the FASB carefully analyzes the comments it will stimulate, polishes up the draft and monitors the results of the experimentation.

The board has done a noble deed in sticking to basics—historical cost—for the official reporting model; fears of its being tinkered with are allayed, and so the reaction to the draft will be less heated. But an experiment of such consequences cannot offer so many choices, it cannot be so complicated, nor can its objectives or uses be so elusive.

Let me suggest—as a first step—a simple approach to the determination of what I believe shareholders are looking for: a rough estimation of the portion of reported historical cost earnings that needs to be reserved as some approximation of the current cost of replacing assets in use, before dividends and growth can be accommodated. My suggestion for this reserve is: the excess of current cost depreciation and cost of sales over related historical cost applicable to the shareholders' portion of the capital invested in related assets (vs. creditors' portion), a la the Hyde guidelines previously discussed. This offers what appears to be a simple solution to a complex problem; this approach is illustrated in figure 1. In my view it will provide more relevant and understandable data for the user. But it's not as simple as it looks; refining its elements could provide the basis for considerable future experimentation and research to search out the answers to the inflation question. Obviously, a lot more thought will have to be applied before the inflation puzzle can be solved. Is it within our grasp? The FASB exposure draft seems to suggest that it is if we recognize how far we have to go.

CONSTANT DOLLAR ACCOUNTING: WHICH APPROACH TELLS THE STORY?†

Comments by Stephen A. Zeff and replies by W. E. Hoglund and Philip L. Defliese

Zeff's comments. In his article ["Inflation Accounting: Pursuing the Elusive," *The Journal of Accountancy*, May 1979] on the recent Financial Accounting Standards Board Exposure Draft, *Financial Reporting and Changing Prices*, Philip L. Defliese referred in several places to the special section on "constant dollar" accounting in the 1978 annual report of General Motors Corporation. In fact, the GM disclosure is not an example of the FASB's proposed kind of accounting, notwithstanding the use of the FASB's term "constant dollar accounting" in its annual report.

Defliese was not alone in mistaking the GM analysis for the FASB approach to general price-level accounting. Joseph E. Connor, chairman of Price Waterhouse & Co., in a widely publicized speech, "Recognizing the Cost of Inflation," says that he supports constant dollar accounting and offers the GM "constant dollar" figures as an illustration. But the method which he supports is not the one which GM is espousing.

What method is GM using? It takes the reported net income for a year and multiplies it by the ratio of two price indexes. The numerator of the ratio is the price index of a base year (1973 in the GM report), and the denominator is the price index of the year for which the net income was reported. The restated result is, according to GM, "net income in constant dollars."

There are two problems with the GM approach. First, it assumes that the reported net income for the current year is already expressed in the current year's dollars. This assumption, while valid for sales revenue, is inapplicable to a significant portion of the expenses. In 1978, GM's "depreciation of real estate, plants and equipment" was an amount equal to 34 percent of its net income. The great bulk of the expenditure giving rise to this expense is many years old. Thus, a correct restatement of GM's current-year net income must take account of the age of its depreciable assets. Instead of being $2,390.8 million as shown in its annual report, the 1973 equivalent of GM's 1978 net income is doubtless well under $2 billion. GM defends its shortcut method as "simple," "direct" and easier for stockholders to understand, but I cannot believe that effective communication is served by a gross disparity. Further, I can find no authoritative support in the tentative or final pronouncements of professional accounting

---

†Reprinted with permission from *The Journal of Accountancy* October 1979, pp. 96-97, Opinions of the authors are their own and do not necessarily reflect policies of the AICPA.

bodies in any country, nor in the textbook or periodical literature, for the GM treatment.

Second, the GM disclosure employs a term which the FASB appropriated in December 1978 to signify a quite different measurement from GM's. The use of one term to convey meanings which differ significantly will cause confusion, and I can well understand why two such prominent members of the profession, Defliese and Connor, were led astray.

Hoglund's reply. Zeff's problems with our approach to reporting the impact of inflation on accounting appear to be due entirely to his apparent failure to understand the basic goal, i.e., communication with nonaccountants.

We do not believe the accountant's approach to dealing with the impact of inflation, as spelled out by Zeff, is appropriate simply because it is based on the assumption that the accounting system must be adjusted to deal with the problem of inflation. We do not perceive the problem of inflation to be an accounting problem; thus, we do not believe that any comprehensive restatement of the net income determined under present generally accepted accounting principles is appropriate.

Instead, we believe that the impact of inflation on accounting should be viewed as the impact on the future purchasing power of the net income since, in the final analysis, the net income of a company can be used in only two ways—either distributed as dividends or reinvested (i.e., used for purchases) in the business. In either event, it is the purchasing power of that net income that is significant.

One could quibble about the index used to reflect this purchasing effect, although virtually everyone would agree that the consumer price index should be used as a deflator for dividends. We recognize that we could have applied a different index to the net income retained for reinvestment (such as the wholesale price index or specific indexes applicable to machinery and equipment) but, for understandability, we chose to use the CPI alone.

Another way to view our adjustment is to view the entire net income as being available for distribution as dividends and the restatement as being the purchasing power of the amount.

It appears to us that observers such as Defliese and Connor comprehended this message, and certainly the use of the data by *Business Week*, *Fortune* and *Iron Age* reflected the appropriate use of the data, which, after all, is what accountants should be striving for.

Defliese's reply. Zeff is correct in pointing out that the GM constant dollar method is not the same as the FASB's. He is incorrect in assuming that I was led astray; I was well aware of the difference. Using the same poetic license I took in the article, I made reference to the GM constant dollar presentation (by footnote, as an afterthought) to avoid any inference that GM was unaware of the effect of inflation on its earnings. I didn't have room in my article to expound on a fourth approach to inflation accounting. (Despite the technical flaws which we academic purists must criticize, the GM approach has simplicity and lay understandability going for it.) Judging from the input at the recent FASB hearings on the exposure draft, we can expect more proliferation of methodologies of constant dollar and current costs (and more loose terminology) until the FASB (or the Securities and Exchange Commission) canonizes a preferred method. Let us hope the board sticks to the notion that a period of experimentation is needed for a while. Nevertheless, I must plead guilty to leading some readers astray.

ACCOUNTING FOR INCOME TAXES

NEW STUDY EXAMINES PROBLEMS OF ALLOCATING INCOME TAXES BETWEEN PERIODS†

by
Philip L. Defliese

A recent study published by the AICPA is aimed at clarifying the problem of the tax effect of a transaction which is reported in a different period for tax purposes than for accounting purposes. The study, *Interperiod Allocation of Corporate Income Taxes* (Accounting Research Study No. 9),[1] by Dr. Homer Black,[2] reaches several conclusions which are new, and which, if adopted, will have a significant effect on present accounting practices in this area. These are:

1. That "interperiod tax allocation procedures should be applied comprehensively, that is, to all material timing differences between pretax accounting income and taxable income, including those of a recurring nature over relatively long periods of time." Considerable emphasis is given implicitly to the concept that tax expense relates to specific transactions and that the accounting for the individual transactions and the related taxes should fall within the same period. This across-the-board, item-for-item approach is not yet accepted by all accountants.

2. That, depending on the nature of the item, either the "liability concept" or the "deferred (credit) concept" may be applicable, but that the liability concept should be applied to deferred taxes arising from the use of accelerated depreciation for tax purposes. This will please many tax specialists (who seem to have a preference for that concept), but will be opposed by many accountants who espouse the deferred theory. For example, the "deferred" theorists suggest the *deferment* of the amount of tax actually saved (in the earlier year at the then prevailing rate) resulting from the excess of accelerated depreciation over book

---

†Reprinted from *The Journal of Taxation*, November 1966, pp. 261-264. Copyright © 1966 Tax Research Group Ltd. Reprinted with permission of RIA Group from *The Journal of Taxation*, Vol. 25, No. 5, November 1966.

[1]Such research studies do not constitute statement of policy of the Institute. They are issued to provide informative discussion and exposure of accounting matters for consideration and experimentation prior to official pronouncement by the Institute. The subject has a high priority on the agenda of the Accounting Principles Board, so it can be expected that an official Opinion on it will be published in the not too distant future. This Opinion may or may not agree with the views of the author. Copies of the study are available from the AICPA for $1.50 each.

[2]Dr. Black, who is both a CPA and a Ph.D., is on the faculty of Florida State University. was assisted by Dr. Reed K. Storey, Director of the AICPA Accounting Research Division and his staff.

depreciation, whereas the "liability" theorists propose to "accrue" (in the earlier year) the *postponed* tax calculated at the rate which will be paid (in a later year) when the situation reverses. The only time when this distinction becomes crucial is when tax rates change.

3. That the utilization of carryforward operating losses should not be allowed to benefit the income of the later profit year which permitted its utilization, but rather, should be considered an adjustment of the results of the years which generated the losses. However, such carryforward tax benefits can be given immediate recognition in a loss year in those few cases where there is reasonable expectation that they will be utilized before expiration. Most accountants have always been disturbed by the present practice of distorting operating results (in both the loss year and profit year) by recording loss carryforward tax benefits only in the later profit year.

4. That tax deferments covering long periods of time (usually relating to depreciation) should be *discounted* to present value at an appropriate rate representing either the company's earning power or external borrowing cost. This is a relatively new concept which many accountants will find difficult to accept for several reasons, but mostly because of the many highly theoretical assumptions underlying its use.

The study provides a comprehensive analysis of the concepts and techniques currently employed to afford accounting recognition (in the proper period) of the tax effect of transactions which are reported for tax purposes in periods other than the period in which the transactions are recognized for financial statement purposes. Dr. Black indicates that in the United States most accountants concede that interperiod allocation often is required to state properly periodic net income, but that disagreement exists as to whether interperiod tax allocation applies to all of the major causes of tax "deferment," and the extent to which it applies to tax "prepayments." After an examination of the arguments raised in these latter controversies, he concludes that tax allocation procedures should be applied to all material timing differences and that the "matching of expense and revenues requires a recognition of income tax allocation *assets* as well as deferred liabilities." Criteria for recognizing tax effect assets are included in the study.

PROCEDURE FOR INTERPERIOD ALLOCATION

The study explores in some detail the results of applying each of the three existing methods of accounting for tax timing differences. The methods, which take their names from the underlying concepts, are the "liability" method, the "deferred" method, and the "net of tax" method. The analysis leads the reader to conclude that the use of "net of tax" method is not acceptable and that both the other methods fail to some extent to provide the proper answer to income tax allocation, although, as a practical matter, the results from application of the liability and deferred methods differ only when a change in the tax rate occurs. Accordingly, the author advances his concepts for the application of accrual and deferral accounting to each of the four types of timing differences, as indicated in the accompanying box.

FINANCIAL STATEMENTS

If the recommendations are adopted, income tax expense should ordinarily be shown as a single amount in the income statement. However, because of current emphasis on the estimated tax payable for the period, the study suggests that it would be advisable to disclose this amount either parenthetically in the income statement caption or in a note stating the components of income tax expenses for a period.

The recommended manner of reflecting income taxes in the balance sheet of a profitable corporation is likely to result in three separate items, namely, a current liability, a noncurrent liability, and a noncurrent asset. The first caption would include the unpaid portion of current taxes payable and the portion of the deferred income taxes payable in the next year (or operating cycle), reflecting the estimated tax payments, or arising from any item classified as a current asset.

Thus, the roll-over resulting from continuing replacements with new items cannot serve to classify all deferred taxes as noncurrent. The second item would include the balance of the deferred income taxes. The third classification would include the prepaid income taxes which will be amortized after one year or operating cycle. The study recommends "that the current portion of the deferred tax asset be combined with other prepaid expenses unless the amount is exceptionally large."

IMPLEMENTATION OF RECOMMENDATIONS

The impact of the changes required by the adoption of these recommendations might be material in some instances. The principal effect would be to require additional accrual for tax timing differences not presently recognized, and adjustment of provisions for future taxes which were computed at rates other than the rate expected to prevail at payment. These adjustments would flow through the financial statements as corrections of income of prior periods. However, when timing differences have existed for long periods, the roll-over of items will have leveled off or minimized the effect on annual income; the major effect would be on the balance sheet. Of course, reclassification in income statements and balance sheets will also be required to conform completely with the statement presentation concepts advanced by the study.

OPERATING LOSSES

Present practice in accounting for the tax benefits of operating losses has in roots in Chapter 10B of *Accounting Research Bulletin No. 43*, which in general, provides that taxes which are refundable from carrybacks should be included in the income statement of the year in which the loss occurs, and that tax reductions arising from operating loss carryforwards should be reflected is the year to which such losses are carried unless misleading inferences would drawn from such inclusion, in which case the tax reduction should credited to retained earnings. The latter, however, is rarely followed.

To overcome the criticisms of the existing practice of accounting for carryforward losses, the study suggests two alternatives. They are: "(1) to recognize a possible tax benefit of the carryforward as an asset in the loss year, or (2) to recognize the tax reduction in the carryforward year as a correction of the previous loss." The former carries with it the question of determining if the carryforward will be utilized in future years. Accordingly, "a practical solution is a judicious combination of the two alternatives." After examining the characteristics of a situation which would permit recognition, in the year the loss occurs, of the tax benefit arising from a carryforward, the study concludes that the reasonable expectation of future earnings in the year of loss is infrequent and that in most cases the tax benefits arising from carryforward losses should be deferred to the year of utilization. As opposed to present practice, the benefit from a carryforward should be treated as a *correction of the results of the loss year* and should not increase the income of the year in which the carryforward is applied.

CARRYFORWARDS AND TAX TIMING

Based upon the foregoing, there could be situations when it would be inappropriate to recognize the benefit arising from carryforwards in the year in which the loss occurs since there may not be reasonable expectation of future profits within the carryforward period. The reasonable certainty of taxable income in future periods, however, is the keystone of the case for interperiod allocation of income taxes. It can be seen that the accounting for interperiod allocations and operating losses under certain circumstances may he based on inconsistent assumptions and some adjustment is required to interperiod allocation in these instances.

In those cases where it is inappropriate to recognize the loss carryforward currently, it would likewise seem inappropriate to recognize the future taxes which arise from timing differences in that year. The "deferred" concept theorists concur because they would state that no tax benefit has been obtained which needs deferment. When the carryforward is ultimately realized and results for the year of loss is corrected, such *correction should include recognition of the effect of tax timing differences in the loss year.*

With respect to the liability for future taxes accrued because of timing differences in prior years, if, as a result of the loss, it appears unlikely that such payment will be required, the tax liability for future payments should be treated as a *correction of the income in the earlier period in which the tax liability was accrued*, not as a take-down in the loss year of amounts previously accrued (deferred).

DISCOUNTING FUTURE LIABILITIES

The study recognized that the true advantages from electing to postpone tax payments (e.g., accelerated depreciation) stems from the fact that a dollar now is worth more than a dollar sometime in the future. Accordingly, appropriate accounting for the effects of tax postponement must come to grips with the question of discounting, at least with respect to long-term liabilities. The study describes the three principal arguments against discounting as: (1) the general argument that accountants are not and should not be concerned with present values, (2) the practical argument that discounting is an undesirable and unnecessary complication in accounting for income tax liabilities, and (3) the theoretical argument that discounting is appropriate but the discount rate in the transaction is zero.

The discussion that ensues in the study emphasizes the weaknesses in the logic of the arguments against discounting; pension costing on a present value basis is used as a prime example of accounting recognition of the discounting principle. (Note, however, that this is because outside funding usually takes place.) The author concludes that discounting of long-term tax liabilities is required whenever the interest factor is significant, and further, that an appropriate rate for discounting can be selected once the decision to discount has been made.

It seems, upon reflection, that the question of discounting has been lightly dealt with in the study. Undoubtedly, those accountants who feel discounting is not appropriate in the situation will secure some comfort from the fact that the author, while attacking the arguments against discounting, does not present his argument for discounting in such detail as exists elsewhere in the study. The question of how to deal with the accumulating "interest" charge in the financial statements is not discussed. Some insight into the failure to be more specific is implicit in the statement that "the best way to develop the experience necessary to find the circumstances in which discounting is and is not significant is for a large number of companies in varying situations to use the discounting procedure."

In all likelihood, discounting of deferred taxes will be opposed by those accountants who consider tax allocation as a deferred credit and not a liability (hence, not subject to discounting), and will be accepted by those who prefer the liability concept of the immediate flow-through of all the benefits (on the theory that half flow-through is better than none).

SCOPE OF THE STUDY

The study addresses itself to the basic principles and procedures for interperiod income tax allocations. The principles outlined are recommended for application by all corporations including those in specialized industries to the extent such principles apply. The study did not consider the problem of accounting for incomes taxes by companies regulated for rate-making the allocation of consolidated income taxes among members of an affiliated group, or the special tax allocation problems arising from provisions in the Code relative to exploration and development costs and intangible drilling costs of extractive industries. These matters have been assigned to others for study by the Institute. Also, the author did not give special consideration to the problem of accounting for the investment credit since this matter has been the subject of two opinions issued by the Accounting Principles Board.

There seems to be general agreement on procedures for intraperiod tax allocation, i.e., as between income and surplus, and the study did not further consider this concept.

It is important in forming a judgment on the value of the study to keep in mind that the author begins with the premise that interperiod tax allocation is an accepted practice and he does not discuss either the basic nature of income tax or the validity of the concept of interperiod tax allocations.

If the accounting profession and the business community concur with the author's views (or a major portion of them) the study will serve to provide a basis for a further reduction of alternatives among generally accepted accounting principles. However, tax men will then be faced with the need to furnish clients with more comprehensive analyses of the annual flow-through of tax timing differentials on almost an item-for-item basis.

APPLICATION OF INTERPERIOD ALLOCATION

Type of timing difference	*Recommended accounting*
1. Revenues or gains taxed after accrued. Examples: Use of installment sales method for taxes but not for accounting purposes; use of completed contract basis for taxes and percentage of completion for accounting.	Interperiod income tax allocation in this situation is the accrual of an expense and a *liability*. Revenue is recognized currently and when reported later for tax purposes the related tax will be paid. The current expense and estimated liability are *accrued at the tax rate expected to apply when the revenue is taxable.*
2. Expenses or losses deducted after accrued. Examples: Provisions for costs of guarantees and product warranties, deferred compensation, etc., which are not deductible for taxes until paid.	In this circumstance, a tax prepayment results when an expense is accrued, but cannot be reported as a deduction to reduce current tax payments. The amount of the prepaid tax depends on the *tax paid in the period in which the timing difference originates.* Ordinarily, the prepayment is amortized in the later period when the expense accrual is deductible for tax purposes. Unless the expense is expected to reduce tax payments when it becomes deductible, however, the tax must be charged as an expense of the period when paid.
3. Revenues or gains taxed before accrued. Examples: Rents and royalties collected in advance; proceeds of carved-out oil payments.	This situation is a classic example of a prepaid expense. Cash is received and a tax on it is paid; the revenue or gain is recognized in the future, not currently. Amortization of the prepaid tax is an expense of the period when the revenue or gain is recognized.
4. Expenses or losses deducted before accrued. Examples: Use of accelerated depreciation for taxes and straight-line for accounting; expensing R & D costs as incurred and amortization them for accounting.	Interperiod income tax allocation in this situation is the accrual of a tax expense and a *liability*. The presence of the tax deduction in the period in which the timing difference originates reduces current tax payments. A tax expense is accrued (at a rate expected to prevail when the tax is paid) because in a later period when the expense is recognized for accounting purposes no deduction will be available and the tax paid will be increased.

In the author's view, the methods recommended to be applied in situations 1 and 4 represent the "liability" concept while the methods recommended for situations 2 and 3 are an application of the "deferred" concept.

DEFERRED TAXES—FOREVER†

by

Philip L. Defliese

THERE is only one point in the Rosenfield-Dent article on which everyone can agree: the controversy over interperiod income tax allocation can be settled only by vote.

That vote was taken in 1967 (when a two-thirds vote was needed) by the Accounting Principles Board, composed of 20 prestigious and practical-minded accountants who were keenly interested in giving investors a meaningful measure of the annual earning power of U.S. companies. That objective, as well as the attendant espousal of accrual accounting and matching of costs and revenues in the determination of periodic income, has since been reaffirmed by the Financial Accounting Standards Board in FASB Concepts Statement no. 1, *Objectives of Financial Reporting by Business Enterprises*.[1]

BACKGROUND OF OPINION NO. 11

The article's implication that APB Opinion no. 11, *Accounting for Income Taxes*,[2] was issued without adequate study is a biased viewpoint at best. A careful reading of the opinion and a knowledge of subsequent events reveal that all the pros and cons were then well considered and that no new ideas or opinions on the subject have surfaced since. Considering that corporate management generally dislikes anything that diminishes reported income, either temporarily or permanently, I believe that it was a courageous act by a board largely comprising practitioners. After considerable debate, the APB ultimately espoused the deferred method of income tax allocation. Rosenfield and Dent refer to it as a theory. I believe it is a practical solution. The board carefully weighed the "various concepts of accounting for income taxes" before requiring

---

†In this article Philip L. Defliese presents his rebuttal to the article, "No More Deferred Taxes," by Paul Rosenfield and William C. Dent that appeared in *The Journal of Accountancy*, February 1983, pp. 44-55. A reply by Rosenfield and Dent followed the comments by Defliese; however, their reply is not reprinted here. Reprinted with permission from *The Journal of Accountancy*, August 1983, pp. 94-96, 98, copyright © 1983 by American Institute of CPAs. Opinions of the authors are their own and do not necessarily reflect policies of the AICPA.

[1]Financial Accounting Standards Board Concepts Statement no. 1, *Objectives of Financial Reporting by Business Enterprises* (Stamford: FASB, 1978).

[2]Accounting Principles Board Opinion no. 11, *Accounting for Income Taxes* (New York: AICPA, 1967).

"comprehensive interperiod allocation."[3] The APB concluded that the deferred method was the "most useful and practical approach"[4] to implement the concept. Board members agreed conceptually with the liability and net-of-tax methods but opted for the deferred method to avoid the problems of changing income tax rates and of awkward presentations.

Accountants get bogged down on the issue of which tax rate to apply—especially with fluctuating effective income tax rates (largely the influence of many permanent differences rather than timing differences). The practical approach devised by the APB in selecting the deferred method was to compute each year's income tax provision by the use of that year's effective rate—on an accrual basis. The required use in the balance sheet of deferred debits and credits—which are mixtures of asset and liability effects—was a practical solution to a presentation problem. The opinion, I believe, carefully explained why they "as such do not represent receivables or payables in the usual sense."[5] Balance sheet purity was a lesser concern.

THE RECONSIDERATION OF DEFERRED TAXES

Since then, the corporate world has lived with, understood and mostly embraced deferred taxes. The U.S. income tax code, whose increased complexity has been brought about by the proliferation of incentives creating timing differences, has now made deferred taxes an essential ingredient of periodic income determination. Nevertheless, the issue has once again been raised—this time by the FASB.

The deferred credit figure, an item much misunderstood by the unsophisticated, has accumulated to substantial amounts in many growing companies as the divergencies between tax and accounting income have increased. Those amounts are a cause for alarm by those who never fully accepted the 1967 decision and by balance sheet purists with narrow views of its elements. The FASB's new conceptual framework project has offered an opportunity for this reexamination, and the FASB has decided to press forward with this reexamination despite the fact that the crucial and controversial segments of recognition and measurement are yet to be agreed on and issued.

THE ROSENFIELD-DENT POSITION

The Rosenfield-Dent approach to taxes is essentially a cash-basis one with additional disclosures presumably sufficient to allow users to calculate periodic income. The APB overcame the dichotomy between cash- and accrual-basis accounting by requiring a statement of changes in financial position as an integral

---

[3]*Ibid.*, par. 34.

[4]*Ibid.*, par. 35.

[5]*Ibid.*, par. 35.

part of the reporting process to enable users to compare accrual income with cash or working capital flow. Analysts have little difficulty understanding deferred taxes in this environment. To revert to cash-basis accounting would be a retrogression and a complete abdication of financial reporting objectives by the profession. FASB Concepts Statement no. 1 states: "Information about enterprise [periodic] earnings and its components measured by accrual accounting generally provides a better indication of . . . performance than information about current cash receipts and payments."[6] Over the years, economists and accountants have disagreed among themselves, and with each other, on the meaning of periodic income. Nevertheless, accountants shouldn't give up the attempt to make what they consider their best determinations. Truth, in accounting, requires more than solely devotion to truthful principles.

Some devotees of the efficient market hypothesis take the extreme position that, as long as all relevant facts are fully disclosed, the accounting principles used aren't important. The "market," they believe, will reach the correct conclusions and stock prices will adjust accordingly. Rosenfield and Dent would have us provide explanations in the notes of the tax effects not recognized in determining periodic income and let the efficient market sort it out. However, the efficiency of the market in absorbing disclosures depends on the emphasis given them in press releases and how the information is interpreted by the media. The abbreviated earnings reports published in most newspapers will be inadequate for that purpose, and it may take weeks (as it sometimes does now) for sophisticated analysts to reach conclusions and affect the market.

ANOTHER VIEW OF THE ROSENFIELD-DENT POSITION

Rosenfield and Dent base their conclusions on their interpretation of selected quotes from FASB Concepts Statement no. 3, *Elements of Financial Statements of Business Enterprises*, particularly the definition of *liabilities* as "probable future sacrifices of economic benefits arising from present obligations of a particular entity to transfer assets or provide services to other entities in the future as a result of past transactions or events."[7] They overlook the definition of *assets*, whose "future economic benefits"[8] may be impaired by a lack of tax deductibility and ignore the net aspect of the "future sacrifices" of liabilities that have a future tax recovery aspect—all based on past transactions. To paraphrase their thrust, they say that, because there is no liability for future taxes until taxable revenue is generated in the future, no tax accrual is needed.

The incongruity of that position can be illustrated by a simple transaction in which a $100 million gain is reported in year one without a tax provision,

---

[6]FASB Concepts Statement no. 1, par. 44.

[7]FASB Concepts Statement no. 3, *Elements of Financial Statements of Business Enterprises* (Stamford: FASB, 1980), par. 28.

[8] *Ibid.*, par. 19.

because the tax is paid in year two when the receivable is collected. Of course, Rosenfield and Dent would recommend disclosure of the income tax aspects of the transaction in the notes, but what about the floor traders who see only what the broad tape chooses to print?

To say that a tax obligation can arise only when taxable revenue is earned in the future is to ignore the going-concern assumption on which all financial reporting rests, a concept also reaffirmed by the FASB. Only two assumptions are available

1. A company will be profitable in the future, particularly if it already is. (If it is profitable one year and has a loss in the succeeding year, the tax carry-back recovery will be reduced by the timing difference.)

2. A company currently isn't profitable and won't be profitable in the future—in which case we must question it as a going concern. (Since no tax benefit has been derived, no deferred taxes are recognized.)

Consequently, probable future benefits or sacrifices (obligations)—tax effects—based on past events must be recognized. Whether those benefits and sacrifices are presented as liabilities or as reductions of assets (net of tax) isn't pertinent to the conceptual issue. In the previous illustration, it isn't relevant whether the deferred tax is shown as a liability or as a reduction of the realizable value of the receivable. Does anyone really believe that, in a profitable environment, the tax won't be paid?

Ordinarily, the debate over deferred taxes gravitates to the "rollover" issue—whether tax benefits of anticipated future investments should be considered. Adherents of that view say that deferred taxes will never be paid because, over the long term, new items—asset purchases—arise that replace the reversal of the old, leading to perpetual deferment. According to Rosenfield and Dent, however, rollover isn't an issue. They would never recognize deferred taxes, even if the reversal was within one year. (The rollover issue isn't debated here.)

DEFERRED TAXES AND THE CONCEPTUAL FRAMEWORK

If another vote is to be taken on deferred taxes, I hope that it will be delayed until all the pieces of the new conceptual framework are in place and well accepted. I also hope that another vote would be based on logic and reasoning, although in accounting, unfortunately, they are always in the eyes of the beholder.

No amount of study—empirical or conceptual—can definitely prove whether deferred taxes are necessary. The issue rests entirely on differing opinions regarding concepts of periodic income and how the objectives of financial reporting can be achieved. I believe that the concepts statements produced so far are so general that any viewpoint can be considered compatible. Although the framework is still incomplete, the FASB has created a "comprehensive income"[9] concept as a catchall for all changes in equity and has deferred the definition of *earnings*. It has implied, but avoided direct consideration of the issue, that the asset-liability approach to income determination (comprehensive or otherwise) should prevail over the revenue-expense approach. That approach emphasizes that the beholder is viewing the balance sheet's year-end position at the "split-second of midnight." Our bookkeeping origins tell us that a "balance sheet" is a list of account balances after the year's profit or loss is determined. Are we moving in a completely new direction?

Rosenfield and Dent point out that deferred taxes began with the idea that accounting periods should each be allocated an amount of income tax expense that bears a "normal relationship to the income shown in the income statement."[10] Subsequent refinements of that idea limited deferred taxes to timing differences that were expected to reverse. Accrual accounting, matching and allocation were the underlying principles relied on, and so far the FASB hasn't abandoned them. The reference to deferred taxes as an interest-free loan from the government has become prevalent, and all knowledgeable users now understand it. Whether, because of rollover, the resultant deferred debits and credits will continue to increase depends on circumstances. Recently, with the shrinking of some capital-intensive enterprises, we have seen some reductions—proof that the concept works.

Opponents of deferred taxes, particularly academics, are sometimes influenced by their own philosophies. For example, those who believe that current value accounting should replace historical cost accounting often oppose deferred taxes for somewhat the same reasons as do Rosenfield and Dent. However, some would acknowledge that value determinations should recognize the degree to which an asset has or hasn't tax deductibility. After a struggle with the current value issue, the FASB finally recognized that for now historical cost accounting must continue as the basis for our primary financial statements.

TAXES WITHIN THE HISTORICAL COST FRAMEWORK

Because of this, emphasis must be given to historical cost, uninfluenced by any extraneous issues. Conceptually, the carrying amount of an asset in a historical cost framework should be what was paid for it less what has been depreciated (allocated to income determination) and less any excess tax benefit recovered. When, as with accelerated depreciation, the government has advanced money (through reduced taxes), it becomes a temporary reduction of invested cost (that is, net of tax). Even the government has recently renamed depreciation accelerated cost recovery, and public utility regulators, after much confusion and congressional prodding, now almost uniformly deduct deferred taxes from plant

---

[9] *Ibid.*, par. 14.

[10] Accounting Research Bulletin no. 23, *Accounting for Income Taxes* (New York: AIA, 1944), p. 185.

assets in the rate-making process. When an installment receivable will in all likelihood be taxed on collection, the tax represents a reduction of the amount receivable by the enterprise (net realizable value)—or a liability to be paid on collection. It doesn't matter how it is presented on the balance sheet, except to balance sheet purists, as long as the concepts that make up the historical cost framework are recognized.

The recognition and measurement concepts of assets and liabilities—even in a historical cost framework—have yet to be settled by the FASB. In doing so, it will no doubt be influenced by the definitions promulgated in FASB Concepts Statement no. 3. There the board states that an asset "embodies a probable future benefit . . . to contribute . . . to future net cash inflows."[11] Hence, recognition would have to be given to the extent to which cost has been recovered in advance by accelerated tax depreciation, a sure impairment of the future benefit an asset could contribute.[12]

Although it has proclaimed its neutrality on the interperiod tax allocation issue, the FASB has ruled the deferred method as incompatible with its "elements"—no doubt at the prodding of some people long opposed to deferred items in the balance sheet. It did, however, acknowledge the relevance of the liability and net-of-tax methods and indicated a "possible compatible rationale for the results of the [deferred] method."[13] I hope that, after concluding consideration of the recognition and measurement concepts, the FASB may find that interperiod tax allocation is conceptually sound and that the deferred presentation is the most practical approach to implement the concept.

CONCLUSION

Much is to be said on behalf of sound interperiod allocation of costs and revenues, even though some may claim the effect is to smooth periodic income. Interperiod tax allocation isn't a smoothing device. It is an attempt to produce a conceptually sound approach to periodic income. Investors need to have a good understanding of a company's annual earning power. Years ago, George 0. May is said to have stated, "The determination of periodic income would be indefensible if it were not indispensable." Let us not throw out the baby with the wash water.

---

[11]FASB Concepts Statement no. 3, par. 20(a).

[12] The net-of-tax aspect of asset valuation has been accepted practice since the promulgation of APB Opinion no. 16, *Business Combinations* (New York: AICPA, 1970); see par. 89.

[13]FASB Concepts Statement no. 3, par. 165.

DEFERRED TAXES—MORE FATAL FLAWS†

by
Philip L. Defliese

IT isn't often that Paul Rosenfield and I can agree on any aspect of the subject of Deferred Taxes, but I must heartily agree with his Commentary in the September 1990 issue of *Accounting Horizons* to the effect that FASB 96 is fatally flawed by opting for the liability method for deferred taxes. I have always maintained, as he does, that deferred taxes do not constitute liabilities—present or future. For that reason he usually plumps for total nonrecognition, whereas I have always been in the corner of comprehensive tax allocation—based on the net-of-tax theory. Nevertheless, in his willingness to accept the deferred method of tax allocation espoused by APB 11 I detect a mellowing, and perhaps some recognition of the logic that has motivated comprehensive tax allocation supporters over the years.

Modern accounting got along reasonably well without a "conceptual framework" for almost a century, as cash basis evolved into accrual accounting. The FASB Concept Statements are really afterthoughts, or perhaps a summation (authoritatively expressed) of what has evolved. In the process of that articulation, the determination of periodic income was somewhat subjugated to a balance sheet determination concept that was never seriously applied. The old Accounting Research Committee (predecessor of the APB) said it well: "With the increasing importance of the income statement there has been a tendency to regard the balance sheet as a connecting link between successive income statements..." (ARB 43, Introduction, Par. 3 *not superseded*). In that era a balance sheet was what its name implied—a sheet of balances remaining after net profit was determined.

Does the equity section of a balance sheet ever truly portray financial or economic position? Although the terms "surplus" and "net worth" have been discarded as meaningless or misleading, the present equity section now contains a new set of dangling debits and credits. Disregarding for the moment the issue of current value, and considering the many off-balance-sheet issues that constantly arise, and the current concern over financial instruments, we must conclude that it is an oversimplification to consider that comprehensive income is the difference between two equity balance sheet amounts (exclusive, of course, of equity transactions). This is not to say that a balance sheet does not have its uses, but it certainly should not be used as a determinant of income. The FASB's

†Reprinted from *Accounting Horizons*, March 1991, pp. 89-91, with permission of the American Accounting Association.

infatuation with the balance sheet as such a determinant is overdone. Matching of costs and revenues to determine income was always the overwhelming thrust of the APB, and although the FASB Concept Statements give that notion some recognition, it is mostly by sufferance.

When accelerated tax depreciation came along in the '50s, most accountants felt the need to defer the tax benefit to the period when the related accounting charge would take place. Matching was logical and fair. Except for a brief flurry of roll-over, early pronouncements on tax allocation were largely predicated on the matching concept—without too much concern over the balance sheet placement. In some instances it was permissible to deduct the deferred credit from the related asset as additional depreciation, and the net-of-tax concept was born. There can be no question that when accelerated tax depreciation is taken, the cost basis of the asset is impaired, or used up, and that this should somehow be reflected in an appropriate place on the balance sheet. A cost recovery (in advance) has taken place and the remaining balance is a fairer reflection of the unrecovered investment the entity has in the asset. Many utility regulatory commissions still make this subtraction today in arriving at the rate base for setting a rate of return.

In accounting parlance there is a fine line of distinction between a "valuation" account and an "allocation" account. Depreciation, which started out as a valuation account, is now universally considered as an allocation account. An installment receivable that generates taxable income when collected requires tax allocation, except to the most virulent anti-tax allocators. Net-of-tax advocates sometimes split on the issue of whether the tax should be deducted from the asset (as valuation or allocation) or shown as a liability. Consistent application of the net-of-tax method would call for the former. The same applies to the anticipated tax recovery of accrued liabilities that will become future tax deductions.

Net-of-tax and liability advocates usually don't disagree on the need for tax allocation; the practical difference lies in the rate to be applied—current or future—and on the need to adjust the residual when rates change. Net-of-tax people believe that a tax benefit already obtained doesn't change, and object to rate revision adjustments—this justifies and simplifies the procedure. In their view, future rate changes are future events that should be reflected in future statements.

The APB was hopelessly split on which rationale to apply to tax allocation. Some members were concerned that use of the net-of-tax concept would require across the board application in the income statement and thus clutter the portrayal of operating results. As a result, the compromise went to the deferred method—there was then no conceptual framework straightjacket and deferred charges and credits were not only acceptable balance sheet elements, but commonplace as accrual accounting became more refined.

Upon closer examination it seems that the net-of-tax approach is easier to fit into the current conceptual framework. For example, assets are defined in the Elements statement as "probable future economic benefits obtained or controlled...as a result of past transactions or events" (Con 6, Par 25) and the "elements defined are...resources...and the *changes therein* from transactions and other...circumstances *involved in its use of resources...to earn a profit.*" (Con 6 Par 10, emphasis supplied) An asset that has used up its tax deductibility in advance should exhibit that fact.

Net-of-tax theory does not, of course, solve the thorny issue of realizability of deferred tax assets, however shown. Practice under APB 11 on this issue was reasonably good, except for some unusual cases. We should depend on good audit judgment in this area and not concern ourselves with cookbook guidelines. Considering the usual availability of deferred credits as offsets (often completely so), we seem to be making a tempest in a teapot on this point.

One further thought. Financial analysts make much of the "debt/equity" ratio—a ratio that presumably is useful to evaluate the posture of an entity when it comes upon hard times. (Considering the fuzziness of "debt" and "equity" these days this may be misguided.) When a company finds itself in dire straits it is usually in a loss position and in that event deferred tax "liabilities" will certainly not be "paid." If the debt/equity ratio is to be useful for any purpose, it would seem that deferred taxes should be excluded, and I suspect that many analysts do just that. The net-of-tax position solves the problem!

It is unfortunate that we have placed accounting on the Procrustean bed of a conceptual framework that, like many economic theories, is a matter of opinion. Before we add to the mish-mash our accounting standards are now in, let's stop compounding the fatal flaws.

THE ROLE OF THE ACCOUNTING PROFESSION

THE INFLUENCE OF SEC ON ACCOUNTING PRINCIPLES AND PROCEDURES AND THE PRACTICE OF AUDITING[†]

by
Philip L. Defliese

THE question is frequently asked, particularly by students of accounting, "What effect has the SEC had upon the accounting professions?" This question has two different meanings. Very often it is intended to mean "What effect has the SEC had upon the growth of the accounting profession?" There is no doubt that the rules and regulations promulgated by the SEC since the middle Thirties in administering the Federal Securities Acts have had a rather definite influence upon the growth of the accounting profession. However, it should be remembered that throughout this period business has expanded considerably and that the growth of the accounting profession has been largely stimulated by this general business expansion. To the practicing accountant, the question of what effect has the SEC had upon the accounting profession has a much more important meaning. The practicing accountant is more concerned with the effect which the SEC has had upon the formulation of accounting principles and the development of auditing procedures. The discussion that follows is concerned with this latter effect.

BASIS FOR ACCOUNTING REGULATION BY SEC

It is desirable at the outset to clarify what the SEC means to accountants, both public and private. The private or corporate accountant is included here because it should be remembered that financial statements which are filed with the SEC and stock exchanges originate with, and are the responsibility of, the corporate (management) accountant. He also has an interest, somewhat indirectly, in the SEC's effect upon the public accountant's procedures because it is inconceivable that the public accountant could ever examine financial statements

---

[†]Presented at the Twelfth Annual Conference of Accountants, The University of Tulsa, April 23, 24, 1958. Reprinted from *1958 Conference of Accountants: Accounting Papers* (Tulsa, OK: Department of Accounting, College of Business Administration, The University of Tulsa, 1958), pp. 65-76, with permission of the Conference of Accountants at The University of Tulsa.

The author acknowledges the assistance of his partner, Louis H. Rappaport, CPA, in the preparation of this paper. Mr. Rappaport is author of *SEC Accounting Practice and Procedure*, Ronald Press.

without the corporate accountant becoming directly involved. Consequently, both public and private accountants have a deep interest in the work of the SEC.

The SEC is an agency of the federal government charged with administering the Securities Act of 1933, Securities Exchange Act of 1934 and other acts governing the sale or exchange of securities. Pursuant to such acts, the Commission has seen fit to delegate to its Chief Accountant its authority concerning the review of financial statements filed with it, and the auditing procedures involved in their certification. In this respect the Commissioners have acted wisely because they have given the administration of a very important segment of its responsibilities to a permanent staff capable of dealing with such problems. Obviously, it would be difficult for non-accountant commissioners appointed for limited terms to deal with the many accounting problems that are presented to it. In dealing with the Commission, the accountant almost always is concerned with financial statements filed with it; therefore he usually deals with the Chief Accountant or members of his staff.

Just how does the SEC affect the practice of the public accountant? Apart from the examination of the accounts of brokers, dealers in securities and members of exchanges, auditors usually become involved with the SEC through their examination of financial statements filed with the SEC. The Securities Act of 1933 is generally referred to as a "disclosure statute." It requires that specified financial and other information be furnished to prospective buyers of securities. It also requires the filing of annual reports after the securities have been sold, which reports then become available to the general public. The Securities Exchange Act of 1934 also provides for the filing of annual reports by companies with securities listed on national exchanges. As indicated previously, a point very frequently overlooked is that financial statements and other financial data contained in these filing are representations of the managements of the respective corporations and are the prime responsibility of such managements despite the fact that the statements are certified by independent public accountants. Accordingly, *all* accountants, public and private, should have a real interest in the activities of the SEC.

The Securities Act gives the Commission broad powers to make, amend and rescind any rules and regulations that may be necessary to carry out the provisions of the law. The Commission is authorized to define accounting, technical, and trade terms used in the law and has the power to prescribe the form in which required information shall be set forth in the financial statements. The Commission may prescribe the methods to be followed in the preparation of accounts, in the appraisal or valuation of assets and liabilities, in the determination of depreciation and depletion, in the differentiation between recurring and nonrecurring income, in the differentiation between investment and operating income, and in the preparation of consolidated financial statements of companies controlling or controlled by the issuer or under common control with the issuer. The Commission has similar powers and in some cases even broader powers under the Holding Company Act of 1935, the Investment Company Act of 1940 and other acts. Generally, these powers are unrestricted except that they may not be used in a manner which is inconsistent with the requirements imposed by other Federal regulatory bodies. The Commission also has the power to hold hearings and conduct investigations, subpoena records and conduct audits; it has the power to discipline accountants by suspending or disbarring from practice before the SEC.

Although the SEC has the authority to prescribe the accounting principles to be followed in financial statements filed with it, the Commission has not, with certain exceptions, invoked its authority to dictate how such financial statements shall be prepared. In Regulation S-X it has set forth its requirements as to the form and content of financial statements filed under the several laws administered by it. In its decisions and Accounting Series Releases it has stated its opinion concerning a limited number of accounting principles and practices. However, as to the large body of accounting principles underlying the preparation of financial statements, the SEC has for the most part been content to rely on generally accepted principles of accounting as they exist, or develop with the passage of time. This is all to the good. It would be regrettable if the SEC were to prescribe *one* set of accounting principles and to have business generally follow *different* principles for purposes other than filing with the SEC. Likewise, the SEC does not ordinarily prescribe the auditing procedure to be followed by the independent public accountant in his examination of financial statements to be filed with the Commission. Nevertheless, the Commission is aware of its authority and its responsibility in both these fields under these Acts. It has on a number of occasions exercised this authority by speaking out in favor of or against certain practices and principles. These are all a matter of record and it is interesting to study their history in relation to the development of accounting principles and auditing practices.

INFLUENCE ON AUDITING PROCEDURES

It would be well to consider first those instances which have had an impact upon the practice of auditing. These are somewhat more spectacular than those involving the development of accounting principles. Beyond any doubt, the SEC case which had the greatest impact on the public accounting profession was that involving McKesson and Robbins, Incorporated. Because of the magnitude of the fraud, the manner in which it was accomplished, and the sensational developments following the exposure, the facts in the case were widely publicized during 1938 and 1939. Accountants, however, are concerned principally with the SEC's investigation of the fraud and the report which followed. The basic facts concerning this case are generally well-known. It will be recalled that the master deception perpetrated by the top management of the company resulted in a gross overstatement of assets and operations. The principal purpose of the investigation which was instituted by the SEC was to determine (1) the character and scope of the audit made by the certifying accountants; (2) whether the audit by the accountants conformed to generally accepted standards; and (3) whether the existing generally accepted auditing standards were adequate to assure the reliability of financial statements. This was the most searching investigation ever conducted by a governmental organization of an audit made by a public accounting firm and the practices of the profession in general. The accountants who had certified the McKesson financial statements testified at the hearings as to the scope of their examinations and the detailed steps and procedures followed. They also testified with respect to a wide variety of other matters, such as the make-up of their firm, their procedures for investigating new clients, organization and training of staff accountants, review of clients' systems of internal control, review of work of subordinates and many other matters. In addition, a number of expert witnesses representing other accounting firms and educators testified as to what in their opinion constituted generally accepted auditing standards and procedures at that time. The testimony of the expert witnesses established that there was wide disagreement regarding the procedures to be employed in the examination of inventories and receivables. At one extreme was the view of one witness that the accountant was not concerned with physical quantities, quality, or condition of the inventory; representations of management were accepted and that fact reported in the balance sheet. At the other extreme was the view that accountants are obliged to do such work as they consider necessary to establish to their own satisfaction that the inventories are as represented and this includes physical contact with the inventory. With respect to receivables, the majority of authoritative opinion at the time supported the view that confirmation was not essential in cases in which substantial collection of the accounts prior to the conclusion of the audit is proved.

Even before the SEC made known the results of its investigations in the McKesson affair the accountancy profession began to put its house in order. The American Institute of Accountants was especially concerned about the impact of the McKesson fraud on the public's confidence in certificates of independent public accountants. A special Institute committee on auditing procedure, a newly created body, prepared a report entitled "Extensions of Auditing Procedure" and submitted it to the Council of the Institute. The report set forth the additional procedures regarding inventories and accounts receivable which the Committee believed should be regarded as generally accepted practice, and which are today the basic requirements concerning inventories and accounts receivable. This pronouncement was subsequently adopted by the Council and the membership of the Institute and became Statement on Auditing Procedure No. 1, dated October, 1939. In view of this timely action by the American Institute, the SEC felt that is was not necessary to prescribe specific auditing procedures with respect to inventories and accounts receivable or for that matter any other areas in the examination of financial statements. It reserved the right to take action at a later date should the new extended procedures prove ineffectual or inadequate. This has not been necessary.

Whether or not similar action on the part of the Institute would have occurred in the absence of a SEC is conjectural. The Commission should be credited for having initiated the investigation and for having brought it to a rapid conclusion. The case marks a turning point in attitude toward technical matters for the Institute. Prior to this time its technical pronouncements were isolated and scant. Committees on Accounting Procedure and Auditing Procedure were formed at about this time which began issuing the authoritative technical bulletins and statements with which members of the accounting profession are so familiar today. (The Commission's Accounting Series Releases had begun in 1937.) The case also emphasized the need for selection and election of auditors by stockholders early in fiscal year, the need for a thorough review of internal control and, all in all, strengthened the independence of the public accountant, a subject discussed later in this article.

The McKesson case also gave rise to the first official pronouncements concerning the auditor's responsibility for the detection of fraud. In its report the SEC said "we believe that, even in balance sheet examinations . . . , accountants can be expected to detect gross overstatements of assets and profits whether resulting from collusive fraud or otherwise . . . we feel that the discovery of gross overstatements in the accounts is a major purpose of such an audit even though it be conceded that it might not disclose every minor defalcation."

The American Institute made its first similar pronouncement in Statements on Auditing Procedure No. 1. This statement was restated in the Codification of Statements on Auditing Procedure 1-24 and now reads: "The ordinary examination incident to the issuance of an opinion respecting financial statements is not designed *and cannot be relied upon* to disclose defalcations and other similar irregularities, although their discovery frequently results."

A careful comparison of these two views will reveal that they are not exactly alike. However, the differences are subtle and have even since been the subject of discussion among practicing public accountants. It is expected that the Committee on Auditing Procedure of the American Institute of Certified Public Accountants will soon undertake further to define the responsibility of the auditor concerning the detection of fraud.

Although the cases that followed the McKesson case are somewhat less spectacular, they are nonetheless important with respect to the points at issue which they clarify. From the viewpoint of the day-to-day practice of public accountants, the decision in the Interstate Hosiery Mills, Inc. case in 1939 is one of the most important of the Commission's decisions. The Company had filed false financial statements with the SEC and the exchange on which the Company's securities were listed for trading. The financial statements overstated substantially the Company's assets and earnings. The author of the falsifications was a staff member of the certifying firm of accountants. Exposure came in 1938 from the accidental discovery that the staff member had forged several checks on the Company's bank account. Representatives of the Company and the accounting firm called on him in an effort to obtain an explanation of what he had done. He said only that he must have been crazy, that he received nothing for what he had done, and that he did not know why he had done it.

The exchange suspended trading in the Company's securities and the SEC instituted an investigation to determine whether the Company's securities should be delisted. One of the principal issues at the hearing was whether the firm had exercised due care in reviewing the work of its staff member. The testimony at the hearing did not show that the accounting firm's review of his work was any less extensive than that ordinarily made by accounting firms. Expert witnesses testified as to the usual review procedure followed by independent public accountants. The SEC stated that, in its opinion, this procedure required thorough revision. The review upon which an accounting firm assumes responsibility for work done by subordinates, said the SEC, must be a series of more than perfunctory questions as to the performance of particular items in an audit program; explanations of unusual items should not be accepted by a reviewer without detailed support in the working papers. The review should be designed, in the SEC's view, with two objectives in mind: first to insure the integration of the original work papers with the financial statements, second to analyze in a searching manner the ultimate facts developed in the course of the actual audit. This type of review has now become general practice.

There have been a number of other cases which generally have involved findings of improper professional conduct in connection with certification of financial statements by accounting firms practicing before the Commission. For the most part these cases involve questions concerning the use of generally accepted accounting principles in a given instance or whether or not a firm was, in fact, independent as judged by its actions. Rarely have they involved fraudulent actions on the part of the accountants. Considering the number of filings that have been made with the Commission since its inception, these cases have indeed been very rare. Generally speaking the greatest impact upon auditing practice was made by the McKesson and Interstate Hosiery cases.

Another influence which the SEC has had upon auditing practice in the field of events subsequent to the date of financial statements. The SEC has always taken the position that a prospectus and registration statement spoke as of its effective date. Financial statements included in such registrations may sometimes be as much as six months old. Events may have taken place subsequent to the date of certification which have a material effect upon the financial position and results of operations shown in the prospectus. The SEC has insisted that such events be disclosed and, when necessary, that the financial statements be corrected. Although accountants have always extended their examinations, to a limited degree, to transactions after the balance sheet date in an effort to support their opinion on the financial statements, no clear understanding existed of the nature of and extent to which these procedures were to be employed. When the SEC's policy regarding subsequent events became known it was necessary for the auditor, at about the effective date of a registration statement to "have another look." This inquiry was generally directed to events which transpired between the certification date and the effective date of the registration. The scope of such a review had never been defined nor had there been any declaration of the nature of the items requiring disclosure until the American Institute's Auditing Procedure Committee issued a statement in 1954 on this subject. Included in the statement was a full discussion of the subject, in general, and in relation to SEC practice in particular, giving recommendations for the treatment of post-balance sheet events occurring prior to, as well as subsequent to, certification date. This is an example of how a procedure initiated by the SEC was gradually adopted in practice and then formalized by Institute pronouncement.

INFLUENCE ON ACCOUNTANTS' INDEPENDENCE

Another great influence the SEC has had upon the public accounting profession is in the field of independence. The concept of independence on the part of certifying accountants was not created by the SEC or by the draftsman of the federal securities laws. Independence is the foundation of the public accounting profession. While the accounting profession and industry have been aware of the importance of independence on the part of public accountants, the SEC deserves most of the credit for accelerating the development of the independence concept. In its regulations and decisions—both formal and informal—the SEC has been particularly insistent that accountants who certify statements for filing with it be independent. The views of the SEC and the American Institute on the matter of independence are not exactly alike. The SEC precludes independent status if an accountant has *any* financial interest in his client or occupies any position as officer, director, or employee, while the American Institute would preclude the status only if he held a substantial interest. In either viewpoint, however, the independent state of mind would have to exist.

The SEC emphasizes the specific relationships between an accountant and his client which give rise to a presumption of *lack* of independence, that is, the SEC will not recognize an accountant as independent if any of the proscribed relationships exist.

The Institute emphasizes the fact of independence—the state of mind which the word denotes. It recognizes that an accountant may be independent in spite of close relationships with his client—or, on the other hand, that he may lack independence in spite of the most correct appearances. The Institute, therefore, has not chosen to prohibit a great variety of relationships which might conceivably tend to introduce a subconscious bias into the accountant's judgment, but rather relies mainly on his actions to determine whether independence has actually been impaired. If accepted accounting and auditing standards are observed, and all material facts are fully disclosed, it may be presumed that independence exists. The publicity and support which the SEC has directed toward this matter of independence, as well as to other problems involving accounting principles or auditing practice, has been a boon to the public accounting profession over the past two decades.

INFLUENCE ON ACCOUNTING PRINCIPLES

As previously mentioned, the SEC has for the most part been content to rely on generally accepted principles of accounting as they exist or develop with the passage of time. There have been, however, a few instances in which the SEC felt that certain practices or procedures, although having some basis under accounting principles, should not be permitted; these will be discussed later. The Commission also took the position rather early in its existence (1938) that where the financial statements filed were prepared in accordance with accounting principles for which there was no substantial authoritative support, such financial statements would be presumed to be misleading or inaccurate despite disclosures contained in the certificate of the accountant or in footnotes to the statements. In clarifying this point the Commission said that in cases where there was a difference of opinion between the Commission and the registrant as to the proper principle of accounting to be followed, disclosure would be accepted in lieu of correction of the financial statements themselves *only* if the points involved were such that there was substantial authoritative support for the practices followed by the registrant and the position of the Commission had not been previously expressed in rules, regulations or other official releases.

It is perhaps not surprising that most of the early SEC decisions relating to accounting matters dealt with newly formed corporations that issued large amounts of stock for assets having little or no value. Promoters often have not hesitated to set up assets in amounts having no relation to the cost or value of the assets acquired or the value of the stock issued. The Commission prevented many of these corporations from proceeding with the sale of their securities to the public and issued many decisions on accounting for property acquired for stock, property under option, promotional services, appraisals, and the like. Many of these cases hinged upon the use of the par value of stock which in earlier days had some significance and which today may or may not have significance. As a consequence of its experience in this area it can be stated that the Commission is generally opposed to the accounting recognition of appraised values which write up assets in excess of their historical cost. Although at one time such write ups were considered by accountants to be permissible, the SEC's consistent view that upward restatements of *only* property, plant and equipment is not in accordance with present day accepted accounting principles has had the effect of forcing this view upon the profession.

In recent years considerable thought has been devoted by accountants, businessmen and economists to the subject of depreciation and high costs. During periods of greatly increased price levels, management is faced with the problem of replacing plant facilities at costs much greater than those of the original facilities. Many have suggested that the problem be met by periodically recording current appraised amounts for all property with comparable increased depreciation charges against current income. The American Institute's Committee on Accounting Procedure has taken the position that this would not increase the usefulness of reported corporate income figures if some companies charged depreciation on appraised values while others adhered to cost. The Committee believes that consideration of radical changes in accepted accounting procedures should not be undertaken at least until a stable price level would make it practicable for business as a whole to make the change at the same time.

The Commission is, however, favorably disposed to the establishment of new accounting values established in the course of a quasi-reorganization in which a corporation, without creating a new corporate entity, and, without resort to formal court proceedings, is enabled to eliminate a deficit in earned surplus and to establish a new earned surplus account for the accumulation of earnings subsequent to the effective date of the quasi-reorganization. By a series of releases the SEC has required that in all quasi-reorganizations the following conditions exist: (1) earned surplus as of the date selected is exhausted; (2) upon consummation of the quasi-reorganization no deficit exists in any surplus account; (3) the entire procedure is made known to all persons entitled to vote on matters of general corporate policy and the appropriate consents to the particular transactions are obtained in advance in accordance with law and charter provisions; (4) the procedure accomplishes with respect to the accounts substantially what might be accomplished in a reorganization by legal proceedings—namely, the restatement of assets in terms of present conditions, as well as appropriate modifications of capital and capital surplus, in order to obviate so far as possible the necessity of future reorganization of like nature.

Reductions in the carrying value of assets at the effective date of the reorganization may not be made beyond the point which gives appropriate recognition to conditions that appear to have resulted in relatively permanent reductions in asset values; as for example, complete or partial obsolescent, lessened utility value, reduction in investment value due to changed economic conditions, or, in the case of current assets, decline in indicated realization value. A procedure of this kind should not be employed recurrently but only under circumstances that would justify an actual reorganization or formation of a new company, particularly if the principal purpose of the quasi-reorganization is the elimination of a deficit in earned surplus. The Commission requires that any deficits written off in the course of a quasi-reorganization should be disclosed for a period of at 1east three years following the reorganization in order to provide additional disclosure of the occurrence and its significance. Earned surplus accumulated since the quasi-reorganization is usually dated for a period of ten years. The ground rules thus established by the SEC for quasi-reorganizations have become generally accepted procedure today.

It seems almost needless to point out that principles of taxation are not the same as generally accepted principles of accounting. Because of the divergences between them, Congress attempted in 1954 to bring them more clearly into agreement by amendment of the Internal Revenue Code. This attempt was not too successful and it is expected that further attempts will be made which it is hoped will be successful. There have been instances when the financial statements included in registration statements had been prepared on a tax basis and were certified by public accountants as being in conformity with generally accepted principles of accounting. Financial statements have been filed, for example, in which life insurance premiums were charged to surplus for the sole reason that they were not deductible for tax purposes. Other statements have been filed with SEC in which the current provision for federal income taxes was also charged to surplus presumably on the basis that it represented a sharing of profits with the Government. Today most accountants are well aware of the differences between tax accounting and good accounting and act accordingly.

Because taxable income is frequently quite different today from accounting income there has been the gradual development of what is known as the principle of "tax-effect accounting." This is the application of the "matching cost and revenue" theory to income taxes. In the early days of the formulation of this principle the SEC took a position directly opposed to this practice and did not permit income to be charged with an amount representing the estimated reduction of income tax due to, for example, an item such as amortization of emergency facilities for tax purposes when such amortization was not recorded for accounting purposes. The American Institute took a contrary viewpoint, in favor of the principle, and has ever since generally supported the principle of allocation of income taxes. The SEC has modified its views on tax-effect accounting and now permits it provided a disclosure is made of that portion of the provision for income tax in the income statement which is not payable currently. In other words as long as the actual tax payable for the current year is indicated it is permissible to show a greater charge for taxes in the income statement based upon the income reflected in that statement. This is one instance where an accounting series release (#53) is still on record and has not been officially modified by the Commission although the release has been eroded in practice. In order that practitioners and the public may know the SEC's views on tax-effect accounting, it would appear desirable for the Commission officially to update its views on this subject or withdraw the release in question.

As indicated earlier, the Securities Acts administered by the SEC were generally known as disclosure acts and the SEC saw its responsibility as one requiring full and fair disclosure of all facts which a prudent investor ought to know in determining whether or not an investment in particular securities should be made. For the accountant this means that there should be full and fair disclosure of all material facts necessary to make the financial statements not misleading; that they actually reflect a fair presentation of financial position and results of operations. Also, as indicated earlier, the SEC was not content with merely full disclosure of material facts, that full disclosure would not necessarily cure what the Commission might consider an incorrect treatment of an accounting principle. Despite disclosure, the burden of proof for the use of an accounting principle that was not generally accepted was placed squarely upon the accountants preparing such statements and those certifying such statements. In a few instances the SEC has seen fit to slap the wrists of certain registrants and certain accounting firms for deviating slightly from this principle. There has also been one occasion when the SEC was slightly criticized for not requiring full disclosure of a particular fact or not requiring strict adherence to generally accepted principles in the light of all the facts. However, these occasions have been very few and only serve to prove, rather than disprove, the degree of vigilance with which the SEC has carried out its responsibility for not only *full* disclosure, but *fair* disclosure of all material facts in relation to the financial statements of a business.

As inferred previously, the SEC and the accounting profession have not always seen eye-to-eye with respect to what constituted fair disclosure or proper accounting treatment. The issue which gave rise to a great deal of amiable controversy between the Commission and the accounting profession, and which in the author's opinion is not yet really fully resolved but appears to be reaching general acceptance, is the one concerning the choice between an "all inclusive" income statement and that which is referred to as the "current operating performance" income statement. The American Accounting Association, comprised largely of accounting professors and teachers, has long held the view that an income statement should be all-inclusive—that all items of profit and loss should be included in the determination of net income regardless of their nature or size. Management accountants and public accountants in the late 30's and early 40's soon saw that this type of income statement, while it might contain *disclosure* of any abnormal, nonrecurring, distorting type of item, might nevertheless lead the laymen astray as to the meaning and portent of the amount of net income. It is well recognized that the ordinary layman investor looks at the net income figure, and particularly the earnings-per-share figure, as his benchmark for comparison and for guidance in choosing between issues of securities. Consequently, any abnormality within the income statement which might not be adequately publicized or too apparent might result in a misleading inference by the ordinary investor.

The American Institute recognized this problem and issued a bulletin in 1947 which recommended a deviation from the "all-inclusive" type of income statement in certain circumstances and urged rather strongly the use of a modified current operating income type of statement. This bulletin recommended that while there should be a general presumption that all items of profit and loss recognized during the period were to be used in determining the figure reported as net income, that an exception should be made to this presumption for items which, in the aggregate, were *material* in relation to the Company's net income and which were *not* clearly identifiable with, or resulted from, the *usual* or *typical* business operations of the period. Thus, it recommended the exclusion from the determination of net income of such extraordinary items as (1) those which related to operations of prior years, such as the elimination of unused reserves and adjustments of income taxes, or (2) material charges or credits resulting from unusual sales of assets not acquired for resale and not of the type in which the company generally dealt, or (3) material losses of a type not usually insured against such as those resulting from wars, riots, earthquakes, floods and similar catastrophes which were not a recurrent hazard, or (4) the write-off of a material amount of intangibles (assuming there is a proper basis for such write-off) or, (5) the write-off of material amounts of unamortized discount or premium at the time of retiring or refunding of bond issues. Such nonrecurring items were required to be charged or credited directly to earned surplus and to be excluded in any determination of net income or earnings-per-share for the year. This type of income statement has been fairly well accepted by management and the public accounting profession and has become the one in general use. For many years the SEC took exception to this form of income statement even though the accounting profession generally stood steadfastly behind it. In proposing a new revision of Regulation S-X in 1950, the SEC wanted all profit and loss items, regardless of their nature or size, included in the determination of net income. At this point the accountants of the many companies listed on the exchanges, and the public accountants, objected to this manner of presentation. While it was recognized that both concepts provided disclosure of what had taken place, the question was one of *full* and *fair* disclosure—so that no one might be misled. This difference of opinion was ultimately compromised by permitting the addition to or deduction from net income of such adjustments which might ordinarily be credited or charged to surplus and gave rise to what is generally known today as the "special item." Such special item is excluded from the determination of net income, but is added to or subtracted from net income at the bottom of the income statement giving rise to a new caption known as "net income and special item." This compromise satisfied the SEC because the reader of an income statement is immediately put on notice concerning any additional profit or loss items incurred by the company during that year; yet it has the advantage of excluding such special item from an unequivocal determination of net income and, of course, of excluding it from the determination of earnings-per-share. Present practice is to quote earnings-per-share on the basis of net income and, in addition, the special item effect per share is usually also given. Thus, the investor may visualize earnings per share on the basis of the ordinary operations of the business (from which he may make some estimation of what future operations will be like) and he is also made aware of the fact that the company has sustained a nonrecurring profit or loss amounting to a certain amount per share. This is one example of how the SEC and the accounting profession have worked together in the solution of the mutual problem of determining what constitutes full and fair disclosure of the results of operations of a business.

The matters discussed thus far are mainly historical. What about the present and future influence of the SEC on accounting principles and procedures and the practice of auditing? In the past, differences of opinion between the SEC and the accounting profession on matters of accounting principles or auditing procedures have been settled rather amicably, and there is every reason to believe that this will continue. Furthermore, the organizations of accountants, public and private, have taken steps to crystallize and formalize their opinions and to establish procedures whereby such opinions are brought before the SEC for its consideration before adoption. The American Institute of CPA's, for example, has, in addition to its Committees on Accounting Procedure and Auditing Procedure, a Committee on Relations with the SEC. These committees in dealing with their respective problems will always lay their proposed pronouncements before the SEC, for its consideration and comment, before attempting to formalize them. The American Accounting Association, the Controllers Institute and the other professional accounting organizations have comparable committees which operate in similar fashion.

Likewise, the SEC, principally through its Chief Accountant, confers with these committees in connection with the interpretation and drafting of its accounting rules and regulations. As a result there exists an atmosphere of complete cooperation and candor between the accountants and the SEC. For example, just recently the Commission proposed a revision of Regulation S-X designed to clarify its position concerning the question of the independence of the public accountant. The proposed revision was designed to answer many of the questions which are regularly brought before the Commission seeking to determine whether in given circumstances an accountant is, in the judgment of the SEC, independent. Following the practice just mentioned, the Commission exposed the proposed revision of the Regulation to several committees and members of the accounting profession for comment. The comments resulting from this exposure indicated that some questions were still unanswered by the proposed revision. As a consequence, the SEC, upon revising the Regulation, issued an explanatory release which further clarified its position and stated that it would exempt certain deviations from the application of the rule. This is an example of how the present set-up is working and how it is expected to continue to work. The author can foresee only a continuation of this spirit of cooperation and is convinced that in the future there will be fewer differences of opinion between the SEC and the accounting profession because of their mutual respect and their dedication to a common purpose—the full and fair presentation of the financial positions and results of operation of American businesses.

THE CHALLENGE OF THE PRESENT†

by
Philip L. Defliese

RATHER than attempt to become a visionary and address myself to the challenge of the profession's future, I shall confine my remarks to the challenge of the present. It is more compelling, it is with us, and if we look after it, the future will take care of itself.

While I prefer to look upon myself as an idealist, my many years in the profession have made me a realist and a pragmatist. I know, for example, that as your Chairman I occupy for the short space of a year an honorary post whose primary function is to chair a Board of Directors chosen by nominating committees for 3-year terms. With such limited power I do not expect to make an impact other than to attempt to set the tone and provide some measure of leadership. Hereafter when I speak for the Institute I shall be constrained to speak the Board's views, which may not always coincide with mine. Consequently, I shall take this opportunity to speak plainly before I undertake the role you have asked me to assume.

First, let me state that I believe strongly in the concept of a professional institute and that our organization is growing and evolving as it should. We now have a full-time President who looks after the day-to-day operations—both technical and administrative—and we are fortunate in having as capable and dedicated a professional as Wally Olson to occupy that position, plus the able assistance of John Lawler and the rest of the Institute staff. The structure is constantly changing and such evolution is essential for a thriving and growing profession.

Your outgoing chairman has stressed the need for unity in the profession. I echo that need but hasten to add that more than unity is the need to share with one another the results of our research, development and expertise so that our professional behavior can equal that of the medical and scientific professions. As individual professionals we are obligated to innovate and create, and then to share the outcome for the common good and the public interest. An Institute is an assemblage of diversely-minded individuals. It must seek a consensus, and cannot, of itself, always create progress. But it must be the vehicle for sharing, moderating and promulgating the progress made by its members.

The present finds the image of the profession at low ebb. We are constantly being criticized by the press, financial analysts and the SEC, and the horrendous litigations facing us—both civil and criminal—compounds this problem. In the

---

†Inaugural Address, 1974. American Institute of Certified Public Accountants. Reprinted with permission from the files of the American Institute of Certified Public Accountants. Opinions of the authors are their own and do not necessarily reflect policies of the AICPA.

recent past, the proliferation of alternative accounting principles has been blamed. I have never accepted this premise because I have always felt that the inadequacies of our auditing techniques were to blame. In 1971, speaking before the Wheat Committee, I said:

> ...many of the 'horror' stories of accounting—those involving lawsuits and accusations of fraud against the auditors by the SEC—are not as much a matter of accounting principles as a matter of auditing and reporting standards... Those problems fall within the purview of the Institute's auditing procedure committee, which is trying valiantly to catch up.

The Wheat Committee report resulted in the creation of the FASB and we are now on the road toward an orderly resolution of the problems with accounting principles. That is a long road and patience is needed while that group gears up and fills the pipeline—an activity that is now evidencing itself. While I opposed separating this function from the profession, I support strongly its purpose and urge upon others the necessary forbearance.

But the problem of auditing is still with us, creating more crises daily. It is here that the profession has the greatest challenge and must take positive steps to restore its image in the business world. As I see it we must do three things promptly:

1. We must broaden and define the role and functions of the auditor to satisfy a public need.
2. We must establish quality control procedures and disciplinary formats to demonstrate that we are capable of satisfying the public need and disciplining ourselves.
3. We must re-examine the scope and structure of our ever-enlarging profession so that it will encompass the necessary disciplines and expertise to cope with the public need.

Fortunately, beginnings have been made in all three areas and all I need to do is emphasize the direction they should take.

In the first area—the audit function—the appointment of the new Audit Commission marks a giant step in recognizing the major problem. This Commission will explore the expectations of the public and the means whereby the auditor can fulfill those expectations. Heretofore our pronouncements have been self-serving and restrictive. We must open the window to the needs of the public investor and assume greater responsibility rather than less. We must take a positive approach toward what we can do, rather than focusing on what we can't do. We must assume greater responsibility for the appropriateness of the application of accounting principles and the many judgments that entails. We must research, create, and innovate, individually and collectively, and share the results as true professionals. The Institute's auditing staff is being enlarged to cope with this added thrust, once the Commission issues its recommendations.

In the second area—quality control and discipline—the establishment of voluntary peer reviews of local and multi-office firms is a great step forward. Admittedly, the imposition of peer reviews by the SEC has been a catalyst. While many mayor firms have for some time had internal peer review programs, the movement toward outsider reviews is salutary. Long-range—after considerable experimentation—the program will be more effective if it becomes compulsory. The movement toward compulsory continuing education will also be helpful if properly implemented. However, we should not expect that these programs will eliminate audit failures. At the heart of our problem is a public expectancy of infallibility, when we know that human error can never be removed from a profession as judgmental as ours. Nevertheless greater efforts must be made—the profession must demonstrate its intentions.

The disciplinary area is more complicated; in this respect I refer specifically to technical standards. As a membership organization without licensing power, subpoena power, or privilege, the Institute can only do the best under the circumstances. Necessarily, its wheels must grind slowly; because of these limitations, it cannot pursue cases until all related litigation is completed. However, considerable progress is being made. The recently adopted new enforcement plan calling for joint trial boards with state societies will eliminate much duplication and provide greater uniformity to the enforcement mechanism. But it is only a first step; hopefully, all State Boards will ultimately become an integral part of this process.

In the meantime we are faced with a powerful overseer that has recently become active in this area and flexed its muscles—The SEC. Its recent accusations of fraud—both civil and criminal—against individuals and firms—has shocked the profession and the business community. Here we face an over-structured disciplinary mechanism that can at one time act as a prosecutor, judge and jury. I would not care to prejudge these cases but there is common belief that there is some overreaction here. Auditors who have been nurtured in an environment of objectivity do not ordinarily deliberately commit fraud, even though hindsight applied to judgmental decisions can give that impression.

As Sam Derieux has indicated, the Institute has begun discussions with the accounting and enforcement divisions of the SEC to explore the premises under which they operate and determine how the profession can cope with the existing environment. I hope that thereby we can create a detente in this area while we seek a more equitable structure. In my view there is needed an integrated vehicle nationally and locally by which the profession can operate vis-à-vis the SEC in the disciplinary area. There is no doubt that if the profession does not discipline itself the SEC will—and should. Federal and state legislation or regulation may be needed to provide a new structure that will satisfy this need. I intend to appoint an Ad Hoc Committee to explore this problem in depth—but don't look for a quick and easy solution.

Finally, the scope and structure of our profession must be re-examined. This has more long-range implications, but the challenge to begin is here. The report of Lou Kessler's committee is now out for discussion. Many will disagree with its conclusions, but I cannot see much room for disagreement with its philosophy, which is a recognition that the profession is composed of many specializations. Those who may look upon its recommendations as a dilution of the CPA concept should instead see it as a broadening of the accounting profession. We should remember that the "A" in "CPA" stands for "accountant" not "auditor." Although steeped in the auditing tradition, professional accountants do much more than auditing. We already have today a de facto multi-discipline profession—audit, tax, and management accounting services. And no one in or out of the profession can truly challenge the high levels of expertise achieved in each area. In the major firms an auditor would hesitate to render a sophisticated tax opinion or install an involved EDP system. Nor would a tax or MCS man give an audit opinion. The recognition of these specializations need not detract from the valued contributions of the many general practitioners who nevertheless practice taxation and do more management consulting than they realize. Long-range I look forward to a broadly-based CPA exam which will serve as the entry point of our profession from which a man will then pursue specialization certifications in either auditing, taxation or management consulting, or all three. This may take some time, and some grandfathering, but unless we look forward to it, we may find three distinct professions instead of one. In my view, we are now one integrated profession, and it is this type of integration that gives us strength and the ability to serve the public need most.

In closing, let me thank you for the honor of being your Chairman for the coming year. I shall pursue the points I have covered with the Board of Directors and shall work with them to further the aims of the Institute as they see them.

ACCOUNTING, FORECASTING AND CONSULTING FOR MANAGMENT USE[†]

by
Philip L. Defliese

INTRODUCTION

TO say that we are living in a fast-moving world is to repeat an overworked cliché. Accountants who attended this Congress five years ago are well aware of the rapid changes that have taken place since in accounting, economics and finance. Many of them, particularly those affecting accounting, have already been discussed.

The most dramatic occurrence has been the onset of a deep worldwide recession, which has often been compared to the great Depression of the thirties, coupled with the economic anomaly of unprecedented worldwide inflation. Even more dramatic has been the nature of the recovery in the U.S. from the most severe recession since World War II—which many say was the only event that could have rescued us from the great Depression. Although unemployment in the U.S. remains high by historical standards, there is no doubt that the industrial recovery has been more rapid than many expected.

Economists know better than to compare the 1973-75 recession with the Depression of the thirties. Capitalist and Government attitudes are no longer of the laissez faire variety that led to that debacle, and I need not dwell on the cushion effect of tax reductions, unemployment insurance, social security and welfare payments which serve to pump prime an economy. Our macro-economists, although surprised at the speed, are not surprised at the result. Accountants, whose interest in macro-economics is growing (as I shall cover later), who are the professional micro-economists of today, are not very surprised at the speed.

One, often overlooked, major difference between today and the thirties is the speed of communication of economic and financial data and events through our vast media (which can have bad effects as well as good) not only to the public at large but also to the decision-makers of industry. They have at their finger tips an unprecedented array of accounting and economic information generated in

[†]This paper was presented at the Eleventh International Congress of Accountants in Munich, October 10-14, 1977. Reprinted from *The Chartered Accountant* (India), March 1978, pp. 524-533, with permission of The Institute of Chartered Accountants of India. Portions of the paper were published in *The Accountant* (England), November 10, 1977, pp. 595-597; and in *Industrial Accountant* (Pakistan), January-March 1978, pp. 17-20.

The author gratefully acknowledges the assistance in preparation of this paper furnished by his partner, Roy D. Thylin.

split-second fashion by the most sophisticated computers and business models available—models that almost make the decisions before we can take the time to analyze the output.

In the thirties, it took years before we learned the extent of the widespread extreme overproduction that had taken place as a result of the booming twenties. We have since learned that rapid charges in consumer attitudes constitute the key. Today our sophisticated computers not only alert us instantaneously to sales trends, but, combined with inventory controls, trigger production and supply changes that prevent excessive inventory build up. By late 1974 inventory liquidation had begun and by 1976 production wheels had begun to turn to replenish the liquidated stock. Thus there was no price collapse creating large scale bankruptcies to ripple through the economy, such as we saw through the thirties. Most industry has remained healthy and profitability has returned.

This may sound like an oversimplification and overstatement of this aspect of the recovery. Obviously, the U.S. recovery is one facet of a complex, interrelated worldwide economy. But the impact on the U.S. recovery of accounting, forecasting and consulting techniques which the accounting profession has brought to a high degree of sophistication cannot be minimized. While the general public may be unaware of this, the decisionmakers of industry appreciate the role we play. However, we are only on the threshold of a new era of involvement in the macro-economic future of the world. We need to re-examine what we have achieved and coordinate our efforts to improve our techniques, develop new ones, and spread our ideas. While we will never be able to overcome the cyclical nature of business, we can do our utmost to smooth it.

I shall cover in the following discussion the emergence of management accounting and its role as distinguished from that of financial accounting. Accounting generated data are an integral part of the information management needs for effective decision-making, planning and control. With liquidity a widespread concern, the concepts of cash flow, return on investment and scientific inventory management are being increasingly utilized as performance measures and in decision-making. Forecasting in today's uncertain environment has changed the nature of the planning process and has expanded the use of business modelling. Rapidly changing computer technology has raised questions about handling the vast amounts of data made available. Investors also want more information concerning investment opportunities, and the demand for dissemination to the public of what heretofore has been considered management accounting information has increased. The rapid changes taking place has emphasized management's need to seek expertise, and accountants are playing a significant role as consultants to management.

MANAGEMENT ACCOUNTING

The Emergence of Management Accounting

As soon as a civilization develops beyond the simplest level and economic affairs increase in complexity, it becomes necessary to maintain records to transactions between individuals. Records of wages paid, taxes due and other accounts can be traced back to 4500 B.C. Those records were usually kept in columnar form, providing a net position of receipt and payments. The double entry system of accounting was introduced in the 15th century when it was used principally to record buying and selling transactions. It was not until the industrial revolution ushered in the era of expanding business organization and increasing competition that interest in accounting and financial control arose. Even during that time of heightened business activity, the accountant was looked upon as a "scorekeeper." Most of his time was spent reporting on the past instead of looking toward the future. It was not until late in the 19th century that accounting evolved into a management tool.

The first manuals on cost accounting were published and the concepts of fixed and variable costs introduced in the last quarter of the 19th century. In 1891, Sir John *Mann* stated that "cost records should be kept to exam and explain past results and to form a guide for future trading." Throughout the 20th century, emphasis on the use of accounting information in forward planning and control has been growing. The first complete standard cost system was introduced in 1911; its development was linked to the emergence of the scientific management movement espoused by F.W. *Taylor* in his book, *The Principles of Scientific Management.* Budgetary control was also introduced at this time. Overhead items were budgeted, actual costs were compared to the budget, and variances were investigated. However, it was not until the period during the immediately following World War II that budgeting came into widespread use. Cost summarization data were needed for decision-making, and different cost data were required for different decisions at various levels of management. It became a job of the accountant to provide each manager with data relevant to his decision-making process. The existence of two branches of accounting, both summarizing the same events but from different points of view, was finally acknowledged. The age of management accounting had arrived.

The Role of Management Accounting

Management accounting and financial accounting are not unrelated, but they differ in that they serve different classes of decision-makers. Financial accounting may be described as the preparation and collection of documents relating to business transaction and the preparation and interpretion of financial statements summarizing those transactions. Its primary purpose is to produce financial statements that reflect the comparative results of the economic activities of the enterprise during recent periods. Financial accounting operates under special rules, procedures and conventions for generating information that is made available to both management and the public.

Management accounting, on the other hand, may be described as the presentation of accounting data in such a way as to assist management in its function of promoting maximum efficiency and formulating and coordinating future plans and subsequently measuring their execution. It is more comprehensive and broadly based than cost accounting and utilizes quantitative information from internal and external sources. Its primary purpose is providing different levels of management with comparisons to predetermined standard costs and budgets and disclosure of variances for timely decision-making, planning and control.

Timing also plays a different role in each of the branches. Financial accounting reports or statements are usually prepared at specified times (monthly, quarterly, annually) and require varying degrees of accuracy. As the need for accuracy increases, the time required to assemble the necessary data also increases. Management accounting reports are generated more frequently, and the need for accuracy is subordinated to the need for timely information. This is not meant to imply that accurate data are not required in management accounting, but only to emphasize that complete accuracy must be sacrificed if it delays the information until it is too late for effective management action.

The Role of Financial Accounting

Management's use of accounting data is wide and vaied; the most well-known use is financial reporting, which is a product of the financial accounting system and serves as management's "report card" to shareholders. The financial statements are concerned primarily with stewardship of assets and the evaluation of results of a past short-term period.

It must be remembered that, given a specific set of facts, alternative accounting methods might be used which would produce strikingly different results. Accounting is still an art, not an absolute science. Authoritative bodies throughout the world are promulgating standards of reporting and financial disclosure intended to ensure that information about which a reasonable, prudent investor ought to be informed is included in the statements. For discussion purpose, the reasonable, prudent investor is defined as a person or institution that purchases debt or equity securities on an open market, relying on data made public by the issuer and the advice of those who analyze such data. His buy, sell or hold decisions are heavily dependent on information in the company's financial statements.

Despite the efforts being made to set standards, accountancy is still a collection of conficting conventions and financial statements often lack clarity and comparability. Part of the blame rests with the accountants for failing to agree earlier on what the objectives of financial accounting are, or should be.

Financial accounting information, despite its limitations, is also used for internal purposes, and many industrialists would now agree that internal reporting is as important, if not more important, than external reporting. Its use is further limited, however, in that values are expressed basically in terms of historical cost. In times of inflation and rapid changing purchasing power of the monetary unit, financial statements have become a melange of present and past values, often making the results less meaningful. Accountants have a duty to alert management to this factor.

Cash Flow and Return on Investment

In recent years, the rewards of business have been declining in relation to the investment required to produce them. Management must now take increased interest in the return it receives on the assets invested. Business has been forced to take on additional debt. While some of the debt may be attributed to expansion, some is a result of industry's inability to earn enough of a return to provide the capital needed to maintain itself in a viable state. Traditional financial accounting not only hides this trend, but also may give the impression that a company is "sailing along" when in fact it is headed towards disaster. By relating cash flow to assets, management can acquire incisive information about the economic viability of its facilities.

Return on investment may be defined as the reward for the commitment of resources, which include time, technology, manpower and materials as well as money. Simply stated, it is the rate that equates the present value of future cash flows with the original investment. Care must be taken in computing cash flows and invested assets if reliable return on investment figures are to be obtained. Financial accounting profit may serve as the basis of the cash flow computation, but management must be aware of the conventions used to calculate that profit and must adjust it as necessary. Items such as depreciation and amortization must be added back to the profit figure. Interest on debt and interest and depreciation implicit in obligations resulting from long-term lease agreements should also be added back to adjust for the particular financing methods employed by an enterprise. While financing will affect the company's earnings per share, it does not affect the return of investment. Earnings per share represents an expression of the stockholders' stake in the company's earnings; return on investment, on the other hand, is a function of the business itself.

Off-balance sheet financing should also be reflected in the total investment figure utilized for computing return on investment. As a general rule, a value of ten times annual rental payments for assets with useful lives of 20 years or more may be added to the balance sheet figure in arriving at invested assets. As in the case of cash flow, the investment figure should not be affected by the company's method of financing. All assets, regardless of who holds title to them, used by the company to generate the cash flow should be included in the calculation of return on investment.

Practically speaking, management can most fully utilize the return on investment concept in analyzing individual investment opportunities. Financial institutions work with the return on investment concept every day. The manufacturing side of business often does not deal with these ratios. Yet, virtually all individual investment decisions can be expressed in a maner that will provide a result directly comparable to financial models. The return on investment concept of equating the present value of future cash flows with the original investment recognizes the time value of money. Resources are invested now to increase future cash flows and return on investment. All other factors being equal, the investment with the highest return will usually be selected.

The expected return may also be an indicator of successful product innovation; that is, the more significant the improvement in the product, the greater the reward. Returns can also be weighed against risk factors. Simply stated, a project or investment with a 30% expected return and a 50% chance of success would be comparable to a project or investment with a 15% return and a 99% chance of success. Most projects are not "all or nothing" propositions, and the likelihood of partial success must be taken into consideration in reviewing the overall expected return on the project. When reviewing return on investment of several alternative projects, management must be aware of any intentional or unintentional biases built into the projected returns, which are only as valid as the input assumptions on which they are based.

Cost of Capital

While the method of financing does not affect the return on investment, management must constantly be aware of the cost of capital employed in the business. Companies have access to three sources of funds (debt, external equity and internal equity), which all have associated costs. The cost of capital may be defined as the minimum amount one must expect to earn on a project to pay the costs, implicit as well as explicit, of funds used to finance it. The expected earnings should be such that the stock price, adjusted for splits and dividends, does not decline. It should be noted that this concept is an outgrowth of management's responsibility for the stewardship of assets and maintenance of the stockholders' investment.

Management uses the cost of capital primarily for capital budgeting purposes, but it may also be used as the discount factor in present value computations or as a reference point in evaluating the expected rate of return of several alternative investment opportunities. Profits determined for financial accounting purposes do not allow for the cost of equity capital employed in the business, which is an economic evaluation; thus, such profits are usually inflated in an economic sense.

Planning and Control

Management also relies on the use of accounting data in the area of planning and control. Planning is the determination of where a business should be headed and the best route to follow to arrive at the desired destination; control is the process of making sure that each element of the business is meeting its commitments and quickly exposing areas in which plans must be changed to ensure the best possible results.

Control is concerned with the rapid, efficient and economic execution of tasks within the management plan and budget. Managers need frequent information on individual operations or jobs to provide accurate work measurement and evaluation. In modern business, accounting is viewed as part of the management information and control systems, primarily in the areas of budgetary procedures. While managers must monitor the day-to-day operations of the company, they must plan for the future as well. No matter how busy a manager may be, the majority of his time should be devoted to forward planning. All too often, however, the day-to-day decisions take precedence, and forward planning becomes a haphazard sideline as time permits. The implementation of "management by exception" can help to alleviate this problem—managers' attention should be directed to items deviating from the plan, and corrective action should be taken as necessary.

The most important segment for control in many companies is inventory. Some managements mistake inventory recordkeeping for inventory management, but inventory management goes much further than recordkeeping in that it provides answers to the basic issues: How much stock should be bought or produced and when should the purchase or production order be placed?

Traditionally, inventory management performance has been measured in terms of average turnover for either total inventory or classifications of inventory. However, this can be misleading. For example, in a company whose entire inventory moves an average of five times a year, which may be in line with that of other companies in the industry, item analysis reveals that 30% of the company's items are moving 25 times annually and 70% are turning over only twice a year. The company is in trouble but the average inventory turnover figure does not reflect this fact. The correct approach to measuring performance is on a item-by-item basis, because each item behaves differently and customers buy individual items, not groups or categories of items.

Inventory management concepts have expanded in recent years from large, sophisticated companies to companies of all sizes. The basic theory of scientific inventory management for repetitively ordered or stock items involves short-range forcasting of demand using exponential smoothing techniques (a type of weighted moving average); calculation of safety stocks based on the probability of stockouts and the variability of forecast demand and replenishment lead time; and economic order quantities which balance the variable cost of placing orders against the variable cost of carrying inventory. Management may thus quickly react, but not overreact, to bring inventory into balance with changing demand. Effective inventory management, combing accounting and short-range forcasting information enables a company to provide maximum customer service with minimum inventory investment.

FORECASTING

Forecasting and Decision-Making

The intricacies of the modern economic environment have forced the professional managers to look forward. The attainment of corporate goals requires that management use its discretion in choosing among the variety of alternatives available to deal with particular situations. By selecting among these options, management charts a course of action. That is, by deciding it manages. The decision process involves the identification and analysis of a problem, the consideration of possible solutions, and the selection and finally implementation of a course of action. Forecasting impacts on the first three elements: identification and analysis of problems and consideration of alternative courses of action.

Forecasting identifies problems by anticipating future events based on a set of assumptions, which are based in turn on a composite of known and predicted elements. In essence, forecasting is a tool which management employs in the decision-making process to control risk in uncertainty. The forecast result may be, for example, that the company's share of a particular market, which was projected on the basis of total industry growth, specific demographic patterns, and expectations as to the likely actions of competitors, will cause an increase in demand beyond present productive capacity. The forecast result may as well have indicated that no shortage of capacity will exist; that would have identified a non-problem and served to eliminate an element of uncertainty.

A forecast is not an end in itself. Management forecasts for various reasons, such as to anticipate profit opportunities, loss possibilities, capital requirements or financing needs. Once a forecast is made, management must consider what to do about it. A variety of alternatives may present themselves and the forecasting vehicle may be used again to select again among the choices. This anticipates a fair level of sophistication, including a model governed by several variables and constants. Selecting each of the alternatives in turn will determine different combinations of these variables and constants so that the impact of different decisions can be seen and considered. Further, the forecast becomes a standard for monitoring events as they take place so that comparisons to expectations and appropriate adjustments can be made on a timely basis.

For purposes of this paper, a forecast is a company's estimate of the outcome of future events based on macro-economic data, industry statistics, market surveys, etc., either in conjunction with the company's own historical data or by itself. The extrapolation of purely historical data to future periods in the absence of outside data does not constitute a forecast.

In the decision-making process, management relies on information, which may be internal, external, past or future. Whatever the source, the use of the data is based on management's expectations and may be expressed in terms of trends or goals. At one extreme, the vehicle may be based entirely on management's "feel"; at the other extreme, it may be based on a sophisticated econometric model. Most often, management operates somewhere along this continuum.

Variable Mode Forecasting

In today's environment, the future has never been more uncertain. Generally, both economists and businessmen failed to predict the depth of the 1973-75 recession, which was aggravated by unexpected high inflation coupled with low growth. The next decade is equally unpredictable. However, this does not negate the need to forecast; rather, it increases the importance of forecasting and emphasizes the need for injecting more variables into forecasts. Forward planning has become a critical function in the management process, although its nature is presently undergoing dramatic change. Instead of concentrating on a single plan, management now uses a flexible series of contingency or alternative plans. Also, plans are reviewed and revised more frequently in light of changing conditions. Many forecasts based on the most probable outcome are being replaced by series of forecasts that include a range of possibilities.

The emphasis on flexibility has increased the burden on the forecasting system. However, the computer can help management in assessing the impact of rapidly changing variables, and the use of planning models, which enable a company to consider more alternatives in its planning, has greatly increased.

What is modelling? A business model is a series of mathematical statements reflecting some or all of the financial and operating aspects of a business and the known relationships among them. A simple model showing financial relationships follows:

(*Verbal*)
Revenue = Market Potential x Market Share x Price
(*Mathematical*)
R = M x S x P
(*Verbal*)
Cost = Market Potential x Market Share x Unit Variables Costs + Fixed Costs
(*Mathematical*)
C = M x S x U + F

A business model serves the function of testing the effects of alternative assumptions concerning these components and relationships. Modelling, then, is the selection of those aspects of a business that can be quantified, the construction of a series of mathematical statements reflecting the relationships among the selected components, and the evaluation of the results produced by the model under alternative assumptions.

Business modelling is much more complex tban the simple illutration given above. Many problems deal with ten, fifty, or even hundreds of variables and with many interrelationships and restrictions, such as various revenue and expense items, raw material prices, interest rates, capital investment, cash flow, income taxes, earnings, etc. The preparation of schedules for a five-year plan could require many, many hours of calculations; subsequent "what-if" evaluations could multiply the number of hours required. For effective planning, enabling management to evaluate the impact of many alternatives, the process should be computerized. The model in effect, becomes a computerized planning vehicle designed to influence decision-making by revealing the consequences of alternative values of financial variables.

It is difficult to mention an area of business operations that does not lend itself to business modelling. Modelling is currently used extensively in short-term and long-term business planning, including cash flow and financial forecasts; merger and acquisition studies; pricing and other marketing problems; international taxation and foreign currency fluctuations; manpower planning; distribution studies; inventory studies; labour negotiations; advertising planning;

shop scheduling—in fact, anywhere there is a need to evaluate the effects of assumptions.

Financial models are frequently operated in a time-sharing model. (Time-sharing systems allow an individual user access to a large central computer system, usually via a terminal device. Standardized time-sharing programmes are generally available, and users may develop their own programmes and store them in a reserved library within the system.) Time-sharing programmes used in the modelling process may be categorized as follows:

- Analytical programmes. Analytical programmes are designed to detect historical patterns or trends, which can be expressed either in the form of ratios, percentage changes, and seasonal factors or in mathematical form, such as simple or multiple regressions, correlations, or sample values. Analytical progammes are most useful in analyzing operating patterns (monthly, quarterly, annual) for short-term and long-term planning.
- Calculating programes. Calculating programmes as the name implies, are employed primarily to speed up the manual work associated with mathematical calculations. In this category are programmes used for calculating net present value, cost allocations, mortgage schedules, depreciation schedules, tax computations, etc. They are used either individually or in concert with a number of other programmes, as in a capital investment analysis application where mortgage, amortization, interest, and net present value calculations are used as a group.
- Financial planning programmes. One form of financial planning model is structured in the form of a matrix, each row designating an income statement or balance sheet account, and each column a period, such as a month, quarter, or year. Future period values for an account can be entered directly, they can be based on calculations performed by the programme, using relationships specified by the user, or they can be calculated directly by one of the subroutines (such as depreciation, mortgage payment, and interest payment) which are built into the programme and can be "called" whenever required by the user. The use of this type of programme eliminates the need to programme a financial model anew each time different variables are used. It is a tremendous time saver, not only in structuring the programme, but also (especially when compared with manual schedule preparation) where the "what-if" situation is prevalent. The row and column model just described is deterministic in nature; that is, one value for each account is used in running the programme.

At times, it is desirable to deal with a range of values for a variable, with probabilities associated with the range of estimates. There are modelling programmes that can accommodate a range of values for each variable and the relationships that exist among the variables. For example, if the problem involves the calculation of potential profit, with a range of estimates given for market size, market share, cost and price, the potential profit would be expressed in the form of the chance that profit will be equal to or less than $1, $B, $C, etc. This form is called a probabilistic modelling programme, and is extremely useful in new venture studies, where a great deal of uncertainty may exist, and in conjunction with deterministic models, where it is most important to narrow the range on certain accounts for which uncertainty exists.

A forecast model normally uses both internal and external information sources. In addition to a company's own historical input, the model will often incorporate industry and national or worldwide data. The information may be directly related, for example, competitors' reported gross margins, or indirectly related, such as trends in the relocation of families and businesses. Depending on the purposes and sophistication of the model design, different amounts of external data will enter into the process.

While the computer can help assess the impact of hundreds of variables, the current trend is toward more selective use of data. To achieve flexibility and speed in the forecasting process where external data are used, management should concentrate on the ten or fifteen factors most critical to their business, for example, rate of inflation, interest rates, consumer spending on nondurable goods, basic raw material prices, etc.

If contingency or alternative plans are developed, tbey may be used to enable management to react quickly to changing conditions. "Worst case" plans may project, for example, 10% or 15% sales declines, specify expense reductions which should be made, and determine the priorities of the reductions.

Information System Design Considerations

A management information system that will monitor results as part of the forecasting process must be designed to suit the individual characteristics of the particular enterprise. It is important that the system be relatively simple and reasonably well understood, yet it must be able to instantaneously process and make available large masses of data and relate them to the forecast. The need for processing voluminous data brought with it widespread use of computer systems and quantitative methods.

Information has a time value. Knowing that you should have been on the ship after it has left means the process is too slow. At the other extreme, if early knowledge that you want to sail is so costly that you can't buy passage, the system also fails. Obviously a balance must be struck, but finding it is often quite difficult. When large scale computer storage became technologically and economically feasible, many sought to construct huge integrated system to provide instantaneous updated information. Sometimes this has been overdone.

Computer technology has had a strong impact on the cost/time relationship of information. The ability to handle, and make available for use, vast amounts of data has opened new vistas in the decision-making process. It has allowed management to cope with problems which have become more sophisticated as our business world has matured. Along with the computer revolution have come questions about the dedication of resources to the handling of these data.

A distributive computer system consists of multiple small processing units that are geographically dispersed plus a central, large processing unit. The smaller, dispersed units function independently of the larger host, but communicate with the host on some periodic basis. This is in contrast to the continuous communication that takes place in real-time systems.

The trend toward distributive systems challenges the conventional wisdom of building bigger, faster, more efficient computing systems. The question becomes whether companies can afford to know what the largest systems might tell them. Further, the technological advances of computer processing have outpaced management's ability to cope with the results. The need to keep information processing at a level consistent with management's decision-making ability may well explain the popularity of distributive systems. Management may properly feel that they have learned enough, and that their relationship with the computer has matured to to the point where the more manageable-sized elements of distributive systems leave them in control of the black box instead of in fear of it.

While the computer is capable of collecting large masses of data and applying simple operational decision-making criteria, it cannot apply subjective criteria. The system must, therefore, provide a selective process whereby only the data relevant to the decision-making process are forwarded to management. An abundance of irrelevant information can be as devastating to the decision-making process as the lack of vital information. Total information needs of management need to be anticipated and the necessary information kept available at all times. This is not to suggest that it is possible to provide all information desired or that technically available information is always economical to obtain. Information generation is not costless and the cost/benefit principle should be applied to all information system designs.

The earliest information systems tended to focus on separate divisional or decision-maker needs. As organization grew and systems became complex, the use of common data files for multiple purposes became widespread. Operational systems and information systems were integrated in order to interrelate and process all relevant data together. The most widely used information system is one in which the same underlying source is used to generate information for both external reporting purposes and management use. Financial transactions may be summarized in several ways to monitor operations of a division or department, progress of a particular product line, compliance with predetermined budgets or standards, or other management goals. These same transactions are accumulated throughout the reporting period and become the basis of the financial statements. They also constitute economically available information about future costs and form the basis for forward planning and budgeting. The review of financial data by independent accountants and the integration of the two accounting systems lend reliability and consistency to managerial accounting data.

Reporting systems should be structured so that each manager is accountable for his own operations. Care must be taken, however, to insure that methods used for collection of information and control of operations do not evoke undesirable responses. Maximization of departmental profits does not necessarily mean maximization of orgnizational profits. Long-range needs of plant capacity, product diversification, capital requirements, etc. must sometimes take precedence over short-range objectives. The method of measuring departmental profits, therefore, becomes very important if a department manager perceives maximization of profits as his primary goal. Accounting data should be used as a supportive tool not a punitive one. There should be adequate involvement and participation at all levels of management in setting up systems, designs and controls. Since the success of most management decisions hinges on motivating the individuals involved to conduct their activities in a manner most consistent with management's objectives, employees should have clearly defined objectives and should receive feedback on the extent to which they are achieving those objectives.

The Expansion of Public Reporting Requirements

Investors want more information concerning investment opportunities and they want the information faster. As a result, there has been increased demand for the dissemination to the public of what heretofore has been considered management accounting information. The U.S. Securities and Exchange Commission (SEC) requires registrants to disclose total sales or revvunue and income before taxes and extraordinary items for business segments or similar products and services that account for 10% or more of a company's total results in these areas. The Financial Accounting Standards Board (FASB) has proposed a similar requirement which would require disclosure of revenue, profit (or loss) contribution, operating profit, and identifiable assets of segments that account for 10% or more of a company's total in any of these areas. These bodies feel that segment reporting is necessary to assist financial statement users in analyzing and understanding the enterprise's financial statements by permitting better appraisal of the enterprise's past performance and future risks and profits. The different rates of growth, profitability and risk among different segments of an enterprise complicate the task of evaluating earnings prospects and make disclosure of segment results a necessity.

The SEC also requires management to provide a narrative explanation of significant changes from period to period for the use of investors in appraising the results shown in the financial statements. Annual reports to shareholders and related proxy material must include certified financial statements for the last two fiscal years, a summary of operations for the last five years, management's analysis of the summary of operations, line-of-business data for the last five years, brief descriptions of the business, identification of directors and executive officers, including occupation and place of employment and a host of additional information intended to allow investors to "read between the lines" of the financial statements and get a clearer picture of the company's progress.

There has also been increased pressure for companies to release interim reports to shareholders and the public. While some companies have issued interim reports in the past, their use was somewhat limited until all companies registered with the SEC are required to file quarterly reports.

The objectives of interim reporting are not necessarily the same as those of annual financial reporting. In the United States, it is believed that the usefulness of interim financial information rests on its relationship to the annual results of operations. Accordingly, each interim period is considered an integral part of the fiscal year, and certain accounting principles may require modification to better relate interim results to results of operations for the year. The SEC also requires disclosure of selected quarterly data in annual reports and requires the registrant's independent accountants to make a limited review of the data.

Forecasts for External Use

The use of forecasts is not limited to internal applications. Opinions differ widely on the external use of forecast data. Management's use of forecast data for external consumption serves a public relations function. By reporting its expectations to security analysts and financial publishers, management keeps the company's name in the minds of the financial public. To the extent that significant improvement is forecast, activity among present and prospective holders of the company's securities is likely to increase share prices in the securities markets.

The conservative use of this approach in practice is ample evidence of its double-edged quality. The financial public is aptly described as "once burnt, twice shy." A temporary advantage resulting from overly optimistic forecasts will likely turn to a more permanent disadvantage. Bad press and lack of general interest are the predictable reaction to a company's management that has misled would-be investors.

Regulatory authority has also taken an interest in forecasting, largely to help assure that management's insights are not restricted to a select group. The SEC has made a proposal that would permit forecasts, and would require public disclosure of projections that have been furnished to any outsiders, a subsequent comparison of historical results with the projections, and a description of significant differences. The chorus of negative reaction to these proposals was deafening and the issue presently lies quietly on the sidelines. Concerns that were raised, and apparently caused the temporary if not permament shelving of the questions, included tbe assumption of liability for the failure to achieve, or nearly achieve, forcasted results. The guideline ranges proposed by the SEC provided a too narrow margin for error, and the so-called "safe harbour" rules to limit liability were unacceptable to many.

Legitimate concern about reporting responsibilities and the related legal liabilities could force management into an overly conservative stance, seriously limiting the utility of forecasts for external purposes. Furthermore, variations in approach could lead to substantial comparability problems between companies.

Should independent accountants be publicly associated with forecasts? We, as accountants, are keenly sensitive to the possibility that direct association could imply a greater degree of certainty than is justified. Published forecasts can be useful to the public only if they are based on a consistently applied and rational set of principles governing both the development of assumptions and the computation of the projection.

The question of attesting to managerial assumptions is at the root of the issue. Does the accountant have a rational basis for challenging managerial assumptions about the future? What particular qualifications do accountants have for launching such a challenge in view of the fact that their discipline does not cover macro-economic projections, marketing outlooks, or intuition? Professional accountants do have a unique kowledge of business and business conditions, and they have both the discipline and the independence to be an ideal outside party to check on forecasts. Their role, however, must first be carefully structured so that they can effectively bring their training and knowledge to bear.

Public reporting of forecasts might ultimately be useful to the investing public, but only when the relative degree of certainty and uncertainty entailed in financial forecasts ean be clearly defined, expressed and understood by the investing public.

CONSULTING

Use of Consultants

Consulting may be defined as the application of internal or external expertise as a support function for management; it encompasses all personnel who interrelate with management in the accounting and forecasting process. Although the use of management consultants is now a generally accepted practice, this has not always been the case. In the past, few managers would call in a consultant because it was thought to be an admission that they were unable to run the company. Employees saw their jobs being threatened by efficiency experts. Why, then, has management consulting grown so rapidly? The chief contribution of management consultants has been assistance in the analysis of management problems and the recommendation of complete, practicable, and timely solutions suited to the company's need. The consultant brings to a problem objectivity, broad experience, analytical skills and undivided attention. He is able to make independent and impartial observations of the situation, free from personal interests. Since a consultant sees many diverse companies, he may have dealt with a certain problem several times, whereas internal management may see it only once in a lifetime. Managemeat must also monitor the daily operations of the company and cannot devote undivided attention to the problem at hand. A consultant, on the other hand, has only one responsibility, that is, to solve the problem. Thus, he can devote his full attention to this critical task.

However, a consultant may not be allowed to work in a vacuum. A successful consulting relationship requires cooperation and dialogue between the consultant and management and employees who will work under the new system. Before any work begins, management and the consultant must have a mutual understanding of the problems under consideration, the objectives of the engagement, and any time constraints involved. The consultant should also be an integral part of the implementation phase of the project to assure that his suggestions "work."

While management consultants are often external to the company, there is much to be gained from efficient use of internal expertise. The most widely used area of internal consultation is electronic data processing. The systems analyst and the data processing manager must constantly work with corporate management to ensure that system design and reporting are consonant with management needs.

An often overlooked internal consultant is the internal auditor. The internal audit function supplements routine management checks through its independent approach and review methods. Because of his specific knowledge of the company's operations, policies and procedures, the internal auditor has a unique opportunity to be an effective consultant. He should assist management in attaining its goals by furnishing information and recommendations pertinent to management's duties and objectives. Specifically, the job of the intereal auditor is to independently and objectively analyze, review and evaluate existing procedures and activities, to report on conditions found, and, whenever deemed necessary, to recommend changes or other action for management and operating officers to consider. While financial auditing is an important segment of the internal autitor's reponsibilities, much of his effort should be devotes to operational auditing. The operational audit is primarily a review of efficiency and the economic use of resources. The resulting report calls attention to breakdown in control and serves as a road map to corrective action. The audit is a sensitive detection mechanism which furnishes management with advance warnings of imperfections.

Internal auditing does not relieve operating officers of the responsibility to comply with prescribed policies and procedures. The internal auditor should be indepentent of the corporate officers who are directly responsible for the operations he reviews.

External consultants come from many sources. Many firms provide general business consulting on various areas of expertise, including market research, econometric model building, paper flow analysis, organization studies, etc. Most major public accounting firms offer consulting services through separate management consulting service divisions. Additionally, the independent accountant may also provide a consulting service during the course of his audit; he reviews the company's operations and control procedures and usually comments on deficiencies or possible improvements that he observes.

Some firms have integrated an operational control review with the financial audit. Whereas internal accounting controls are tested annually, operational controls may be tested in cycles so that all functional areas of the business are reviewed within a three to five year period. Controls may be evaluated in relation to "preferred practices" which have been found through experience to be successful or optimal. A deviation from a preferred practice is usually an indication that resources are being wasted. Observations and comments are ordinarily conveyed to management in a management letter or report to management in which the auditor outlines the significance of his findings, including "dollarization" of deficiencies and his suggestion for improvement.

Although management consulting by public accounting firms is now a common practice, the underlying tacit question remains—does this jeopardize the accountant's independence? Most public accountants feel that independence is not jeopardized because consulting is performed by a separate division of the firm and decisions are made by management. The critical question becomes how the public views the situation. A recent survey indicated that the public generally does not see a distinction between the various divisions within a public accounting firm. Many people think that the consultant and the auditor are the same person. The fact that a firm may have specialists on data processing, inventory control, production or marketing who are capable of rendering expert advice in these areas is not clear to the public. Even with public education, the problem of the appearance of independence will remain. Public accountants have assumed a peculiar relationship with the investing public; and many people perceive their responsibility as that of safeguarding the public interest, not the client's.

Nevertheless, public accountants assert their ability to remain indepentent in the attest function while their consultants provide much valuable advice in the area of management information system design and implementation. In their view, assisting the decision-makers to make decisions is not decision-making, and thus they are set apart from management. To date, there has not been any serious challenge to this contention based on actual circumstances. To deprive clients of such valuable assistance in the interest of image would be counterproductive.

CONCLUSION

The future will likely bring a sharper focus to the interrelationships among accounting, forecasting and consulting. The techniques for gathering and sifting information for management's use in decision-making have become very sophisticated, so that accounting is actually affecting the course of the economy, not merely recording it.

Recent developments in the association of public accountants with unaudited data highlight this increasing involvement in financial reporting. They will be viewed more and more as "the auditors of record" and will have some responsibility for all public financial reporting of their clients.

External financial reporting of the future appears headed toward relating on a frequent basis, actual results of operations to accomplishment of the company's goals as expressed in its forecasts. At that stage, forecasting, recording results and reporting will have come full circle, with accounting information at its centre.

PHILIP L. DEFLIESE: A BIBLIOGRAPHY†

"Staff Training at a New Climax—An Introduction." *L. R. B. & M. Journal* 38 (July-September 1957): 8-9.

"The Influence of SEC on Accounting Principles and Procedures and the Practice of Auditing." In 1958 *Conference of Accountants: Accounting Papers* (Accounting Papers of the Twelfth Annual Conference of Accountants, The University of Tulsa, April 23, 24, 1958). Tulsa, OK: Department of Accounting, College of Business Administration, The University of Tulsa, 1958, 65-76.

"Auditing When Internal Control is Inadequate." *The Journal of Accountancy* 108 (September 1959): 37-43.

"Audit Report Problems of Regulated Companies." (Address at Annual Meeting of American Institute of Certified Public Accountants, September 1960), 19 typewritten pages.*

"The 'New Look' at the Auditor's Responsibility for Fraud Detection." *The Journal of Accountancy* 114 (October 1962): 36-44. *The Pakistan Accountant* 4 (July, September 1966): 19-26.

"A Practitioner's View of the Realization Concept." *The Accounting Review* 40 (July 1965): 517-521.

"Public Utility Accounting—Comparable or Chaotic?" (Excerpts from speech before the National Conference of Electric and Gas Utility Accountants, New Orleans, May 2, 1966.) *The Journal of Accountancy* 122 (August 1966): 65-71.

"New Study Examines Problems of Allocating Income Taxes Between Periods." *The Journal of Taxation* 25 (November 1966): 261-264.

"A New Look at Utility Rate-Making." *Lybrand Journal* 49 (1968): 5-14.

"The State of the Firm—1970: New Decades Demand New Concepts." *Lybrand Journal* 51 (1970): 3-8.

†Items followed by an asterisk were not reprinted in this volume.

"Accounting Principles Board's Conclusions Deserve Time to Operate." *The New York Times* (September 13, 1970): 10

"The APB and Its Recent and Pending Opinions." (Address before the Conference Institute, New York, November 19, 1970.) *The Journal of Accountancy* 131 (February 1971): 66-69. Also published, in a slightly abridged version, under the title, "The Accounting Principles Board and Its Recent and Pending Opinions." *The New York Certified Public Accountant* 41 (April 1971): 279-283, 314.

"Accounting Principles." An Interview of Philip L. Defliese. *The New York Times* (May 9, 1971): 1, 9.

"APB Chairman in London." An Interview of Philip L. Defliese. *Accountancy* (England) 82 (July 1971): 411-414.

"Changing Accounting Objectives for Utilities Discussed at Accounting Conference." (Address before the Annual EEI-AGA Accounting Conference, Chicago, Illinois, May 8-10, 1972.) *Edison Electric Institute Bulletin* 40 (May-June, 1972): 107, 142. A somewhat longer version of this topic was published under the title "Changing Accounting Objectives—What About Utilities?" *Public Utilities Fortnightly* 90 (July 20, 1972): 17-21.

"Profit Forecasts." *The CPA Journal* 43 (March 1973): 171-175.

The Objectives of Financial Accounting. New York: Coopers & Lybrand, 1973: 22 pages. Preface also reprinted under the title, "The State of the Accounting Art," in *The CPA Journal* 44 (April 1974): 25, and portions of the paper were published under the title, "Accounting Practice—Design for Change," *in Financial Executive* 42 (January 1974): 14-18, 23.

Should Accountants Capitalize Leases? The Economic Case Against It at Present. New York: Coopers & Lybrand, 1973, 24 pages. Portions also published under the title, "Accounting for Leases: A Broader Perspective," in *Financial Executive* 42 (July 1974): 14-23, and under the title, "The Economic Case Against Capitalization of Leases—A New Look at Facility Accounting," in *Institutional Issues in Public Accounting*, Chapter 10, Robert R. Sterling, ed. Lawrence, KS: Scholars Book Co., 1974, 345-361, which also contains related commentary by Ross M. Skinner (362-369), and the transcript of a conference discussion involving Defliese, Skinner and others (370-373).

"New Era for Auditors: Interim Reports." *Financial Executive* 42 (December 1974): 22-24, 26, 28, 32.

"The Search for Standards: U.S. and Abroad," Transcript of Conference Discussion Involving Philip L. Defliese, Stephen A. Zeff, and others. In *Accounting in Transition: Oral Histories of Recent U.S. Experience*, Thomas J. Burns, ed. Columbus, OH: College of Administrative Science, The Ohio State University, (1974): 19-43.

Business Combinations Revisited: A Temporary Defense of the Status Quo. New York: Coopers & Lybrand, 1974: 22 pages. Also published with slight variations as "Business Combinations Revisited." In *DR Scott Memorial Lectures in Accountancy*, Volume VI, Alfred R. Roberts, ed. Columbia, MO: Department of Accountancy, College of Administration and Public Affairs, University of Missouri - Columbia 1974: 46-65; and "Business Combinations Revisited: A Temporary Defense of the Status Quo." *Ohio State Law Journal* 35 (1974): 393-411. Portions reprinted under the title "Business Combinations Revisited." *Financial Executive* 43 (September 1975): 42-47.

"What Makes Profits Look 'Obscene'." *Business Week* (August 4, 1975): 10-11.

"Luncheon Address: [Perspectives on Auditor's Responsibilities]." *Collected Papers of the American Accounting Association's Annual Meeting*. August 18-20, 1975. Sarasota, FL: American Accounting Association, 1975, 405-411.

"The Accountant's Role in the New World Order." (Substance of an address at a luncheon meeting of the London Chartered Accountants on October 2, 1975). *The Accountant* (England) 173 (October 9, 1975): 413-414. Also reprinted with minor modifications in *The Journal of Accountancy* 140 (December 1975): 71-73.

"Definition of Materiality: The Multi-Facet Perspectives—The Accountant's View," by Philip L. Defliese and Roderick K. Macleod. In *Materiality: An Evolving Concept Under the Securities Laws*, Course Handbook Series Number 197, Douglas R. Carmichael and Alan B. Levenson, cochairmen. New York: Practising Law Institute, 1975, 27-40.

"The Challenge of the Present." Inaugural Address, 1974. In the files of the American Institute of Certified Public Accountants. 8 typewritten pages.

Montgomery's Auditing, by Vincent M. O'Reilly, Murray B. Hirsch, Philip L. Defliese, and Henry R. Jaenicke. 11th ed. New York: John Wiley & Sons, Inc., 1990. *Montgomery's Auditing*, by Jerry D. Sullivan, Richard A. Gnospelius, Philip L. Defliese, and Henry R. Jaenicke. 10th ed. New York: John Wiley & Sons, Inc., 1985. *Montgomery's Auditing*, by Philip L. Defliese, Kenneth P. Johnson and Roderick K. Macleod. 9th ed. New

York. Ronald Press, 1975. *Montgomery's Auditing*, by Norman J. Lenhart and Philip L. Defliese, 8th ed. New York, Ronald Press Company, 1957.*

"Capitalization and Amortization of Leases." Chapter 10 in *The Modern Accountant's Handbook*, James Don Edwards and Homer A. Black, eds. Homewood, IL: Dow Jones-Irwin, 1976, 175-200.

"The Search for a New Conceptual Framework of Accounting." *The Journal of Accountancy* 144 (July 1977): 59-67.

"The Changing Business Scene." Introduction in *Current Value Accounting: A Practical Guide for Business*, Warren Chippindale and Philip L. Defliese, eds. New York: AMACOM: A Division of American Management Association, 1977, 1-4.

"The Management of an Accounting Practice: A Search for Principles and Alternatives." In *1997 Accounting Research Convocation* (Papers Presented at the 1977 Accounting Research Convocation on the Subject of Patterns of Change), Jonathan J. Davies, ed. University, AL: Graduate School of Business Administration, The University of Alabama, 1978, 133-153.

"Accounting, Forecasting and Consulting for Management Use." (Presented at the Eleventh International Congress of Accountants in Munich, October 10-14, 1977.) *The Chartered Accountant* (India) 26 (March 1978): 524-533. Portions of the paper were published in *The Accountant* (England) 177 (November 10, 1977): 595-597, and in *Industrial Accountant* (Pakistan) 17 (January-March 1978): 17-20.

"Inflation Accounting: Pursuing the Elusive." *The Journal of Accountancy* 147 (May 1979): 50, 52, 54, 58-63.

Zeff, Stephen A., W. E. Hoglund, and Philip L. Defliese, "Constant Dollar Accounting: Which Approach Tells the Story?" A comment and replies. *The Journal of Accountancy* 148 (October 1979): 96-97.

"Update on the New Conceptual Framework Project." In *Contemporary Issues in Accounting*, Dhia D. AlHashim and James W. Robertson, eds. Indianapolis, IN: Bobbs-Merrill Company, Inc. 1979, 37-54. A nearly identical article was published in *The Journal of Accountancy* 145 (March 1978): 74-79.

"Deferred Taxes—Forever." *The Journal of Accountancy* 156 (August 1983): 94-96, 98.

"Deferred Taxes—More Fatal Flaws." *Accounting Horizons* 5 (March 1991): 89-91.

THE ACCOUNTING HALL OF FAME

THE Accounting Hall of Fame was established at The Ohio State University in 1950 for the purpose of honoring accountants who have made or are making significant contributions to the advancement of accounting since the beginning of the twentieth century. Through 1998, 61 leading accountants from the United States and other countries have been elected to the Hall of Fame.

While selection to the Hall of Fame is intended to honor the people so chosen, it is also intended to be a recognition of distinguished service contributions to the progress of accounting in any of its various fields. Evidence of such service includes contributions to accounting research and literature, significant service to professional accounting organizations, wide recognition as an authority in some field of accounting, advancement of accounting education, and public service. A member must have reached a position of eminence from which the nature of his or her contributions may be judged.

Elections to the Hall of Fame are made by a Board of Nominations consisting of up to 45 eminent accountants from each of the following three groups: public accountants, educators, and industrial and governmental accountants. Each Board member serves a fixed term. Starting in 1973, Board membership became international. In addition to members from the United States, the Board has included members from Australia, Canada, England, Japan, Mexico, and other countries.

Nomination and election to the Accounting Hall of Fame by the Board are made annually by mail in two steps. Individual members of the Board are asked to nominate a living or deceased accountant for possible election to the Hall of Fame. From these preliminary nominations, a ballot is prepared containing the names, alphabetically listed, of not more than four candidates who have been nominated most frequently. The members of the Board of Nominations then cast their votes for one of the four nominees. The candidate on the ballot receiving the most votes is elected to the Hall. In the event that several candidates receive the same number of votes, more than one candidate may be elected.

Evidence of election to the Accounting Hall of Fame takes three forms. A certificate issued under the seal of The Ohio State University and signed by the President of the University and a representative of the Board of Nominations is presented to each person elected (or to the person's representative when the person elected is deceased). The names of the elected persons are inscribed on a scroll, and a photographic portrait of each person elected are permanently displayed in the corridors of the Fisher College of Business at The Ohio State University. The presentation of the certificate usually takes place at the annual meeting of the American Accounting

Association. Living members of The Ohio State University faculty are not eligible for election to the Accounting Hall of Fame.

THE ACCOUNTING HALL OF FAME MEMBERSHIP

1950
George Oliver May
Robert Hiester Montgomery
William Andrew Paton

1951
Arthur Lowes Dickinson
Henry Rand Hatfield

1952
Elijah Watt Sells
Victor Hermann Stempf

1953
Arthur Edward Andersen
Thomas Coleman Andrews
Charles Ezra Sprague
Joseph Edmund Sterrett

1954
Carman George Blough
Samuel John Broad
Thomas Henry Sanders
Hiram Thompson Scovill

1955
Percival Flack Brundage

1956
Ananias Charles Littleton

1957
Roy Bernard Kester
Hermann Clinton Miller

1958
Harry Anson Finney
Arthur Bevins Foye
Donald Putnam Perry

1959
Marquis George Eaton

1960
Maurice Hubert Stans

1961
Eric Louis Kohler

1963
Andrew Barr
Lloyd Morey

1964
Paul Franklin Grady
Perry Empey Mason

1965
James Loring Peirce

1968
George Davis Bailey
John Lansing Carey
William Welling Werntz

1974
Robert Martin Trueblood

1975
Leonard Paul Spacek

1976
John William Queenan

1977
Howard Irwin Ross

1978
Robert Kuhn Mautz

1979
Maurice Moonitz

1980
Marshall Smith Armstrong

1981
Elmer Boyd Staats

1982
Herbert Elmer Miller

1983
Sidney Davidson

1984
Henry Alexander Benson

1985
Oscar Strand Gellein

1986
Robert Newton Anthony

1987
Philip Leroy Defliese

1988
Norton Moore Bedford

1989
Yuji Ijiri

1990
Charles Thomas Horngren

1991
Raymond John Chambers

1992
David Solomons

1993
Richard Thomas Baker

1994
Robert Thomas Sprouse

1995
William Wager Cooper

1996
William Henry Beaver
Charles Arthur Bowsher
Donald James Kirk

1997
Thomas Junior Burns
John Campbell Burton

1998
Arthur Ramer Wyatt

THE ACCOUNTING HALL OF FAME: THOMAS J. BURNS SERIES IN ACCOUNTING HISTORY

Volume 1: Samuel J. Broad: A Collection of His Writings (1993)
(ISBN 1-883356-00-8)

Volume 2: T. Coleman Andrews: A Collection of His Writings (1996)
(ISBN 1-883356-02-4)

Volume 3: James L. Peirce: A Collection of His Writings (1997)
(ISBN 1-883356-03-1)

Volume 4: Philip L. Defliese: A Collection of His Writings (1999)
(ISBN 1-883356-04-0)